THE GERMAN SYMPHONY BETWEEN
BEETHOVEN AND BRAHMS

*To my wife Anna, our son Robin and our daughter Elodie,
born as I first put pen to paper in 2006
and to whom I can now give much more time.*

The German Symphony between Beethoven and Brahms
The Fall and Rise of a Genre

CHRISTOPHER FIFIELD

LONDON AND NEW YORK

First published 2015 by Ashgate Publisher

2 Park Square, Milton Park, Abingdon, Oxfordshire OX14 4RN
52 Vanderbilt Avenue, New York, NY 10017

Routledge is an imprint of the Taylor & Francis Group, an informa business

First issued in paperback 2020

Copyright © Christopher Fifield 2015

Christopher Fifield has asserted his right under the Copyright, Designs and Patents Act, 1988, to be identified as the author of this work.

All rights reserved. No part of this book may be reprinted or reproduced or utilised in any form or by any electronic, mechanical, or other means, now known or hereafter invented, including photocopying and recording, or in any information storage or retrieval system, without permission in writing from the publishers.

Notice:
Product or corporate names may be trademarks or registered trademarks, and are used only for identification and explanation without intent to infringe.

British Library Cataloguing in Publication Data
A catalogue record for this book is available from the British Library.

The Library of Congress has cataloged the printed edition as follows:
Fifield, Christopher.
 The German symphony between Beethoven and Brahms : the fall and rise of a genre / by Christopher Fifield.
   pages cm
 Includes bibliographical references and index.
 ISBN 978-1-4094-5288-1 (hardcover)
 1. Symphony--Germany--19th century. I. Title.
 ML1255.G44 2015
 784.2'184094309034--dc23

2014031362

ISBN 978-1-4094-5288-1 (hbk)
ISBN 978-0-367-59940-9 (pbk)

Bach musicological font developed by © Yo Tomita

Contents

List of Tables   *vii*
List of Music Examples   *ix*
Preface and Acknowledgements   *xix*

1	Introduction	1
2	The German Symphony in the 1830s	7
3	The German Symphony in the 1840s	81
4	Leipzig, its Gewandhaus and Conservatoire	125
5	The German Symphony in the 1850s	151
6	The German Symphony in the 1860s	185
7	The German Symphony 1870–1876	251

Select Bibliography   *285*
Select Discography   *293*
Index   *297*

List of Tables

2.1	Performances of Kalliwoda's seven symphonies at Leipzig 1826–52	17
2.2	Kalliwoda's seven symphonies and those of six of his contemporaries	21
2.3	119 performances of symphonies at Leipzig 1 January 1835–31 December 1840	78
3.1	New symphonies published between 1830 and 1876	82
5.1	Programmes of Leipzig's Gewandhaus concerts	165
7.1	Average age of a composer writing his first symphony	279

List of Music Examples

1.1	Schubert: Symphony No. 9 in C *Great* D. 944. Finale, bars 386–93	2
2.1	Spohr: Symphony No. 2. Finale	11
2.2	Kalliwoda: Symphony No. 1. Introduction	20
2.3	Kalliwoda: Symphony No. 1. First movement, first subject	20
2.4	Kalliwoda: Symphony No. 1. First movement, second subject	22
2.5	Kalliwoda: Symphony No. 1. First movement, second subject	22
2.6	Kalliwoda: Symphony No. 1. First movement, development	22
2.7	Kalliwoda: Symphony No. 1. Second movement, theme	23
2.8	Mozart: *Cosi fan tutte* K.588 Act 2 No. 29. Duet	23
2.9	Kalliwoda: Symphony No. 1. Second movement, accompaniment	23
2.10	Mozart: Symphony No. 40 K.550. Second movement, bars 20–22	24
2.11	Kalliwoda: Symphony No. 1. Third movement, Scherzo	24
2.12	Schumann: Symphony No. 4 Op. 120. Third movement, Scherzo	24
2.13	Kalliwoda: Symphony No. 2. First movement, introduction	26
2.14	Kalliwoda: Symphony No. 2. First movement, fugue subject	26
2.15	Kalliwoda: Symphony No. 2. First movement, first subject	26
2.16	Kalliwoda: Symphony No. 2. First movement, second subject	27
2.17	Kalliwoda: Symphony No. 2. First movement, fugal development	27
2.18	Kalliwoda: Symphony No. 2. Third movement, Scherzo	28
2.19	Mozart: Symphony No. 39 K.543. Third movement, Scherzo	28
2.20	Kalliwoda: Symphony No. 2. Third movement, Trio	28
2.21	Mozart: Symphony No. 41 *Jupiter* K.551. Finale opening	28
2.22	Kalliwoda: Symphony No. 2. Finale, fugal opening	28
2.23	Kalliwoda: Symphony No. 2. Finale	28
2.24	Kalliwoda: Symphony No. 1. Finale	29
2.25	Kalliwoda: Symphony No. 3. Five-note motif	30
2.26	Kalliwoda: Symphony No. 3. First movement, cello solo and canon	30
2.27	Kalliwoda: Symphony No. 3. Second movement, opening	31
2.28	Kalliwoda: Symphony No. 3. Second movement, conclusion	31
2.29	Kalliwoda: Symphony No. 3. Second movement, bars 5–8	31
2.30	Kalliwoda: Symphony No. 3. Third movement, bars 1–4	32
2.31	Kalliwoda: Symphony No. 3. Third movement, bars 8–12	32
2.32	Kalliwoda: Symphony No. 3. Trio	32
2.33	Kalliwoda: Symphony No. 3. Finale	32
2.34	Kalliwoda: Symphony No. 4. Second movement, Romanze	33

2.35	Kalliwoda: Symphony No. 5. Introduction	34
2.36	Kalliwoda: Symphony No. 5. First movement	34
2.37	Kalliwoda: Symphony No. 5. First movement, second subject	35
2.38	Kalliwoda: Symphony No. 5. Third movement, opening	35
2.39	Kalliwoda: Symphony No. 7. Introduction	38
2.40	Kalliwoda: Symphony No. 7. First movement, first subject	38
2.41	Kalliwoda: Symphony No. 7. Second movement, Scherzo	38
2.42	Kalliwoda: Symphony No. 7. Third movement, March	38
2.43	Kalliwoda: Symphony No. 7. Finale	38
2.44	Kalliwoda: Symphony No. 6. First movement introduction	40
2.45	Kalliwoda: Symphony No. 6. First movement, first subject	40
2.46	Kalliwoda: Symphony No. 6. Second movement	40
2.47	Kalliwoda: Symphony No. 6. Scherzo	40
2.48	Kalliwoda: Symphony No. 6. Finale	41
2.49	Burgmüller: Symphony No. 1. First movement, slow introduction	46
2.50	Burgmüller: Symphony No. 1. First movement, first subject	46
2.51	Burgmüller: Symphony No. 1. Second movement	46
2.52	Burgmüller: Symphony No. 1. Second movement, oboe solo	46
2.53	Burgmüller: Symphony No. 1. Third movement, Scherzo	47
2.54	Burgmüller: Symphony No. 1. Third movement, Trio	47
2.55	Burgmüller: Symphony No. 1. Finale, first theme	47
2.56	Burgmüller: Symphony No. 1. Finale, second theme	48
2.57	Burgmüller: Symphony No. 2. First movement, first motif	49
2.58	Burgmüller: Symphony No. 2. First movement, second motif	49
2.59	Burgmüller: Symphony No. 1. Finale. Bridge passage to recapitulation of Ex. 2.55	49
2.60	Beethoven: Symphony No. 7. Finale	50
2.61	Burgmüller: Symphony No. 2. First movement, orchestral recitative	50
2.62	Schubert: Symphony No. 9. Second movement	51
2.63	Burgmüller: Symphony No. 2. Second movement	51
2.64	Burgmüller: Symphony No. 2. Scherzo, opening	52
2.65	Beethoven: Symphony No. 5. Trio	52
2.66	Beethoven: Symphony No. 8. Finale	52
2.67	Burgmüller: Symphony No. 2. Scherzo elision to Trio	53
2.68	Burgmüller: Symphony No. 2. Scherzo elision to Trio	53
2.69	Beethoven: Symphony No. 8. Trio	53
2.70	Lachner: Symphony No. 1. First movement, first subject	58
2.71	Lachner: Symphony No. 1. First movement, second subject	58
2.72	Lachner: Symphony No. 1. Second movement, opening	58
2.73	Lachner: Symphony No. 1. Second movement, bars 17–24	59
2.74	Lachner: Symphony No. 1. Scherzo, a four-part canon for strings	59
2.75	Lachner: Symphony No. 1. Scherzo, the theme inverted	59
2.76	Lachner: Symphony No. 1. Trio	59

2.77	Lachner: Symphony No. 1. Finale, opening	59
2.78	Lachner: Symphony No. 5. Introduction	61
2.79	Lachner: Symphony No. 5. Introduction	61
2.80	Lachner: Symphony No. 5. First movement, six-note motif	61
2.81	Lachner: Symphony No. 5. First movement, first subject	61
2.82	Lachner: Symphony No. 5. First movement, quasi-recitative	62
2.83	Lachner: Symphony No. 5. Second movement	62
2.84	Lachner: Symphony No. 5. Second movement	63
2.85	Lachner: Symphony No. 5. Third movement, Minuet	64
2.86	Lachner: Symphony No. 5. Trio, conclusion	64
2.87	Lachner: Symphony No. 5. Finale, opening	64
2.88	Lachner: Symphony No. 5. Finale, second subject	64
2.89	Lachner: Symphony No. 5. Finale, double fugue	65
2.90	Lachner: Symphony No. 6. First movement, first subject	73
2.91	Lachner: Symphony No. 6. First movement, first subject fugue	73
2.92	Lachner: Symphony No. 6. First movement, second subject fugue	73
2.93	Lachner: Symphony No. 6. First movement, second subject	73
2.94	Lachner: Symphony No. 6. First movement, the two fugal subjects combined	73
2.95	Lachner: Symphony No. 6. Second movement beginning	74
2.96	Lachner: Symphony No. 6. Third movement, Scherzo	74
2.97	Lachner: Symphony No. 6. Third movement, Trio	74
2.98	Lachner: Symphony No. 6. Finale	74
3.1	Kittl: Symphony No. 2. First movement, opening 'Summons'	85
3.2	Kittl: Symphony No. 2. First movement, 'Start of the hunt'	85
3.3	Kittl: Symphony No. 2. Second movement, 'Rest from the hunt'	85
3.4	Kittl: Symphony No. 2. Third movement, Scherzo 'Drinking chorus'	85
3.5	Kittl: Symphony No. 2. Finale, 'The end of the hunt', fanfare-chorale	86
3.6	Verhulst: Symphony in E minor. First movement, first subject	96
3.7	Verhulst: Symphony in E minor. First movement, second subject	96
3.8	Verhulst: Symphony in E minor. First movement, development	97
3.9	Verhulst: Symphony in E minor. Second movement, theme	97
3.10	Verhulst: Symphony in E minor. Second movement, first variation	97
3.11	Verhulst: Symphony in E minor. Third movement, Scherzo	97
3.12	Verhulst: Symphony in E minor. Third movement, Trio	97
3.13	Verhulst: Symphony in E minor. Finale, opening	98
3.14	Gade: Symphony No. 1. Introduction, Danish folk melody	104
3.15	Gade: Symphony No. 1. Finale, Coda, brass C major response	105
3.16	Gade: Symphony No. 1. First movement, accompanying passage by the strings at letter A	105
3.17	Gade: Symphony No. 1. Second movement, Scherzo	105

3.18	Gade: Symphony No. 1. Second movement, Trio	105
3.19	Gade: Symphony No. 1. Third movement, opening	105
3.20	Gade: Symphony No. 1. Third movement, cellos at letter B	105
3.21	Gade: Symphony No. 1. Finale, opening	106
3.22	Gade: Symphony No. 1. Finale, second theme at letter B	106
3.23	Schnyder von Wartensee: Symphony No. 3. First movement, opening	119
3.24	Schnyder von Wartensee: Symphony No. 3. First movement, double bass solo	119
3.25	Schnyder von Wartensee: Symphony No. 3. First movement, canon in augmentation	120
3.26	Schnyder von Wartensee: Symphony No. 3. Second movement, opening	120
3.27	Schnyder von Wartensee: Symphony No. 3. Second movement, March	120
3.28	Schnyder von Wartensee: Symphony No. 3. Second movement, Trio	120
3.29	Schnyder von Wartensee: Symphony No. 3. Third movement, Scherzo, opening	121
3.30	Schnyder von Wartensee: Symphony No. 3. Third movement, second theme	121
3.31	Schnyder von Wartensee: Symphony No. 3. Third movement, Trio section	121
3.32	Schnyder von Wartensee: Symphony No. 3. Third movement, Scherzo, enharmonic transition	121
3.33	Schnyder von Wartensee: Symphony No. 3. Scherzo, transition to recapitulation	122
3.34	Schnyder von Wartensee: Symphony No. 3. Rondo finale, opening	123
3.35	Schnyder von Wartensee: Symphony No. 3. Finale, episodic transition	123
3.36	Schnyder von Wartensee: Symphony No. 3. Finale recalls first movement opening	123
5.1	Lachner: Symphony No. 8. First movement, introduction	154
5.2	Lachner: Symphony No. 8. First movement, principal theme	154
5.3	Lachner: Symphony No. 8. First movement, second subject	154
5.4	Lachner: Symphony No. 8. First movement, bassoon cadenza	155
5.5	Lachner: Symphony No. 8. Second movement, bars 13–20	156
5.6	Lachner: Symphony No. 8. Second movement, variation	156
5.7	Lachner: Symphony No. 8. Second movement, variation	156
5.8	Lachner: Symphony No. 8. Second movement, flute solo variation	156
5.9	Lachner: Symphony No. 8. Third movement, Scherzo	157

List of Music Examples xiii

5.10	Lachner: Symphony No. 8. Third movement, Trio	157
5.11	Lachner: Symphony No. 8. Rondo finale, opening	157
5.12	Lachner: Symphony No. 8. Rondo finale, theme in augmentation	157
5.13	Lachner: Symphony No. 8. Rondo finale, chromatic modulation	158
5.14	Franck: Symphony in A. First movement, opening	161
5.15	Franck: Symphony in A. Second movement, opening	161
5.16	Franck: Symphony in A. Third movement, Scherzo	162
5.17	Schumann: Piano concerto. First movement, second subject	162
5.18	Franck: Symphony in A. Third movement, Trio, oboe and cello in canon	162
5.19	Franck: Symphony in B♭. Second movement, Scherzo	163
5.20	Franck: Symphony in B♭. Second movement, Scherzo	163
5.21	Franck: Symphony in B♭. Third movement, opening	163
5.22	Franck: Symphony in B♭. Third movement, chromatic variation	164
5.23	Franck: Symphony in B♭. Finale	164
5.24	Rietz: Symphony No. 3. First movement, opening	172
5.25	Rietz: Symphony No. 3. First movement, second subject	172
5.26	Rietz: Symphony No. 3. Second movement, quasi Minuet, opening	173
5.27	Rietz: Symphony No. 3. Second movement, quasi Trio	173
5.28	Rietz: Symphony No. 3. Third movement, theme	173
5.29	Hiller: Symphony in E minor. First movement, opening	176
5.30	Hiller: Symphony in E minor. First movement, second subject	176
5.31	Hiller: Symphony in E minor. Second movement, main theme	176
5.32	Hiller: Symphony in E minor. Second movement, variation	177
5.33	Hiller: Symphony in E minor. Third movement, Scherzo	178
5.34	Hiller: Symphony in E minor. Third movement, Trio	178
5.35	Hiller: Symphony in E minor. Third movement, Coda	178
5.36	Hiller: Symphony in E minor. Finale, opening	178
5.37	Hiller: Symphony in E minor. Finale, second theme	178
5.38	Reinecke: Symphony No. 1. First movement, slow introduction	181
5.39	Reinecke: Symphony No. 1. First movement, first subject	181
5.40	Reinecke: Symphony No. 1. First movement, second subject	181
5.41	Reinecke: Symphony No. 1. Shifting accents for lower strings	181
5.42	Reinecke: Symphony No. 1. Second movement, opening	182
5.43	Reinecke: Symphony No. 1. Second movement, variation	182
5.44	Reinecke: Symphony No. 1. Third movement, Scherzo	183
5.45	Reinecke: Symphony No. 1. Third movement, Trio	183
5.46	Reinecke: Symphony No. 1. Third movement, Coda with quasi cadenza for clarinet	183
5.47	Reinecke: Symphony No. 1. Third movement Cadenza linking to Finale	184

6.1	Reinthaler: Symphony in D. First movement, opening	190
6.2	Reinthaler: Symphony in D. Second movement, opening	190
6.3	Reinthaler: Symphony in D. Third movement, Scherzo	191
6.4	Reinthaler: Symphony in D. Third movement, Trio	191
6.5	Reinthaler: Symphony in D. Finale, slow introduction	191
6.6	Reinthaler: Symphony in D. Finale	191
6.7	Volkmann: Symphony No. 1. First movement, opening	194
6.8	Borodin: Symphony No. 2. First movement, opening	194
6.9	Volkmann: Symphony No. 1. First movement, pedal point	194
6.10	Volkmann: Symphony No. 1. First movement, bars 71–4	194
6.11	Volkmann: Symphony No. 1. First movement, bars 80–83	194
6.12	Volkmann: Symphony No. 1. First movement, second pedal point	195
6.13	Volkmann: Symphony No. 1. First movement, development, bars 122–8	195
6.14	Bruckner: Symphony No. 4. First movement, rhythmic motif	195
6.15	Volkmann: Symphony No. 1. Second movement, introduction	196
6.16	Schumann: Symphony No. 4. Second movement, opening	196
6.17	Brahms: Symphony No. 3. Second movement, opening	196
6.18	Volkmann Symphony No. 1. Second movement, pedal point	197
6.19	Volkmann Symphony No. 1. Third movement, Scherzo	197
6.20	Volkmann Symphony No. 1. Third movement, Trio	198
6.21	Schumann: Symphony No. 3. Third movement, Scherzo	198
6.22	Volkmann: Symphony No. 1. Finale, opening	198
6.23	Brahms: Symphony No. 4. First movement, development	198
6.24	Volkmann: Symphony No. 1. Finale, development (canon)	199
6.25	Raff: Symphony No. 1. First movement, first subject	204
6.26	Raff: Symphony No. 1. First movement, second subject	205
6.27	Raff: Symphony No. 1. First movement, fugal development	205
6.28	Raff: Symphony No. 1. Scherzo, introductory fanfare for horns	205
6.29	Raff: Symphony No. 1. Second movement, Scherzo	205
6.30	Raff: Symphony No. 1. Second movement, Trio	205
6.31	Raff: Symphony No. 1. Third movement	207
6.32	Raff: Symphony No. 1. First movement, vibrato in the violins	207
6.33	Raff: Symphony No. 1. Third movement, vibrato for solo cello	207
6.34	Raff: Symphony No. 1. Fourth movement, main motif	207
6.35	Raff: Symphony No. 1. Fourth movement, main theme	208
6.36	Raff: Symphony No. 1. Fourth movement, hints of Berlioz	208
6.37	Berlioz: *Symphonie fantastique*. Finale, introduction	208
6.38	Raff: Symphony No. 1. Fourth movement, letter B, main theme in the brass	208
6.39	Raff: Symphony No. 1. Finale, opening Funeral March	209
6.40	Raff: Symphony No. 1. Finale, brass chorale March	209
6.41	Raff: Symphony No. 1. Finale, main theme	209
6.42	Raff: Symphony No. 2. First movement, opening	210

6.43	Raff: Symphony No. 2. Second movement, opening	210
6.44	Raff: Symphony No. 2. Third movement, Scherzo	210
6.45	Raff: Symphony No. 10. Third movement	211
6.46	Tchaikovsky: Symphony No. 5. Second movement	211
6.47	Raff: Symphony No. 4. First movement, first subject	212
6.48	Raff: Symphony No. 4. First movement, second subject	212
6.49	Raff: Symphony No. 4. Second movement, Scherzo	212
6.50	Raff: Symphony No. 4. Third movement, theme	213
6.51	Raff: Symphony No. 4. Finale, introduction	213
6.52	Schnyder von Wartensee: Symphony No. 3. First movement, introduction	215
6.53	Raff: Symphony No. 6. Finale, opening	215
6.54	Bruch: Symphony No. 1. First movement, first subject	222
6.55	Bruch: Symphony No. 1. First movement, second subject	222
6.56	Bruch: Symphony No. 1. First movement, second subject, strings	222
6.57	Bruch: Symphony No. 1. Second movement, Intermezzo, opening	223
6.58	Bruch: Symphony No. 1. First movement, development	223
6.59	Bruch: Symphony No. 1. Second movement, first subject	224
6.60	Bruch: Symphony No. 1. Second movement, second subject	224
6.61	Bruch: Symphony No. 1. Second movement, syncopation	224
6.62	Bruch: Symphony No. 1. Third movement, Scherzo	225
6.63	Bruch: Symphony No. 1. Third movement, Trio	225
6.64	Bruch: Symphony No. 1. Fourth movement, opening	226
6.65	Bruch: Scottish Fantasy. First movement, opening	226
6.66	Bruch: Symphony No. 1. Finale, opening	227
6.67	Bruch: Symphony No. 1. Finale, second subject	227
6.68	Bruch: Symphony No. 2. Finale, principal theme	232
6.69	Dietrich: Symphony in D minor. Opening motto theme	234
6.70	Dietrich: Symphony in D minor. Second movement, horn theme	234
6.71	Dietrich: Symphony in D minor. Second movement, climax	234
6.72	Dietrich: Symphony in D minor. Third movement, Scherzo	235
6.73	Dietrich: Symphony in D minor. Third movement, first trio	235
6.74	Dietrich: Symphony in D minor. Third movement, second trio	235
6.75	Dietrich: Symphony in D minor. Finale	236
6.76	Dietrich: Symphony in D minor. First movement, second subject	236
6.77	Dietrich: Symphony in D minor. First movement	236
6.78	Draeseke: Symphony No. 1. First movement, Introduction	241
6.79	Draeseke: Symphony No. 1. First movement, first subject	241
6.80	Draeseke: Symphony No. 1. First movement, development	241
6.81	Draeseke: Symphony No. 1. First movement, development	242
6.82	Draeseke: Symphony No. 1. Second movement, Scherzo	242
6.83	Draeseke: Symphony No. 1. Third movement, opening	242
6.84	Draeseke: Symphony No. 1. Fourth movement, opening	243

6.85	Draeseke: Symphony No. 2. First movement, first theme	245
6.86	Draeseke: Symphony No. 2. First movement, second theme	245
6.87	Draeseke: Symphony No. 2. First movement, third theme	245
6.88	Draeseke: Symphony No. 2. Second movement, opening, March	246
6.89	Draeseke: Symphony No. 2. Second movement, first episode	246
6.90	Draeseke: Symphony No. 2. Second movement, final bars	246
6.91	Draeseke: Symphony No. 2. Third movement, Scherzo, opening	247
6.92	Draeseke: Symphony No. 2. Third movement, Trio	247
6.93	Draeseke: Symphony No. 2. Third movement, Scherzo climax	247
6.94	Draeseke: Symphony No. 2. Third movement, Scherzo, conclusion	248
6.95	Draeseke: Symphony No. 2. Fourth movement, Rondo, opening	248
6.96	Draeseke: Symphony No. 2. Fourth movement, second theme	249
6.97	Draeseke: Symphony No. 2. Fourth movement, fugue subject	249
7.1	Gernsheim: Symphony No. 1. First movement, opening	255
7.2	Gernsheim: Symphony No. 1. First movement, first subject	255
7.3	Gernsheim: Symphony No. 1. First movement, second subject	256
7.4	Gernsheim: Symphony No. 1. First movement, transition on pedal	256
7.5	Gernsheim: Symphony No. 1. Second movement, main theme	257
7.6	Gernsheim: Symphony No. 1. Second movement, thematic elaboration	257
7.7	Gernsheim: Symphony No. 1. Third movement, Scherzo	257
7.8	Gernsheim: Symphony No. 1. Third movement, Trio	258
7.9	Gernsheim: Symphony No. 1. Fourth movement, first subject	259
7.10	Gernsheim: Symphony No. 1. Fourth movement, second subject	259
7.11	Gernsheim: Symphony No. 1. Fourth movement, bridge passage	260
7.12	Brahms: Symphony No. 1. Fourth movement, bridge passage	260
7.13	Gernsheim: Symphony No. 1. Fourth movement, first subject developed	260
7.14	Gernsheim: Symphony No. 1. Fourth movement, development	260
7.15	Gernsheim: Symphony No. 1. Fourth movement, bridge passage to coda	261
7.16	Brahms: Violin concerto. Finale, bars 141–3	261
7.17	Goetz: Symphony No. 2. First movement, first subject	264
7.18	Goetz: Symphony No. 2. First movement, second subject	264
7.19	Goetz: Symphony No. 2. Second movement, Intermezzo, fanfare bars 1–7	264
7.20	Goetz: Symphony No. 2. Second movement, Intermezzo, dance bars 8–12	265
7.21	Goetz: Symphony No. 2. Second movement, Intermezzo, flute cadenza leading to main section	265
7.22	Goetz: Symphony No. 2. Second movement, Intermezzo, trio	265

7.23	Goetz: Symphony No. 2. Second movement, Intermezzo, coda	265
7.24	Goetz: Symphony No.2. Third movement, opening	266
7.25	Goetz: Symphony No.2. Fourth movement, finale, bars 5–7	266
7.26	Grimm: Symphony in D minor. Duplet + triplet motto rhythm.	270
7.27	Grimm: Symphony in D minor. First movement, motto rhythm	271
7.28	Grimm: Symphony in D minor. First movement, motto rhythm with upper and lower pedal points on D	271
7.29	Bruckner: Symphony No. 3. First movement, duplet + triplet motto rhythm	271
7.30	Grimm: Symphony in D minor. First movement, second subject	272
7.31	Grimm: Symphony in D minor. First movement, second subject	272
7.32	Grimm: Symphony in D minor. First movement, second subject	272
7.33	Grimm: Symphony in D minor. Second movement, opening	273
7.34	Grimm: Symphony in D minor. Second movement, motto rhythm	273
7.35	Grimm: Symphony in D minor. Second movement, middle section	273
7.36	Grimm: Symphony in D minor. Third movement, Scherzo	274
7.37	Grimm: Symphony in D minor. Rondo finale, opening theme	275
7.38	Grimm: Symphony in D minor. Rondo finale, second theme	275
7.39	Grimm: Symphony in D minor. Rondo finale, third theme	275
7.40	Brahms: Rhapsody for piano Op. 119 No. 4.	276
7.41	Grimm: Symphony in D minor. Discarded finale, first subject	276
7.42	Grimm: Symphony in D minor. Discarded finale, second subject	276
7.43	Grimm: Symphony in D minor. Discarded finale, coda	277
7.44	Grimm: Symphony in D minor. Second movement, coda	282
7.45	Brahms: Symphony No. 1. First movement, Introduction	283

Preface and Acknowledgements

This book investigates, decade by decade, the German symphony from the mid-1820s to the mid-1870s, starting from the impact and aftermath of Beethoven's ninth in 1824 and ending with the emergence of Brahms's first in 1876. Beethoven's colossal final symphony can be compared to a huge meteor, which hurtled to earth and left a vast crater on impact. From that crater emerged composers of symphonies such as Spohr, Kalliwoda, Lachner, Raff, Reinecke, Bruch, Volkmann, Gernsheim, Dietrich, Draeseke and Grimm. These relatively unknown musicians have often been dismissed hitherto as epigones of Beethoven, Mendelssohn and Schumann, but investigation of their symphonies reveals that they too had their own distinctive brand of originality. The turbulent years for German music continued beyond the century's halfway point. Wagner was redefining German opera, Liszt had turned to the symphonic poem, while in music periodicals, critics were setting out minimum requirements for acceptance, success and longevity of the symphony in both analytical previews of scores and reviews of performances. From 1843 the musical epicentre of the many states of pre-unified Germany was Leipzig, where teaching of composition at the Conservatoire and performances at Gewandhaus concerts became the focus for new works. The city's influence lasted until the end of the century and is evaluated. Finally, the book defines and illustrates the various qualities that were necessary to progress the German symphony through a process of reassessment and lead it to the point where, a half-century after Beethoven's mould-breaking ninth, Brahms finally unlocked the door to revival and renewal.

Apart from a few exceptions such as Kittl's *Jagd*, Raff's *An das Vaterland* or Hiller's *Es muss doch Frühling werden*, programmatic symphonies with titles to guide the listener are more closely related to the symphonic poem.[1] Already broad in scope by focussing on the German symphony, the decision was taken to exclude not only France's few post-Berlioz symphonists (such as Gounod and Saint-Saëns) but also those emerging from eastern Europe and bearing the green shoots of nationalism (such as Dvořák and Tchaikovsky). Also not included are those from the neighbouring Austrian Empire (1804–67) and its Austro-Hungarian successor (1867–1918), although as it happens, the half-century journey of the symphony under discussion begins with Beethoven and ends with Brahms, both of them emigrants from Bonn and Hamburg respectively to Vienna. Symphonists such as Matthäus Nagiller, Josef Netzer and Johann Rufinatscha warrant thorough investigation, but in the context of this book they should be perceived as parallel

---

[1] Article by Roger Scruton in *The New Grove Dictionary of Music and Musicians* 6th edition, 20 vols (London, 1980) (henceforth Grove 6), Vol. 15, 283, col. 2.

threads leading to Bruckner and Mahler rather than to Brahms, a vast topic in itself when considering the direction that the symphony took in the last quarter of the nineteenth century.² Some Germans based in Switzerland (Hermann Goetz, for example) are covered, as are some non-German symphonists who studied at Leipzig. That city is hugely significant in maintaining the lineage of the symphony from Haydn through Mozart, Beethoven and Schubert on to Mendelssohn, who was primarily active at Leipzig. In turn this city became the epicentre of German music-making and the natural successor to Vienna following the death of Schubert in 1828. By virtue of its conservatoire, music publishers, musical press and the Gewandhaus, Leipzig merits a chapter to itself.

The paucity of literature about symphonists between Beethoven and Brahms (excluding work on Mendelssohn and Schumann) is striking. A handful of theses or articles about Spohr, Wagner, Mendelssohn, Reinecke and Schneider is mentioned in the relevant period in *Die Musik in Geschichte und Gegenwart*, while the topic is alluded to in biographies (Franz Lachner) or reminiscences (Carl Reinecke).³ Hermann Kretschmar's *Guide to the Concert Hall* (1886), based on essays he had written for audiences attending concerts he had conducted over the years 'to prepare the listener for the performances of unknown or difficult compositions', is the most comprehensive analytical study of many of the symphonies under discussion.⁴

In more recent years musicologists have begun to explore the subject, particularly in respect of the period 1850–76 between Schumann and Brahms. In Germany, Rebecca Grotjahn, while eschewing musical analysis, provides statistical evidence of performances of a comprehensive list of works written during that quarter century 1850–76.⁵ Her fine book covers historical aspects, including socio-historical detail, and the institution of the symphony concert before 1850. She uses Leipzig's Gewandhaus orchestra as a model when describing the many developments that then took place, deals with concert programmes and repertoire, and also touches on reception in the journal *Die Signale*. Matthias Wiegandt starts with a general discussion on the subject of the epigone in music, then studies only the symphonies of Raff and Reinecke.⁶ Similarly Matthias Falke studies the three symphonies by Bruch and the first by Volkmann, before concluding with theories

---

² Nor the enormously influential teacher Simon Sechter, who did for Austrian composers, almost from Schubert (but whose death intervened) to Bruckner, what the Leipzig Conservatoire did for its students.

³ *Die Musik in Geschichte und Gegenwart* (henceforth *MGG*), cols 1896–7. A notable exception is Clive Brown's biography of Spohr, which includes comprehensive analysis of that composer's symphonies.

⁴ Hermann Kretschmar, *Führer durch den Konzertsaal Sinfonie und Suite* Vol. I part ii (Leipzig, 1898).

⁵ Rebecca Grotjahn, *Die Sinfonie im deutschen Kulturgebiet 1850–1875: ein Beitrag zur Gattungs- und Institutionengeschichte* (Sinzig, 1998).

⁶ Matthias Wiegandt, *Vergessene Symphonik* (Sinzig, 1997).

of interpretation.[7] All three authors mention most of those composers who qualify as *Kleinmeister* (in Germany today this is a somewhat disparaging term that hints at plagiarism), but they do not go on to measure the significance of their roles or their forgotten symphonies. The Oxford-based German musicologist Barbara Eichner has a concluding chapter entitled 'Symphonic Visions from the Periphery' in her study into German national identity, while David Brodbeck's recent essay 'The Symphony after Beethoven after Dahlhaus' gives a general overview of the topic.[8]

Full scores of many of the works discussed are lodged at the British Library, but these days reprints of an increasing number can be bought from German publishers. First performances of new symphonies were played from manuscript scores and parts. Only after close monitoring of the public's response at such premieres would a decision be taken by a publisher whether or not to print the performing material; most were not, and so many of them have had to be evaluated from reports in the musical press of the day. Music examples are largely in short score made up from printed works. I have translated all material from the original German.

I am most grateful to Alan Howe for providing me with recordings of symphonies, for confirming my translation of some of the denser nineteenth-century German I encountered and for casting an eye over the finished product. I am also extremely grateful to Margaret Williams for setting the music examples and to Theda Lehmann for guiding me along or rescuing me from the paths of computer technology. Numerous enquiries at the British Library were always treated with efficiency, courtesy and consideration by its staff. I am grateful to the following for help or advice: Peter Horton at the Royal College of Music Library, staff at the Bavarian State Library, Münster and Göttingen city archives, Département de la Musique at the Bibliothèque nationale de France, Stephen Banfield, Alexander Rumpf, Monica Werra, Christian Kirscht, Irmgard Pelster, Harold Mann, Tobias Koch, Matthias Falke, Matthias Wiegandt, Rebecca Grotjahn, Ulrich Konrad, Styra Avins, Ronald Sebben, Clive Brown, Walter Frisch, Michael Musgrave, Robert Pascall and the late Alan Krueck. Last but far from least, my dealings with Ashgate have (and not for the first time) been made much easier thanks to the courtesy and professionalism of Emma Gallon, Kayleigh Huelin and Felicity Teague. If I single out my editor Laura Macy, it is because her enthusiasm and encouragement spurred me on to write this book,

---

[7] Matthias Falke, *Die Symphonie zwischen Schumann und Brahms: Studien zu Max Bruch und Robert Volkmann* (Berlin, 2006).

[8] Barbara Eichner, *History in Mighty Sounds* (Woodbridge, 2012), 229–72; David Brodbeck, 'The symphony after Beethoven after Dahlhaus' in *The Cambridge Companion to the Symphony* (ed. Julian Horton) (Cambridge, 2013), 61–95.

Chapter 1
Introduction

> I secretly hope I will achieve something, but who dares to try anything after Beethoven?[1]

This book shines a light into a half-century of shadows in the history of the German nineteenth century symphony, namely the years 1826–76. How widespread Schubert's secret hopes, as expressed in this chapter's opening quotation above, on the future of the symphony, were disseminated before they were made known in 1858, 30 years after his death, is unclear. Even so, at that date the symphony was in the throes of a second, longer crisis, and composers would not have relished reading Schubert's words. This crisis was identified by Carl Dahlhaus most recently in 1989, when, like Wagner before him, he pronounced the death of the symphony as having occurred in 1850 after Schumann's last contribution to the genre.[2] We should, however, raise the possibility of a disingenuous Schubert misleading us, for in 1825, just a year after Beethoven's ninth symphony, he answered the question himself with a ninth symphony of his own. For lesser mortals it was different. The late Alan Krueck described Beethoven's position as 'so powerful in the period 1830–70, that even the most talented men shrank from this symphonic god like penitent apostles struck dumb with awe'.[3] For half a century from 1824, Beethoven's ninth became an impossible act to follow.[4] It was only after Schumann discovered Schubert's masterpiece in a drawer at his brother Ferdinand Schubert's house in Vienna in 1838, that he realised that 'it was still possible to make an original contribution to a genre whose potential had been seemingly exhausted by Beethoven, and it certainly stimulated him to take up symphonic composition again' after his aborted attempt in 1832.[5] Throughout this book, we shall find many references to Beethoven's ninth when dealing with his German symphonist descendants, either in reviews and analyses or in the

---

[1] Josef von Spaun, *Aufzeichnungen über meinen Verkehr mit Franz Schubert* (1858) quoted in Konrad Küster, 'Leipziger Perspektive' in *Aspekte historischer und systematischer Musikforschung*, Schriften zur Musikwissenschaft Vol. 5 (eds Christoph-Hellmut Mahling and Kristina Pfarr) (Mainz, 2002), 210.

[2] Richard Wagner, *Oper und Drama* (1851) in Carl Dahlhaus, *Nineteenth century Music* trans. J. Bradford Robinson (Berkeley, CA, 1989), 265.

[3] Alan Krueck, *The Symphonies of Felix Draeseke* (PhD dissertation, University of Zurich, 1967), 15.

[4] Mendelssohn's *Lobgesang* (Symphony No. 2) makes a brave, if uneven, attempt at retaining the choral element.

[5] John Daverio, *Crossing Paths: Schubert, Schumann and Brahms* (Oxford, 2002), 18.

music itself, ranging from similarities or even outright plagiarisms to mere hints or recognisable quotations. It had already started within a year of the first performance when, in 1825, Schubert quoted it with a pair of clarinets in the *finale* of his own *Great* C major symphony (Ex. 1.1), although, despite his unqualified enthusiasm for Beethoven's masterpiece, Schumann curiously failed to mention this understated tug of the forelock.

Example 1.1   Schubert: Symphony No. 9 in C *Great* D. 944. Finale, bars 386–93

Midway through the period under discussion Mendelssohn and Schumann both made their mark for a decade and in so doing, illuminated the progress of the symphony. Each man's talent and influence, the one as a teacher, the other as a writer and both as composers, played a crucial part in revitalising the genre through the 1840s. Between them, they fed the concert repertoire with at least half a dozen symphonies, two of Mendelssohn's five (Nos 3 and 4) and all four by Schumann. These six works are mentioned but not covered in any great detail in their own right, beyond reference to the influence they exerted on composers encountered on the road to Brahms a quarter of a century later. They are by no means summarily dismissed, but they are fully covered elsewhere in numerous other books. The symphony was territory that neither man comfortably inhabited; instead, between them, they reigned supreme in the fields of chamber music, oratorio, piano music and Lieder. According to Marcel Brion, 'the evolution of Schumann's art was a constant development of its language, with no end to his learning. [His] symphonies ... may be regarded as stages in the conquest of a more stringent musical form'.[6] The consequences of his contribution, both in his symphonies and more importantly his writings, were confusing. On the one hand he was noticeably non-formulaic in his own symphonies, yet on the other, in his writings he solidified a set of pre-requisites for the genre, which were then so rigidly taken up and applied by critics, musicians and public alike that too often they stifled the inspiration of hopeful symphonists. Those who came after Beethoven were simply not given the chance to develop in their own time and in their own way until the arrival on the scene of Brahms, who produced his first symphony as a mature work and as one that immediately took its place in the concert hall. Even so, it too had its own quarter-century of gestation before he

---

[6] Marcel Brion, *Schumann and the Romantic Age* (trans. G. Sainsbury) (London, 1956), 274.

deemed it ready or worthy of performance in the year (1876) in which Wagner's *Ring* cycle was also first heard. By that date the symphonic poem (for example Liszt's *Faust* and *Dante* symphonies) had been fully accepted as a genre. This in turn encouraged a radical rejection of the traditional symphony as impossible after Beethoven and led to its redirection through a process of synthesis. The concerto, meanwhile, had advanced (for example, Tchaikovsky's for the violin) and it was also time for the symphony to reinvent itself at the highest level. In 1878 the German music scholar Friedrich Chrysander was among the first to acknowledge that 'the [first] symphony by Brahms ... belongs to those musical works that are significant not only through their specific musical content but also through the position they occupy in the development of music'.[7] Nevertheless, the half-century leading to this success is strewn with near misses, so near that many of them may now be deemed worthy of reassessment and even revival. What was it that made them stand out from the run-of-the-mill compositions that soon fell by the wayside? What made a good symphony? The best composers brought *originality* to a symphony, *developed* it and posthumously *influenced* symphonists who came after them. These criteria, originality, development and influence, were therefore the three vital ingredients in the recipe for success, a yardstick that this book will also seek to apply. The press of the day constantly demanded originality, high-quality thematic material and skill in its development, but all such elements were to be present within the traditional symphonic structure, particularly in the application of a sound contrapuntal technique. An optimum length developed, but this was a consideration that (a cynic might say, predictably) only seemed to arise when the material was mediocre and therefore boring. Texture and colour were expected in the mastery of orchestration, critical at a time when instruments were growing in size and volume, more musicians were being trained, and bigger halls were available to growing numbers of audiences.

What the press was not looking for was a newly established style or even harmonic progressiveness, presumably because mould-breakers such as Wagner, Liszt and their New German followers were providing more than enough of either in other genres. *Colorit* or *Farbenfülle* (colour), *Behandlung* (treatment) and *Entwicklung der Formen* (development of form) were common words or phrases in a critic's armoury.[8] Like Beckmesser (the pedantic trouble-maker in Wagner's *Die Meistersinger*), they marked their slates noisily when they heard or read anything of which they disapproved, such as a symphony in only three movements, an absence of a fugue, unmemorable themes or dense scoring. A phrase such as 'applauded without opposition' appeared frequently, for new music was generally assumed to be guilty until proven innocent, particularly if the

---

[7] Friedrich Chrysander in *Allgemeine Musikalische Zeitung* (henceforth *AMZ*), Vol. 13 No. 6, 6 February 1878, col. 94 as quoted in David Brodbeck, *Brahms: Symphony No. 1* (Cambridge, 1997), 86.

[8] For example *Die Signale*, Vol. 27 No. 3 (1869), 40; *AMZ*, Vol. 4 No. 10, 10 March 1869, col. 79.

composer was unknown and untested.⁹ *Scherzo*s and slow movements fared better and were the most popular with the public, because their respective structured patterns were familiar. While a *scherzo* usually showed obvious character by being loud, exciting and rhythmically robust, a tuneful *Adagio* could wear a full range of emotion on its melodic sleeve. The first movement, if the material was good enough, was expected to fit into a template of sonata form. This left the *finale* as a problem, the more so because Beethoven had come up with a brilliant solution. For those who came after, including Mendelssohn, who was brave enough to attempt the same choral solution but to no avail, the *finale* problem became the Achilles heel of any new symphony.

A decade after Beethoven's ninth, Gottfried Wilhelm Fink, one of the earliest editors to write about the symphony, placed the genre on a pedestal as the pinnacle of instrumental music.[10] Quoting E.T.A. Hoffmann from some 20 years earlier, Fink added that the symphony had become 'the opera of instruments', which by then (i.e. 1835) gave a composer free rein, with all possible means at his disposal, including order of movements, harmony and instrumentation, to enchant the listener. Fink pointed out that combinations of orchestral instruments required more independence and freedom in a composer's treatment and control of sound and colour, in a way that was unachievable when writing for the more uniformly monochrome sound of a string quartet. Almost as a throw-away line, he begged the question whether the symphony should be constructed on a narrative or a poem, for he viewed it as a dramatised, sentimental *novella*; whatever the chosen description, feelings were an essential ingredient, otherwise a symphony became merely a collection of meaningless sounds.[11] The argument between absolute and programme music had begun.

There were, of course, alternatives to writing a symphony for performance in the concert hall during the first half of the nineteenth century, such as the concert overture, which appeared regularly in programmes. Since the eighteenth century, the overture in opera or ballet was played first, but in the context of a concert programme this was not always the case. Neither was it always extracted from an opera. Sometimes (as in the case of Beethoven's *Coriolan* overture) it preceded a spoken drama or recitation; and in that particular case, it was even heard for the first time (in 1807) literally as a concert overture in its rightful place to start the concert. In many ways the concert overture became the soft option to writing a symphony. After a slow introduction, it became a symphonic first movement in a loosely structured sonata form. Those that bore a title may have conveyed a programmatic message, either a direct literary reference or by an implication of mood using words such as *pastorale* or *solenelle*, while others carried no more than a mundane nomenclature such as an opus number or the key. Concert overtures

---

[9] *AMZ*, Vol. 49 No. 30, 28 July 1847, col. 517.

[10] Fink (1783–1846) edited *AMZ* 1828–41.

[11] *AMZ*, Vol. 15 No. 23, 9 June 1813, cols 373–4; G.W. Fink, *Über die Symphonie* in *AMZ*, Vol. 37 No. 34, 26 August 1835, col. 557.

were frequently produced on demand as occasional pieces; and in order to enhance an audience's pleasure, a composer would incorporate familiar melodies such as chorales or anthems following a tradition going back to Weber and beyond.[12] In the second half of the century, another genre presented itself as a way out for composers who had taken the symphony as far as they could, when a revival of the eighteenth-century suite and serenade became a less challenging alternative to such composers as Johann Kalliwoda, Franz Lachner, Robert Volkmann and Joachim Raff. This retrospective approach was part and parcel of Mendelssohn's Bach revival in the post-Beethoven years, while later in the century Brahms cast his eye even further back in his admiration for the music of Palestrina or Schütz.

In his survey of post-Beethoven symphonic music, Hermann Kretschmar commented:

> The works of the Romantics were a last flicker of the old light; the lean years of the symphony began and not even the best intentions of an open competition could change that. If four or five new symphonies appeared on the programme of a winter season and were even half worthwhile, that was the best one could expect.[13]

Schumann himself seems to have triggered signs of a revival in the genre's fortunes after writing a composite *critique* of symphonies by Gottfried Preyer, Karl Gottlieb Reissiger and Franz Lachner in 1839, the year Schubert's ninth was first heard.[14] In fact, as Sanna Pederson has noted,

> Schumann's criticisms made manifest the tension between venerating past masters and realising the tremendous expectations for the glorious future. Now that Beethoven's symphonies were established, their true greatness had to be maintained in two ways, Schumann repeated over and over. First, their tradition had to be preserved and honoured and second, composers had to realise this tradition further by composing works that were new and progressive. The task of writing symphonies was weighed down with enormous significance.[15]

Schumann must have intimidated many a young composer when he wrote in 1840 that crossing the symphonic Rubicon had become impossible after Beethoven,

---

[12] Such as Weber's *Jubel* Overture (1818), which concludes with the anthem *God Save the King* to the words 'Heil dir im Siegerkranz' written for the 50th anniversary celebrations of the accession to the throne of King Friedrich August I of Saxony.

[13] Hermann Kretschmar, *Führer durch den Konzertsaal: Sinfonie und Suite*, Vol. I part ii (Leipzig, 1898), 265.

[14] Heinrich Simon (ed.), *Gesammelte Schriften über Musik und Musiker* (Leipzig, 1888).

[15] Sanna Pederson, 'On the task of the music historian: the myth of the Symphony after Beethoven' in *repercussions*, Vol. 2 No. 2 (1993), 19.

and that any such subsequent work represented nothing more than an interesting signpost for its composer's own development, rather than a contribution to the universal progress and development of the genre. He dismissed such symphonists as mere epigones, for the music they produced was nothing more than 'mirror images'.[16] Ironically, both he and Mendelssohn then spent the next decade (1840–50) grappling with their own symphonic problems.[17] Although Lachner's sixth symphony came off relatively unscathed in Schumann's article (having already taken his fifth apart three years earlier, as we shall see), the symphonies of Preyer and Reissiger were shot down in flames, consigning them to subsequent oblivion.[18] On the other hand, some of Lachner's symphonies are at least heard today, on disc if not in the concert hall, so Schumann generally recognised a worthy work when he saw it. Yet Lachner may well have taken the criticism to heart, for his last two symphonies (his seventh and eighth) are separated by a dozen years (1839–51). What is more, this pillorying and deflation of symphonic aspirants, which started with the death of Beethoven in 1827 and continued for decades, was not just confined to Schumann's pen but also to lesser writers wielding as much power and influence from their journalistic bases. A more enlightened critic, however, would encourage a composer to view Beethoven not as an impediment but as a guide and touchstone. Such advisers, however, were too rare; and while the press could take on its share of responsibility for keeping the symphony alive, too often its finger hovered uncomfortably close to the self-destruct button when analysing and reviewing new works.

---

[16] *Neue Zeitschrift für Musik* (henceforth *NZfM*), Vol. 7 No. 12 (1840), quoted in Martin Kreisig (ed.), *Robert Schumann: Gesammelte Werke über Musik und Musiker* 5th edition, 2 vols, Vol. 1 (Leipzig, 1914), 461.

[17] Mendelssohn's *Scottish* and *Italian* symphonies are meant here; both had their origins far earlier in the composer's lifetime and, leapfrogging the decade of the 1830s, went on to cause him considerable problems; see R. Larry Todd, *Mendelssohn: A Life in Music* (Oxford, 2003), 276 and 430.

[18] Gottfried Preyer (1807–1901), Viennese organist, composer, conductor and pedagogue; Karl Reissiger (1798–1859), German composer, conductor and pedagogue.

Chapter 2
The German Symphony in the 1830s

Every symphony became a surprise symphony.[1]

In the 1830s it was general practice in German-speaking countries to have a mixed content in concert programmes. In one evening the public might listen to a symphony, part of an oratorio, and a virtuoso playing a concerto as well as taking another solo spot. Large works were cut or performed in part. The juxtaposition of works took no account of the attention span of the audience, while chosen combinations sometimes beggared belief. In 1803 Mozart's *Requiem* was interrupted after the Hostias for a bassoon concerto and an overture. Even more bizarrely, at Vienna in 1839 an aria from Donizetti's *Lucia di Lammermoor* was inserted between the first two movements of Schubert's *Great* C major symphony.[2] Until Mendelssohn took over at Leipzig in 1835 most orchestral works were by Haydn, Mozart and Beethoven, but he then ensured that more music by his contemporaries was included. In 1840 at Leipzig, Beethoven's name is still found most commonly on programmes, followed by Mozart and Haydn. Especially liked were Weber, Cherubini and Spohr, whereas Bach, Handel and Gluck were found singly, while singers unsurprisingly favoured Rossini, Bellini and Donizetti. Other works were by the significant German contemporary composers of the day such as Marschner, Schneider and Kalliwoda.

Where concert programming was concerned, audiences of the mid-nineteenth century demanded a substantive symphony after a functional overture followed by obligatory virtuosic displays from solo instrumentalists or singers. Apart from Telemann's efforts in Frankfurt in the 1720s, it was in Leipzig in 1781 that a series of Subscription Concerts as entertainment was established, and the practice soon spread throughout Germany and its cities. After 1835, the symphonic works that filled the programmes for such concerts were the historically proven masterpieces from the deified Haydn, Mozart and Beethoven, to which was now added a splash of Mendelssohn and Schumann and the odd token work by a living composer. William Weber places 'the rise of the masters to musical sainthood … during the 1850s and 1860s. It was only then that their works came to dominate the concert repertoire and their names were put up on high for all to behold. Their elevation marked a fundamental change in the orientation of European musical taste, for never before had the music of dead composers been played so often or ascribed so

---

[1] Roger Shattuck, *The Banquet Years* (London, 1958), 262 quoted in Allan Scott Morris, *The Wellsprings of Neoclassicism in Music: The 19th century Suite and Serenade* (PhD dissertation, University of Toronto, 1998), 13.

[2] Eduard Hanslick, *Geschichte des Concertwesens in Wien* (Vienna, 1869), 291.

lofty a status in musical life'.[3] It would appear, however, that such worship of the selected few took place earlier than he asserts.

The large number of past works being performed were being heard for the first time by many discerning audiences, who then demanded their repetition at subsequent concerts. This therefore left little room for new works, unless they dislodged such acknowledged masterpieces as the symphonies of Haydn and Mozart. So not only did new composers of symphonies have to contend with being refused admission onto the concert programmes, they were also given an unattainable benchmark penned by Gottfried Wilhelm Fink, namely the so-called *grosse Symphonien* (implicitly by Beethoven), which brought both high expectations and inevitable comparisons from reviewers. Even the word *grosse* had two meanings, both of which (*great* = worth, *grand* = size) were highly loaded in their implications. The ultimate expectation from a symphony in the immediate post-Beethoven years was for unity with diversity, 'a coherent impression created out of many different ideas and instruments', as Fink described it.[4]

The 1830s were uncertain years during which the symphony struggled to find an identity as it travelled along its post-Beethoven route, but there was never any doubt that it had to. The problem for the next generation of composers was the expectation confronting them to continue where Beethoven had left off with one of the most challenging calls of 'Follow that!' in the history of music. Yet (and unfairly so) no account was taken of the two and a half decades it took him to make the transition from the decidedly eighteenth-century Classical first symphony *via* the *Eroica*, fifth and *Pastoral* to the Romantic ninth, all four of whose collective shadows inevitably loomed large thereafter. A composer living and working in post-Beethoven Germany who produced a symphony had a mountain to climb before he might have it performed.[5] With that performance achieved, he might look upon such an occasion with pride, for it probably meant that he had convinced a conductor, an orchestra and an administrator, perhaps all three, of its worth. He could also guarantee that, before long, within the covers of one of the increasing number of music journals of the day, a detailed analysis of the published score or a thorough critical response to a first performance would be in print. The reviewer at this time might also have been the founding editor of the very same music

---

[3] 'Mass Culture and the Reshaping of European Musical Taste, 1770–1870' in *International Review of the Aesthetics and Sociology of Music*, Vol. 8 No. 1 (June 1977), 5.

[4] Fink, 'Symphonien' in *Encyclopädie der gesammten musikalischen Wissenschaften der Tonkunst* (ed. Gustav Schilling) (Stuttgart, 1838), quoted in Walter Frisch, '"Echt symphonisch": on the historical context of Brahms' symphonies' in *Brahms Studies 2* (ed. David Brodbeck) (Lincoln, NE, 1998), 115.

[5] The masculine pronoun is used here because, as Grotjahn observes (*Die Sinfonie im deutschen Kulturgebiet 1850–1875*), female composers only appear, if at all, on the fringes of symphonic production. In the period she deals with (1850–75), she names only Aline Hundt (1849–73) and Emilie Mayer (1812–83). She blames a lack of women in music directors' posts, thus denying them the opportunity to programme their own music.

journal. He was someone who wielded extraordinary power, exercised immense influence and built a formidable reputation based upon his personal response, taste, prejudice, judgement and historical view, all of which opinions were entirely subjective. He was 'a musical *arbiter elegantiarum*'.[6] Whether, as a result of such criticism, careers were made or broken is hard to judge; certainly paths could be made smoother or rockier. In their collective view, the height of the bar had been set by Beethoven in 1824. One might be forgiven for thinking that, despite offering a glimmer of hope, Parry's article on the Symphony for Grove might have discouraged many a young composer when he wrote that,

> It might seem almost superfluous to trace the history of the Symphony further after Beethoven. Nothing since his time has shown, nor in the changing conditions of the history of the race is it likely anything should show, any approach to the vitality and depth of his work. But it is just these changing conditions that leave a little opening for composers to tread the same path with him.[7]

As the century progressed, ever-increasing sizes in halls produced larger audiences (or ever-increasing sizes in audiences led to the building or rebuilding of larger halls to accommodate them), while instruments were made louder and larger to fill the halls with sound; and for that, appropriate music had to be written. While the writing of choral music for large forces became an obvious way to satisfy such growing demands, in the field of purely orchestral music it was the symphony that now had to develop in similar fashion. Romanticism took hold, the symphony as a genre grew in stature, and in so doing it acquired a mystique among composers, performers and audiences alike. From 1799 and for at least the next three and a half decades, symphonies were given human emotional characteristics. They contained 'not one individual emotion ... but an entire world, an entire drama of human emotions'.[8] Then they became 'the expression of a sentiment of an entire multitude',[9] and finally 'a story, developed within a psychological context, of some particular emotional state of a large body of people'.[10] Even that

---

[6] Hans-Hubert Schönzeler, 'The Romantic Classicists' in *Of German Music* (London, 1976), 219. The term *arbiter elegantiarum* means a judge of matters of taste and those influential reviewers of the day included E.T.A. Hoffmann, Johann Friedrich Rochlitz, the Rellstabs (father Johann and son Heinrich), Ludwig Bischoff, Friedrich Chrysander and Robert Schumann.

[7] C.H.H. Parry 'Symphony' in *A Dictionary of Music and Musicians* 1st edition, Vol. IV (ed. George Grove) (London, 1879), 27–8.

[8] 'The characteristic inner nature of the musical art and the psychology of today's instrumental music' in *Wackenroder's Confessions and Fantasies* (trans. M.H. Schubert) (University Park, PA, 1971), 193.

[9] Heinrich Koch in 1802, quoted in Mark Evan Bonds, *A History of Music in Western Culture* (Chapel Hill, NJ, 2003), 375.

[10] Gottfried Wilhelm Fink in 1835, ibid.

non-symphonist Wagner, having pronounced the symphony as dead in 1851,[11] went on to fire a typical Parthian shot just two weeks before his death on 13 February 1883. According to Cosima Wagner's diary her husband said, 'In the sonatas etc., [Beethoven] made music himself; in the symphonies the world made music through him'.[12] This universality was not intended as a devious way to send out a subliminal political message of nationalism, but rather as embracing a more individualised view of humanity.[13] Why, if they provoked such profound thoughts in so many serious minds, have symphonies produced after Beethoven, with a few exceptions, been so readily dismissed?

Kretschmar described the Romantic era as one in which 'the fruitful years of symphonic writing were completely extinguished' by what he identified as 'external circumstances and the way of intellectual thought'. These 'external circumstances' were the events of the years known as the *Vormärz*, between the revolution in France in 1830 and the more widespread upheavals of March 1848, during which Germany finally stopped watching from the sidelines and took its own road to unity just over two decades later. The 'old fruitfulness' of Haydn's 104 symphonies, Mozart's 41, even Beethoven's nine, was reduced to far fewer by the time of Mendelssohn (five) and Schumann (four), after which single-figure totals became more commonplace. By 'intellectual thought', Kretschmar meant a more questioning approach to the artistic and creative process. While symphonists of the 1830s stood comparatively unnoticed in Beethoven's intimidating shadow (with his 'unendingly mounting demands'), it was also the lack of quality in 'the content of their musical ideas' that doomed the symphonies they did write before they had even begun to impact upon concert life.[14] This was the Biedermeier period, which reached deep into urban bourgeois society by deliberately substituting complexity, intellectual and technical facility with a simple, superficial approach that listeners could imitate. Salon pieces and simple songs encouraged house music, and in turn brought their owners, players and audiences to concert halls. On the other hand this was the era of the virtuoso, in which they heard Chopin, Liszt and Paganini, who impressed with their charisma and astounding technical facility, way beyond imitation at home by their ardent, admiring audience. It was also the decade that saw an increase in the publication of books explaining musical form as a handbook

---

[11] 'Die letzte Symphonie Beethovens ... auf sie ist kein Fortschritt möglich' ['Progress is not possible after Beethoven's last symphony'] – Richard Wagner, *Gesammelte Schriften und Dichtungen* Vol. 3 (2nd edition, Leipzig, 1887).

[12] Martin Gregor-Dellin and Dietrich Mack (eds), *Cosima Wagner's Diaries*, entry for 31 January 1883 (trans. Geoffrey Skelton), Vol. 2 1878–83 (Munich, 1976), p. 1001.

[13] The non-programmatic symphony is meant here, which therefore excludes Berlioz's highly personal *Symphonie fantastique*.

[14] Kretschmar, Vol. II part i, 265.

to composition, albeit with few, if any, concessions to any probable lack of familiarity or knowledge of music's technical language on the part of the reader.[15]

There were a few exceptions among the symphonists working during this first symphonic crisis of the 1830s.[16] The first was Louis Spohr (1784–1859). His 10 symphonies span nearly half a century (1811–57) and, without setting an agenda for future decades, perpetually address the development of new ideas within new structures, and experiment either with orchestral sounds using various instrumental combinations or with rhythmic passages, sometimes even whole movements of strikingly novel complexity. Following Beethoven's model, the first two are cast in the Classical mould. The first (1811) owes much to Mozart (for whom Spohr held a deep reverence), but E.T.A. Hoffmann also hailed it as a highly significant work that raised great hopes for the future, and it went on to hold an annual place in Leipzig's Gewandhaus concerts virtually until 1830.[17] Both it and the second symphony, which followed in 1820, seem to have been composed after Spohr had written a concert overture as a preparatory exercise, a practice that Mendelssohn would follow a generation later. This second symphony, coming nine years after the first, was written hastily in three weeks during his first visit to London, and was specifically designed to make a good impression upon his English public.[18] As Clive Brown points out, the *finale* of the second symphony (1820) (Ex. 2.1), while of lightweight quality, possesses 'a principal theme with its warm harmonisation which has something of the amiable flow characteristic of later nineteenth-century D major symphonic *finales* (Brahms [No. 2] and Dvořák [No. 6])'.[19]

Example 2.1   Spohr: Symphony No. 2. Finale

Spohr's third symphony (1828) was a successful work that held its place in concerts until the end of the century. Johann Friedrich Rochlitz, a contemporary

---

[15] Marx, Dehn, Fink, Czerny and Gathy were writing treatises, handbooks, manuals and articles.

[16] In German musicology today the term *symphonische Krise* tends to be used rather than Dahlhaus's description of a first and second age of the symphony or *Zeitalter*.

[17] *AMZ*, Vol. 13 No. 48 (27 November 1811) col. 797ff. quoted in Clive Brown, *Louis Spohr: A Critical Biography* (Cambridge, 1984), 70n7.

[18] Mozart had written his *Linz* symphony in similar haste when he visited the city in the autumn of 1783.

[19] C. Brown, 140.

of Beethoven but longer lived, first tackled Spohr in 1828 on the matter of writing symphonies in the post-Beethoven era that had just begun.[20] The highly influential Rochlitz (first editor of the *Allgemeine Musikalische Zeitung* when the music publishing house of Breitkopf & Härtel launched it in 1798) was a friend and admirer of the composer, and the two were in fairly regular correspondence. In a letter to Spohr in response to news that the new third symphony was on its way, he asked the rhetorical question, 'Who else should now write symphonies?'[21] One senses here an unspoken 'but you', while 'now' can be read as 'since the death of Beethoven'. He also observed that 'the symphony as a genre was once again attracting interest, not so much as entertainment but in a more serious vein, a nobler, worthier manner'.[22] How ironic that such a question should be asked in the very year of Schubert's death, and one wonders what Rochlitz would have been asking had he known about the composer's *Great* C major symphony, the manuscript of which, as we have noted, was still in Vienna until 1838, when Schumann sent it to Leipzig for its premiere under Mendelssohn on 21 March 1839. This was a landmark that, as we shall discover, made a huge impact on the nineteenth century symphony. Despite his unawareness of the existence of that monumental work, Rochlitz implies that the symphony was making a comeback after the cataclysmic shock to the system caused by Beethoven's ninth four years earlier in 1824. With extraordinary prescience, his conclusion, while highlighting a necessity for new forms, also warns against petty criticisms by self-important reviewers and critics of new attempts by composers of symphonies throughout the next half-century:

> However you may write the symphony, it will be received with joy and thanks; indeed in these circumstances quite definitely *double* joy and thanks. It seems to me that absolutely new (or perhaps only rarely and very imperfectly used) forms can be devised for symphonies, which would have the double advantage of continuing to make it easier for the composer to be original in design while also preventing tiresome comparisons on the part of semi-experts and dabblers, who, however often they may be told, almost always unjustly criticise one movement out of two and so destroy their own pleasure![23]

If Spohr did not go down the road of structural originality with his third symphony, he did so with his fourth in 1832. For the first time since Beethoven's *Pastoral* symphony (1808), a German symphony carried a title, in this case *Die Weihe der Töne* ('The consecration of sound'). The composer elaborated further

---

[20] Johann Friedrich Rochlitz (1769–1842).
[21] Letter dated 23 July 1828. Ernst Rychnovsky, 'Ludwig Spohr und Friedrich Rochlitz: Ihre Beziehungen nach ungedruckten Briefen' in *Sammelbände der Internationalen Musik-Gesellschaft*, Vol. V (1903/4), 283.
[22] Ibid.
[23] Ibid.

by describing it as 'a characteristic sound picture in the form of a symphony', so its description takes precedence over its structural format. The various 'pictures' include the evocation of 'the deep silence of nature before the creation of sound', followed by a movement in conventional sonata form. Another depicts the role of music variously as a lullaby, a dance tune and a serenade, each with a different melody and time signature, appearing first alone then ingeniously combined (the orchestral accompaniment to the party scene in the first act *finale* of Mozart's *Don Giovanni* comes to mind). There is music to inspire courage in war (a military march), a trio in which sounds of a departing army are heard (as a gradual *diminuendo* from *fortissimo*), anxious feelings of those left behind followed by a return of the march (a gradual *crescendo*) culminating in thanks for victory (chorale prelude entitled *Ambrosianer Lobgesang*).[24] The *finale*, beginning with a *Larghetto*, depicts the burial of the dead in a funeral chorale *Begrabst den Leib* followed by an *Allegretto* subtitled 'Consolation in tears'. Brown not only identifies this latter melody as having a close kinship to the consolatory theme in the *finale* of Tchaikovsky's *Pathétique* symphony but also draws attention to the similarity between Spohr's symphony and Berlioz's *Symphonie fantastique* (1830), a work that Spohr could not have known until 1835, three years after he had written his own fourth symphony when Schumann wrote a review of it in *NZfM*. Like Berlioz, Spohr asked that either the programme or the original poem by Carl Pfeiffer be made available to the audience before the performance, and while both composers significantly modified conventional symphonic form in order to accommodate the programme, the results are very dissimilar largely because Spohr's sense of instrumental colour lacks Berlioz's new sonorities 'despite beautifully calculated richness, exquisite balance and a perfect blend of sounds'.[25] The fourth symphony had a good track record in Germany (17 times at Leipzig's Gewandhaus between 1834 and 1869), though, following a pattern which will often be repeated, Spohr's symphonies dropped out of the standard concert repertoire after his death.

Over a period of 15 years, Rochlitz continued to comment on Spohr's symphonies in letters from Leipzig, from where he rarely travelled.[26] He made a final complimentary observation of their popularity to the composer shortly before his death in 1842:

> I welcome all the more the opportunity to learn of your worthy, praiseworthy life, not merely from tiresome newspaper articles, but from your works, and at the same time to experience every winter – to my great joy – the unmistakeably

---

[24] Just three years earlier (1829) Mendelssohn had revived Bach's *St Matthew Passion*, as a consequence of which chorales (sung or instrumental) began to appear in symphonies. The following year (1830), Mendelssohn produced his *Reformation* symphony, the first German choral symphony since Beethoven's ninth (1824).

[25] C. Brown, 221.

[26] Hans Ehinger in *Die Musik in Geschichte und Gegenwart* (henceforth *MGG*), 11 (Munich, 1989), cols 590–93.

far-reaching effect of those of your works, principally the symphonies, not upon me and others who have the ability to grasp and understand [them], but also upon the mixed crowd that is our concert audience. That is how it is with your symphonies, but not with your oratorios, and that makes me very sorry.[27]

Despite the tragic loss of close members of his family during the 1830s, Spohr's fifth symphony (1837) is a cheerful work written for the Vienna *Concerts spirituels* after the success there of the fourth.[28] With it he believed he had 'introduced many new effects as well as much that is unusual in the orchestration'. Brown, who considers the fifth to be the best of Spohr's symphonies, notes its unusual scoring of three trombones in the slow movement, rich wind writing throughout, and the favoured use of the lower register in the string writing, all of which contributed to a warm Romantic colouring.[29]

Innovation continued to feature in Spohr's symphonies as the genre entered into the 'momentary daylight' of the decade of the 1840s, during which he would be joined by Mendelssohn and Schumann as symphonists. The sixth symphony bears the title 'Historical, in the style and taste of four different periods'. In turn, each movement investigates the styles of composers of the pre-1840 past at specific dates, Bach (a prelude and fugue) and Handel (a pastorale) in 1720, Haydn and Mozart (with shadowy and overt reference to the slow movements of the *Prague* and 39th symphonies) in 1780, and Beethoven in 1810 (reminiscences of the *scherzo* from his seventh symphony, though all on a rather subdued dynamic level).[30] The surprise lies in the *finale*, which is a satirical view of 'the newest of the new' music of the day (1840) focussed mainly on Auber and Adam, but it was a joke that misfired.[31] By not having any guidance in the programme, audiences missed the point, while even the critics could only make assumptions. Spohr abhorred effects for their own sake, which he made clear with music that is frankly trivial, the orchestration extravagant, the whole bordering on the vulgar, with piccolo and percussion playing stridently to the fore in places. Musicians of the day disagreed among themselves on whether or not to praise it. Mendelssohn would have preferred Spohr to showcase his own music, in particular his overtures, which he much admired, rather than the music of others. Schumann, on the other hand, spotted Spohr's hand at every twist and turn in the movement. When he wrote it, Spohr may also have had the Leipzig Gewandhaus' Historical Concerts in his sights, for from February 1838 they were an established series in the city and, led by Mendelssohn's example as well as setting his own, it was becoming

---

[27] Rochlitz to Spohr, 8 September 1842 in C. Brown, 310–11.
[28] Despite having lost his brother, wife and daughter, he also made a happy remarriage.
[29] C. Brown, 243.
[30] Spohr had once before used Mozart's Symphony No. 39 as a model for his first symphony back in 1811.
[31] Auber's *La Muette de Portici* was an opera Spohr was obliged to conduct too much for his liking at Kassel.

fashionable to explore music's more distant past. As Brown concludes, 'leaving aside its musical worth, it has considerable interest as possibly the earliest serious nineteenth century attempt at a species of pastiche'.[32]

After this mix of retrospective and contemporary, Spohr continued to develop new ideas in his endeavours to take the symphony along new paths. His seventh symphony (1841) is a large-scale work for, as he describes it, double orchestra, though in effect one of them is a chamber ensemble of 11 solo instruments (wind quartet, two horns and a string quintet). It therefore looks back to the eighteenth-century *Concerto grosso* principle, grouping and contrasting a small *concertino* with a large body of *ripieno*, and bears the title 'The temporal and divine in the life of Man'. The unconventionality of this metaphysical work is further reflected by having just three movements, each of which is prefaced by a four-line verse and bears a title, 'Child's world', 'Age of passion' and 'Final victory of the divine'.

The eighth symphony (1847) has no programmatic content and, like Beethoven in his own eighth symphony, Spohr (with its commission from the conservative Philharmonic Society in London in mind) returns to Classical mode and conventional four-movement format.[33] Brown detects 'Brahmsian affinities in its expansive melodic style and even Tchaikovsky [again] in the rich scoring of the slow movement', which, as in Spohr's fifth, also includes trombones. The English paper *Morning Chronicle* praised it after its premiere on 1 May 1848:

> Now that Mendelssohn is dead [six months earlier], Spohr holds the position of the first composer of the day, without a possible rival. No master has done to advance the art in the highest department of composition [symphony] than he, and as he has excelled and produced masterpieces in every style, his genius may be pronounced universal and a place be assigned to him by the side of Bach, Handel, Haydn, Mozart, Beethoven and the lamented musician just mentioned, who may appropriately be called the kings of art.[34]

Henry Chorley, on the other hand, dismissed it as nothing new from Spohr's pen and correctly predicted that it would not be heard again, while Hans von Bülow's contribution to the 'Prophetic Musical Calendar for 1859' was, 'Spohr composes his eighth symphony yet again without realising it'.[35] While there is more than a grain of truth in these judgements, they are too harsh when applied to the symphony as a whole, for it has a trio that develops and extends the composer's imaginative innovation, turning it virtually into a violin concerto, a retrospective glance perhaps at his own former career. Disappointingly, it is the *finale* that is extremely patchy in quality, at times slipping into the comic style of a Gilbert

---

[32] C. Brown, 245.
[33] The eighth symphony was written to a commission from the Philharmonic Society, but the work was actually first played in public under Spohr at Kassel on 22 December 1847.
[34] 2 May 1848 quoted in C. Brown, 308.
[35] Both quoted in ibid., 308–9.

and Sullivan operetta, giving good grounds for their later reference to Spohr in *The Mikado*.

Spohr's last two symphonies were both written in the 1850s, the ninth bearing the title *Die Jahreszeiten* ('The Seasons'). Although the conventional four movements are discernible, its originality lies in its two-part structure, Winter/Spring and Summer/Autumn. Brown considers the opening Winter to be 'the weakest movement, containing nothing which is graphically descriptive or even evocative of that season'.[36] It was the quality of content that declined rather than his ever-imaginative treatment of form, and it affected Spohr's unpredictable tendency to surprise any unwary listener. He retained almost to the end a remarkable willingness to keep abreast of new trends. There is a dichotomy here, for Spohr, whose name was worthy of a place on Novello's vocal scores alongside the usual suspects from Bach to Mendelssohn, conducted Wagner's music (a staged *Tannhäuser* and excerpts from *Lohengrin* in concert) during the last 10 years of his life. Nevertheless it was clear that he was running out of ideas and, substantiating von Bülow's dry observation, beginning to repeat himself, despite retaining his mental faculties. Even the English were tiring of him. *The Spectator* described him as 'truly *ultimus Romanorum* – the last of the great symphonists'.[37] *Musical World* summed it up: 'Spohr has taught us, by previous essays, to expect so much, that the announcement of a new symphony from his pen is almost tantamount to the promise of a new *chef d'oeuvre* for the art. That we have been disappointed on the present occasion cannot be denied'.[38] Spohr wrote a tenth symphony in 1857, which he tried out with his orchestra in Kassel, but did not consider worthy of publication and suppressed it. Fortunately he did not go so far as to destroy it and it is now published, though adds nothing beyond what he had achieved with his best. Indeed, most of Spohr's symphonies from the third to the ninth strive for, and to a large extent achieve, progress by innovation. He stood head and shoulders above most German composers who essayed a symphony during that bleak decade of the 1830s.

Johann Kalliwoda (1801–66) was another composer who wrote symphonies during the two post-Beethoven decades, but whose reputation today lies mainly in the field of chamber music.[39] He emerges as a significant figure. His seven symphonies were written between 1825 and 1843, during almost 40 years as court conductor at Donaueschingen (in the state of Baden-Württemberg), an appointment that began in December 1822. Such was his reputation (as a violinist as well as a composer) that all of Kalliwoda's symphonies were performed at Leipzig more or less as they appeared. The first (like Spohr's first) was heard nine times between 1826 and 1838.

---

[36] Ibid., 319–20.
[37] *The Spectator* 23 (1850) quoted in C. Brown, 1137.
[38] *Musical World* xxv (1850), 766 quoted in C. Brown, 320.
[39] Though Bohemian, here he is considered German.

Table 2.1   Performances of Kalliwoda's seven symphonies at Leipzig 1826–52

Symphony No.	Year	Total number of performances
1	1826 (2), 1828 (2) 1829, 1830, 1833, 1834, 1838	9
2	1827, 1829, 1830	3
3	1832 (2), 1834	3
4	1835 (2)	2
5	1840 (2), 1852	3
6	1841	1
7	1843	1
	Total	*22*

With Spohr and Kalliwoda, we have examples of composers who, having appeared at a prestigious venue as an instrumental virtuoso, then consolidated that success with performances of their own music. They represented the last of a line of the eighteenth-century, first Viennese school of composers, who directed performances of their own music from either the keyboard or the violin. By the 1830s that performance practice had succumbed to more complex music as well as larger and louder instruments. The rise of the virtuoso soloist then led naturally to the separation of the two activities, one of them the star player, the other the new career of the silent star conductor, Mendelssohn being an early and fine example of the latter. Kalliwoda, meanwhile, was still trading on his reputation as an exemplary violinist while also building another to match it as a composer. His final count of published works reached 243; and contemporary reviewers and later biographers were united in their positive verdict on him as a composer. An obituary in the local paper in Donaueschingen reported that, while he wrote numerous respectable works, he attained the highest rank in the topmost genre of instrumental works, the symphony, an achievement that quickly resulted in the spread of his reputation throughout Germany.[40]

In terms of style, Kalliwoda's seven symphonies reveal a mix of the first Viennese school of Mozart and Beethoven, into which he pours his own brand of early Romanticism with Weber as template. Weber died just as the period under discussion begins and his influence is sometimes discernible, though it was not so much through his own two symphonies (1807) but through his more frequently played overtures and concertos.[41] Despite Kretschmar's opinion that Weber's two symphonies were 'beloved by orchestras for a long time', there is a glaring

---

[40] *Donaueschinger Wochenblatt* 7 December 1866, quoted in Laszló Strauss-Neméth, *Johann Wenzel Kalliwoda und die Musik am Hof von Donaueschingen* (Hildesheim, 2005).

[41] Kalliwoda, having graduated, joined the Prague opera as violinist in 1816, when Weber was a staff Kapellmeister.

omission here of the words 'and audiences'.[42] The Leipzig Gewandhaus concerts to 1881 included them just three times, twice during his lifetime (1814 and 1825) and once (1839) after his death in 1826. Weber was uncomfortable as a symphonist and both are uneven. Their best music lies in their rich slow movements or brilliant finales. Both works were written for the Court at Karlsruhe where he was briefly employed, and both managed to avoid any similarity to the *Eroica* written just two years before. Weber himself admitted to an overture style for the first movement of the first symphony, rather than the classically constructed sonata form, and he himself dismissed it in 1815.[43] A handful of performances followed during his life (Mannheim and Munich), but being written for a Court may well have limited their chances of further hearings, though more likely it was Weber's own lack of conviction in the worth of both works that inhibited their chances of being heard.

The more confident Kalliwoda had better luck with his symphonies at Leipzig. His music possesses an infectious rhythmic energy. His scherzos and finales show his Slavic origins (with hints of the later Dvořák and, once again, even Tchaikovsky), as well as the inevitable debt to Beethoven (the pastoral element of the sixth and the idiosyncratic rhythms of the seventh and ninth symphonies). Kretschmar's overview was written at the end of the nineteenth century and it is remarkable that he gave such elevated status to a composer, who by then was largely forgotten:

> Kalliwoda should be considered the last and most important exponent of the original style of the North German School, whose music held an important place in the repertoire from the mid-1820s for a quarter of a century. Fate seemed to want to bestow upon him the status of a first-class Master. Versatile, confident in every musical form, often new, original but also natural and simple, he repeatedly gave the impression of being one of the chosen, and came near to the last step before immortality. Although Kalliwoda's eminent talent did not develop to the full, for in each of his works there lacks that final finish with excessive long-windedness of construction here and disproportion of sections there, a study of his symphonies is nevertheless very enjoyable. Each one contains a pearl of originality.[44]

In 1910, Kalliwoda's biographer Karl Strunz acknowledged that 'the name Kalliwoda is long forgotten'.[45] He went on to describe an exceptional but unfulfilled talent, because, in his view, the composer's creativity was never matched by originality. His weaknesses lay in several areas, including the matter of form, where he indulged in excessive breadth of construction, unequal proportionality of section and a general lack of momentum. He could also not resist pandering

---

[42] Kretschmar, Vol. I part i, 226–7.
[43] John Warrack, *Carl Maria von Weber* (London, 1968), 56–7.
[44] Kretschmar, Vol. I part i, 222–3.
[45] Karl Strunz, *Johann Wenzel Kalliwoda (1801–1866)* (Vienna 1910), 1.

to public taste and thus never really formulated his own personal style.⁴⁶ The relationship between Schumann and Kalliwoda is significant.⁴⁷ Kalliwoda stopped writing symphonies in the early 1840s, just as Schumann began to write his. Despite their friendship, some of Kalliwoda's music was dismissed by Schumann as 'commonplace'.⁴⁸ Yet with typical exaggeration, he also described the symphonies as 'flickering lightning illuminating Roman and Greek ruins' (in other words, the Romantic illuminating the Classical).⁴⁹ They exchanged dedications in small-scale works, though in 1835 Schumann described Kalliwoda as 'a cheerful harmonious person, whose later symphonies, with a more laboured foundation, did not reach the imaginative heights of his first', a significant comment but one that obviously could only pertain to the four that then existed.⁵⁰ Though, as we shall see, his review of Kalliwoda's fifth symphony is very enthusiastic, he could also write, 'What annoys me is when it is said that a symphony by Kalliwoda is no symphony by Beethoven. Naturally he who tastes caviar will smile when a child finds an apple tasty'.⁵¹

Kalliwoda's seven symphonies are among the best of his achievements; and Strunz, despite his criticisms, conceded that the music still had a resonance in 1910.⁵² They were written during the 16 years between the composition of the last symphonies of Schubert and the first of Schumann. In 1825, a year after Beethoven's ninth and the year Schubert wrote his last, Kalliwoda's first (in F minor) was premiered in Prague. Table 2.2 puts his seven symphonies in the context of those of his contemporaries. Note that Mendelssohn's *Italian* symphony, commissioned in 1833 by the Philharmonic Society in London, was not heard in Germany until 1849, two years after the composer's death. It also illustrates the impact and influence Schubert's ninth may have had after its first performance in 1839.

If expectations were high that symphonic development was an open invitation to Beethoven's younger contemporaries and immediate successors, the success of Kalliwoda's first two symphonies indicated that he was among them; indeed the first (1825) became popular immediately and was published (1826) by Breitkopf &

---

⁴⁶ Ibid., 16.

⁴⁷ Schumann met Kalliwoda for the first time on 23 August 1831. Georg Eisman (ed.), *Robert Schumann Tagebücher (1827–1838)*, Vol. 1 (Leipzig, 1971).

⁴⁸ Quoted in Strunz, 16.

⁴⁹ Robert Schumann, *Gesammelte Werke über Musik und Musiker* 4 vols, Vol. 1 (Leipzig, 1854), 160 quoted in Strunz, 17.

⁵⁰ Robert Schumann, 'Hector Berlioz' in *On Music and Musicians* (ed. Konrad Wolff; trans. Paul Rosenfeld) (London, 1947), 165.

⁵¹ Schumann, *Gesammelte Werke über Musik und Musiker*, Vol. 1, 29.

⁵² At the time of writing, four have been recorded and published: Symphony Nos 1 and 5 *Das Erbe Deutscher Musik* (ed. Albrecht Dürr) Vol. 7 Breitkopf & Härtel (Wiesbaden, 1998); Symphony Nos 2 and 4 *Symphony, 1720–1840* Series C Vol. XIII (ed. David E. Fenske) (New York, 1984). A study has also been written: Strauss-Neméth, *Johann Wenzel Kalliwoda und die Musik am Hof von Donaueschingen* (see page 17, footnote 40).

Härtel.[53] A review of the Leipzig premiere was preceded by an assessment of the symphonic genre, whether or how the tradition might be developed beyond the works of the three Viennese masters.[54] The question was asked, as it would be for the next half-century, could a younger composer develop the symphony further, matching the freshness and spirit of the earlier era, or would there be the danger of imitation, of becoming nothing more than a diluted copy of the great masters?[55] This was especially so if themes or phrases seemed familiar and were then recognised as having their roots in the Viennese triumvirate. Having studied the score of Kalliwoda's first symphony and despite having come to it with no preconceptions, the reviewer professed himself surprised, that he, audience and players alike would be so pleased by the work.[56] He was reminded of Mozart's mature style, while later commentators mentioned Schubert (his fourth) and Mendelssohn.

A slow introduction (Ex. 2.2) is followed by a theme heavily phrased in pairs and hinting at Schumann (Ex. 2.3), while Bruch some 40 years later might have written the second subject (Ex. 2.4), though that humourless man would never have added the cheerful Rossinian afterthought (Ex. 2.5). Strauss-Neméth notes Kalliwoda's remarkable exploration of keys in the development, with some enharmonic switches, such as this one (Ex. 2.6) leading from A♭ major, eventually reaching remote D minor. From the outset, Kalliwoda's thematic material appears in both major and minor modes to heighten means of expression; and, as we shall see, his choice of mode is invariably crucial to the success or failure of his later symphonies.

Example 2.2   Kalliwoda: Symphony No. 1. Introduction

Example 2.3   Kalliwoda: Symphony No. 1. First movement, first subject

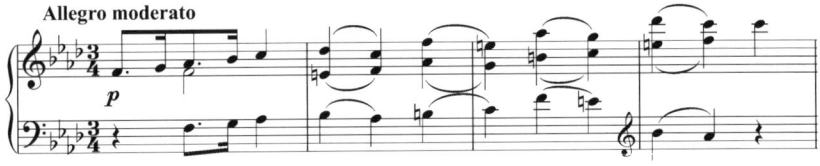

---

[53] Kalliwoda's violin playing also kept him in the public eye until about 1845.
[54] *AMZ*, Vol. 29 No. 11, 14 March 1827, cols 177–82.
[55] See also Siegfried Kross, 'Das "zweite Zeitalter der Symphonie" – Ideologie und Realität' in *Probleme der symphonischen Tradition im 19 Jahrhundert* ed. Siegfried Kross and Marie Luise Maintz (Tutzing, 1990), 23.
[56] *AMZ*, Vol. 29 No. 11, 14 March 1827, col. 178.

Table 2.2 Kalliwoda's seven symphonies and those of six of his contemporaries

Kalliwoda	Mendelssohn	Schubert	Spohr	Schumann	Lachner	Burgmüller
No. 1 1825	No. 1 1827	No. 9 1825 c	No. 2 1820		No. 1 1827	
No. 2 1829	No. 5 1830		No. 3 1828			
No. 3 1830	No. 4 1833 c		No. 4 1832		No. 2 1833	No. 1 1833
					No. 3	No. 2 1834–36
					No. 4 1834	
No. 4 1835					No. 5 1835	
			No. 5 1837		No. 6 1837	
No. 5 1840	No. 2 1840	No. 9 1839 p	No. 6 1839		No. 7 1839	
No. 7 1841	No. 3 1842		No. 7 1841	No. 1		
				No. 4 c 1841		
No. 6 1843				No. 2 1846		
			No. 8 1847			
	No. 4 1849 p		No. 9 1850	No. 3	No. 8 1851	
				No. 4 1851		

Note: c = year of composition; p = year of first performance

Example 2.4   Kalliwoda: Symphony No. 1. First movement, second subject

Example 2.5   Kalliwoda: Symphony No. 1. First movement, second subject

Example 2.6   Kalliwoda: Symphony No. 1. First movement, development

The second movement, by far the longest, is a substantial work praised at the time for its fullness of expression, its masterly invention and development. There are signs of Mozart here: first we have a main theme (Ex. 2.7) recalling the duet 'Volgi a me' for Ferrando and Fiordiligi in the second act of *Cosi fan tutte* (Ex. 2.8), while a contemporary review suggested a similarity in the accompanying figuration (Ex. 2.9) to the *Andante* of Mozart's Symphony No. 40 (Ex. 2.10).[57]

---

[57] Ibid., col. 180ff.

Example 2.7   Kalliwoda: Symphony No. 1. Second movement, theme

Example 2.8   Mozart: *Cosi fan tutte* K.588 Act 2 No. 29. Duet

Example 2.9   Kalliwoda: Symphony No. 1. Second movement, accompaniment

Example 2.10   Mozart: Symphony No. 40 K.550. Second movement, bars 20–22

Their keys may differ (Kalliwoda in F minor, Schumann in D minor), but the opening of the *scherzo* is remarkably similar to the latter's fourth symphony (1841) (Exx 2.11 and 2.12). It also has in common the canonical interplay of the theme between treble and bass. In view of the mutual admiration between Schumann and Kalliwoda, it is hard to avoid the conclusion that Schumann was paying his respects 16 years later, though there is no hard evidence. R. Larry Todd describes this as a 'striking, though so far overlooked, quotation', but Kretschmar mentions it in his assessment of Kalliwoda's symphonic canon as a 'coincidental similarity'.[58] Albrecht Dürr, editor of the most recent full score, goes further and describes Schumann as deliberately paying homage to his colleague and senior by nine years.[59]

Example 2.11   Kalliwoda: Symphony No. 1. Third movement, Scherzo

Example 2.12   Schumann: Symphony No. 4 Op. 120. Third movement, Scherzo

---

[58] R. Larry Todd, 'On quotation in Schumann's music' in *Schumann and His World* (Princeton, NJ, 1994), 102; 'Eine zufällige Ähnlichkeit', Kretschmar, Vol. I part i, 223.

[59] Foreword by Albrecht Dürr in *Das Erbe Deutscher Musik*, Vol. 7 (Wiesbaden, 1998), viii.

Although Schubert uses the description *Menuetto* until and including his fifth symphony (1816) and Beethoven does so in the third movements of his first and eighth, Kalliwoda goes for a hybrid version of *Menuetto*, namely *Allegro scherzo*. Like the second movement of Beethoven's eighth (*Allegretto scherzando*), the first word indicates the tempo while the second is a characterisation of the material. We meet this again in his third symphony, where *Menuetto* is followed by *allegretto marcato molto*. The four remaining symphonies use the term *scherzo*. The fast *finale* has striking similarities to the first movement, giving the symphony a cyclical structure but without recycling any actual material. The themes in Kalliwoda's symphonies typically juxtapose *Sturm und Drang* and *cantabile*, the standard Romantic 'duality of two contrasting themes' between masculine first subjects and feminine second subjects.[60] In the year of Beethoven's death, Kalliwoda's first symphony was perceived as 'a truly excellent symphony. The composer is still a young man and this is his first attempt in the genre, and we must pin the greatest hopes on him'.[61] Such publicity was dangerous to the unwary, a burden that Schumann laid upon the young Brahms a quarter of a century later. It carried with it great expectations and set Kalliwoda a challenge, but despite progress through experience and maturity, none of his subsequent symphonies achieved the comparatively widespread popularity of the first. It became his most oft-performed work in the first half of the nineteenth century after its premiere at Prague in December 1825 followed by Berlin, Breslau, Königsberg, Halle, Jena, Gotha, Magdeburg, Mannheim, Stuttgart, Munich and (the litmus test of them all) Leipzig, where it was played no less than nine times between 1826 and 1838.[62] Both this symphony and the next are scored for double woodwinds, two each of horns and trumpets, a single bass trombone to reinforce the bass line, timpani and strings.[63]

Kretschmar considered that Kalliwoda made 'significant progress' with his second symphony in 1829.[64] August Gathy described it as 'a fiery composition with fresh melodies, straightforward harmony and free from artificial, modern form'.[65] Whether or not it moved the genre along is a moot point, but once some dull, overlong bridge passages in the first movement have been negotiated, it becomes a fine, highly attractive work. Once again it includes plenty of retrospective glances from the very opening, where a quiet tattoo on the timpani bears a striking similarity to the start of Beethoven's violin concerto (Ex. 2.13).

---

[60] James Webster in Grove 6, Vol. 17, 504.
[61] *AMZ*, Vol. 29 No. 11, 14 March 1827, col. 182.
[62] Alfred Dörffel, *Geschichte der Gewandhausconcerte zu Leipzig 1781–1881* (Leipzig, 1884), Statistik, 31.
[63] All Kalliwoda's symphonies have a bass trombone; the scoring varies only in the number of horns (two or four).
[64] Symphony No. 2 in E♭ Op. 17 in Kretschmar, Vol. I part i, 223.
[65] August Gathy, *Musikalisches Conversations-Lexicon* (Leipzig, 1835), 246, quoted in Strauss-Neméth, 144.

Within 10 bars, Kalliwoda turns to counterpoint with a brief four-part fugue for strings in the more sombre tonic minor (Ex. 2.14), until the first subject appears. Its melodic content again recalls Haydn, with phrasing in note-pairs across strong beats (Ex. 2.15), while elements of Rossini create a sunny mood. The weakness of this opening movement, however, lies in the strong similarity between the first and second subjects (Ex. 2.16) despite some chromaticism in the latter. The development, largely dominated by the return of the fugue (Ex. 2.17) in a substantially detailed and crafted format, is an impressive testimony to Kalliwoda's contrapuntal skills.

Example 2.13   Kalliwoda: Symphony No. 2. First movement, introduction

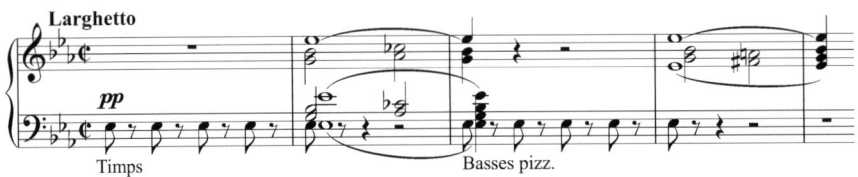

Example 2.14   Kalliwoda: Symphony No. 2. First movement, fugue subject

Example 2.15   Kalliwoda: Symphony No. 2. First movement, first subject

Example 2.16   Kalliwoda: Symphony No. 2. First movement, second subject

Example 2.17   Kalliwoda: Symphony No. 2. First movement, fugal development

A feature of Kalliwoda's style is the charming lyricism of his long-breathed melodies, like his exact contemporary Schubert, who had died just a year before. This is particularly true of this symphony's beautiful second movement, a theme and set of variations, which includes dialogues between solo horn and oboe, bassoon and flute, shifting the listener's attention from strings to winds. Its *Menuetto* is less appealing and has yet to break from the Viennese tradition and develop its own Bohemian folk rhythms and melodies. The key of E♭ major has military associations with trumpets and drums in the symphonies of Haydn and Beethoven, but here it is the content, shape, scoring and instrumental distribution of Mozart's Symphony No. 39 (in the same key) as his model (Exx 2.18 and 2.19).[66] The highly attractive trio, more a waltz (Ex. 2.20), acknowledges Mozart's *Jupiter* symphony by imitating the *finale*'s opening four-note motto (Ex. 2.21) but here in triple time. Kretschmar's view of Kalliwoda's 'significant progress' is contradicted by a typically Classical, bustling *rondo-finale*, contrapuntal from its fugal start (Ex. 2.22), which, like Mozart's overture to the opera *Die Zauberflöte*,

---

[66] 'E flat [major] ... considered to be the "German key"' – Raymond Monelle, *The Musical Topic: Hunt, Military and Pastoral* (Bloomington, IN, 2006), 81.

is entrusted to the second violins. Again Kalliwoda's scoring is cleanly delineated with substantial passages taken by all woodwinds while strings remain silent, but when we compare the finales of the first two symphonies, we find significant instances of self-borrowing, resulting in repetition rather than originality (Exx 2.23 and 2.24).

Example 2.18   Kalliwoda: Symphony No. 2. Third movement, Scherzo

Example 2.19   Mozart: Symphony No. 39 K.543. Third movement, Scherzo

Example 2.20   Kalliwoda: Symphony No. 2. Third movement, Trio

Example 2.21   Mozart: Symphony No. 41 *Jupiter* K.551. Finale opening

Example 2.22   Kalliwoda: Symphony No. 2. Finale, fugal opening

Example 2.23   Kalliwoda: Symphony No. 2. Finale

Example 2.24   Kalliwoda: Symphony No. 1. Finale

Kalliwoda's second symphony was written five years after he entered the service of Prince Karl-Egon II at Donaueschingen, where it was first performed on 14 March 1827. Two years later, on 5 March 1829, Leipzig heard it for the first time with Schumann among the audience. Its reviewer welcomed it and looked forward to the prospect of a third. In its preamble the subject of the symphony as a genre was once again tackled head-on. The writer derided anonymous composers who 'play to the gallery' and accused them of being nothing more than 'false artists', who merely sought applause from an unsuspecting public instead of striving for 'honest art' and a 'true attitude'. Kalliwoda, on the other hand, stood accused of modesty – this, coupled with true spiritual content, made his personality seem doubly likeable. His music stood out thanks to his technical competence, but had someone other than Kalliwoda written it as beautifully, while people would probably still have liked it, they would certainly not have been half so delighted *with* it or thought half so highly *of* it.[67]

Kalliwoda made significant progress with his third symphony (D minor Op. 32, 1830). It was thought his best work to date by most critics and biographers, despite lacking the success of the first. A review of a performance in Stuttgart in 1830 singled out for praise expert handling of modulation, understanding of harmony, and colourful instrumentation, all of which put him head and shoulders above many composers of the day.[68] Two years after it was first heard at Donaueschingen, Fink praised it as 'splendid' after a 'magnificent' performance at Leipzig.[69] Apart from its third-movement minuet and trio, Kalliwoda's third symphony is based on a five-note motif, said to have been played repeatedly by one of his children on the family piano. Strauss-Neméth describes the motto as having 'an Oriental colour'.[70] This family tale is related by Fink, who, following an increasingly metaphysical fashion in German criticism at the time, wonders how the flame of great music (which he considered this symphony to be) can literally be ignited by the act of a child, who, whether through naïve speech or music, was able to inspire its father to great heights. One can see in this example, he continues, how a child can impact upon more sophisticated adult achievement, if both are on the same wavelength.[71] As it happens, however random and unexpected its intervallic

---

[67] Strauss-Neméth, 144, paraphrasing and quoting *AMZ*, Vol. 31 No. 12, 25 March 1829, col. 200.

[68] *AMZ*, Vol. 32 No. 33, 18 August 1830, col. 539 quoted in Strauss-Neméth, 142.

[69] At Leipzig on 2 February 1832: *AMZ*, Vol. 34 No. 14, 4 April 1832, col. 222.

[70] Strauss-Neméth, 142, where the music example is incorrect; the final two notes should be B♭ and A.

[71] Fink in *AMZ*, Vol. 34 No. 14, 4 April 1832, col. 222.

sequence may be (Ex. 2.25), this selection by his child lent itself rather well to harmonic experimentation and contrapuntal exercise; and true to form, Kalliwoda exploited both to the full.[72]

Example 2.25   Kalliwoda: Symphony No. 3. Five-note motif

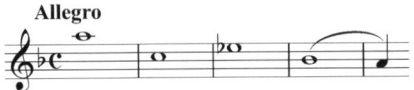

The third symphony, however, has original features that go beyond the motto principle. Unusually there is a brief rising *arpeggio* passage for solo cello in the first movement (reallocated towards the end of the movement to solo violin). This was a rare use of a solo string instrument, the significance of which will become more apparent in the fourth symphony. Elsewhere Kalliwoda juxtaposes instrumental families within an orchestral dialogue.[73] His second subject melody is clothed in Schubert and sits well as a canon (Ex. 2.26); indeed, his maturing imagination and command of orchestration continue to produce some strikingly beautiful passages, one in particular for string and woodwind solos in the slow movement. It starts (Ex. 2.27) and ends (Ex. 2.28) with wind chords like Mendelssohn's overture to *A Midsummer Night's Dream*, written five years earlier and which reveals an early sign of that composer's influence on Kalliwoda. Then follow more passages for accompanied solo cello (Ex. 2.29), after which we hear several episodes in variation form including various instrumental solos and counterpoint to develop the material.

Example 2.26   Kalliwoda: Symphony No. 3. First movement, cello solo and canon

---

[72] It is not clear which of his children is meant, but his son Wilhelm Kalliwoda (1827–93), also a composer, became a conductor at Karlsruhe.

[73] The part is for cello and double bass written on two staves. Three bars before the second subject, the word 'solo' appears in the cello line, while the basses have whole bar rests in the line below. It is surely for solo cello despite the absence of the word *tutti*, when the full section (including basses) clearly joins after three bars.

Example 2.27   Kalliwoda: Symphony No. 3. Second movement, opening

Example 2.28   Kalliwoda: Symphony No. 3. Second movement, conclusion

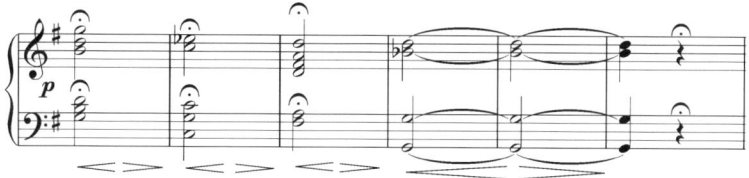

Example 2.29   Kalliwoda: Symphony No. 3. Second movement, bars 5–8

Menuetto is a somewhat ill-fitting description of the third movement, which is a Slavonic dance consisting of two components (Exx 2.30 and 2.31), followed by a trio (Ex. 2.32) whose energy and fast tempo recall the *scherzo* of Beethoven's ninth but with a lighter touch. As if to emphasise the incongruity of this eighteenth-century description, the proportions between *menuetto* and trio are extremely contrary to tradition, the latter being four times longer (170 bars) than the former (43 bars). The principal theme of the *rondo finale* also has eighteenth-century roots, this time in the so-called 'Mannheim Rocket' (an upward-directed *arpeggio*, though Kalliwoda omits the customary *crescendo* that underpins it). The rhythmic shape of its first seven notes also recalls the *finale* of Mozart's G minor symphony K.550 (Ex. 2.33). The second subject is played by winds and three of the four horns (complete with a high concert F to test their principal). In this third symphony, Kalliwoda scores for four horns (rather than two) in differing pairs of crooked keys. The shape and outline of this passage is striking and typical of Kalliwoda's distinctive melodic thought, laced with a pastoral flavour and horn fanfares such as those found in Weber's *Der Freischütz*.

Example 2.30   Kalliwoda: Symphony No. 3. Third movement, bars 1–4

Example 2.31   Kalliwoda: Symphony No. 3. Third movement, bars 8–12

Example 2.32   Kalliwoda: Symphony No. 3. Trio

Example 2.33   Kalliwoda: Symphony No. 3. Finale

Stuck in his remote outpost in south-west Germany, Kalliwoda needed not only to make but also maintain contacts for the sake of his career, and so he dedicated the third symphony to the committee of Leipzig's Gewandhaus, which did his prospects of a performance there no harm. Although Kretschmar found the *finale* unequal to the rest of the work and lacking in conciseness, he regarded the first movement as 'one of the most characteristic symphonic movements ever written; in its spare stiffness and severity it hardly has an equal, and the child's theme is in a class which only a genius could develop successfully'. In his view, the symphony, taken as a whole, was 'a masterpiece of the period, worthy of a place in the repertoire', which unfortunately has not happened.[74] Strunz also regarded it as the most important of Kalliwoda's symphonic canon, 'bold and brilliant', the first movement a classic example of a compact symphonic movement, and he reminds us that 'Schumann spoke highly of it with love and brought its beauty

---

[74] Kretschmar, Vol. II part i, 223–4.

into the sunlight'.[75] The third symphony, despite some predictable sequences, repetitions, phrase structures and familiar contrapuntal devices, is nevertheless a highly attractive work and well worthy of performance.

The fourth symphony (C major Op. 60, 1835) enjoyed a mixed success at its Leipzig premiere.[76] Contemporary reaction was reserved, calling it 'quite strange and different from its predecessors',[77] yet Mendelssohn thought highly enough of it for a repeat there within a matter of months.[78] There are several novel features that may well have confused its first audiences, such as an introduction lasting 70 sombre bars and which, in the case of some of the orchestral parts, bears the marking *Marcia funèbre*.[79] The second movement, however, is a particularly beautiful *Romanze* with solos for horn and oboe but, more significantly, a cello with its own independent part throughout, often taking centre stage like a conventional soloist (Ex. 2.34). We can deduce from this that there must have been a particularly good principal cellist in his Donaueschingen orchestra.

Example 2.34   Kalliwoda: Symphony No. 4. Second movement, Romanze

Solos for string instruments in symphonies, especially when lasting a full movement as in a concerto, are rare after Haydn.[80] The Swiss (domiciled German) Joachim Eggert wrote a lengthy solo for the orchestral leader in the trio of his first symphony (1811), after which Kalliwoda wrote a 'taster' in his third (1830) and a substantial one here in the fourth (1835). After him came Schumann (once again borrowing ideas from his friend) in the slow movement of his fourth (1841), Spohr in the trio movement of his eighth (1847), both writing for a solo violin, while Franz Xaver Schnyder von Wartensee singled out the principal double bass player for a cadenza in his *Military* Symphony (1848) in a bizarre reminiscence of his former friend Beethoven.[81]

---

[75] Quoted in Strunz, 17.
[76] At Leipzig on 12 March 1835.
[77] *AMZ*, Vol. 37 No. 14, 8 April 1835, col. 237.
[78] On 23 November 1835.
[79] Strauss-Neméth, 149; but no such marking appears on the set at the British Library, shelf mark h.1510.b.
[80] For example No. 7 *Le Midi*, 1761 and No. 45 *Farewell*, 1772.
[81] See Chapter 3, page 119.

A cheerful *scherzo* follows in Kalliwoda's fourth, and from now on he uses that nomenclature. It is full of Beethoven's energy and (with the bassoon taking a prominent part) Rossini's wit, but the trio lacks sufficient contrast, despite some felicitous scoring and tuneful phrases here and there. The *finale*, which Strunz characterises as 'breathing rich art', takes off hesitatingly.[82] It breaks off twice at pauses, then proceeds by revisiting the slow movement for 17 bars, with this time not the cello but the principal bassoon, who, in a virtuosic display of florid passagework in *legato* demi-semiquavers extensively covering the middle and upper ranges of the instrument, plays some delightful music. The ensuing movement is an anticlimax, the material never promising enough interest to be developed effectively nor to hold the attention (again it is the second subjects that are more attractive than the first). Even the final mode of the symphony is unclear, for rather than use the model of the day, Beethoven's fifth, which resolves the issue with a *finale* wholly in C major, Kalliwoda leaves it literally to the last moment with a *tierce de Picardie* in the final chord. This is an early example of the symphonic journey 'from darkness to light', a paradigm that developed throughout the nineteenth century and into the twentieth, from Beethoven's fifth to the colossal symphonies of Bruckner and Mahler.

Among all his symphonies, Kalliwoda most resembles Beethoven in the first two movements of his fifth (B minor Op. 106, 1840). Reverting once again to a pair of horns, the scoring is more translucent, though he still retains the single bass trombone, while Beethoven only ever uses either a pair or three in his symphonies. Once again the work begins with a substantial (56 bars) slow introduction, including a beautiful, tender eight-bar passage for violas and divided cellos, repeating the textures in the *Andante* of its immediate predecessor. Otherwise the introduction threatens to become dull, with over-persistent emphasis on a dotted-rhythm fanfare (Ex. 2.35) that features in the movement proper (Ex. 2.36).

Example 2.35 Kalliwoda: Symphony No. 5. Introduction

Example 2.36 Kalliwoda: Symphony No. 5. First movement

---

[82] Strunz, 17.

We shall see how Schumann lays much emphasis on the 'tender' quality of Kalliwoda's music in second subjects, slow passages or even entire movements. Often the scoring at such places consists of woodwinds spanning two or three octaves, such as the second subject here (Ex. 2.37). This is the first time Kalliwoda puts the *scherzo* second in a symphony, a strange decision because the *Allegro con brio* of the first movement is a brisk one-in-a-bar, so there is effectively no change of tempo between the two movements.[83] Borrowing from Beethoven includes the 'Humperdinck' dotted rhythm of the ninth symphony and its chunky scoring, while in Kalliwoda's third movement the woodwind's metronomic accompaniment is modelled on the slow movement of the eighth. Unusually the first bar is a four-note foretaste of the accompaniment just for double basses, whose subsequent part in this movement is often independent of the cellos. In the second bar the second violins and violas add an off-beat accompaniment, followed in the third by the woodwinds mentioned above, all of which ticks away like a clock beneath a charming *Ländler* in the first violins and cellos (Ex. 2.38). This movement was singled out by Kretschmar as the public's favourite from the first five symphonies, an understandable choice.[84] Its robust *finale* has strongly rhythmic and distinctively melodic roots in the music of Kalliwoda's native Bohemia.

Example 2.37   Kalliwoda: Symphony No. 5. First movement, second subject

Example 2.38   Kalliwoda: Symphony No. 5. Third movement, opening

Ludwig Finscher, who remarks that each symphony by Kalliwoda shows 'a different aspect', also points out that in the fifth the middle movements are 'short character pieces'. He draws our attention to positive similarities between

---

[83] Strauss-Neméth points out that the *scherzo* comes third in the piano version a year later (1841), although there is no evidence that this order was used in performance (154).

[84] Kretschmar, Vol. II part i, 224.

Mendelssohn's fourth and Schumann's third, both of which come after Kalliwoda's fifth and which he describes as matching them 'in form if not quite in quality'.[85] Schumann, despite a stated preference for the earlier Kalliwoda symphonies, was positive on the subject of the fifth when he described,

> how sincerely it pleased us; it is a really special work, and as far as we are concerned, what strikes us from beginning to end is its constant tenderness and loveliness; it is arguably unique in the symphonic world. If the composer had wanted to compose music for *Undine*, it would be the easiest matter to identify those qualities, but as he has chosen not to, so his symphony is to be even more highly regarded. How well the composer has misled us with this work!

Continuing in the same vein, Schumann believed that Kalliwoda had somehow become indifferent to his own talent, because he was a court conductor in a small remote town away from the cultural mainstream.[86] Yet he could produce a symphony that, in its instrumentation alone, confirmed him as an advanced master of his art.[87] Strunz makes the same point and wonders how Kalliwoda's creativity might have benefited more had he been in Leipzig, especially once Mendelssohn and Schumann had moved there.[88] Schumann's rapturous reception of the fifth symphony concluded, 'In the forest of German composers, Kalliwoda is a flourishing, verdant tree and we hope to meet him again in the field of the symphony, where he has now held his place for the fifth time'.[89] It is significant that Schumann wrote this review, with its emphasis on tenderness and loveliness, just as he started to compose his own symphonies and it reflects as much upon himself as it does upon Kalliwoda's work he is describing. For Schumann, Kalliwoda (and Schubert after the events of 1839) was living proof that one could write a symphony inspired by a more lyrical aesthetic than that of Beethoven. Despite the fact that, true to Schumann's prediction, Kalliwoda's symphonies would disappear from the repertoire during the composer's lifetime (he correctly and wisely made no such prediction for Schubert), it is also true that Schumann thought highly enough of them to borrow at least two elements for his own second (but fourth published) symphony in 1841. The first was the use of a solo string instrument throughout the slow movement, but in Schumann's case it was cello with oboe, then violin. The

---

[85] Ludwig Finscher, 'Sinfonie' in *MGG*, 2nd edition, 9 (Munich, 1998), cols 71–2.

[86] But a century later, in 1921, one of the most prestigious music festivals for contemporary music was founded there by Richard Strauss, Pfitzner, Busoni and former Gewandhaus conductor Artur Nikisch. It still exists.

[87] Schumann, *Gesammelte Werke über Musik und Musiker*, Vol. 3, 38; *NZfM*, Vol. 12 No. 36 (1 May 1840), 143.

[88] Strunz, 14.

[89] Schumann, *Gesammelte Werke über Musik und Musiker*, Vol. 3, 38; *NZfM*, Vol. 12 No. 36 (1840), 143.

second (already described, see Exx 2.11 and 2.12), was the thematic borrowing from the *scherzo* of Kalliwoda's first symphony for that of his own. Kalliwoda's fifth takes a step further along his own road of symphonic development. As the third had been after the first two, so the fifth advanced beyond all four. Although there are impressive moments in the two even-numbered symphonies to this point (the *Romanze* in the fourth is among the best of Kalliwoda's music), the three odd-numbered works show upward movement on the graph of quality spanning the 15 years 1825–40. All three, in the minor mode, contain his best *Sturm und Drang* music, followed by lyrical feminine second subjects in the major, in other words a mix of progressive Romanticism tempered by retrospective Classicism.

Kretschmar dismissed the two remaining symphonies (the sixth and seventh) as neither adding anything to Kalliwoda's development as a symphonist nor advancing the genre; but that is too harsh, for the composer's assured fluency remains striking, even if the music itself lacks imagination in places and constantly reminds us of his earlier achievements. The symphony published as the seventh (G minor without Opus, 1841) was in fact written two years before the sixth (F major Op. 132, 1843); therefore, although retaining their published numbers here, they will be dealt with in their order of composition rather than that of publication. The slow introduction to the seventh has a menacing tension from the outset and, always one to repeat a good idea, Kalliwoda starts the basses ahead of the orchestra, but this time joined by the funereal tread of timpani. The lengthy (46 bars) introduction (Ex. 2.39) is based on a simple rising *arpeggio*, but there is by now an all-too-familiar formulaic treatment of material in the *Allegro non tanto* such as its *unisono* start (Ex. 2.40).[90] It is, however, the trio of the energetic, canonic *scherzo* (once again strangely placed as second in view of key and tempo) that is the highlight of the symphony (Ex. 2.41). Kalliwoda's writing for horns and woodwinds (and now timpani) has become a strong feature. Strauss-Neméth criticises the third movement march (*Adagio*) (Ex. 2.42) as too thickly scored with overloud dynamics in trumpets and timpani, but there is a prominent, fine clarinet solo and stirring climaxes from the full orchestra. By leading straight into the *Allegro vivace* (Ex. 2.43), we have the only example of conjoined movements in Kalliwoda's symphonies. Somehow, even when the dynamo of his imagination is running down (more *unisono* passages forming an unmemorable opening theme) and his structures are beginning to creak because of their flimsy conciseness, he still nevertheless manages to produce a novel moment of effective brilliance.

---

[90] The first subject quietly in unison, the second an attractive sequence of melodious phrases in the relative major.

Example 2.39   Kalliwoda: Symphony No. 7. Introduction

Example 2.40   Kalliwoda: Symphony No. 7. First movement, first subject

Example 2.41   Kalliwoda: Symphony No. 7. Second movement, Scherzo

Example 2.42   Kalliwoda: Symphony No. 7. Third movement, March

Example 2.43   Kalliwoda: Symphony No. 7. Finale

William Neumann considers the seventh 'a very respectable work', yet 'lacking all the beautiful attributes' and 'special qualities' of the earlier symphonies, which he describes as having 'tasteful melodic invention, beautiful form, able, clear, easily comprehensible work, appealing simplicity and naturalness'.[91] Strauss-

---

[91] William Neumann, *Komponisten* (Kassel, 1856), 90.

Neméth notes a lack of uniformity or connection between its four movements and, like the fourth, another case of modal dilemma. The composer was disappointed by its poor reception at Leipzig on 18 February 1841, which may have led him to withold its publication for two years, although, as far as one can ascertain, even that did not lead to further performances. At Leipzig, Kalliwoda's last two symphonies were each heard only once.[92] In an attempt to disseminate it and raise its popularity perhaps, the composer reworked the seventh as a sonata for piano duet in 1846. One reviewer encouraged readers not to spoil the composer's symphonic game on account of one less successful throw of the dice. 'The seventh symphony by the beloved master should be made welcome'; and he went on to explain its poor reception by criticising the disadvantageous position it was given when placed first on the programme. 'The instruments, the musicians themselves, are often not yet warmed up at that time, while the public has not yet settled down and made itself comfortable.'[93] Programme structure was a contentious issue at Leipzig. During Julius Rietz's regime as music director (1848–52 and 1854–60), symphonies were placed in the second half of a concert, especially those of Beethoven, as if quarantined because 'their reception and musical riches were best enjoyed if they were isolated from other works'.[94] On the other hand, during Carl Reinecke's tenure (1860–95), he continually pleaded to the administration for the main work to be at the start, so that any tension resulting from the demands of listening could be relaxed by going from a hard work to an easy one.[95]

Kalliwoda's sixth symphony (F major Op. 132, 1843) also received a less-than-rapturous reception, being generally dismissed as mundane and lacking in originality. To accept this without question is to overlook some fine music. It begins gently and simply with the main material presented by *unisono* strings (Ex. 2.44), adding harmony and accompaniment as it feeds into the *Allegro*. Here the theme appears in Rossini's garb, a comparison mentioned on more than one occasion in the study of Kalliwoda's music (Ex. 2.45). The slow movement's haunting beauty (Ex. 2.46) more than makes up for its four-square shape, while a wonderfully energetic third-movement *scherzo* (Ex. 2.47) recalls the *Eroica* or Weber's two symphonies. In total contrast, Kalliwoda writes a trio in slow duple time with a *pizzicato* bass line underpinning its lovely melody, and it sounds uncannily like Schubert's string quintet in C major. The *finale* (Ex. 2.48), typically packed with contrapuntal challenges, is unfortunately the least impressive symphonic movement of any of Kalliwoda's seven symphonies. It was described as

---

[92] Dörffel, Statistik, 31. Dörffel incorrectly identifies the symphony performed on 18 February 1841 as No. 6 in F. It was actually premiered on 7 December 1843.

[93] *NZfM*, Vol. 8 No. 25 (1841), 102.

[94] Eberhard Creuzburg, *Die Gewandhaus-Konzerte zu Leipzig 1781–1931* (Leipzig, 1931), 91.

[95] Ibid., 107.

clever, well ordered, fluent and, in fulfilling a natural inner need for development, not lacking piquantly fine details; in addition it is melodious, pleasing to the ear and interestingly scored. ... It lacks a wealth of loftier ideas, which, new and stirring, would carry it above the realms of the commonplace, giving at least a fleeting pleasure.[96]

If he was seeking a new direction for the symphony, Kalliwoda could only revisit its traditional formats (there is more than a hint of Beethoven's *Pastoral* in the *finale*); and, though a pleasant work, it is ultimately superficial and too reminiscent of his earlier symphonies, a sign perhaps that, with his fifth, he had already come to the end of his journey down the symphonic road.

Example 2.44   Kalliwoda: Symphony No. 6. First movement introduction

Example 2.45   Kalliwoda: Symphony No. 6. First movement, first subject

Example 2.46   Kalliwoda: Symphony No. 6. Second movement

Example 2.47   Kalliwoda: Symphony No. 6. Scherzo

[96] *NZfM*, Vol. 10 No. 52 (1843), 206.

Example 2.48   Kalliwoda: Symphony No. 6. Finale

Despite an enormous list of published and unpublished works totalling some 450 compositions, Kalliwoda stopped writing symphonies comparatively early in his career, for he lived for a further 23 years.[97] He did so as Schumann began to produce his first in the genre and when Mendelssohn had composed his last and most popular in its day, his third (*Scottish*). The instant popular success of both these works, together with the indifferent critical reception of his own sixth and seventh symphonies considered as contributing nothing new, may well have determined the timing of his decision. Furthermore Schumann took a wildly fluctuating view of Kalliwoda's symphonies and, despite paeans of praise, gave them no chance of survival on the concert platform, while the rest of his orchestral output was dismissed as lightweight. To a certain extent Schumann was right, though what doomed Kalliwoda's music was its conservative style, which the public had initially found appealing (hence many performances of the first symphony and a piano version for four hands that ran to a second edition) yet of which they soon tired. Although, as we shall see, other composers such as Lachner and Volkmann turned from the symphony to the suite or serenade, Kalliwoda's favoured format became the concert overture, of which some two dozen were written 1820–64, spanning virtually his whole composing life. Until his death in 1847, Mendelssohn was a valued and vital champion of Kalliwoda's music at Leipzig, whereupon there is a marked decline in its number of performances (see Table 2.1, page 17), with only the fifth symphony in 1852 and that after a gap of 12 years.[98]

The disappearance there of Kalliwoda's music could have been caught up in Rietz's reluctance to explore post-Mendelssohn repertoire during his tenure of music director in the 1850s, despite the fact that Kalliwoda's symphonies (1826–43) could hardly have been viewed as modernist. Rietz's successor Reinecke held the view that 'the Gewandhaus was primarily the place to care for the proven, valued old music and therefore he had no obligation to try out the new'.[99] It was also normal for the works of all but the great either to fade gradually or to vanish instantly with their deaths. Spohr's symphonies dropped out of the

---

[97] Despite his theatre duties at Donaueschingen, Kalliwoda's instrumental works remain his strongest achievements, though he was prolific in all fields, including 10 masses, various song collections, two operas, choruses, many works for violin and orchestra, and three each of piano trios and string quartets.

[98] Overtures, variations, and concerted works for winds. Dörffel, *Statistik*, 31.

[99] Katrin Seidel, *Carl Reinecke und das Leipziger Gewandhaus* (Hamburg, 1998), 84.

Gewandhaus repertoire after 1859, with only five performances of the third and two of the fourth in the next 20 years. Reinecke makes little mention of Kalliwoda in his memoirs, except to list him among the 'minor' composers of the mid-1830s, whose works he remembered hearing, namely 'Kalliwoda, Reissiger, Lindpaintner and others of the day'.[100] During the two decades after Beethoven, Kalliwoda, having caught the attention of the Gewandhaus management and Leipzig's public with his violin playing and then consolidated it with a successful first symphony, went on to hold both second places after Spohr, many of whose 10 symphonies experiment with and develop the form, extending it from the post-Classical era to Romanticism. From his remote outpost, Kalliwoda thus managed to send his symphonies into their concert orbit despite (unlike Spohr or Mendelssohn) having no status, influence or school of composition to provide him with pupils or disciples. Spohr also exceeded him in international reputation, for, largely due to their own efforts, both he and Mendelssohn were extremely popular in England, where they conducted and performed their own music. By 1840 Kalliwoda had peaked with his fifth symphony, a timely moment for Mendelssohn to produce his best work in the genre, and for Schumann to begin.

Commentators today generally take a more positive view of Kalliwoda. Küster praises the quality of the symphonies, which were written at a time when new works were constantly compared to the Viennese classics and new directions demanded. The term 'epigone' became a Damoclean sword above the head of an aspiring composer of symphonies, yet more of them were given a first hearing in the 1830s than after 1845. Küster credits Kalliwoda with several achievements, among them his thoroughly individual sound at a time of instrumental experimentation and development, also with pouring his personally devised formal, motivic structures into a classical mould. 'He is technically secure in the minor mode with chromaticism, while in the major he enjoys a different, almost naïve success thanks to familiar phrasing and harmony.'[101] Ludwig Finscher describes the symphonies as 'combining energetic, well-defined, unique themes, their development having sweeping romantic gestures'. He praises their unusually colourful and virtuosic scoring and despite 'occasional triviality', concludes that 'each symphony has its own characteristics.[102] In 1875, Hermann Mendel's summary of Kalliwoda's achievement as a symphonist was seriously qualified as 'six [sic] symphonies belonging to the cleverest, most remarkable produced in the post-Beethoven era, albeit in descending order, as his talent did not take an upward turn for the better after the extremely successful reception given to the first one'.[103] Today Strauss-Neméth disagrees: 'Put like that, this statement is not tenable, for between the first,

---

[100] Carl Reinecke, *Erlebnisse und Bekenntnisse: Autobiographie eines Gewandhauskapellmeisters* (Leipzig, 2005), 19. In these memoirs, written 1902–1904, he uses 'Die Kleinmeister', a disparaging term today.

[101] Küster, 31, 33.

[102] Finscher 'Sinfonie' in *MGG* 9, col. 72.

[103] Hermann Mendel, *Musikalisches Conversations-Lexicon* Vol. 5 (Berlin, 1875), 523.

third and fifth there is clearly a recognisable improvement, while even the sixth and seventh achieve the quality of the first, albeit they stand in the shadow of the fifth'.[104] A more recent view of Kalliwoda's importance is his current entry in Grove: 'The symphonies also provide an interesting case study in the problems faced by a composer whose allegiance to late eighteenth century ideals was tinged by an incipient Romantic spirit. Several writers ... praised their clarity of form, graceful, at times Italianate melodies, skilful developments, finely wrought contrapuntal textures and deft orchestration.'[105] Neumann, while in general agreement with Schumann, is more generous in his praise of Kalliwoda:

> Since the genius of Beethoven and above all his symphonies aroused love and enthusiasm in audiences and players alike, it has become very difficult to achieve any success in this genre, which the public will acknowledge. Many composers in recent and contemporary times have tried to perform their Muse-inspired works. There are, however, two rocks on which such attempts usually run aground. If such works get too close to Beethoven, they are easily dismissed as imitations. If they stand too far off, generally they do not appeal. Happily Kalliwoda has sailed between the two rocks.[106]

Norbert Burgmüller (1810–36) was a composer whose tragic life was played out in the best Romantic tradition. His two symphonies date from the first half of the 1830s and were written in Düsseldorf, by no means a centre such as nearby Cologne and with only a nascent, rudimentary infrastructure to support musical activity run by amateur players and lovers of music. Burgmüller's background, his upbringing and the course of his short life played a huge part in the character of his music. His father Johann (1766–1824) was Düsseldorf's first Stadtmusikdirektor (city music director) from 1807 until his death, while one of Norbert's older brothers, Friedrich (1806–74), earned a fortune writing studies for piano (played to this day) and salon music. Norbert began music lessons with his father, but at the age of 14 his life was changed by Johann's unexpected death. An aristocratic patron, Count Franz Bertram von Nesselrode-Ehreshoven (1783-1847), came to the rescue and provided the funds to send the boy to Kassel, where he studied for four years (1826–30), violin with Spohr and composition with Moritz Hauptmann. In 1830, while establishing himself as a composer and teacher in Kassel, he began an affair with Sophia Roland, a singer at the opera house there; whether this explains his permanent break with Spohr (its court conductor) remains unclear. Burgmüller seems to have inherited his father's single-mindedness, loose morals and anti-social attitudes; and for the last six years remaining to him, he seemed

---

[104] Strauss-Neméth, 134.
[105] John Daverio, 'Kalliwoda, Johann Wenzel' in *The New Grove Dictionary of Music and Musicians* (henceforth Grove) 7th edition, 29 vols (London, 2001), Vol. 13, 330–31.
[106] William Neumann, *Die Componisten der neueren Zeit* Biographien Vol. 41 (Lindpaintner–Kalliwoda) (Kassel, 1856), 82, quoted in Strauss-Neméth, 131.

bent on a course of self-destruction. Still engaged to Norbert, Sophia left Kassel for Paris where she hoped to improve her career; in so doing she met a wealthy aristocrat and married him instead, thus improving her prospects. The jilted Burgmüller was devastated.

This traumatic experience destabilised his already fragile mental and physical state (recurring fits were probably the first signs of epilepsy) and he soon moved back to the family home at Düsseldorf. Once there, he fell in with a group of artists and playwrights, his drinking became excessive, and according to one description, he became 'bizarre, an enemy of the ways of the world, of social convention, and of all restraint, he had nothing but contempt for the distinguished works of previous masters'.[107] Later in that troubled year (1830) he married the French governess of his patron, although it was an unhappy union, for he now pined even more for Sophia, who died the same year. It had always been his hope that he would be appointed music director at Düsseldorf, but his attempts failed. During the years when Mendelssohn occupied the post (1833–35), Burgmüller responded very positively, and the two men (a year apart in age) became mutually admiring friends, Mendelssohn conducting Burgmüller's piano concerto with the composer as soloist. He seemed to overcome his shyness, melancholy and social awkwardness, but just as his musical life seemed to take a turn for the better with performances, interest and growing acclaim, tragedy struck. On 7 May 1836, *en route* to Paris to visit Friedrich, who was doing well, Norbert stayed in Aachen to take the waters. As he lay in his bath, it is assumed that he had an epileptic fit and drowned, but rumours of suicide have never been dispelled. Mendelssohn composed a funeral march (Op. 103) for his burial. He was 26 years old. In a memoir written shortly before Burgmüller's death, Wolfgang Müller von Königswinter recalled the composer's own words that voiced his frustration with life. It was tantamount to a *cri de coeur*:

> This provincial artistic life is becoming intolerable; I can gain nothing from it, whether as an observer or participant. I was not ready to cope with the world. I believed only in music; at first I was too stupid and did not think it necessary, and now I am too obstinate, if not perhaps too proud, to adapt myself to the ways of mankind.[108]

Burgmüller's output, half of which appeared in print in the 1860s, consists not only of the two symphonies but also four string quartets, a piano concerto, sonata, four orchestral *entr'actes*, an overture, a duo for clarinet and piano, and four sets of songs. There is no choral music or opera. All the ingredients for the *Sturm und Drang* of his life are manifest in his first symphony (C minor Op. 2, 1830–33),

---

[107] F.-J. Fétis, *Biographie universelle des musiciens* 2nd edition (Paris, 1867), 116–17.
[108] Wolfgang Müller von Königswinter, *Erinnerungen an Norbert Burgmüller* in *NZfM*, Vol. 12, Nos 1–6, 10–12 (1840), 1ff.

played at Düsseldorf under Mendelssohn on 13 November 1834.[109] It was well received, in particular for

> its deeply thoughtful originality and surprising freshness, immediate impact and comprehensibility, its unusual boldness and fullness of harmony, its character, which indeed reminds us of the author himself ... all this distinguishes this composition, giving it such an advantage over the many other similar ones of recent times that the work should meet with the greatest interest from music lovers.[110]

There are moments recalling Beethoven and also Spohr's third symphony, which, by 1833, was already five years old, and (together with Kalliwoda's first, 1826 but discounting Schubert's then unknown eighth and ninth) was the first symphony of any significance (and recognised by the public as such) to be written since Beethoven's ninth in 1824. There are clear similarities between Burgmüller and Spohr in style, tempi (first movements are *Andante grave – Allegro moderato*), and some time signatures (*scherzo*s in $_4^6$). Burgmüller's music is strikingly chromatic and, like Spohr's, his *finale* is an effective counterweight to the substantive opening movement, and not merely a pendant *rondo*. The slow introduction to the first movement has a sinister bass-line tread (Ex. 2.49), while *arpeggios* above a tonic pedal (Ex. 2.50) continue well into the *Allegro moderato*. The music now becomes turbulent, its ascending and descending diminished sevenths having more than a passing resemblance to the 'gathering waters' that 'rush along' in *Elijah* (1846).[111] The highly expressive *Adagio* (particularly its opening dozen bars for strings) recalls Beethoven's overtures rather than his symphonies. It begins in a tranquil mood (Ex. 2.51) but, by way of accompaniments, accents and fluctuating dynamics, soon takes on a touch of foreboding. Various outbursts for full orchestra (though without the three trombones in this movement alone) drive the music along until a lengthy impassioned solo for oboe, under which the strings stir restlessly in measured fast-moving accompaniment (Ex. 2.52). A repeated fragment of it takes on a deeper significance and is passed around the orchestra at several points until unusually claimed by the solo timpani, appearing three times in the last eight bars, with the oboe, now more plaintive but still on high.

---

[109] It is scored for double winds, two horns, two trumpets, three trombones, timpani and strings.

[110] Unidentified review quoted in the foreword by Klaus Zehnder-Tischendorf in Musikproduktion Höflich's score.

[111] Mendelssohn admired Burgmüller's first symphony. He conducted not only its Düsseldorf premiere but also its first Leipzig performance on 18 January 1838.

Example 2.49   Burgmüller: Symphony No. 1. First movement, slow introduction

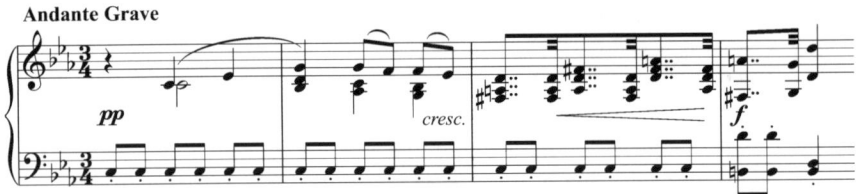

Example 2.50   Burgmüller: Symphony No. 1. First movement, first subject

Example 2.51   Burgmüller: Symphony No. 1. Second movement

Example 2.52   Burgmüller: Symphony No. 1. Second movement, oboe solo

The *scherzo* (Ex. 2.53) is energetic, confidently stating and restating *fortissimo* a punchy phrase for full orchestra, including the full family of trombones rather than just a bass to reinforce the lowest-lying line. The trio, on the other hand, is primarily for all instruments except the strings; and with no tempo change, we are in a more bucolic episode that might have come from an opera by Weber (Ex. 2.54). The material is very like the *scherzo* yet with quieter dynamics. The coda restates the opening phrases of the trio, but it is soon interrupted by the *scherzo* in a headlong dash to a final four-bar *prestissimo*. Burgmüller cleverly avoids conventional four-square phrasing, and on occasion slips in three- or five-bar groupings within an overarching 16-bar phrase, so the balance becomes 4+3+4+5. The *finale* too is exciting, beginning quietly with strings playing an *arpeggio*-shaped theme, mostly over a tonic pedal (Ex. 2.55). It takes us neatly back to the spirit of the first movement, giving the symphony a cyclical shape. This restlessness and a contrasting *cantilena* melody in woodwinds (Ex. 2.56) alternate through the movement, varied by a differently coloured orchestration at each repetition. A rhythmic recall of the start of the *finale* of Beethoven's seventh symphony occurs at a junction of the two subjects, the significance of which will become even more interesting in Burgmüller's second symphony. Burgmüller wrote his symphonies in the wake of Beethoven, but he sought to be an entirely independent figure and we recognise in his melodies and chromatic harmony a full-blooded Romantic. Even so, there are discernible doses of Weber, Spohr and Beethoven (but with less influence of Haydn or Mozart), although, compared to other composers of the day like Kalliwoda, such doses are usually small. There is also one significant element absent from Burgmüller's symphonic music – and that, apart from a small amount of canonic imitation in the first subject of the *finale*, is counterpoint. At no point in this or his next, and last, symphony does he break off for an expected, if not obligatory, fugue.

Example 2.53   Burgmüller: Symphony No. 1. Third movement, Scherzo

Example 2.54   Burgmüller: Symphony No. 1. Third movement, Trio

Example 2.55   Burgmüller: Symphony No. 1. Finale, first theme

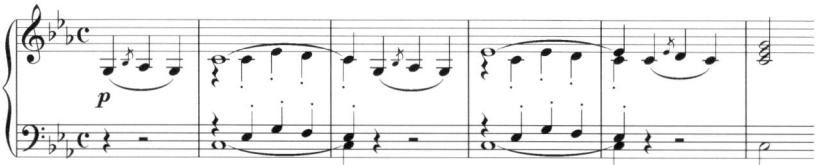

Example 2.56   Burgmüller: Symphony No. 1. Finale, second theme

Burgmüller's second symphony (D major Op. 11, 1834–36) is incomplete. It is also more lightly scored, with no trombones, just pairs of winds, horns and trumpets with timpani and strings. The first two movements were finished and performed under Julius Rietz at a memorial concert for Burgmüller in Düsseldorf on 22 April 1837, a year after he set off on his journey to Paris, with its fatal sojourn in Aachen. The *scherzo* is fully scored, but at the request of the Burgmüller family, it was Schumann who scored the trio from bar 184 in December 1851 using the extant short score. Ten days later, Schumann began work on rescoring his own D minor symphony, so the task of scoring Burgmüller's trio might have prompted him to work on his own music. Thus a three-movement version of Burgmüller's second symphony is performable, but there is no possibility regarding the *finale*.[112] A fragment of 58 bars of an *Allegro* was discovered in 1983, which belies contemporary reports that it was never started. Schumann also attempted a *finale*; 121 bars were found in the manuscript of his Mass Op. 147 in 1988, but it seems he soon abandoned the idea. 'Burgmüller would snatch the pen from my hand.'[113]

The contrast between this symphony and its predecessor is a stark one, a juxtaposition that would be repeated 40 years later when Brahms produced his own first two symphonies, and which coincidentally share the same sequence of key signatures, namely C minor followed by D major.[114] There is neither a slow introduction nor *Sturm und Drang*. Instead we hear a more pastoral mood, an opening 33-bar pedal underpinning this *Allegro moderato*, its repeated rising cello *arpeggio* phrases evoking future sounds of *Vltava* or the tranquillity of *Waldweben* in *Siegfried* (Ex. 2.57). From the vigorous motif in the movement (Ex. 2.58) and bearing in mind the *finale* of the first symphony (Ex. 2.59), we conclude that Beethoven's seventh symphony was clearly a work Burgmüller admired (Ex. 2.60), but it also stands comparison with Kalliwoda's first symphony (Ex. 2.5) for

---

[112] The author conducted this three-movement symphony in London on 13 February 2010, possibly its UK premiere.

[113] Benno Vorwerk, 'Norbert Burgmüller' in *Beiträge zur Geschichte des Niederrheins* 4 (1889), 177.

[114] Brahms refers to Burgmüller's music in a letter from Düsseldorf (27 August 1854) to Clara Schumann: 'I found a wondrous Rhapsodie (Op. 13), deeply moving, and among his songs I found some splendid ones' – Styra Avins, *Johannes Brahms: Life and Letters* (Oxford, 1997), 60.

further evidence of such admiration. What is more, it is in a triple-metre construct (Beethoven's was in duple) and the rhythmic displacement at various points before the expected conclusion of the phrase produces syncopations of the kind that later became the hallmark of Schumann and Brahms. After all, it was when Schumann encountered Burgmüller's first symphony that he embarked on writing his own. We hear the second subject only after an extraordinary four-bar episode modelled on the orchestral recitative at the start of the *finale* of Beethoven's ninth. The full orchestra builds to a climactic *ff* quasi-*fermata* on a diminished seventh, after which cellos and double basses descend through its four notes *con fuoco* collecting the remaining strings on the way to a chordal conclusion (Ex. 2.61). Eight bars later (strengthened with violas) the episode is repeated (and again in the recapitulation). By showing due deference to the ninth and acknowledging all the responsibilities it placed upon him as a member of the next generation of symphonists and those to come, Burgmüller's symphony shines with the confidence of knowing that within it he has something new and different to offer, confirming that he is perfectly capable of taking the genre further along its developmental path. Only his death could, and did, intervene.

Example 2.57   Burgmüller: Symphony No. 2. First movement, first motif

Example 2.58   Burgmüller: Symphony No. 2. First movement, second motif

Example 2.59   Burgmüller: Symphony No. 1. Finale. Bridge passage to recapitulation of Ex. 2.55

Example 2.60   Beethoven: Symphony No. 7. Finale

Example 2.61   Burgmüller: Symphony No. 2. First movement, orchestral recitative

While we can draw certain conclusions from such Beethoven moments and readily understand why a composer would want to include them in his works (and there are more to come in the *scherzo*), there is an enigma in Burgmüller's second symphony that will probably remain unsolved. It is the second-movement *Andante* that bears an uncanny similarity to Schubert's own *Andante con moto* in his *Great* C major symphony. Schubert had been dead five years, and his symphony, a decade old, was hidden in a drawer in Vienna at his brother's home until 1839. Whether or not it had ever been seen or studied by anyone is unproven. We shall encounter this riddle again when we come to Franz Lachner, but we do know that Burgmüller never met Schubert and never went to Vienna. Whether he ever met Schubert's friend Lachner is not known. The tempo, minor mode, time signature, character of the accompaniment, its steady tread of string quavers, and above all the long oboe solo of 24 bars, are common to both works (Exx 2.62 and 2.63). It should also be noted that Burgmüller's three-movement work is as long as its four-movement predecessor; so had he added a substantial *finale*, the result would have been comparable to Schubert's 'heavenly length' and his two-movement 'Unfinished' published 30 years later.[115] Burgmüller's *Andante* is monothematic, has absolutely no change of tempo throughout with a metronomic tick of continual quavers, but develops and varies the material with either quicker note values in the accompaniment or changes of instrumentation.

Example 2.62   Schubert: Symphony No. 9. Second movement

Example 2.63   Burgmüller: Symphony No. 2. Second movement

Burgmüller's *scherzo* and trio in his second symphony have much in common with those in Beethoven's fifth, seventh and eighth symphonies. The music is cheerful, witty, and packed with power and energy from its opening hectic passages for strings, like the trio in Beethoven's fifth (Exx 2.64 and 2.65). The cheeky figure in the last bar, with its syncopated silent first beat, recalls the opening of the *finale* of Beethoven's eighth symphony (Ex. 2.66). Just as Beethoven's seventh connects the *scherzo* and trio, so too does Burgmüller (Exx 2.67 and 2.68), though his trio is not marked as such in the score, neither (a curious omission) is there any change of tempo, which is clearly called for (Beethoven indicates the slower *Assai meno presto*). The trio is based around the familiar horn call epitomised by the trio of Beethoven's eighth (compare Exx 2.68 and 2.69); and Burgmüller, like Beethoven before him, treats the pair of bassoons as substitute horns to form a 'horn quartet'

---

[115] For Schumann's description of Schubert's symphony see page 71.

in the trio's opening horn call. For reasons of crooking, the work is scored for just two horns. Sixteen bars later Schumann takes up the scoring until the end.[116] The first part of Burgmüller's *scherzo* has a conventional repeat from a double bar; the longer second part has no repeat. The trio is written out (no double bars) and needs an *accelerando* over four bars to regain the tempo of the returning *scherzo*, to which it is once again linked without a break. There is a reprise of the trio, the homophonic melody now below a sustained upper pedal in the violins (Beethoven again).

Example 2.64   Burgmüller: Symphony No. 2. Scherzo, opening

Example 2.65   Beethoven: Symphony No. 5. Trio

Example 2.66   Beethoven: Symphony No. 8. Finale

---

[116] In the full score, 'Von hier bis zum Schluss instrumentirt von Rob. Schumann': Kistner & Siegel (Leipzig, 1864).

Example 2.67   Burgmüller: Symphony No. 2. Scherzo elision to Trio

Example 2.68   Burgmüller: Symphony No. 2. Scherzo elision to Trio

Example 2.69   Beethoven: Symphony No. 8. Trio

Burgmüller was not alone composing in the shadow of the more experienced and highly popular Spohr. By 1836 Kalliwoda had written his fourth symphony and Lachner his fifth, but Spohr's position remained unassailable. Despite many overt signs of *hommage à* Beethoven in Burgmüller's two symphonies, he was original, took the genre forward and exerted posthumous influence, the three prerequisites for German symphonists active in the half century 1826–76. Tragically Burgmüller's symphonic output was curtailed by his early death, while the public's perception of his legacy was unfortunately clouded by the melodramatic headlines it generated.

Schumann, as a broker of the careers of others through his journalism, proved vitally important for Burgmüller's posthumous reputation.[117] He had reviewed

---

[117] Schumann edited the *Neue Zeitschrift für Musik* until 1843, and was music director in Düsseldorf when he scored the trio of the second symphony in December 1850.

the 1838 performance of the first symphony very positively; it was the duty of musicians 'to pay that honour to the dead which we did not show to the living'.[118] Just a year later it appears likely that he had neither seen nor heard Burgmüller's second symphony, for, in an article on a symphony by Gottfried Preyer, he wrote, 'Sometimes I wish that a young composer might give us, just once, a light, merry symphony in a major key, without trombones and doubled horns but then of course that is more difficult'.[119] More Burgmüller-related articles, serialised memoirs and reviews followed for the next two years, keeping the dead composer's name before the public. In some ways Schumann over-egged the pudding as Burgmüller was not that well known in many places beyond Düsseldorf, but it was his own enthusiasm for the music that drove him to do so, the more so in view of his current preoccupation with Schubert's manuscripts that he had discovered in Vienna. His most comprehensive article, really a belated obituary, appeared on 30 August 1839, just five months after the *Great* C major symphony was heard for the first time. He recognised Burgmüller as an extraordinary composer, even if he overdid the hyperbole by comparing the piano Rhapsody Op. 13, much praised by Brahms to Clara, to the experience of discovering Goethe's *Erlkönig*:

> Since the early death of Franz Schubert, no other has been more painful to endure than that of Burgmüller. Instead of Fate for once decimating mediocre [foot soldiers] from our midst, it has taken one of our most talented generals. Whereas Schubert enjoyed some kind of recognition in life, Burgmüller hardly had the beginnings of such public acclaim and was known only to a small circle, perhaps even to them only as a "curiosity" rather than as a musician. So it becomes a duty to honour the dead, something we did not show him when he was alive, even if he was in part responsible. In fact we know little about him. A symphony [No. 1] remains a happy memory despite having encountered it just once. ... He possessed such brilliant talent, only the blind could have been unaware of it; I am sure that sooner or later the rich melodies of his music would have convinced the masses, even if his actual artistic skills would have bypassed their understanding. ... The publisher, who has more works by Burgmüller, should print them quickly; he will not regret it.[120] Publishers often strike me as fishermen. Unaware of what luck or coincidence might bring, they cast their nets and catch a mixed harvest of flotsam and jetsam, large and small, until suddenly they feel the heavy weight of an unusual guest in their net, and jubilantly haul in a priceless treasure from the depths. Such a catch was Burgmüller.[121]

---

[118] Robert Schumann, *Gesammelte Schriften über Musik und Musiker* 2 vols (ed. Martin Kreisig) Vol. 1 (Leipzig, 1914), 430.
[119] Henry Pleasants (ed.), *The Musical World of Robert Schumann* (London, 1965), 150.
[120] The publisher was Kistner & Siegel.
[121] See footnote 114 above. *NZfM*, Vol. 11 No. 18 (30 August 1839), 70–71.

A reviewer wrote of the 'great originality and astonishing novelty' of the first symphony, the music reaching directly to its audience, 'extraordinarily pleasing to one and all' in its 'uncommon boldness and harmonic richness, pleasing character and beautiful effects'.[122] After the mystery surrounding the cause of his death, an inevitably distorted mix of fact and fiction tried to connect the *Sturm und Drang* of his music to the turbulence of his life, producing such nonsense as, 'A more anxious but highly noble spirit appears tempered by life's experience, ... as if the music of his soul, unhappily trapped in the hostile element of this earth, breaks free and flies to the heavens, where it belongs'.[123]

In 1864 his former teacher, Moritz Hauptmann, wrote not only that was there no trace of Burgmüller's mental illness in his music, but also that the second symphony was a better work than the first. Hauptmann encouraged performances of Burgmüller's music, likening it to music buried in an alum mine; once unearthed, its original properties of youthful freshness and vigour would be found preserved and unchanged.[124] The second symphony was performed at Leipzig on 24 November 1864.

> [It] was of special interest because of the personality of its composer, and for its own intrinsic value. The work did not reveal music of forced wildness, which one might have expected from the manner in which the unhappy composer lived his life; instead it was bold, passionate (*Allegro*), melting, soft (*Andante*), finishing with a happy, cheerful *scherzo*, each of its three movements developing with easy clarity. His melodies, which flow so agreeably into and out of each other, have such a warm feeling that in the *Andante* one can be reduced to tears. One would not exaggerate by placing our friend and his work among the ranks of the greatest composers.[125]

Another paper described the symphony as,

> a clever work, to which we show due respect and recognition. The *scherzo* is exceptionally fine and effective, almost combustible. It was a pleasure getting to know this work, and if there were the opportunity for another performance, it would certainly be wanted by music lovers.[126]

Burgmüller's hometown newspaper went further: 'Beethoven himself would not have been ashamed to put his name to the second symphony, however exaggerated

---

[122] Hermann, 'Musikalisches aus Düsseldorf' in *Ein Centralorgan für Rheinland und Westfalen* 1834.
[123] *Düsseldorfer Zeitung*, 1837.
[124] Hauptmann has in mind E.T.A. Hoffmann's *Mines of Falun* (1819).
[125] 'Correspondences' in *Die Sonntagspost*, 25 November 1864.
[126] *Leipziger Tageblatt*, November 1864.

that might sound.'[127] Occasional performances of the symphonies can be found later in the century, such as one in 1882.[128] It was a great success, recognised for its high-quality music, and was deemed worthy of standing alongside any symphony by Schumann.[129] By 1891, Leipzig was only performing the *scherzo* of the first symphony, to the regret of a reviewer, who hoped for a performance of the full work before long.[130] Max Bruch referred to Burgmüller as someone highly regarded when he himself was young (1860s) but whose name by then (1913) no longer had any resonance. Reviews in 1936, when the first symphony received another performance in Germany, placed his music between Weber's *Euryanthe* and Schumann, having a 'fraternal' relationship with Schubert, and firmly upon a road that leads directly to Brahms.[131]

A year before Burgmüller's death, Franz Lachner, whose life (1803–90) spans most of the nineteenth century, had just enjoyed success with his fifth symphony.[132] He is probably best remembered for his tussles with Wagner, who, by scheming to insert Hans von Bülow at Munich in order to promote his own music dramas in the city under King Ludwig's patronage, made life so uncomfortable for Lachner that he retired in 1868 (the year of *Die Meistersinger*) after 16 years as court conductor. Despite conducting some of Wagner's stage works, he was not in sympathy with his musical thought. The son of a clockmaker, after studies in Munich, Franz moved in 1823 to Vienna, where he took an organist's post in the Evangelical Church. The income paid for lessons in counterpoint and composition from the renowned pedagogue Simon Sechter, Bruckner's future teacher.[133] Lachner entered the music circles of Vienna, giving him access to Beethoven and leading to friendship with Schubert. In 1827 he joined the Kärntnerthor Theatre, where he began to build a reputation both as a composer and as a conductor. Vienna was a Mecca for young musicians. It was the city where Gluck, Haydn, Mozart, Beethoven and Schubert worked, but after their deaths (spanning the years 1787–1828) the attraction to young composers lost its gloss during the 1830s in favour of Leipzig, Dresden and Munich. It would only revive when Brahms, Bruckner, Mahler, Wolf and the Strauss family were based there from the mid-1860s. Having heard his first three symphonies in Vienna between 1828 and 1834, he moved on to the court opera at

---

[127] *Düsseldorfer Zeitung*, 1864.

[128] Given by the Rostock Musical Association under Hermann Kretschmar, the city's music director 1880–87.

[129] 'Vermischte Mittheilungen', *Musikalisches Wochenblatt*, 18 May 1882, 253.

[130] At the sixth Gewandhaus concert of the season. *Leipziger Nachrichten*, 1891.

[131] *Hamburger Fremdenblatt* and *Westfälische Zeitung* 1936, listed on the Burgmüller website (no longer available).

[132] Franz had three brothers: Theodor (1788–1877), Vincenz (1811–93) and Ignaz (1807–95), all of whom became composers and conductors.

[133] Simon Sechter (1788–1867) was rumoured to write a fugue daily for 60 years. This would total 21,915.

Mannheim on a life-long contract.[134] On his way there, however, he was invited to conduct his third symphony in Munich, 11 years after the cold reception that had precipitated his move to Vienna. This time, the symphony proved a great success and received 'stormy applause'.[135] Immediately negotiations were begun for a post there, but first he was committed to at least two years at Mannheim, where he raised orchestral standards and breathed fresh life into the city's music-making. So it was only in 1836 that Lachner finally moved to Munich and for over three decades (from 1852 as chief conductor) took charge of the city's opera and concert life.[136] Despite leaving Vienna, he was welcomed back there in November 1836 to conduct a highly successful performance of his fourth symphony.[137]

Lachner's first symphony was published in the year of Schubert's death (1828), but it was possibly written two years earlier.[138] We find his style already established, his mannerisms, favourite instrumental colours, contrapuntal devices and four-square thematic phrase shapes. Over the 23 years spanning the composition of his eight symphonies (1828–51), we see little change in substance, while Sechter encouraged the contrapuntal element at the heart of Lachner's symphonic writing. A study of some of Lachner's eight symphonies (Nos 2, 4 and 7 remain unpublished) reveals that the quality of the outer movements rarely reaches the high standard of the inner slow and *scherzo* movements. The problem with the first movement of the first symphony is its monothematic material, the substance of which cannot be sustained by the length of its sonata form. The principle of thematic relationship as a means of establishing unity was not unusual after Haydn, but in Lachner's case there are too many repetitions of phrases and too many predictable melodic or harmonic sequences that become wearisome, while the motifs themselves lack inspiration. Apart from the change from major to minor modality, too great a similarity in both lyrical character and structure exists between the two subjects as we can see (Exx 2.70 and 2.71). According to Steinbeck, the first movement was performed privately on 8 January 1826, but, tantalisingly, it is not known if Schubert was present, as a few places in the development section here indicate that there may have been a relationship between it and the *Great* C major.[139] The slow movement starts with 16 bars of the thematic material played *pizzicato* and *pianissimo* by the strings (Ex. 2.72), after which violas and cellos (both of them *divisi*) repeat it *arco* (Ex. 2.73). This *is* pure Schubert with all the beauty found in the slow

---

[134] Reference is made to a 'lebenslänglichen Vertrag' (life-long contract) in a paragraph announcing his departure from Mannheim two years later in *AMZ*, Vol. 38 No. 1, 6 January 1836, col. 13.

[135] Ibid.

[136] His younger brother Vincenz succeeded Franz in both his Vienna Kärntnerthor and Mannheim posts, remaining in the latter for 30 years (1836–66).

[137] *AMZ*, Vol. 38 No. 7, 17 February 1836, col. 107.

[138] Wolfram Steinbeck, 'Lachner und die Symphonie' in *Franz Lachner und seine Brüder Hofkapellmeister zwischen Schubert und Wagner* Kongressbericht Munich 2003 (Tutzing, 2006), 133–44.

[139] Steinbeck, 137–8.

movement of his string quintet. The *scherzo* of this first symphony is both clever and highly attractive. It is a four-part canon from the first bar (first violins) working down to cellos and, from the double bar, restated in inversion by the same instruments in the same descending order; and Sechter would surely have approved of his pupil's work (Exx 2.74 and 2.75). Lachner uses a sudden enharmonic switch to B major (Schubert again) to introduce the trio, a charming *Ländler* led by clarinet and flute with a gentle string-textured accompaniment (Ex. 2.76). The opening upward rush of strings in the *finale* (Ex. 2.77) is very like the opening of the *scherzo* in Burgmüller's second symphony still to come a decade later (Ex. 2.64).

Example 2.70   Lachner: Symphony No. 1. First movement, first subject

Example 2.71   Lachner: Symphony No. 1. First movement, second subject

Example 2.72   Lachner: Symphony No. 1. Second movement, opening

Example 2.73   Lachner: Symphony No. 1. Second movement, bars 17–24

Example 2.74   Lachner: Symphony No. 1. Scherzo, a four-part canon for strings

Example 2.75   Lachner: Symphony No. 1. Scherzo, the theme inverted

Example 2.76   Lachner: Symphony No. 1. Trio

Example 2.77   Lachner: Symphony No. 1. Final, opening

The third symphony (D minor Op. 41, 1834) and the fourth (E major, unpublished) were both written in 1834. A report of a performance of the third in Munich in early 1837 mentions public demand for it following its premiere there in November 1835, when it caused a great sensation. It got even more applause than his fifth, which was in circulation by then. 'The *Andante* and *scherzo* are most ingenious, while the outer movements have the advantage of being shorter, therefore easier to take in and more easily understood, than the same movements in the fifth'.[140] The fourth had a successful performance in Vienna about the same time and was described as 'a genuine, splendidly worked masterpiece'.[141] Of Lachner's remaining five symphonies we shall look at the fifth, which raises the issue of competitions, the sixth, with Schumann's response to it, and (in Chapter 5, 1850s) the eighth and last, written after a gap of a dozen years.

While Lachner was in his post at the Mannheim Opera, he submitted his fifth to a competition for a new symphony sponsored by the *Gesellschaft der Musikfreunde* and held at Vienna in October 1835. It attracted 57 entries, and the fact that it took place at all is indicative of the concerns of musicians at the time for the plight of the symphony. Judging by the uneven quality of the winning work, however, no star appears to have been born, nor does it appear that any of the other entrants went on to make a name as a symphonist. Lachner's winning entry, announced on 11 January 1836, appears to have ticked all the correct boxes for the jury of seven conductors: Joseph von Eybler, Johann Gänsbacher, Adalbert Gyrowetz, Conradin Kreutzer, Ignaz von Seyfried, Michael Umlauff and Joseph Weigl. As was customary, all the entries bore a motto and were submitted under pseudonyms; and Lachner's identity was revealed only after he had received the prize of 50 ducats.[142] Although the composer had given it the title *Sinfonia passionata*, it became known as the *Preis-Symphonie* (C minor Op. 52, 1835), its scoring standard for symphonies of the day, namely double woodwinds, four horns, two trumpets, three trombones, timpani and strings, with a piccolo added in the first and third movements.

The symphony's subdued introduction appears reverentially Mendelssohnian, but once he gets into his stride, Lachner develops a tuneful motif in his own brand of chromatic sequences (Exx 2.78 and 2.79). Motifs lie at the heart of his style and we find that one consisting of six notes (for violas and bassoon) becomes the principal one of the movement (Ex. 2.80). The *Allegro* bursts forth with exciting energy from the full orchestra, followed by a conventionally constructed edifice in sonata form (Ex. 2.81). At the *fermata* Burgmüller's second symphony (Ex. 2.61) comes to mind, for although the works were written at the same time, if geographically far apart, they both take their cue from Beethoven's innovative *recitative* in the ninth symphony. While Burgmüller's quotation is unequivocally plagiaristic (but adding violas in two of the four statements) and with the same aggressive interruption,

---

[140] *AMZ*, Vol. 39 No. 11, 15 March 1837, 184.
[141] *AMZ*, Vol. 39 No. 7, 17 February 1837, 107.
[142] Lachner's was No. 28 of the 57 and submitted as *Sinfonia passionata* with a three-line motto taken from Goethe's play *Torquato Tasso*, Act 1, Scene 3, lines 388–90 (1770), here in Anna Swanwick's translation (London, 1864):

'Und wie der Mensch nur sagen kann: hier bin ich!   'A man can say but simply, "Here I am",
Dass Freunde seiner schonend sich erfreu'n,   That they, with kind forbearance, may rejoice;
So kann ich auch nur sagen: nimm es hin!'   So I can only say, – Receive my work!'

Lachner's takes Beethoven's idea but translates it into some colourful, wistful *quasi-recitative* phrases for flute, oboe and clarinet, making a far calmer statement of the first subject (Ex. 2.82). Another model is the dialogue between piano and orchestra in the *Andante* of Beethoven's fourth piano concerto, characterised by Liszt as Orpheus taming the lions with his lute. The long second subject has its own theatrical excitement, announced by a solo quartet of horn, bassoon, trumpet and trombone accompanied by *tremolando* strings, but as it progresses with brief interjections of the first subject motif from woodwinds, it also resorts to sequential repetition and verges on the bombastic, though its recapitulation is improved by a more subtle rescoring for flute, clarinet and bassoon (Ex. 2.83).[143]

Example 2.78   Lachner: Symphony No. 5. Introduction

Example 2.79   Lachner: Symphony No. 5. Introduction

Example 2.80   Lachner: Symphony No. 5. First movement, six-note motif

Example 2.81   Lachner: Symphony No. 5. First movement, first subject

---

[143] In his Organ Suite No. 3 (1904) and in the version as a Concerto for two pianos (1915) Op. 88a, Max Bruch used the same notes and rhythm of the four-note motif (bars 2–4).

Example 2.82   Lachner: Symphony No. 5. First movement, quasi-recitative

Example 2.83   Lachner: Symphony No. 5. Second movement

All the material in this first movement is given a thorough workout in the development section, either in the form of a brief *fugato* or a complex fugue, in order to meet the expectations of the pedagogical jurors on the competition's panel. Did Lachner take the prize element too literally and try to impress by covering all the formulaic conventions? One suspects not, for much of what is in the fifth symphony in terms of style, musical language and structure can be found in the other shorter symphonies. For an audience of the day, however, it became a matter of coping with *longueurs*. This first movement is too long and not helped by frequent false signs of ending, only for the music to be revived and made to jump through further contrapuntal hoops, like a series of exercises. In the middle movements there are more promising signs, although their quality remains uneven.

In the slow movement (*Andante con moto*), there are several touches of that Schubertian beauty already encountered in Lachner's music (imperfect cadences and melodic falling sevenths), albeit blurred at times by some unattractively dense scoring (Ex. 2.84). The strings play alone from the start for 20 bars, the textures thickened by violas in two parts then cellos and, after them, double basses, but Lachner continues to write finely crafted solos for winds or horn despite unimaginatively functional accompaniments. There is another outburst of fugal counterpoint and a rash of predictable sequential passages. Lachner has a tendency, either through inexperience or mistrust of an instrument's power in his day, to double woodwind pairings at the octave, or to double melodies in different instrumental territories. Often the cello/bass line is reinforced by the addition of bassoons and bass trombone, making the textures thick and bottom-heavy, dispositions that Brahms would eventually hone and refine. Yet, when it is at its most lyrical, the music is charming and beautiful, the end of the slow movement particularly striking with the final four-part chord of A flat major in *divisi* violins on high.

The minuet has the rhythmic spirit and canonic structure of bygone ages within its infrastructure, a *pastiche* technique Lachner will develop further from the 1860s in numerous, popular orchestral suites. Orchestration is again less successful with some leaden-footed bass-lines, but the material, despite lacking spontaneity through formulaic repetition, is attractive and given sufficient contrast with its triplet and dotted rhythms (Ex. 2.85). One could argue that Lachner's pragmatic approach to impress the jury results in an excessive use of the canon, but it also continues to miscalculate some instrumentation here, reinforcing the first violins with piccolo over wide melodic leaps of a tenth resulting in unwelcome shrill sounds. As in the lengthy first movement, he does not know when to stop and there are over-extended phrases in the coda. With its subdued dynamic levels and somewhat muddied low-lying string textures, the trio, like the extended opening bars of the slow movement, has a quiet, dirge-like feel and with no tempo contrast between minuet and trio (the scherzo-trio contrast on the other hand is usually more successful). In its second part, however, when the focus is more on winds and horns, matters cheer up and the landscape brightens. This passage has much more of Schubert about it and there is a clever touch as the main motif of the minuet is introduced by the first violins during the last bars of the trio (Ex. 2.86). The *finale* is a kaleidoscope of colour and sound. It starts with the strings in mischievous mood, after which a melodramatic change takes place with the full orchestra unleashed in a torrent of sequential phrases, but, as in the first movement, the quality of the material is indifferent, its dotted rhythmic passages repeated to excess (Ex. 2.87). The second subject, however, has a pleasant, lightweight reminiscence of Mozart, including the *Jupiter* symphony motto (Ex. 2.88). This is more evident later in a double fugue, where the first subject appears in augmentation, which clearly did more than enough to satisfy the judges (Ex. 2.89).

Example 2.84   Lachner: Symphony No. 5. Second movement

Example 2.85   Lachner: Symphony No. 5. Third movement, Minuet

Example 2.86   Lachner: Symphony No. 5. Trio, conclusion

Example 2.87   Lachner: Symphony No. 5. Finale, opening

Example 2.88   Lachner: Symphony No. 5. Finale, second subject

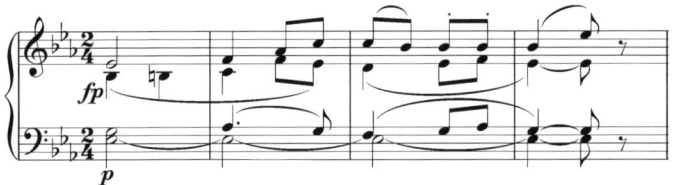

Example 2.89   Lachner: Symphony No. 5. Finale, double fugue

For 1835, the length of Lachner's fifth symphony (one hour) is comparable to the proportions of Beethoven's ninth and Berlioz's *Symphonie fantastique*, but what of Schubert's ninth, which also lasts 50 minutes? Lachner had been a personal friend and possibly knew of its existence, perhaps even its content. There is, however, no evidence that he did; and in any case, unlike Schubert's symphony, it does not have either the thematic material or the musical infrastructure capable of sustaining a work for so long. Lachner is at his best when he understates rather than overstates his case; his handling of the orchestra is far less refined here than in the more mature eighth symphony (1851), despite the fact that by 1835 he was already in his thirties and had eight years' practical experience behind him as a conductor, both on the concert platform and in the opera house.[144] In his fifth symphony, Lachner never indicates gradual changes of tempo; there is a total absence of *ritardando*, *rallentando* or *accelerando* markings in the score, while a *fermata* will suddenly appear as an interruption. Nor does the music lend itself to any form of interpretative *rubato* on the part of a conductor. Similarly, changes of dynamic level are relatively scarce and also more likely to be sudden rather than gradual. The piccolo (a third player is required rather than being doubled by the second flute) is confined to the first and third movements, making its omission from the tempestuous *finale* odd.

As well as 50 ducats, the prize also included publication by the firm of Tobias Haslinger in Vienna followed by two performances, which took place on 18 February 1836 at a *Concert spirituel* and again on 24 March, conducted on both occasions by one of the judges, Ignaz von Seyfried.[145] Mendelssohn programmed it on 27 October in his second season at Leipzig, though it must have been a hard

---

[144] 'There was nothing approaching a fully professional concert orchestra in Vienna until six years after Beethoven's death, when Franz Lachner gave a series of carefully rehearsed concerts with the orchestra of the Hofoper' – Clive Brown in 'The Orchestra in Beethoven's Vienna', *Early Music*, Vol. 16 No. 1 (February 1988), 9.

[145] See Kretschmar quotation (Chapter 1, footnote 13). Second prize was awarded to Ignaz Dobrzyński (Warsaw) with his second symphony; third went to Joseph Strauss

act to follow music by Beethoven, whose third *Leonore* Overture was played twice in order 'to satisfy the audience's endless [cries of] "Da Capo!"'.[146] In the season 1836–37 alone it was performed a dozen times, twice in Vienna, then Breslau, Munich, Leipzig, Frankfurt, Hamburg, Augsburg, Berlin, Königsberg, Mannheim and Prague.[147]

Turning to its reception, Lachner's fifth was caught up in the changing fortunes of the symphony taking place in the 1830s. First reviews were based on the two Viennese performances in the spring and autumn of 1836; but even by the second of those, the full score was not available to writers for music periodicals. Reviewers writing about new works therefore usually included a *caveat* that their opinion was based on what they heard, not on what they read. Haslinger published the score in the summer of 1837, so until then the public had to wait for 'a thorough and detailed critique' according to the report after the performance in Munich early that year.[148] Nevertheless the general consensus was favourable, each movement being applauded at Munich. *AMZ* had from the start alluded to rumours of political infighting behind the scenes, which ensured that Lachner, rather than the runner-up Dobrzyński (whose symphony was 'without basis alleged to be much more beautiful'), took the first prize, but it also acknowledged that Lachner's symphony was 'genuinely a real masterpiece'.[149] The review by Fink of the Leipzig performance under Mendelssohn shows a geographical as well as a cultural divide with Vienna. A similar reaction occurred even further north at Hamburg after the performance there on 26 November 1836 under Friedrich Grund.[150] Several reviews refer to less favourable receptions the farther north from Vienna it was heard. According to Fink, the first movement received

> only average clapping, the second and third passed unnoticed and the fourth got lukewarm, negligible applause. In short the crowned symphony was not liked here; most found it too long and boring; the whole work showed no musicality in ideas and coherence, which must be expected of a great symphony; and it was said quite openly how bewildering it was that this work could have been chosen by those prize-awarding gentlemen in Vienna. If this was not the opinion of all, it was of the majority.

(Karlsruhe). Details are listed in the 'Historical Introduction' to the full score published by Tobias Haslinger, Vienna, 1837 (British Library shelf mark h.3260).

[146] Dörffel, 89.

[147] At least five other composers, Carl Gottlieb Reissiger (1798–1859), Benedict Randhartinger (1802–93), Wenzel Gährich (1794–1864), Gottfried Preyer (1807–1901) and Adolf Hesse (1809–63), had their entries performed at some of these centres during the same period. Küster, 216.

[148] *AMZ*, Vol. 39 No. 10, 8 March 1837, col. 184.

[149] *AMZ*, Vol. 38 No. 29, 20 July 1836, col. 478.

[150] Friedrich Wilhelm Grund (1791–1874). Composer, conductor and teacher in Hamburg 1819–63.

... To begin with, Vienna did not like *Don Giovanni*! Personally I know a time when symphonies by Beethoven, universally honoured today, aroused very differing opinions. Those in favour would constantly urge those who opposed to "listen to them again and again. You have not understood them!" What is sauce for the goose is sauce for the gander. "But can you compare this symphony to one by Beethoven?" No! It's quite different and therein lies the main reason. One has both grown accustomed to and fallen in love with Beethoven's masterful, exaltedly romantic genre but not at all with this one. No one has found imaginative coherence in it; nor I, but after only one hearing I shall not presume to maintain that none is there. Justice demands that one should err on the safe side. Lachner, whose symphonies have now given great satisfaction in Vienna, Mannheim and Munich, is not so trifling a figure that I could immediately dare to disagree.[151]

The unnamed reviewer of the performance in Dresden on 10 August 1836 took up the issue of alleged political manipulation of the result in favour of Lachner and expanded it to a deeper, searching and more challenging question, that of the value of competitions. He alleged that there was partisan support from cities for composers who were either famous sons or spent their working lives there, which begs the question, would Lachner's symphony have won first prize if the competition had been held in other musical centres such as Berlin, Munich or Kassel? Cities were known to have prejudices for and against certain works or their composers. Weber's *Euryanthe* was feted in Dresden but poorly received in Vienna, while Rossini's operas initially fared badly in Berlin. If the purpose of competitions, continued this unknown reviewer, was to introduce a composer to the public, then normally they would only have that one work by which to judge him, but this was untrue in Lachner's case because he already had four symphonies behind him. The public had no evidence to support the judges' decision that any one particular symphony was the best. It would, therefore, have been fairer to have a semi-final concert in which three shortlisted works were played in public. If, as a result, Lachner had still won from Vienna, it would have been *consensus gentium* (with the peoples' agreement), rewarding the composer and allaying any fears of a suspicious public. As it was, the seven judges made their own decisions independently (it is not known if conferring was permitted); and though not questioning the impartiality of this all-Viennese septet, the anonymous reviewer concluded that it would have been fairer to have had one member from each of the main cities of Vienna, Berlin, Munich and so on. There may have been 10 good symphonies that fell by the wayside, but, he concluded, for only one to be chosen cannot have been good for the progress of the Art nor for the discovery of a genius.[152] Three years later, in 1838, we do find impartiality despite the complication of a stalemate. A competition in Mannheim to write a song attracted 193 entries. This time the judges were scattered around Germany, but no majority verdict could be

---

[151] *AMZ*, Vol. 38 No. 45, 9 November 1836, cols 746 and 751.
[152] *AMZ*, Vol. 38 No. 35, 31 August 1836, cols 579–80.

reached, so the last word was given to three new judges, who selected the winner from those favoured by the five original judges. One has to hope that, anxious to avoid accusations of nepotism, Franz Lachner would have declared an interest and not voted for his brother Vincenz, who took second prize.[153]

From a review of a performance of Lachner's fifth symphony in Prague in the spring of 1838, we learn that, despite being a non-repertoire work, it was played by the best orchestra of the city's Conservatoire conducted by its director Dionys Weber.[154] Lachner's first symphony was also played just one season earlier in Vienna in similar circumstances, a pupils' concert organised by the *Gesellschaft der Musikfreunde*, while a performance of its first movement was subsequently demanded by Emperor Ferdinand.[155] This was therefore the second time one of his symphonies was played by the orchestra of a conservatoire. The reviewer at the Prague concert has little good to say about the music, whereas he has nothing but praise for the playing:

> That Lachner's fifth symphony, a real novelty, won first prize in the competition is no evidence in itself that the genre is flourishing in Germany. ... The main problem with the work is its gigantic length, caused by too many repetitions, something that the average well-established symphony has long overcome, for it can damage the infrastructure. ... What is more, Lachner has not taken into consideration that, for a performance of this symphony, a colossus of an orchestra is needed, but such a thing is not at the disposal of all cities, so either it cannot be played or only by making unsatisfactory cuts. This performance was full of precision, fire, confidence and taste, and when one takes into account that Director Weber is working with an orchestra of young men and boys, who have only been in the Conservatoire since 1834 and have only played together since July 1837, one really must concede that he has worked wonders to achieve such results.[156]

In a long critique in *NZfM*, Schumann dismissed the *Preis-Symphonie* as being 'without style, a cobbled-together mix of music, namely German (the openings and counterpoint), Italian (*cantilena*) and French (connecting passages and endings)', which one could listen to when in a good mood but which lacked sufficient skill to prevent the boredom 'evident in the faces of the Leipzig audience'; in short,

---

[153] The Lied was 'In die Ferne'. The original judges were Lachner in Munich, Fink in Leipzig, Lindpaintner in Stuttgart, Joseph Strauss in Karlsruhe and Schnyder von Wartensee in Frankfurt. The winner (selected by the three new judges, Spohr in Kassel, Reissiger in Dresden and an unnamed Mannheim judge) was Julius Otto (1804–77), a teacher and cantor in Dresden. *Intelligenzblatt No. 12 zur AMZ*, Vol. 40 No. 40, 3 October 1838, col. 48.

[154] Dionys Weber (1766–1842) was the founding director of the Conservatoire from 1811 until his death.

[155] *AMZ*, Vol. 39 No. 23, 7 June 1837, cols 373–4.

[156] *AMZ*, Vol. 40 No. 16, 18 April 1838, col. 259.

it was unacceptably long for them. To put it another way, Schumann continued, for someone who had feasted for a year on part of the *Adagio* in Beethoven's string quartet Op. 127, this symphony would need endless eternity. The work has a depressingly sprawling breadth, he complained – Beethoven's ninth runs to 226 pages, this symphony to 304 – and it is consequently full of rhythmic monotony. Schumann found the first movement 'the best and freshest' of the four and, having praised its passion (the elemental *Sturm und Drang* appealed to him) in what is plainly mischievous mockery, fantasised a nonsensical programmatic interpretation of the work: 'Someone observed that the beginning expresses the struggle for the prize, the *Adagio* the first doubts of a successful outcome, the *scherzo* a glimmer of hope and the last movement a surge of cheerful confidence.' Perhaps, he surmised, the stress of writing a symphony on demand for a competition inhibited its composer and so he proposed that in future only works already completed should be submitted.

Schumann also pointed out the three-note upbeat figure (Exx 2.80–2.84) frequently to be found in the first two movements, which recalled Beethoven's fifth symphony and how this rhythmic motto had since become a rhythmic *petard* on which many a luckless composer had been hoisted.

> While we worship Beethoven's C minor symphony, Lachner's aroused no such obeisance, its material not worthy of development. This weakness was particularly true of the *Adagio* [*sic*], whose point is made in the first part of Schubert's *Sehnsucht* waltz far more tellingly than in the whole of this movement, which is a hundred times longer, ends on every page and never stops. The *scherzo* is without humour, the trio without wit. Only in the last movement, are there a couple of attractive motifs, nicely interwoven and subjected to traditional fugato-like treatment.

Schumann, overwhelmed by its mediocrity and frustrated by a lack of serious errors or structural weaknesses, reduced his comments to 'dull' or 'quite good', or 'sighs and thinks about something else'. His *coup de grâce* was the audience's response,

> already so diminished that even the most massive effects fell upon deaf ears. A few applauded perfunctorily, probably as much for the impeccable performance as for the symphony itself. The majority heaved a sigh of relief to have it all – at long last – behind them![157]

At this point one feels obliged, as clearly Fink did in February 1837, to come to the aid of the beleaguered Lachner, increasingly vilified for his success in the competition. In a piece entitled 'A bit about Franz Lachner', Fink, who claimed

---

[157] 'The Prize Symphony' in Pleasants, 100–102; the original article is in *NZfM*, Vol. 5 No. 38, 8 November 1836, col. 151ff. I have paraphrased some awkward translation.

no personal acquaintance with the composer, clearly felt a balanced reply to Schumann's piece three months earlier was required. It was only fair, he wrote, to allow those with a different opinion to have their say; and, after all, Munich and Vienna gave the fifth symphony an enthusiastic response, unlike Leipzig and Hamburg. He noted that contradictions were not surprising given the bias and preconceptions disseminated by all manner of means and then somewhat patronisingly he dismissed any general understanding of the language of musical art, while stressing that quality of performance was vital to the reception of a new work. Fink had received a letter from an unnamed acquaintance of Lachner, who had written a hagiography in his defence. It becomes a shopping list of Lachner's virtues based on his success in Munich.

> I must express my pleasure at Lachner's arrival here. My regard for him grows daily as I get to know him as man, artist and director. We have already heard his fine *Preis-Symphonie* and the oratorio *Moses*. I would call Lachner another Mozart, with whose style he has much in common; although in some works he could also be the Haydn of our time. He has united great art, magical melody and a deep understanding of harmony, without lacking clarity. He never strives for originality, yet is often more original than some who do; in short, he is master of the tools of his art.

He continued in similar vein, including an admission that Lachner's music did not always sound as expected after prior study of the score; these were usually passages that looked particularly empty, but sounded surprisingly full. He praised Lachner primarily for his masterly knowledge of orchestration and could think of no other to match him. How, he concluded, could this man, so modest and lacking in self-esteem, be so viciously misunderstood and persecuted? It was inexplicable and his colleague Fink concurred. A month later there was another performance. It had been 'carefully prepared ... for its first-rate rendition in the large hall of the well-visited English House'.[158] The first movement was preferred, but any positive comments about the rest were qualified by its length. Applause after each movement became weaker, so it could only be considered a *succès d'estime*. The reviewer made the perfectly valid point that Lachner's technical prowess, while pleasing a competition jury, would not necessarily satisfy an audience, who wants music from the heart, not from the head. Reviews criticising its length took the same attitude with Schubert's ninth two years later. It was fulsomely praised, but the view was also taken that, had he lived, Schubert 'would have made [cuts] to this symphony, which lasts five minutes short of an hour'. Its first two movements were adjudged the best, the *scherzo* with its conventional repeats was too long, while the last was an 'operatic *finale* without words'.[159] Another view was that

---

[158] At Berlin in March 1837. *AMZ*, Vol. 39 No. 16, 19 April 1837, 258–9.
[159] *AMZ*, Vol. 41 No. 13, 27 March 1839, 256.

'orchestral things like this attract only a small public, and large symphonies, in particular, have little success at the present time'.[160] Mendelssohn (possibly concerned for the staying power of the second violins) sent word to London ahead of his trip there, during which he planned to conduct Schubert's work for the first time in England.[161] 'It is a very extraordinary composition,' he wrote, 'which has created an uncommon sensation amongst the musicians here [Leipzig]. I should strongly recommend you *not to repeat the first part* of the last movement, perhaps also not the first and the second part of the *scherzo*.'[162] For Schumann, length was not an issue, as he told Clara:

> All the instruments are human voices; it is gifted beyond measure, and this instrumentation, Beethoven notwithstanding, and this length, this heavenly length, like a novel in four volumes, longer than the ninth symphony. I was completely happy and wished for nothing but that you might be my wife and that I too could write such symphonies.[163]

In the April 1903 edition of the *Musical Times*, Algernon Ashton, hoping to generate interest and enthusiasm for centenary celebrations in Britain to mark Lachner's birth, described him as 'one of the greatest contrapuntists and masters of fugues who ever lived. ... Why should these grand classical compositions be allowed to fall into oblivion, whilst the most ghastly trash of latter day composers is performed, even applauded by the public'. On the other hand, elsewhere within its pages the very same periodical reprinted a review in the *Musical World* of 29 April 1836, which slated the first symphony at its first British performance. The occasion was a Philharmonic Society concert in London on 9 April that year, and the report drew attention to Lachner's recent success with the fifth:

> A prize was offered a year since [1835] by Haslinger of Vienna for the best new symphony, and Mr Lachner gained it against fifty [sic] competitors. It would have been worthwhile to obtain a sight of [it] and compare that composition with the one produced on Monday evening. Either Lachner had a worthless squad to contend against or his effort on that occasion has exhausted him, for this is a positively unworthy affair for any concert. It is wholly void of originality and is

---

[160] Raymond Härtel of the publishing firm Breitkopf & Härtel to Mendelssohn, 22 March 1839, quoted in O.E. Deutsch, *Schubert: Memoirs by his Friends* (London, 1958), 394.

[161] In 1844 Mendelssohn tried to programme it with the Philharmonic Society but met with such resistance from the string players that instead he conducted the overture *Fierrabras* (10 June). His fears were therefore justified. It was 1856 before the 'Great' C major symphony was given its first public performance in London.

[162] Mendelssohn to William Watts, Secretary of, and violist in, the Philharmonic Society. Quoted in Deutsch, 398.

[163] Ibid., 400.

too long, even for a composition possessing ten times its merit. The best features in it are the instrumentation and the *Andante*, which nevertheless is but an imitation of Beethoven. The *scherzo* too has a pretty point, which is repeated over and over again. The audience testified in decided terms their disapprobation of the piece.[164]

Lachner's sixth symphony appeared in 1837, was dedicated to the Paris Conservatoire, and was also published by Haslinger. The scoring is conventional except for the addition of a piccolo in the last two movements. In the full score, 'Mälzel's metronome marks' head each movement. It had two successful performances in Munich in 1837, the second by public demand.[165] It is effectively a shorter version of the fifth and one is inclined to make the same criticism, namely unpromising material, overlong repetitive rhythmic phrases, endless dotted notes and a second subject built around homophonic chords (like sacred music by Mendelssohn) in predictable four-bar phrases, which in *fortissimo* sounds grand but soon becomes tiring on the ear. Of most interest, however, after a half-close *fermata* at the end of the development in the first movement, is the recapitulation headed *fugue à 2 sujets*, a four-part double fugue written by an expert. The first subject of the movement (Ex. 2.90) becomes the first subject of the fugue (Ex. 2.91), but the second subject of the fugue is new material with triplet figuration (Ex. 2.92), rather than of the movement (Ex. 2.93). The two fugue subjects then combine (Ex. 2.94). Of the rest, one can point to inventive instrumental colour and imaginative orchestration, producing attractive effects that, as we are seeing, are increasingly demanded by audiences of the day. One occurs in the slow movement, which starts with muted violins in three parts and *divisi* violas, with a solo bassoon doubling the lower viola line (Ex. 2.95). The *scherzo* is striking for its colourful combination of first violins doubled an octave higher by the piccolo (Ex. 2.96). One reviewer found it 'extraordinarily effective' and was reminded of 'Demons and Sirens – Children of Hell with which medieval German master builders decorated cathedrals'.[166] As a contrast, in the trio we find another such combination (a placid melody, this time clarinet doubling the violins an octave lower), while violas form the bass-line in rising and falling *arpeggios* (Ex. 2.97). The *finale* is unusually in triple time with a plethora of dotted rhythms, the second subject a lilting waltz. The whole movement has more of a *scherzo* feel to it. Midway there is an interesting extended passage for clarinets and bassoons accompanied by *pizzicato* cellos and basses *pp*, echoed *ppp* by muted *divisi* violins (Ex. 2.98).

---

[164] *Musical World*, 29 April 1836, quoted in *Musical Times*, Vol. 44 No. 4, 1 April 1903, 234.
[165] *AMZ*, Vol. 39 No. 24, 14 June 1837, col. 393.
[166] *AMZ*, Vol. 38 No. 25, 19 June 1836, col. 487.

Example 2.90   Lachner: Symphony No. 6. First movement, first subject

Example 2.91   Lachner: Symphony No. 6. First movement, first subject fugue

Example 2.92   Lachner: Symphony No. 6. First movement, second subject fugue

Example 2.93   Lachner: Symphony No. 6. First movement, second subject

Example 2.94   Lachner: Symphony No. 6. First movement, the two fugal subjects combined

Example 2.95   Lachner: Symphony No. 6. Second movement beginning

Example 2.96   Lachner: Symphony No. 6. Third movement, Scherzo

Example 2.97   Lachner: Symphony No. 6. Third movement, Trio

Example 2.98   Lachner: Symphony No. 6. Finale

The first performance at Leipzig of Lachner's sixth symphony took place on 17 January 1839, carefully directed, given the best attention by the well-rehearsed orchestra, and with nothing left to be desired. Nevertheless the applause was targeted at specific movements by a discerning audience:

> The first got the most, thanks to its fine and brilliantly scored final fugue. The second and last were not quite received in silence, the whole unenthusiastically throughout. The reason is Lachner's overlong development sections. If the work were shortened by a third, it would achieve the desired result.[167]

That question of length was raised again, when somewhat expectedly Schumann came to Lachner's rescue three years after his demolition of the fifth, with a paean of praise for the sixth and in the 1839 article on Gottfried Preyer's symphony, admitted that the more he heard those symphonies that had been entered for the Vienna competition (and Preyer's was one), the more willing he was to concede that Lachner's fifth had been the best.[168] Of the sixth, he wrote:

> Such masterly order and clarity, lightness and euphony distinguishes this symphony; with one word, so ripe and so sustained is it, that for its sake we are willing to accord its composer a place near his beloved model Franz Schubert. Though he does not approach him in variety of invention, he is at least his equal in his talent for orchestration. When this symphony was performed at Leipzig it was not successful; but the composer need not trouble himself about that since Beethoven and, later, Mendelssohn have somewhat spoiled us; it is no small achievement to stand beside them and receive an honourable mention; in any case, the symphony deserves the familiar reproach of excessive length. Lachner does not always know how to break off at the right moment, unlike witty [composers] who send us home with a joke (a technique often employed by Beethoven). ... Lachner [must] learn how to be brief; he must become less meticulous; he must not allow himself to repeat his fine ideas so often; he should not squeeze the last drop out of them but mix them with others which are new and ever lovelier. Everything as in Beethoven! Thus we always return to this divine composer and can think of nothing more to say today, save that we hope that Lachner may pursue this path towards the ideal of a modern symphony, which since Beethoven's death, we are called upon to build along new lines. Long live the German symphony! May it have fresh prosperity and a new flowering![169]

---

[167] *AMZ*, Vol. 41 No. 4, 23 January 1839, cols 73–4.

[168] Robert Schumann, *Gesammelte Schriften über Musik und Musiker* (ed. Heinrich Simon) (Leipzig, 1888).

[169] Robert Schumann 'Neue Symphonien für Orchester', *NZfM*, Vol. 11 No. 1, 2 July 1839, quoted in Schumann, *On Music and Musicians* (ed. Wolff, trans. Rosenfeld), 246, but paraphrased in places. Rather than 'new lines', Walter Frisch takes the original German ('in neuer Norm') literally and offers 'a new norm', but this is an expression that has never

More significantly, while each in turn of Schumann's own four symphonies explored new territory and developed innovations such as five movements, scherzos with two trios, extensive solos and unifying motivic structures, his conclusion here nevertheless implies that he places his hopes for the 'modern symphony' on Lachner rather than taking the responsibility upon himself. Indeed, Schumann had a habit of placing heavy burdens on the shoulders of others (possibly a sign of increasing mental instability), including his final act of baptism, the laying-on of hands on Brahms in 1853. Ironically his praise probably frightened Lachner off, for after his seventh symphony he preferred the orchestral suite. Perhaps he was intimidated by the discovery of his friend Schubert's ninth in 1839, perhaps a decade of criticism had worn him down, or perhaps Schumann had indeed given him the symphonic 'black spot'. In fact Lachner wrote just one more symphony, in 1851, and in many ways this work (to be discussed in its chronological place) provides more than one clue why, in the quarter-century that then followed, symphonists lost their sense of direction and the symphony its sense of development.

Meanwhile, Lachner's unpublished seventh symphony (1839) appears to have been in three movements and subtitled *Elegie in Form einer Symphonie*.[170] No review of any performance of the work has been found; indeed its provenance is confusing. The Bayerische Staatsbibliothek has a copy of the full score dated 1840 and bearing the description No. 7, [Op.] 58, the movements being 1. *Andante-Allegro assai*, 2. *Scherzo*, 3. *Fantasie* (the final 22 bars are missing but exist in a complete piano version made by Heinrich Esser).[171] Some 42 years later, Lachner reworked the first two movements. The introductory *Andante*, with its intermittent *recitativo* passages followed by an *Allegro assai*, becomes an overture, the *scherzo* retains its name, and together they become the first two movements of his Suite No. 7 in D minor Op. 190 (1881), to which he added a freshly composed intermezzo and chaconne with fugue.[172] The original fantasie and fugue, not used for the suite, is extant at Munich.[173]

We now see a curious case of Lachner's history as a symphonist repeating itself. The gap between the last two symphonies lasted through the 1840s (1839–51); we then find another quiet decade (1851–61) before he starts composing suites and a third (1871–81) between his sixth and (final) seventh suites. Apart from

---

really been satisfactorily explained. In his '"Echt symphonisch": On the historical context of Brahms' symphonies' in *Brahms Studies 2*, 117, Frisch also points out that Schumann's *oeuvres* are very much an endpoint rather than a springboard as far as the symphony is concerned.

[170] Manuscripts for the three unpublished symphonies (2, 4, 7) are held in the Music Department of the Bayerische Staatsbibliothek, München. It remains unclear why the unpublished No. 7 is assigned the opus number 58.

[171] Musikabteilung, Bayerische Staatsbibliothek München, Mus.ms. 5925.

[172] Robert Pascall, 'Lachner spricht echten Suitenton', in *Franz Lachner und seine Brüder* quoted in Steinbeck, 159.

[173] Mus.ms. 5879, 'Fantasie und Fugue aus der *Elegie in Form einer Symphonie*', signed 'Franz Lachner 1837'.

geographical prejudice, what reaction to his new symphonies could Lachner expect from audiences? Writing much later, Selmar Bagge defended Lachner's decision to abandon symphonies for suites as 'a modest admission that [he] dare not proceed in the dangerous proximity of the gigantic master of sonata form, Beethoven'.[174] In Kretschmar's survey, Lachner is acknowledged as an important figure in the revival of the orchestral suite, but as a symphonist he is dismissed as someone who, back in the 1830s, found favour with a competition jury rather than the public.

Let us assume that Schumann is not being sarcastic when he writes in his 1836 article praising Lachner's sixth symphony, 'Every announcement of a new symphony is an occasion for rejoicing and we approach any new work of such dimensions already prejudiced in its favour', a comment that, three years later, took on huge significance when he discovered 'such dimensions' in Schubert.[175] James Hepokoski identifies at least three genuine concerns Schumann had for the troubled symphonic genre by the end of the 1830s. First there were the possible distractions of special effects, trivialities leading to a lack of moral seriousness and consistency of national (German) character, compounded by the absence of a strong ethical component underpinning the musical form; second was the likelihood that traditional form decayed into insipid formula (this could be said of Lachner's entry for the competition); finally, the resulting formal shapes needed justification through a strong expressive content, implicit or explicit, that could draw the movements together as a single concept.[176] Steinbeck concludes by describing Lachner as 'a talented but shrewd non-symphonist who sought salvation in the suite in order to escape from the elements in the symphony which alienated him. Nevertheless he should be praised for ceasing to write them and recognising that his talents lay elsewhere'.[177] What becomes particularly pertinent regarding Lachner, though not the greater Burgmüller, is that weakness of content, even before its treatment in the process of development becomes an issue, lies at the heart of symphonic success or (more likely) failure in post-Beethoven Germany during the decade of the 1830s, before Mendelssohn and Schumann made their contributions in the mini-revival of the 1840s. As we have seen, such revival as did occur was largely based around the symphonies of Spohr, though had Burgmüller lived, who knows what further contribution he would have gone on to make?

Kretschmar, writing from Leipzig at the end of the nineteenth century, could be very patronising towards symphonists, especially those 'who generally have the honour of experiencing a performance only once' and whose music 'follows

---

[174] *Leipziger Allgemeine musikalische Zeitung* (henceforth *LAMZ*), Vol. 1 No. 9, 28 February 1866, 70–71, quoted in Scott Morris, 173.

[175] *NZfM*, Vol. 11 No. 18 (1839), 70–71.

[176] 'Beethoven reception: the symphonic tradition' in *The Cambridge History of Nineteenth- Century Music* (ed. Jim Samson) (Cambridge, 2001), 427.

[177] Steinbeck, 143.

the example of Mozart and the young Beethoven'.[178] Such composers appear in a survey from 1840 (Table 2.3) covering the last six years of the decade (1830s) at Leipzig during Mendelssohn's tenure there and showing his powerful influence within the city and elsewhere in Germany. By the beginning of the new decade (1840s), his reputation had won for Leipzig a universal historical–artistic importance. Each winter season had 20 concerts plus some Extra Concerts and Pension Fund concerts. Although there are inconsistencies in contemporary analyses, such as this one taken from *AMZ*, and while symphonies are not always identifiable because numbers or keys are lacking, it is worth illustrating the huge problems facing composers of new symphonies and the slim chances they had of securing a performance.[179] In the six-year period from 1 January 1835 to 31 December 1840 there were 119 performances of symphonies by 24 composers.

Table 2.3   119 performances of symphonies at Leipzig 1 January 1835–31 December 1840

Composer	Number of performances	Notes
Beethoven	47	All nine were played, only No. 1 just once
Mozart	17	
Haydn	12	
Spohr	8	
Onslow	5	
Schubert	4	All of them were of the ninth
Kalliwoda	4	
Schneider	3	
Lachner	2	
Mendelssohn	2	Premiere and repeat of No. 2 *Lobgesang* December 1840
Abt Vogler	2	
Burgmüller, Dobrzyński, Gährich, Hetsch, Kittl, Lindblad, Méhul, Möhring, Molique, Reissiger, Ries, Strauss and Täglichsbeck	1	Each composer received one performance of one of their symphonies

---

[178] Kretschmar cites 'Molique, Gähring, Möhring, Täglichsbeck, Markull, Lührss, Rosenhain, Leonhardt, Helstedt, Pape etc', Vol. 1 part ii, 266. We cannot assume that these symphonies were not played in places other than Leipzig just because they were not reviewed.
[179] *AMZ*, Vol. 42 No. 27, 1 July 1840, col. 563.

Elsewhere, in the winter season 1839–40 at Breslau, one could hear three symphonies each by Beethoven and Spohr, two by Mozart and one each by Haydn, Weber, Abt Vogler and Adolf Hesse (fifth), while the nine symphonies played at Potsdam were all from the first Viennese school.[180] In neighbouring Berlin they also played Hesse's fifth, described as 'his newest and a respectable work, if owing much to Spohr's form and modulatory style'.[181] We also find performances of orchestral transcriptions replacing the symphony on programmes in the Prussian capital.[182] One was of Beethoven's *Pathétique* Sonata Op. 13, while Mendelssohn conducted the *Kreutzer* Violin Sonata Op. 47 as transcribed by Eduard Marxsen (1806–87). Another example that proved popular was of Schubert's Lied *Erlkönig* made by Josef Nowakowski (1800–1865). Finally, and looking ahead a few months into the new decade, we can ascertain from an overview of 758 published works received for review by the *Allgemeine Musikalische Zeitung* between April and mid-July 1840, that 40 of them (including 11 concert overtures) were orchestral but none of them symphonies ('this time we are not richer'), whereas 351 were for solo piano, 137 were songs, and the rest were for a whole range of single instruments with piano accompaniment as well as operas, choral works and ensemble pieces.[183]

On the other hand, the decade of the 1830s, the one most in the shadow of Beethoven, *had* been rich with some fine works from Spohr, Kalliwoda and Burgmüller. Lachner's symphonies were flawed yet nevertheless epitomised the mire the genre had got itself into by the end of the decade. Partisan attitudes, public competitions and the power of the musical press were the distractions that first Mendelssohn, then Schumann at least partially resolved until the halfway point of 1850.

---

[180] *AMZ*, Vol. 42 No. 21, 20 May 1840, col. 439.
[181] *AMZ*, Vol. 42 No. 4, 22 January 1840, col. 74.
[182] *AMZ*, Vol. 42 No. 26, 24 June 1840, col. 548.
[183] *AMZ*, Vol. 42 No. 32, 5 August 1840, cols 649–55.

Chapter 3
The German Symphony in the 1840s

> Hot blood must run through the veins of the symphony of our time.[1]

From the beginning of the 1840s the German symphony was in the hands of two of the best-known composers of the decade, Mendelssohn and Schumann. However, by its end, the genre itself would be touched by two others. The first was Wagner, beginning his journey from opera to music drama.[2] The other was Liszt, moving to what he would call the 'symphonic poem' for the first time in 1854. Schumann and Mendelssohn had mixed fortunes in the symphonic field, where arguably they were not consistently at their best. Mendelssohn wrote just four orchestral works during the 1840s. Apart from a brief march (1841), there is the *Lobgesang* ('Song of Praise') symphony-cantata (1840), an uneven response to Beethoven's ninth symphony, followed by two far greater works in the respective fields of orchestral and concerted music, the *Scottish* symphony (1842) and the violin concerto (1844), both of which immediately established an uncontested place in concert programmes. Disregarding his *Jugendsinfonie* of 1832, Schumann's four symphonies, each in its own way as lyrical as his Lieder, have held a fairly constant place in the repertoire.[3] While not discussing the symphonies of either composer in detail, it stands to reason that the influence of both composers' works in the genre touched all aspiring symphonists caught in their wake.

During the 1840s most of Spohr's symphonies and some of Lachner's still featured in concert programmes but took their place in the queue according to a developing natural symphonic law, in other words after the triumvirate of Haydn, Mozart and Beethoven followed by Schubert (albeit only his ninth). Despite ingredients of Romanticism infiltrating other (particularly vocal) musical forms, it was still the earlier Classical age that continued to influence the symphony. How was this reflected in programmes? For example, by the time four of Beethoven's symphonies, three of Mozart's and two of Haydn's had been played in a winter season (October to April), what room was left for a new contemporary work? A study has examined the period 1800–1914 and finds an average level of 35 new symphonies published in each decade throughout the long nineteenth century.[4]

---

[1] *AMZ*, Vol. 48 No. 50, 16 December 1846, col. 847.

[2] *Rienzi*, *Der Fliegende Holländer* and *Tannhäuser* were all first staged during the 1840s.

[3] Despite alleged flaws in their scoring and construction, discussed many times, starting with Weingartner in Felix Weingartner, *Die Symphonie nach Beethoven* (Leipzig, 1897).

[4] F.E. Kirby, 'The Germanic symphony of the nineteenth century: genre, form, instrumentation, expression' in *Journal of Musicological Research* Vol. 14 (1995), 197. Regrettably Kirby does not identify any of these published symphonies.

Here, however, we are concerned with the years 1830–76, during which the average per decade fell to 27.

Table 3.1   New symphonies published between 1830 and 1876

Decade	Number of symphonies
1830–1839	20
1840–1849	23
1850–1859	19
1860–1869	33
1870–1876	c.30

From a total of 110 German symphonies published during the first three decades 1800–1829, the average number is higher at 36 per year; and a similar leap occurred not, as Dahlhaus stated, from 1850, when, on the contrary, the figure was at an all-time low of 19, but in the 1860s when it rose to 33, a level virtually sustained in the following first six years of the (Brahms) symphonic decade of the 1870s.[5] So turning once again to Dahlhaus, his description of a symphonic 'dead time' between 1850 and 1876 is not only misdirected by two decades but in fact there never was a 'dead time'.[6] The lowest was the period of 30 years 1830–60, during which time the average number of symphonies published per decade fell to 20, of which there were relatively few performances, which in turn discouraged further symphonic production. There were, however, plenty of performances of symphonies played from manuscript score and parts, but as they remained unpublished, we can only assume that they failed. By the 1880s the number of newly published symphonies had returned to the level of the first decade of the century, i.e. from 50 to 52. Performance venues at courts such as Esterháza and Eisenstadt were lost to cities such as Berlin and Leipzig, though a few smaller ones, such as Sondershausen, Koblenz, Meiningen and Donaueschingen, hung on to the benefit of their respective composers-in-residence. It was not the Saxon court at Dresden that stimulated the production and performance of symphonies but the Saxon city of Leipzig. This was not, however, true of opera, where centres such as Weimar, Dresden and Munich continued to flourish under Liszt, Wagner and Lachner respectively. Whereas opera retained its traditional aristocratic position, the symphony occupied a new bourgeois urban one. While the emerging

[5]   Carl Dahlhaus, *Nineteenth-Century Music* (Wiesbaden, 1980; trans. J. Bradford Robinson, Berkeley, CA, 1989). Kirby's figure here is 43, but that goes beyond Brahms (1876) to cover the full decade 1870–79.

[6]   'Die Jahrzehnte zwischen 1850 und 1870 waren … in der Geschichte der Symphonie eine tote Zeit' – see Carl Dahlhaus, 'Liszts Idee des Sinfonischen' in idem, *Klassische und romantische Musikästhetik* (Laaber, 1988), 392–401.

middle class generated audiences, music colleges provided specialised study for their students who would become future performers, composers and teachers. By 1840 and with Mendelssohn at the helm as its city music director, Leipzig had become the musical epicentre of Germany, while its new Conservatoire (which Mendelssohn also led) was attracting teachers and would-be young composers. Spohr, on the other hand, called his pupils to Kassel.

Meanwhile the great debate about the future of the symphony rumbled on. What remained a matter for discussion was how (or whether, in Wagner's opinion) new symphonists were to have their first word on the subject when Beethoven's ninth was the last, let alone the final contributions to the genre from Haydn, Mozart and Schubert. Comparing like for like, young composers' new symphonies were never measured against the first attempts of their great forebears but against their last monumental achievements, which unsurprisingly denied them any chance of success. All new ones had to pass this litmus test. There were, however, greater opportunities for performance: Mendelssohn did much for new works in Leipzig, while already from 1835, Aloys Schmitt in Frankfurt resisted the Classical-based core repertory and established a new orchestral society to promote new works 'because one is always hearing only Beethoven's symphonies in the Museum [concerts]'.[7] The concert overture, as first conceived by Weber and Beethoven then developed by Berlioz and Mendelssohn, became a convenient opt-out from the symphony. It compressed elements such as a slow introduction, formal structure and contrapuntal development into a single self-contained unit, a fruitful genre that could take the various routes of absolute, descriptive, literary or operatic music, followed soon after by the suite and serenade as another alternative for the pragmatically minded composer.

The year 1840 provides a pertinent snapshot of the conditions under which a new work struggled to find a platform. The Bohemian composer Johann Friedrich Kittl (1806–68) wrote four symphonies, one of them achieving widespread success. The first (D minor Op. 19) was composed in 1836 and first performed on 27 April 1837 under Dionys Weber at the Prague Conservatoire, but if Kittl is known at all, it is by his Symphony No. 2 (E♭ *Jagd* 'Hunt' Op. 9), written in 1837 and also premiered by Weber, this time on 7 April 1838. It was Spohr who, having played it at Kassel on 2 February 1839, then recommended both the work and its composer to Mendelssohn. He in turn conducted it on 9 January 1840 at Leipzig, where it was received with enthusiasm. Kittl shrewdly dedicated it to Mendelssohn before publication by Breitkopf and Härtel. The way was now open for his music to be performed throughout Germany. His Symphony No. 3 (in D Op. 24) was first performed at Prague on 4 May 1842 and 'unanimously regarded by those who know about music as having taken this excellent composer a significant step forward on his artistic path with music as appealing as it is skilful

---

[7] Hildegard Weber, *Das 'Museum'. 150 Jahre Frankfurter Konzertleben 1808–1958* (Frankfurt, 1958), 123.

and workmanlike'.[8] Schott published it; and after a performance in Hanover a few years later, Kittl was congratulated by Marschner, himself surprised at the good reception from the audience, who, he assured him, only loved symphonies by Beethoven.[9] The *Jagdsinfonie* was well received at Leipzig; despite not being a work of genius or rich in exceptional ideas, it was readily comprehensible and tasteful, two essential ingredients as far as current public opinion was concerned. Of the four movements, the last two were praised for being fresh, lively, best scored and most effective, while the slow movement was criticised for lacking richness of ideas and (surprisingly) for being too short compared to the rest of the work (about 25 minutes). One reviewer was disappointed by 'a work that does not live up to expectations, the more so as Beethoven seems to be its model, and because the title limits its boundaries'.[10]

Kittl's style is very simple and avoids counterpoint in any part of the work. There are, however, some striking moments that give the symphony and its movements their various titles.[11] The opening *Adagio* is a three-bar 'Summons' for a pair of trumpets (Ex. 3.1) followed by the 'Start of the Hunt', an exciting passage for four solo horns (Ex. 3.2). As the full orchestra enters, it becomes a joyous, lively gallop ($\frac{6}{8}$), its syncopated strong accents falling on weak parts of the bar. The *Andante* (Ex. 3.3) is simple, its mood comfortable; and with reduced scoring and tranquil dynamic levels, it creates a dreamy atmosphere as the hunters 'Rest from the Hunt'. The 'Drinking Chorus' is a traditional *scherzo* with a recurrent phrase (Ex. 3.4), the second-beat accent a stumble by a drunken bucolic dancer, an image modelled on the equivalent movement in Beethoven's *Pastoral* symphony perhaps. There are two trios: the first features woodwind syncopations and chordal textures, the second focuses on a melody in low strings and winds accompanied by sustained chords in upper instruments of both families, the dynamics with sudden juxtapositions and therefore with few gradual changes.[12] The 'End of the Hunt' is a *rondo-finale* march introduced, as at the start, by trumpets. The music is plain, most of the activity found in the strings, while winds and brass are given a rather dull secondary function filling out the texture. Momentary excitement is generated when the full brass chorus (four horns, two trumpets and a bass trombone) erupt into a fanfare-chorale (Ex. 3.5). While Kittl requires horns and a trombone to

---

[8] *AMZ*, Vol. 44 No. 26, 29 June 1842, col. 528.

[9] *Johann Friedrich Kittl*, author unknown (published by Ernst Balde, Kassel, 1857), 12–19.

[10] *AMZ*, Vol. 42 No. 3, 15 January 1840, col. 53.

[11] Although it is a symphony with a programme, a description here is a useful guide to such works in 1840. It is scored for double winds, four horns, two trumpets, bass trombone, timpani and strings; the *Andante* reduces this to one flute, two each of oboes, clarinets, bassoons and horns, and strings.

[12] Schumann could have heard Kittl's *Jagdsinfonie* in Leipzig, where he was living at the beginning of 1840, and may have taken up the idea of two trios for the *scherzo* movements of his own first two symphonies (1840, 1845).

play the whole passage *fortissimo*, the pair of trumpets must play *piano* after the two octave-fanfares, providing an insight into the achievable dynamic qualities of brass instruments of his day.

Example 3.1   Kittl: Symphony No. 2. First movement, opening 'Summons'

Example 3.2   Kittl: Symphony No. 2. First movement, 'Start of the hunt'

Example 3.3   Kittl: Symphony No. 2. Second movement, 'Rest from the hunt'

Example 3.4   Kittl: Symphony No. 2. Third movement, Scherzo
                     'Drinking chorus'

Example 3.5   Kittl: Symphony No. 2. Finale, 'The end of the hunt', fanfare-chorale

Kittl, like Kalliwoda and Lachner before him, was another composer who abandoned the symphony for a dozen years before returning to write one more (in C major) in 1857, first performed on 7 July 1858, but it remains unpublished. As a practising musician, Kittl is something of an enigma. He was appointed as Dionys Weber's successor at the Prague Conservatoire in 1843 and introduced new works previously shunned, for Prague was still basking in the glow of Mozart's presence 60 years earlier and the cult that this generated thereafter. Kittl conducted music by Schumann, Rietz, Gade, Berlioz, even Liszt and Wagner, but his own music remained conservative in style. In 1844 he heard Lachner conduct in Munich and was enormously impressed by the standard of the superb orchestra.[13] While he lived, his symphonies continued to be performed at Berlin and Leipzig (his first in December 1844), but despite the backing of Wilhelm Taubert (1811–91) and Mendelssohn respectively at those centres, Kittl became preoccupied with his teaching duties. In March 1853 he conducted the *Jagdsinfonie* at the invitation of the members of the orchestra in Frankfurt, and it was liked so much that he was applauded by the players at the rehearsal, a very rare occurrence, and cheered by the audience at the concert.[14] What impressed the players and audience alike at its first performance was its colour, its effects and the maturity of its characteristic style, despite Kittl's relative inexperience.[15] The foreword to the re-edited full score concludes that,

> even if the judgement of the day, which summed up [the *Jagdsinfonie*] as a companion piece to the *Pastoral* symphony, was exaggerated, it is easy to understand the vitality and popularity of the work. Kittl's passion for hunting really inspired its content, the invention is successful and fluent, the form clear

---

[13] What stuck in his memory was the perfect control of its *crescendi* and *diminuendi* in the *Andante* of Auber's overture *Fra Diavolo*.

[14] Kittl's Frankfurt concert was on Palm Sunday 1853. See Neumann, *Die Componisten der neueren Zeit*, 42.

[15] Ibid.

and the orchestration colourful. Without doubt this symphony counts as one of the best Czech symphonies before Dvořák's time.[16]

Horn calls were obviously a vital ingredient of Kittl's symphony given its title, but they had less reason to predominate as much as they do in the fifth symphony by Carl Czerny (1791–1857), despite the military style generated by its key of E♭ major and the pair of trumpets and drums included in the orchestration.[17] Written in 1845 in the conventional four movements of which the outer ones are far too long, this is the typical work of a pianist (on which of course Czerny's reputation as both soloist and pedagogue remains to this day), but occasionally woodwinds and first horn have rewarding solos, while the cellos have a fine melody in the *Andante*. There is no real contrast between *scherzo* and trio, and in the *finale* the string writing is relentlessly active, particularly for the second violins and violas. Though the result is therefore patchy and unsustainable, Czerny's fifth symphony merits a brief mention, because, despite its heavily Beethoven-influenced style, there are some charming melodies and occasionally inventive modulations that often take the music to keys far removed from the key signature of the moment, but ultimately it succumbs to clichés such as *arpeggio*-constructed melodies and predictable sequences increasingly encountered from the 1840s onwards.

Programmes of the 1840s' winter seasons at Leipzig reveal some new works, but pride of place is always given to the Viennese classics, with Spohr, Kalliwoda and Lachner accepted as newcomers. By 1849 these three alone could muster 21 symphonies between them, while all five by Mendelssohn and the first two by Schumann were also established.[18] The press had now stopped moaning at the length of Schubert's ninth; within a year of its premiere its beauties were acknowledged and more appreciated. It also achieved wider recognition thanks to sales of a four-hand piano version published in 1840. An incident occurred with this symphony that typifies the public's response to new works. The performance on 12 March 1840 got no further than the second subject of the first movement, when crowds shouting in the street interrupted the playing with news of a fire in Leipzig. The danger was soon over, but regrettably so too was the performance. One disappointed reviewer hoped for a repeat before the season's end, rather than having to wait for a place in the next. 'New works,' he wrote, 'when they are as first rate as this, should be given repeat performances from the start so the public gets to know and understand them quickly.' He was either in luck or influential, for it was played two weeks later on 26 March and reviewed in the next issue.[19] New composers would have been grateful for such swiftly scheduled follow-up performances, but despite receiving recommendations from satisfied critics,

---

[16] Foreword to the full score, ed. Jarmil Burghauser (Prague, 1960).
[17] It also has a pair of horns but no trombones.
[18] Mendelssohn's *Italian* was not performed in Germany until 1849, while Schumann's fourth had a chequered start until his revised version of 1851 was published two years later.
[19] *AMZ*, Vol. 42 No. 15, 8 April 1840, col. 316.

many new symphonies were not given such further hearings and became what Kretschmar dismissed as 'halfway useful ones'.[20]

There were also composers who had little more than a day in the sun and who relied on connections at Leipzig, especially those teaching at the Conservatoire. Friedrich Schneider (1786–1853) was a distinguished Saxon organist who spent the years 1805–21 in Leipzig, including a spell as organist at St Thomas' Church, before making Dessau his base. As a composer he was prolific, his works including upwards of 20 symphonies, and, like Kalliwoda, Kittl and Lachner, he took a dozen years out (1823–35) before returning to the genre. Perhaps the gap was a consequence of leaving Leipzig, hitherto his obvious starting point for a performance. Ever the pragmatist, he maintained contact and periodically returned there between 1835 and 1848 to conduct one of his new symphonies. The one in A major, played on 20 February 1840, was 'freshly youthful, well constructed, cleverly worked and received with much appreciation. A good performance will guarantee pleasure everywhere'.[21] 'Pleasure' was *le mot juste*, for Dörffel describes in similar terms one of Schneider's last appearances at the Gewandhaus on 13 January 1848 when he conducted his F minor symphony. It too was 'unexpectedly fresh and youthful, each movement received with noisy applause, so master and public certainly went home most happy with one another'.[22]

Friedrich Wilhelm Markull (1816–87), music director at Danzig, was a pupil of Schneider and wrote two unpublished symphonies. The first in D major was played at the Gewandhaus under his direction on 6 February 1845, the second in C minor a decade later at Danzig in February 1855, after which it won first prize in a competition at Mannheim in 1856.[23] His first symphony was played from manuscript score and parts under the composer's direction and given pride of place at the end of a long mixed programme with two soloists, typical of the mid-1840s. Unfortunately it was not spared a drubbing from at least one critic.

Overture *The Naiads*	Sterndale Bennett
Scene and aria from *Il Pirata*	Bellini
Violin Concerto in E (soloist: Otto von Königslow – Hamburg)[24]	Spohr
Cavatine from *Euryanthe*	Weber
Concertino for trombone (soloist Herr Rex)[25]	Ferdinand David
Symphony in D major	F W Markull

---

[20] Kretschmar, Vol. I part ii, 265.
[21] *AMZ*, Vol. 42 No. 10, 4 March 1840, col. 199.
[22] Dörffel, 54.
[23] Neumann, *Die Componisten der neueren Zeit*, 71.
[24] Königslow went on to premiere the first version of Bruch's G minor violin concerto at Koblenz on 24 April 1866.
[25] A popular work, which had six performances in the 10 years 1837–47 and four 1862–76. Dörffel, 15.

Usually it is most interesting to hear a large work by a little or unknown composer. During the performance one conjures up a picture of his taste, his musical stance, and whether he knows how to communicate his individuality using his material. It is of course on a rough-and-ready basis that all listeners make when sitting in judgement, for such opinions are unprepared and spontaneous. Nevertheless such an impression is more decisive if originality or skill is present in the work, not the case when pronouncing upon Mr Markull's symphony. Its motifs are neither new nor interesting, no definable characteristics impress in any of its four movements, it lacks the imprint of spirit, talent, flight of fancy or fantasy. Overall there is a breadth and length that is made more tiring by lack of interest or tension. The development is so protracted, that one easily forgets the original material itself, while even the scoring does not have enough lustre to hold the listener's attention. This description can only offend Mr Markull's efforts, ability and artistry, but what he has offered the musical world with this symphony cannot gratify the hopes that one is accustomed to regarding a composer who, with such a voluminous work, has made an attempt at the hardest of all genres. The applause was very modest.[26]

Just two concerts later, on 27 February 1845, another hopeful composer, this time Carl Lührss (1824–82), conducted his new symphony from manuscript parts. On this occasion Mendelssohn gave him the start of the concert; and although the programme had a similar structure, Lührss had tougher competition not only from his benefactor's major work concluding the programme, but also from the interest shown by the audience in the debut of Maria Wieck (1832–1916), Clara Schumann's 12-year-old step-sister.

Symphony in E♭	Lührss
Aria from *Hans Heiling*	Marschner
Adagio and *rondo* for piano and orchestra (soloist Maria Wieck – Dresden)	Pixis
Two four-part Lieder	Mendelssohn
Piano solos played by Maria Wieck	
Die erste Walpurgisnacht	Mendelssohn

Unlike Markull, Lührss received a much more encouraging notice from his reviewer, although unfortunately the hopes invested in his 'developing talent' would subsequently remain unrealised.

The symphony by Mr Lührss, who is generally unknown to the greater public, reveals a significant and estimable talent. It continually shows achievement through struggle for a young composer who, having published only a few songbooks and small piano pieces, has turned to a bigger work. We at least can

---

[26] *AMZ*, Vol. 47 No. 7, 12 February 1845, col. 109.

see it, not so much as a rushed attempt to join the ranks of the famous masters and make a mark for eternity but as a laudable attempt and with the hardest assignment, to achieve a position and seize the chance to show clever artistry. From this standpoint, Mr Lührss' success in the struggle has undoubtedly been a happy one. If the melodies are not effective or strikingly original, there is nevertheless in the whole work a warmth and tenderness of feeling, if somewhat neutralised by reflection on the one hand and a notable unrest on the other, which is not quite in the right place in the middle movement, so several instrumental effects do not come off quite as the composer might have expected. Yet throughout, the main positives of the symphony include an exalted spirit, a warm colour to the themes and a solid working out and ordering of its musical thought. The progress of the composer's developing talent will be followed with pleasure and interest and one looks forward to many fine works from him. The first movement and the *scherzo* have appealed to other reviewers. The public gave a warm reception and much applause to the energy and care with which the composer conducted the performance.[27]

The issue of where a new work should be placed in a programme and what should be juxtaposed alongside it was now becoming crucial. Most composers (even those of repute) had no power to decide; that was invested in the music director at a court or city, who therefore could make or break a new work. The Hungarian composer–conductor Ferenc Erkel placed Liszt's newly composed *Les Préludes* not only at the end of a programme but also after Beethoven's *Pastoral* symphony, which roused both the composer's ire and the comment that, 'unless one deliberately intends to sacrifice new works which demand greater attention from audience and players alike, the natural order is to place the symphonies of Beethoven, Mozart or Haydn at the end of a concert'.[28] It was also proving of no service to struggling new composers to find their symphonies placed on programmes within touching distance of those by Mendelssohn or Schumann. Comparisons were odious. Looking at smaller towns and courts, we find no reduction in the number of new symphonies beyond what one would expect between large and small centres; indeed in some instances one can see a pattern forming, which would become normal for such enterprising programming over the next three decades. Bremen in 1842 was a good example. The town had a society that usually put on between ten and a dozen concerts per winter season for 700 subscribers paying 5 florins per ticket. The orchestra under Wilhelm Friedrich Riem (1779–1857) was of a fair size with 62 members; the string strength of 41 consisted of 24 violins, 8 violas, 5 cellos and 4 double basses.[29] A retrospective

---

[27] *AMZ*, Vol. 47 No. 7, 12 February 1845, col. 163.

[28] Wilhelm von Csapó (ed.), *Franz Liszt's Briefe an Baron Anton Augusz, 1846–1878* (Budapest, 1911) quoted in Alan Walker, *Franz Liszt: vol.2 the Weimar years (1848–1861)* (London, 1989), 300–301.

[29] Riem had been music director at Bremen since 1814.

of the 1840–41 winter season praised the public, who, having happily heard six of Beethoven's symphonies in one season, also welcomed new symphonies from composers adjudged to have a future, and took it as

> a good sign that our public listens to symphonies with both undivided attention and unmitigated pleasure. Most popular was Beethoven's seventh. Schubert's [ninth] appealed completely to one section, but less so to another, who found it too long, the ideas too protracted. Perhaps no repeats should be made, as the composer has, with one statement, made clear his ideas. [Ludwig] Pape's *Military* symphony was much liked. It is natural, fresh and well defined; there is nothing artificial about it, nor anything humdrum. The public must continue to watch out for this able and gifted young man.[30]

Another summary described how

> a grand symphony was played at every concert, the old favourites of Haydn and Mozart but above all Beethoven, all interspersed with the newest compositions, such as Spohr [No. 4], Preyer, Reissiger, Ries, C.G. Müller, Schubert, Kalliwoda, Lachner and Kittl. In the last season there were three unpublished symphonies, by Schubert [No. 9], Kittl's *Jagdsinfonie* and the *Militärsinfonie* of L[udwig] Pape from Lübeck. At the next concert, the first symphony of Schumann will be given under his personal direction. At the helm is Music Director Riem, while Schmidt is the leader.[31]

At another middle-sized town, Oldenburg (like Bremen, a venue later active on behalf of Brahms), they seemed pleased with Pape's symphony in the spring of 1840. Ludwig Pape (1809–55 and based at Lübeck) was, as Schneider had been a generation earlier, not only a young, energetic, very talented organist and music director, but also a violinist. His *Military* symphony was performed in Oldenburg with huge success; at the end there was an 'extraordinary furore as the audience clamoured in four equal numbers for each of the four movements to be repeated, but rather than play the whole symphony, it was the *scherzo* that won. The symphony bears the hallmarks of Beethoven's gaiety and spirit'.[32] At the same time August Gottfried Ritter (1811–85, an organist and teacher at Erfurt) was having his C minor symphony played at Jena under Friedrich Stade (1817–1902). It was a work in which the first movement owed much to Beethoven, while the last two paid a

---

[30] *AMZ*, Vol. 43 No. 13, 31 March 1841, col. 278.

[31] Ferdinand Simon Gassner, *Zeitschrift für Deutschlands Musik-Vereine und Dilettanten* (Karlsruhe, 1842), 78–9.

[32] *AMZ*, Vol. 42 No. 16, 15 April 1840, col. 342.

debt to Haydn.³³ The performance was successful and well received, though a call was made for extra players as the orchestra was too small and over-stretched.³⁴

Eduard Marxsen wrote an orchestral work in 1844 or 1845 called *Beethovens Schatten* (*Beethoven's Shadow*), which title would presumably reflect his attitude (and that of many others) to the great man and which in turn was impressed upon his pupil from 1843, the 10-year-old Brahms. Marxsen's Symphony No. 5 in G minor was reviewed after the performance that took place at Hamburg on 22 February 1845. It was conducted by Karl August Krebs (1804–80) directing an 80-piece orchestra. Krebs was based in the Hanseatic port city from 1827–50 and had prepared it diligently. The work itself was much applauded by the public. Marxsen was a well-tutored musician, so it was no surprise to find complex counterpoint in the development of the first movement. The *scherzo* had a trio, which drew the comment that a lyrical theme first appeared in the bass, after which it moved to the upper instruments instead of following the conventional repeat. Both the slow and final movements were noted for charming scoring in the former, and brilliance in the latter, where 'all possible contrapuntal methods were to be found, particularly canon' but in such a way that 'those unable to penetrate the technical devices and mysteries of the art of composition' were left none the wiser.³⁵

Of the 23 new symphonies written in the 1840s (see Table 3.1, page 82), more than half were by composers such as Schubert, Kalliwoda, Spohr, Czerny, Mendelssohn and Schumann as well as the emerging Niels Gade.³⁶ These men are singled out here as composers whose symphonies were not only played during the 1840s but, more importantly, published, albeit some of them several years, if not decades, later. Although Lachner's symphonies were also performed, he produced nothing new during this decade. That many symphonies remained unpublished did not necessarily reflect their worth; indeed many of them received glowing reviews and an enthusiastic public response. One was by Gottfried Herrmann (1808–78), who had a symphony performed at Berlin in November 1841 at a concert he organised to showcase his own compositions.³⁷ A versatile musician, he not only conducted his own symphony but also appeared on the programme as soloist in his own violin concerto and a *Phantasiestück* for piano and orchestra. At the time he was music director in Lübeck and probably wanted to make an impression or even a career move to the Prussian capital. With Mendelssohn very active there, Herrmann tactfully began the concert with the greater man's overture *Fair Melusine* conducted by the orchestra's leader Hubert Ries (1802–66).³⁸ Vocal

---

[33] *AMZ*, Vol. 42 No. 17, 22 April 1840, cols 349–53.
[34] *AMZ*, Vol. 42 No. 16, 15 April 1840, col. 342.
[35] *AMZ*, Vol. 47 No. 18, 30 April 1845, cols 310–11.
[36] This study cannot omit the Dane Niels Gade nor the Dutchman Johannes Verhulst, who with their strong Leipzig associations made major contributions to the German symphony.
[37] Gottfried Herrmann was a pupil of Spohr, Hauptmann and Schmitt.
[38] Hubert Ries, whose more famous father Ferdinand was a friend of Beethoven.

solos and an operatic duet ended the first half, while the second consisted of Herrmann's C minor symphony, inevitably called the *Pathétique*, but it did well:

> This highly estimable composition is worthy of praise, but it requires a sighting of the score and several hearings, because it is very complicated, somewhat too long, strange yet too far-fetched in modulation and continually thickly scored. On the whole, the *Adagio* and *scherzo* appealed most to this reviewer. In any case, with this work, surely created following Beethoven's model, we have credible evidence of the instrumental and harmonic knowledge of a resourceful composer, who takes up an honourable place among German instrumental composers, and deserves to become better known.[39]

At Leipzig a short time later, on 9 December 1841, the reaction was quite different. The extent to which these anonymous critics were responsible for such conflicting messages is breathtaking. It was as if they were constantly striving to sit on the widest of all possible fences, when it came to committing opinions to print. This time, however, Herrmann was left in no doubt:

> The very difficult symphony was admirably played but received no applause. Nevertheless, it showed evidence of clever, scholarly knowledge of harmony but lacked invention, taste and judgement to such an extent that one could only describe it as devoid of talent. We remember only some things, for example the middle section of the *Adagio* movement for wind instruments and the long *coda* in the *finale*, which we frankly found incredible that such a well-educated musician could consider fine or effective. Perhaps if the composer would for once undertake to write less pretentiously and more simply and naturally, the real musical element, which appears to be fully suppressed in this symphony, would prevail.[40]

Adolf Hesse (1808–63), an eminent organist based in Breslau, whose fifth symphony was performed there in the winter season 1839–40, followed it with his sixth and last in the Spring of 1844.[41] The reviewer of the first Leipzig performance (9 January 1845) took care to include what was now becoming a customary *caveat* in the event of a misjudgement, that is having to make 'an impression on the reviewer and on the public' after only one hearing and without a score to hand, 'a daring undertaking'. He was happy to report the music's fresh youthfulness, a stream of good musical ideas and the way they were developed, and a deft hand in instrumentation. On the other hand, he could not deny that there was a degree of unrest created by many changes of harmony as well as complexities in figuration and modulation. In all movements except the *scherzo*

---

[39] *AMZ*, Vol. 44 No. 3, 19 January 1842, col. 66.
[40] *AMZ*, Vol. 43 No. 51, 22 December 1841, cols 1101–2.
[41] *AMZ* Vol. 46 No. 11, 15 March 1844, col. 191.

there were well-ordered contrapuntal episodes, even if the overall result gave the work a degree of stiffness. Otherwise the reception it got bode well for the work, with applause at the end of each movement, and for the excellent direction by the composer.[42] Applause being so vital as a measure of success, however quick to judge the audience had to be, those occasions when music was received in stony silence, such as Herrmann's at Leipzig, must have been extremely embarrassing for composer and performers alike.

Alexander Fesca (1820–49), whose 'career was cut short by irregular living', lived and worked at Braunschweig (Brunswick).[43] While reference is made in February 1842 to the preparation of a performance of his first symphony, there is no evidence that the event actually took place.

> The composer and virtuoso pianist Alexander Fesca, currently living here, claims our undivided attention. Such are the varied opinions that his compositions have attracted until now in the press, that they will surely soon unite in a single voice of positive recognition. In fact with his third trio and first symphony, this 22-year-old young artist has set off on the road to what may be a quite unexpected destination. ... The symphony will be prepared for performance.[44]

In the same year, a composer active in another small provincial town in Germany was the clarinettist Friedrich Müller (1786–1871), court conductor in Schwarzburg-Rudolstadt 1831–54. His new Symphony in E♭ was played at Kassel, where it was 'applauded for its content and a good performance'.[45] A year later it was played at Leipzig on 27 January 1842.

> [It has] already described in detail and with much approval.[46] We have nothing to add, other than the fact that it clearly demonstrated how naturalness of invention, clarity and grasp of technique fundamentally improve the effect of every work of art. We must also praise in particular, however, the tasteful and highly practical scoring, a quality that one does not always find in new orchestral works and that does great honour to the composer's knowledge of the orchestra. The performance of the symphony was very good, and all its movements received loud applause. Because of its freshness of thought and concise development, the first appealed to us the most; perhaps the other three would have made a more powerful effect in a somewhat faster account.[47]

---

[42] *AMZ*, Vol. 47 No. 3, 15 January 1845, col. 44.
[43] Alexander Fesca, *The New Encyclopedia of Music and Musicians* (ed. Waldo Selden Pratt), 346.
[44] *AMZ*, Vol. 44 No. 6, 9 February 1842, col. 114.
[45] *AMZ*, Vol. 43 No. 30, 28 July 1841, col. 597.
[46] *AMZ*, Vol. 43 No. 47, 24 November 1841, cols 971–5.
[47] *AMZ*, Vol. 44 No. 6, 9 February 1842, col. 120.

The court orchestra of Oldenburg included Lachner's second and Spohr's fifth symphonies in the ever-enterprising concerts organised there by its musical director August Pott (1806–83) during December 1841. Both works were well played and positively received by a discerning audience.[48] Leipzig, however, was the performance arena upon which all composers set their sights. Occasionally a player from the orchestra would emerge from its ranks with a new work and succeed; this preferment of one of their own (including past players) must have smacked of musical nepotism to outsiders struggling to gain a foothold there. Christian Gottlieb Müller (1800–63), a violinist in the Gewandhaus orchestra from 1826–38, was city music director in Altenburg at the time his fourth symphony (in F) was played at Leipzig on 10 February 1842, four years after he left.[49]

> It has been interesting for us to get to know the symphony by Mr Müller because it has many different new things in it. What is apparent in this work, as in earlier ones by this composer, is much hard work and bold endeavour, as well as experience and sureness regarding material and instrumentation. Concerning the various movements, the first pleased us the most. It has controlled humour and takes after its model, the eighth symphony of Beethoven, with which it shares the same key. Yet somewhat strange is the sudden appearance of the slow *Intermezzo*. The second and third movements satisfied us less. In the second, the reason may lie in the various tempo changes, which were not a unifying feature, and also in its completely different characteristics compared to the first movement. In the third, it was because it lacked energetic themes throughout and had an uninteresting and unchanging duple time signature. Compared to the first, both movements appeared to us to be written in an inappropriate mood. There is no break between the third movement and the *finale*, which, with its vivacity, we prefer to the preceding pair. The orchestra played this symphony with customary assurance, as it did Mendelssohn's overture *Fingal's Cave*, which opened the second half.[50]

Johannes Verhulst's only symphony (E minor Op. 46, 1841) is important because of this Dutch composer's association with Leipzig.[51] It is also a good symphony, worthy of reassessment and revival, now made easier because the full score has been edited and republished.[52] Verhulst (1816–90) was a pupil of

---

[48] *AMZ*, Vol. 44 No. 7, 16 February 1842, col. 147.

[49] Christian Gottlieb Müller in Dörffel, 239. Several of his works were played by the orchestra on more than one occasion. Some of them were concertos for certain players, including a concertino for its principal trombonist Carl Traugott Queisser (1800–46).

[50] *AMZ*, Vol. 44 No. 9, 2 March 1842, col. 189.

[51] An early example of a symphony in the key of E minor, Haydn's *Trauer* (No. 44, 1770) being a possible model.

[52] Symphony in E minor, ed. Jan Ten Bokum. Vereniging voor Nederlandse Muziekgeschiedenis (Amsterdam, 1971).

Mendelssohn and, from 1838–42, conductor of Leipzig's Euterpe concerts. His symphony was performed for the first time on 24 January 1842, possibly as a farewell to the city where he received his formative musical education and became a follower and member of Schumann's *Davidsbund*. Soon afterwards Verhulst returned to his native Holland, where he worked in Rotterdam and Amsterdam for the rest of his life. The symphony is a highly attractive work written with the *élan* of a man in his mid-twenties. After a slow introduction with traces of Beethoven and Mozart (*Don Giovanni*), the mood of the first movement is crystallised as *con agitata* (Ex. 3.6) followed by a calmer second subject (Ex. 3.7). There are lashings of Beethoven's energy and a confident approach to development, best illustrated by the *Eroica* off-beat discords in the thrilling coda, brass stridently pitting an E against chords of F major, and winning the battle as E is finally absorbed by an upward chromatic shift through F♯ to B minor (Ex. 3.8). Either Haydn or an operatic aria by Mozart lies behind the style of the charming *Andante* (Ex. 3.9), but the harmonic explorations and rhythmic elaborations it goes through place it unequivocally in the Romanticism of the 1840s. The first of the ensuing variations (Ex. 3.10) is for the mellow *tessitura* of middle- and lower-voiced instruments, which despite its sombre key of A minor is tongue-in-cheek music. But do the violas realise this? They should do, for in their part alone and not in that of the doubling bassoon, they are instructed to play 'mit Humor', an early example of a viola joke perhaps. From here the music is packed with unexpected twists and turns, rhythmic experiments and thematic unity as that viola melody becomes the principal thematic ingredient for both remaining movements (Exx 3.11–3.13).

Example 3.6   Verhulst: Symphony in E minor. First movement, first subject

Example 3.7   Verhulst: Symphony in E minor. First movement, second subject

Example 3.8   Verhulst: Symphony in E minor. First movement, development

Example 3.9   Verhulst: Symphony in E minor. Second movement, theme

Example 3.10   Verhulst: Symphony in E minor. Second movement, first variation

Example 3.11   Verhulst: Symphony in E minor. Third movement, Scherzo

Example 3.12   Verhulst: Symphony in E minor. Third movement, Trio

Example 3.13   Verhulst: Symphony in E minor. Finale, opening

It is a fine symphony, fully deserving of the praise it received in its day.

> We are happy to confess that we are surprised by the symphony, which is the composer's first to be given in public. If new works such as this arouse suspense bordering on prejudice, we must happily acknowledge that, after this symphony, much good can be expected. We note its intellectual material, interesting and beautiful, and where we find faults, we are convinced that others will also see them, such as a lack of inner contact between the individual movements and a certain unevenness in scoring that, in later works, will disappear both through hard work and experience. The last [two] movements of the symphony pleased us especially; they appear the freshest and most characteristic in inventiveness and instrumentation. The orchestra was marvellous in dealing with its difficult task.[53]

For many countries in Europe, the 1840s was a decade that culminated in revolution, the roots of which could be traced back to 1789 France *via* 1830. It was often a struggle for music directors to achieve their artistic goals as the decade progressed. Musical politics were exacerbated by the heady or threatening atmosphere (depending on which side was taken) of the *Vormärz* during the years leading to the uprisings of 1848. Fallout from changes caused by the social and industrial upheavals naturally had a knock-on effect in the music profession. Satisfying a new public from the emerging middle classes would prove as difficult as meeting the demands of a despotic aristocrat. Composers and conductors could no longer communicate with their surviving royal masters through court officialdom; instead they now had to deal with committees. Munich was a typical cauldron of upheaval, where poor Franz Lachner struggled for decades against the scheming activities of the exiled Wagner and his supporters, in whose opinion he was an extreme Conservative, a Classicist who stood in the way of the Music of the Future. Yet Lachner too was not without his supporters, who welcomed his reforms, however drastic.

> For several years, the Lenten concerts given by members of the Royal Court Orchestra stand out most notably as much by virtue of their perfection in performance as in their superb, truly classical repertoire. While it may be true that in former times there was a similar desire for such music, this was only put into practice when Lachner took over as conductor of the grand concerts

---

[53]   *AMZ*, Vol. 44 No. 9, 2 March 1842, col. 191.

soon after his appointment here five years ago [1837]. Through his powerfully energetic conducting, he achieved his aim to inspire a reaction in favour of true art, which at that time and despite much resistance, was already developing.

If, at one time, it was normal to perform a serious, solid work (usually a symphony) in the first part of a concert, it is now the second part that is reserved for such works. Therefore all compositions are now banned that belong to the genre of mere fashionable and trivial entertainment such as variations, *potpourris*, rondos, fantasias and similar modern Italian *bravura*, as well as operatic pieces. Even the repertoire of this year's Lenten concerts took this serious course and in the first of them we heard Beethoven's C minor symphony [the fifth] given a masterful performance with not even the slightest slip.[54]

Lachner's first and third symphonies were played in this same Lenten period. Both works were now 16 and 10 years old respectively and clearly still popular, as these comments about the third symphony show:

Before he was even appointed here, Lachner, conducting this symphony, appeared for the first time before the local public, which at that time hardly knew his name. We still remember vividly the completely favourable impression that his work made on that occasion.[55] If, on the one hand, clever combinations and solid development were pleasing to the soul, on the other, the ear and the heart were no less satisfied by the freshness, even boldness of the themes (especially in the first three movements) through a certain naturalness in the whole demeanour and arrangement and by the brilliant orchestration. This time the applause was once again enthusiastic.[56]

By the 1840s, Berlioz was acknowledged both as a weighty if eccentric figure and as a composer whose contribution to the symphonic genre was ambivalent. The *Symphonie fantastique* had been in existence since 1830, but how did it impact on Germany? Ferdinand Hiller encountered it in Paris, where he and Berlioz began a friendship that would last until the latter's death in 1869. Berlioz took his time before venturing to Germany. Despite a first meeting between Berlioz and Mendelssohn in Rome in 1831 and Schumann's series of articles in 1835 on the *Symphonie* in *NZfM*, it was only at the end of 1842 that the Frenchman visited Germany for the first time, taking in several centres (Berlin, Leipzig, Dresden, Weimar and Brunswick) between December that year and the following June. Whereas he 'whirled into the musical life of Paris like a firebrand thrown onto a wooden roof', his entry into Germany was very cautious.[57] This was

---

[54] *AMZ*, Vol. 44 No. 22, 1 June 1842, col. 452.
[55] See page 72, footnote 165.
[56] *AMZ*, Vol. 44 No. 22, 1 June 1842, col. 454.
[57] Max Graf, *Composer and Critic: 200 Years of Musical Criticism* (New York, 1946), 222.

particularly the case at Leipzig, where, by 1880, the *Symphonie fantastique* had been performed just once, on 4 February 1843, under his direction.[58] It may have made an impact on the audience, but the reception by the press was mixed. *AMZ* was critical of its harmonic language and eccentric modulations but, as usual, covered itself by saying that its response was based solely on hearing the work without seeing a score.[59]

It had been the plan for Berlioz to conduct his dramatic symphony *Roméo et Juliette* at a charity concert two weeks later on 22 February, and Mendelssohn (despite his wariness of Berlioz) even undertook to take rehearsals for him while he continued his German tour. Regrettably the programme was changed at the last minute, as Berlioz considered the singer for the part of Friar Laurence inadequate. Ahead of his visit to Leipzig, the full score had been reviewed and deemed a work of great importance, for Berlioz had done what Beethoven had done and introduced the chorus into the genre of the symphony. Mendelssohn would continue the process with his second symphony, the *Lobgesang*, so boundaries were being widened with more vocal and even operatic characteristics increasingly introduced into the symphony. The instrumental *recitative* post-Beethoven, for example, had already been taken up by Lachner and Burgmüller, and would be by Franz Xaver Schnyder von Wartensee.[60] Also acknowledged were Berlioz's extraordinary gifts as an instrumental colourist; 'effects' and 'colour' were now established words in the critical vocabulary. Critics came down heavily on composers whose scoring was too dense and whose effects played to the gallery. In their view, such tricks merely served to deflect attention away from weak thematic material that lay at the core of their lacklustre musical creativity.

These were significant times at Leipzig's Gewandhaus. The premiere of Mendelssohn's revised *Die erste Walpurgisnacht* concluded the concert on 2 February 1843, in which Clara Schumann appeared as soloist in Beethoven's Choral Fantasy ('one of the finest concerts of the season').[61] It was followed a month later by the first symphony by the Dane Niels Gade (1817–90). His teacher was Mendelssohn and he became an assistant conductor at the Gewandhaus, when both he and the orchestra's leader Ferdinand David deputised for their increasingly absent music director. Gade's native Copenhagen had already rejected his new symphony for performance, but Mendelssohn recognised its virtues, took it up with alacrity, and conducted its premiere from manuscript score and parts on 2 March 1843. Three years later, after another Leipzig performance, an ecstatic

---

[58] The programme also included two of his overtures, *King Lear* and *Les francs juges*, the *Rêverie et caprice*, in which Ferdinand David was the solo violinist, and two songs sung by Marie Recio.

[59] It was not published until 1846.

[60] See pages 49–50, 61–2, 119 respectively.

[61] *Die Signale für die Musikalische Welt* (henceforth *Die Signale*), Vol. 1 No. 7, 14 February 1843, col. 46.

review of this first symphony referred to 'our Gade'.[62] Over the next 30 years it was given a dozen times at Leipzig alone.[63] The score was soon published and reviewed in an article that was seminal in the context of the German symphony of 1843, although its implication that musicians of other European nations could deny Beethoven's creative powers is hard to take seriously. This was more likely a specific attack on the French, in particular Berlioz, whose symphonies and overtures were mystifying German audiences at the time. Importance was placed upon a composer's skill in scoring, and how expression of musical thought was totally reliant upon such expertise.

> The domain of the symphony is, for the German musician, of the greatest importance, because its cultural independence from the rest of European nations, which simply can no longer deny Beethoven's creative power, is now acknowledged. Berlioz sought in vain to wrest the crown from our country's composers. The German, so readily compliant in giving way to foreign precedence in other forms of music, will make no concession here to the French. It is all the more important that what is described as a symphony is no mere external musical structure that is powerful because of its size, nor simply by instrumentation does it become an expanded form of quartet or sonata style. Musical power must match the content of the ideas and *vice versa*; this content should be worthy of large forces in performance. What the important art and skilful practice of orchestration can achieve, when it comes to powerful effects, is often temporarily brilliant but not enduring, as countless examples in musical literature prove. Taking into account such experience in the work of a young composer is doubly important from the critic's point of view, for it means that content and its externalised representation must be separately identified and tested. The symphony by Gade, whose talents have already been shown to the musical world in a famous prize-winning overture [see footnote 63], testifies to them once again.
> The general impression is that we are seeing the early seeds of individuality that have yet to germinate into complete expression. It is clear which contemporary composer he leans towards [Mendelssohn]. Such a connection is inevitable in the earliest works of even the most gifted composer. We may attribute a large part of its success to extremely skilful and often surprising combinations of instruments, which create a mysterious symphonic charm reproducing the magnificent colour of a painting. This effect is a typical feature of the modern musical era and derives from the profound quality of the Germanic soul. We must add at once that, if the orchestration were not so charming, much of the musical thought itself would be lost, for example if played on a piano; it is the same with

---

[62] *AMZ*, Vol. 48, No. 2, 14 January 1846, col. 30.
[63] Dörffel, Statistik, 19. Copenhagen's rejection was the more surprising as Gade had already won a competition there in 1840 with his impressive Op. 1, the overture *Efterklange af Ossian* (*Echoes of Ossian*).

a painting, which loses its colour when reproduced as a copper engraving. We do not have the right to question, because a symphony must be judged as such and not played by smaller forces such as the piano. The impact made by the themes is inextricably bound to the choice and charm of instruments.

As distinguished from the more general gift of musicality and composition, this young composer, who we welcome unreservedly, has talent as a symphonist. As countless examples from former masters demonstrate, symphonic influence can be exerted. While Beethoven, Weber and Schubert have created extraordinary effects, we should not forget that contrapuntal skill derives from older schools of composition and provides the means of discreetly channelling moments of inspiration. Mendelssohn achieved it by making the seemingly trivial into something interesting. Even in those works where themes cannot be described as original, the hand of the master is evident in the artful interweaving, never pedantic or artificial, of the various strands that take up the theme either simultaneously or one after the other. They set a fruitful example for the young maturing artist. We would not have made these remarks if it were not our opinion that Gade's talent for the symphony is a quite extraordinary one. We hope it will get stronger and that he will acquire a sure hand to master all aspects of his musical art.[64]

Gade's work 'aroused unanimous enthusiasm [and] is a fine new symphony, one of the most uniquely beautiful there is'.[65] Just seven months later, Gade himself conducted the second performance on 26 October 1843. 'It enjoyed the glittering success normally reserved for only the best. We have never encountered such a first work, one which bears the stamp of true talent.'[66] It had already been published by Kistner by this time and clearly high expectations were being placed upon his next, which unfortunately did not match the success of its predecessor despite four performances at Leipzig over the course of the decade. Although Gade's third and fourth symphonies also remained very popular there for many years, true to form, his music soon dropped out of favour after his death in 1890. However, it is hard to understand why the first symphony (the best of the four) did not survive longer than it did after such continual, fulsome praise.

> After a rather dull first movement, matters improve with a vivacious *scherzo* followed by a beautiful slow movement and a fine *finale* starting with a thrilling timpani solo, all ending in a blaze of audience-rousing C major. ... It is so singular, in all simplicity so highly original, that it will certainly find deserved recognition. The motifs and the treatment of the musical ideas appear different and in a new guise compared to other composers. ... It is a work for which

---

[64] *AMZ*, Vol. 45 No. 49, 6 December 1843, col. 879.
[65] *Die Signale*, Vol. 1 No. 11, 14 March 1843, col. 78.
[66] *AMZ*, Vol. 45 No. 45, 8 November 1843, col. 815.

one can predict a longer future than several other contemporary examples of the genre.[67]

It also enjoyed success at Kassel, where it was greeted as being 'distinguished by natural originality, good melodic flow and splendid orchestration ... the second and fourth movements being preferred above the others'.[68] By 1846 the gloss was beginning to wear off, although it also appears that the orchestra at Hamburg was not up to the required standard to give it full justice.

> The wonderful work did not unfortunately appeal to all as it should do but the performance was partly responsible, as the finer nuances were almost totally lacking and the start was very uncertain. In this work, Gade shows himself to be one of the most talented among the new composers of instrumental works, which, from the court of all non-partisan opinion, the warmest reception will testify.[69]

In the summer of 1847, a report of a performance at Berlin tells us as much about the Prussian capital's concert life as it does about its reception of this symphony, the common view being that, as stated at the outset (page 3), new music was assumed to be guilty until proven innocent.

> Naturally the main ingredients of the repertoire here are the overtures and symphonies of Mozart, Haydn and Beethoven. During the course of a winter season and because at most nine or ten concerts take place, one cannot blame the management if they accede to the wishes of the subscribers, that only rarely should a new work by a living composer be programmed. If the masterpieces by the three dead masters are not heard once every year in excellent performances, where should one be able to enjoy them? Niels Gade's new first symphony was applauded without opposition, which here, when a new work is played at a symphony concert, is one of the greatest rarities. Not that genuine, specialist connoisseurs were sitting in judgement here, more likely it was a selective intolerance which swears blindly by authority.[70]

Gade's first symphony (of eight written between 1842 and 1871) owes much to Mendelssohn's new *Scottish* symphony (1842) and, a decade earlier, *Fingal's Cave* overture. The scoring varies from movement to movement, including (following the precedent of Mendelssohn's *Midsummer Night's Dream*) optional double bassoon instead of a tuba, the latter probably rarer than the former. While it was quite common for the piccolo and tuba to play in one or both of the outer movements, the

---

[67] *AMZ*, Vol. 46 No. 52, 25 December 1844, col. 885. The concert was on 19 December 1844 at Leipzig.
[68] Kassel, 7 February 1844. *AMZ*, Vol. 46 No. 19, 8 May 1844, col. 322.
[69] *AMZ*, Vol. 48 No. 5, 4 February 1846, col. 84.
[70] *AMZ*, Vol. 49 No. 30, 28 July 1847, col. 517.

scoring of the *scherzo* is unusual in omitting trumpets and drums yet retaining the three trombones. In the sublime opening we hear a Danish melody played by violas and cellos (Ex. 3.14).[71] This horn passage is a motif frequently heard throughout the work, but Gade's treatment avoids overkill.[72] The answering phrase in the major key will, in the *coda* to the *finale*, eventually conclude the whole work in a blazing *presto* in C major (Ex. 3.15). Gade includes this 15-bar imaginative effect under the folk tune in the first movement, in which all the strings except basses trill their way through their accompanying passage (Ex. 3.16). The delightful second movement *scherzo* owes much to Mendelssohn in its writing for strings and responding wind and brass. This colourful movement ignores conventional repeats and instead has an extended structure of ABABAB plus a *coda*, where B is a slow trio for muted, divided first violins dreamily weaving phrases over a sustained pedal of winds, horns and *pizzicato* lower strings (Exx 3.17 and 3.18). The opening of the *Andantino grazioso*, an extended oboe solo accompanied by *divisi* violas and cellos and *unisono* basses, is very beautiful in its simplicity (Ex. 3.19). Such alto-register scoring omitting violins was now becoming fairly common and in due course would become a regular ingredient in the music of both Bruch and Brahms. Other elements in the movement include a somewhat awkwardly shaped triplet pattern in the cellos, followed by its use as an accompaniment before taking on its own significance (Ex. 3.20). The opening of the *finale*, a shattering fusillade on the timpani followed by blazing brass (Ex. 3.21), must have taken the audience by surprise, destroying the mood of the *Andantino*, which had just finished. Was this Gade's riposte to Haydn's *Surprise* symphony? The material in this *finale* is not up to the quality of the rest of the work, a familiar tale. There is much repetition of figurations and a lot of chordal writing that sounds as if it is about to burst into patriotic song but refrains from doing so; instead we hear a folk melody (Ex. 3.22) with chords placed sparsely beneath. Among the works of the lesser-known names of the time, Gade's first symphony is the find of the 1840s despite the popularity of those by Mendelssohn and Schumann, even bearing in mind that their respective *Italian* and *Rhenish* symphonies were still to come.

Example 3.14   Gade: Symphony No. 1. Introduction, Danish folk melody

[71]   The first movement is derived from Gade's native Danish roots, its material based on his 1838 melody to B.S. Ingemann's poem *På Sjølunds fagre sletter* ('On the fair plains of Sealand'), although there is no reference either to the melody or to the poem in the full score, nor in the 1843 *AMZ* review.

[72]   As it will do (in 1874) in 'Vltava' from Smetana's *Ma Vlast*, which sounds remarkably similar in places.

Example 3.15   Gade: Symphony No. 1. Finale, Coda, brass C major response

Example 3.16   Gade: Symphony No. 1. First movement, accompanying passage by the strings at letter A

Example 3.17   Gade: Symphony No. 1. Second movement, Scherzo

Example 3.18   Gade: Symphony No. 1. Second movement, Trio

Example 3.19   Gade: Symphony No. 1. Third movement, opening

Example 3.20   Gade: Symphony No. 1. Third movement, cellos at letter B

Example 3.21   Gade: Symphony No. 1. Finale, opening

Example 3.22   Gade: Symphony No. 1. Finale, second theme at letter B

The 1843–44 winter season was the twentieth anniversary of Leipzig's Euterpe concerts, an organisation that stood apart from events at the Gewandhaus and prided itself on presenting new music to the public, although compromises had to be made such as a shared pool of players for both organisations. More significantly, however, although 'a symphony was played in each of the ten concerts', four were Viennese classics, and one a tone poem by Ferdinand Brandenburg (*The Nightmare of Three Islands: Corsica, Elba and St Helena*, so was Napoleon its luckless subject?). The five other symphonies were Spohr's fourth, Kalliwoda's fifth, Gade's first, one by Gerhard von Alvensleben, the current music director of the Euterpe concerts (played on 19 February 1843), and one by Johann Dürrner, 'a definite talent with a work that rigorous study has matured and brought its composer honour'.[73] Dürrner was a Lieder composer based at the small Bavarian town of Ansbach until 1844 when he moved to Edinburgh, where he died in 1859. Other new composers included Karl Drobisch (1803–54) and Julius Rietz (1812–77), whose symphonies were played alongside not only the Viennese classics but also Kalliwoda (his seventh and last) and Mendelssohn, who, once established at Leipzig from 1835, only ever conducted his *Lobgesang* and *Scottish* symphonies there.[74]

Karl Drobisch's Symphony in G minor was performed under his own direction from manuscript parts at Leipzig.[75] He spent most of his career as a church musician at Augsburg and we learn a little more about him, despite his lack of fame, thanks to a character study written by Wilhelm Riehl in 1857. Though Drobisch was 20 years older than Riehl, 'his works ... seemed half a century older. He was suspicious of the younger generation, behind which he assumed there lurked a visionary New-Romantic but neither did he think much of the music by his own

---

[73] *AMZ*, Vol. 46 No. 15, 10 April 1844, col. 257.
[74] *AMZ*, Vol. 46 No. 22, 29 May 1844, col. 373.
[75] On 19 October 1843. Dörffel, *Statistik*, 17.

contemporaries'. Antipathetic to Schumann and worshipping only Mendelssohn, Drobisch was

> an absolute musician, who placed vocal music above instrumental, although he himself wrote quartets and symphonies and warned against writing such genres exclusively, lest creativity be diminished by working to such models or within formal constraints. ... However, while Drobisch's warning may have been timely at the turn of the nineteenth century, by the 1840s no one was flogging himself to death writing quartets and symphonies anyway.[76]

Riehl had an insight into Drobisch's method of composing a symphony, namely to take the spirit of a poem as the basis for the music and setting its verse, a process that in turn inspired the principal material for the symphony. He wrote a symphony based on a ballad by Ludwig Hölty (1748–76) and which happened to imitate Beethoven.[77] Some thought it a parody and labelled Drobisch a heretic, others dismissed it merely as an outdated contribution from a composer living in the past, but a kinder description would have been an epigone.

> According to the musical establishment, our musical life appears brightly lit, but it is in fact mostly submerged and in darkness; it is this unknown world that goes about its business quietly but determinedly. Drobisch was a typical musician of his time. He dragged the past into the present, but lost touch with that present and was consequently less regarded than he deserved to be. Such sub-characters, transient figures when placed next to our heroes, make the great drama of world- and art history both colourful and true to life.[78]

Friedrich Müller, whose first symphony was played at Leipzig in 1842 (see page 94), was less fortunate with his second, though it was heard on his own territory at the court in Rudolstadt in October 1844. Its reviewer had an unequivocal opinion of the minimum expectations from a new symphony at that time:

> Anyone who ventures to compose a symphony in our day, one that favours more and more Italian and French tinkling, is at least making an artistic statement. Moreover, anyone who has succeeded in publishing two symphonies in times such as ours must have significant artistic ability, because it is this genre in particular that critics and public alike keep a strict eye on, so that the frivolous spirit of our time does not seize hold and desecrate it. Any poor little fashion-seeking, untrained composer should not dare to compose a symphony of elegant but empty phrases. The essence of symphonic writing lies in a general emotional

---

[76] See W.H. Riehl, 'Karl Ludwig Drobisch' in *Musikalische Charakterköpfe* (Stuttgart, 1857) 8th edition (1899), 278–94.
[77] Hölty's ballads were set to music by Schubert, Mendelssohn and Brahms.
[78] See Riehl, 278–94.

sensitivity but at the same time, and in order to express properly what it involves, all-embracing study must be constantly worked at and practised, but our brilliant younger generation often recoils in fear and seeks to escape.[79]

'Italian and French tinkling' was presumably a thinly veiled reference to the operatic works of Rossini (by then no longer writing operas) and those of the recently deceased Bellini, Donizetti and Cherubini (despite none of them having reputations as writers of symphonies) and even Berlioz, for whom this description is singularly inappropriate. These superior composers now stood accused of leading their emerging German symphonic descendants astray. Meyerbeer might also have been in the frame but, despite spending years in Paris, was presumably still regarded as a Prussian because his family home always remained in Berlin. After Mendelssohn and Schumann, Spohr remained at the head of the pack during the 1840s. 'His fifth symphony is an acknowledged masterpiece.'[80] At Prague, his music was 'received with true musical piety. In all senses of the word, the fifth symphony is every inch a Spohr'.[81] In 1846, as at Rudolstadt two years earlier, the pre-requisites of a symphony were clear:

> Richness of poetry and melody through great knowledge of harmony and its use, nobility and dignity, wonderful organisation and structure of the whole, masterly and exemplary instrumentation. Above all, Spohr understands how to arrive simply and naturally at unrelated keys without cuts and by following the rules of modulation. The [fifth symphony] must be among the most pleasing of its genre ... in which he has laid all the treasures of his heart and soul.[82]

During the 1840s, the quality and standards expected of symphony writing were becoming topical and stringent litmus tests were applied to new works. Sometimes such comment arose in the context of other genres, such as chamber music:

> These days [1844] are not at all rich in string quartets, especially good ones. In terms of quantity and quality, the symphony, sonata and string quartet are clearly in a minority. We need not elaborate on how the demands of the symphony upon the creative artist have increased almost to the point of discouragement; indeed it would not be difficult to demonstrate that they have gone too far. Perhaps the legacy of our great forebears has had too negative an effect. The quartet finds itself almost in the same situation ... indeed with even greater difficulties to overcome than a symphony.[83]

---

[79] *AMZ*, Vol. 46 No. 44, 30 October 1844, col. 729.
[80] *AMZ*, Vol. 46 No. 44, 30 October 1844, col. 741.
[81] 'Jeder Zoll ein Spohr', a pun on the colloquialism 'Jeder Zoll ein König' or 'every inch a king'.
[82] *AMZ*, Vol. 48 No. 15, 15 April 1846, col. 257.
[83] *AMZ*, Vol. 46 No. 52, 25 December 1844, col. 873.

The first symphony by Jakob (Jacques) Rosenhain (1813–94), a pianist of high repute, was performed from manuscript parts on 29 January 1846 under Mendelssohn's direction at the Gewandhaus. It was Rosenhain's first large-scale work and took pride of place as the first new symphony of the season. Predictably its success was measured by the audience's applause, which in this case was 'good if not universal'. Behind the faint praise, 'it was on the whole not uninteresting', we find some positives despite 'dealing with a young and inexperienced pianist–composer'. The *scherzo* was most successful, although its orchestration was misjudged in places, while the respective descriptions of 'polka' to the second movement and 'march' to the *finale* were considered to be the wrong way round. Again we find anti-French comments such as, 'his lengthy time spent in Paris was reflected by some trivial melodies'.[84] According to Rosenhain's biographer, his works were good in all genres and he was a master of form and melody.[85] They were noted for having Beethoven's spirit, Schubert's melodic style and Mendelssohn's formal beauty, without either becoming a mere imitator or sacrificing his own originality. After the performance, Mendelssohn wrote to Rosenhain:

> I must convey to you, in my own name and certainly that of all the musicians, many thanks for your work, for entrusting its first performance in Germany to us and for the pleasure that it gave us! We studied the symphony over three thorough rehearsals and it was played with much fire and love. The public, which is normally very reserved when it comes to new works, applauded after each movement, the most after the second and last. I got more pleasure from the work with each rehearsal; the whole orchestra felt the same, therefore I thank you once again most heartily for it, and remain as ever in friendship and sincerely yours,
> Felix Mendelssohn-Bartholdy.[86]

Rosenhain wrote three symphonies; the one Mendelssohn conducted was played in Baden-Baden by the town's Kurkapelle (spa orchestra), but it must have been some years later because mention is made of Brahms, who was producing Hungarian dances as piano-duets between 1852 and 1869. Like Mendelssohn, reviewer Richard Pohl singled out the second and last movements for particular praise, while a softening of attitude to French music shows that time had passed.

> At first the symphony has an almost tragic character, but it becomes more cheerful. Typical is its solid German workmanship combined with French lightness and grace, qualities that one only seldom finds combined. The second

---

[84] *AMZ*, Vol. 48 No. 5, 4 February 1846, col. 91.
[85] Elise Kratt-Harveng, *Jacques Rosenhain, Komponist und Pianist: ein Lebensbild* (Baden-Baden, 1891).
[86] Ibid., 23–4. Mendelssohn to Rosenhain from Leipzig dated 9 February 1836.

movement is charming and there is a cheekily conceived *finale* in Hungarian style. Nowadays the whole world writes in the Hungarian or Slavic style, even Brahms has not spurned it, but at the time this symphony was composed it was something new. Rosenhain's originality was thereby assured.[87]

His second symphony (F minor, 1844) was premiered in Brussels under Fétis in January 1849 after nine rehearsals and the 'response was unanimous in praise of its classicism, purity, elegance and solid style'.[88] The primary focus of reviews at this particular time lay in frequent references to style rather than formal structure, with which the Germans, contrary to the French, were obsessed. In one review we also discover much more from what the conductor of a symphonic premiere has to say on the subject. This time it was Karl Guhr (1787–1848) after one of Frankfurt's Theatre and Museum Concerts, which he conducted from 1821 until his death in 1848.[89]

> You [Rosenhain] have unfolded your imagination without letting it be constrained by form. There are places, especially in the last movement, where instrumentation, musical thought and thematic development are conjoined in a way as never before. This symphony need not fight shy of comparison with one by Beethoven and wherever it is played, as here, it will be honoured with applause not only from those with musical knowledge but also from amateur enthusiasts.[90]

Although clearly neither a symphony nor German, another variation of the genre that appeared in the mid-1840s at least deserves a mention, if only because of its reception. At Weimar on 22 February 1846 Liszt conducted *Le Désert*, an *ode-symphonique* composed in 1844 by Félicien David (1810–76). It pleased relatively few in the audience, while later that year it was reported that it had been performed at the theatre in Aachen 'in costume with forty extras and two cardboard camels'.[91] David's exercise in Arab exoticism was neither oratorio nor symphony but more significantly neither was it a symphony-cantata like Mendelssohn's newly composed *Lobgesang*. German audiences had accepted this, but, apart from satisfying a natural curiosity, they could not tolerate the style and content of this French work. In making any Franco-German comparison in general and doing so with Beethoven's *Choral* symphony in particular, we find that any similarity is limited solely to each work's use of voices (for male only in David's case) and their mutually descriptive title of 'ode-symphony', though given the presence of

---

[87] Richard Pohl in *Badeblatt* (n.d.), quoted in Kratt-Harveng (see 1–58).
[88] *Frankfurter Conversationsblatt* 7 February 1849, quoted in Kratt-Harveng (see 1–58).
[89] Weber, *Das 'Museum'*, 118.
[90] Kratt-Harveng, 23–4.
[91] *AMZ*, Vol. 48 No. 35, 2 September 1846, col. 599.

a narrator in *Le Désert* it arguably becomes a good example of a *mélodrame*. Nevertheless Beethoven's influence can be spotted elsewhere, for example the slow tread of the processing caravan, which recalls both in rhythm and mood the slow movement of the seventh symphony; the storm in the *Pastoral* symphony has similarities to its desert counterpart; while *Fidelio* frequently comes to mind. As might be expected, however, it had much more in common with David's compatriot Berlioz, in particular *Lélio* (a *mélodrame*) rather than his *Roméo et Juliette* (a *symphonie dramatique*) or *Damnation de Faust* (a *légende dramatique*). In keeping with France's obsession with the exotic, Bizet, Saint-Saëns and Delibes would, throughout the second half of the nineteenth century, take their cue from David with their respective operas, concertos or suites. *Le Désert* did the rounds in Germany including the major centres of Leipzig and Frankfurt, presumably sung and spoken in French as there was no German translation.[92] A performance took place in Cologne on 23 December 1845 conducted by Heinrich Dorn. Its reviewer characterises most of the work as misguided, criticising its lack of exotic oriental colour and for being too much a creation of the salons of Paris. Some of the music was dismissed as completely cultivated vocal music. In short, the complaint was made that it had been transplanted from one moment to the next, from an Eastern desert to a Western salon.[93] Such criticism was unwarranted. Apart from the occasional miscalculation, such as a shrill piccolo above the rest of the orchestra, David, following the eighteenth century precedent of 'Turkish' bass drum and cymbals, produces an extremely vivid and colourful attempt at Oriental music. If he did draw on Austro-German influences for such exoticism in his *ode-symphonique*, the traffic was distinctly one way, for prejudiced German symphonists took nothing in return.

During the 1840s, Kassel became almost as important as Leipzig as a platform for getting new works played, as Spohr's influence at the former became as powerful as Mendelssohn's at the latter. Hermann Wichmann (1824–1905), a pupil of Taubert, Mendelssohn and Spohr at Berlin, had his first symphony played there in February 1843. 'It revealed a sound basic training, talent and good value.'[94] It was repeated three years later on 25 February 1846, when the critic took young Wichmann to task for a variety of perceived faults, yet also concluded by giving him an encouraging pat on the back: 'Only rarely has a first work of this type and of such scope been able to arouse such general interest among all true music lovers.' However, because it was a first work, it had weaknesses such as 'a lack of sufficient development, in particular contrapuntal treatment of the main motif and subsequent phrases, of which so much more might justifiably be expected from a full orchestra expressing these musical ideas – the full orchestra whose rich potential has such widely varied application'.[95] Rather than expose such first fruits

---

[92] Only in 1851 were English and Italian words added.
[93] *AMZ*, Vol. 48 No. 5, 4 February 1846, col. 78.
[94] *AMZ*, Vol. 45 No. 13, 29 March 1843, col. 248.
[95] *AMZ*, Vol. 48 No. 17, 29 April 1846, col. 288.

to the general public, one wonders whether or not it might have been more helpful to the young composer had this performance taken place under the auspices of one of the burgeoning new music schools, even though many of their promoted events were now also covered by the periodicals. A second symphony by Wichmann was played at Kassel, probably in late May or early June 1848. 'It contained some good and effective moments but did not completely fulfil expectations that we cherished, having heard his first. The theme of the first movement is too trifling for a symphony'. The reviewer wanted different, more substantive material because the development section proved more interesting than the ideas themselves.

> Apart from some occasional harshness, all four of the symphony's movements contained much charming harmony and lively rhythms, but the most attractive was the fourth because its theme had the quality of folk music. The instrumental effects were to some extent very remarkable but always pleasant and, now and then, even original.[96]

Heinrich Dorn (1804–92) established a music school that became the Cologne Conservatoire in 1850. In May 1846 his Symphony in C was performed in that Rhineland city. It was given a detailed review, some of which touched on a critic's expectations of the ingredients for a new symphony at this time. The slow third movement 'is the one on which the composer has evidently worked hardest, because it includes a large-scale fugue. ... The great recommendation of the work from start to finish is the unmistakeable evidence it bears that, like an eager disciple, the composer is walking in the footsteps of the incomparable Beethoven'. Dorn's lyricism found favour, as did his abilities in orchestration, which, by avoiding

> overloaded and meaningless effects, sought to engage with the cultured taste of musicians and admirers of high-quality creations. ... It seems a thoroughly considered, serious work, inspired by a warm enthusiasm for beautiful art. This showed in the pleasing nature and clarity of the work, making it acceptable to the wider public. May it soon be given the further performances it deserves, and may any criticism be quickly cast aside in favour of the importance placed upon it.[97]

In keeping with other conductors who programmed their own music in their power bases, Wilhelm Taubert conducted his symphony (F Op. 69, 1846) at Berlin, where he was director of the Berlin Opera 1845–70. This symphony (the first of three) was published in December 1847, but, despite its success with the public, the press had reservations:

---

[96] *AMZ*, Vol. 50 No. 24, 14 June 1848, col. 393.
[97] *AMZ*, Vol. 48 No. 24, 17 June 1846, cols 402–3.

This new symphony is an attractive piece of music, [but] although there is a lively flow in the *scherzo*, it seems that, particularly in this movement, entitled *Alla danza tedesca*, the sharply defined dance rhythms, combined with a melody of little originality, somewhat compromises the dignity that a symphony should never lack. However, far from wanting to judge a work with these remarks (one brief encounter cannot suffice), we gladly acknowledge evidence of the excellent effort by this well-known and much-liked composer, even though we should not conceal the weakness of the impression it made upon us.[98]

Taubert was mentioned in another review three months later, but what is of greater interest here are the other issues of the day that it also tackled, namely programme selection and construction, which were too often hamstrung by feeding a constant appetite for the Viennese classics while also trying to find room for new works by new composers:

Since the resignation of [Karl] Möser [1774–1851], orchestral concerts have been taking place in the hall of the Royal Theatre under Capellmeister Taubert.[99] Instead of one overture we have two, as well as the usual two symphonies. Vocal music is out of the question, while, regarding new music, we can only recall Lachner's D minor symphony [No. 3], which had already been conducted by the composer in the opera house and where, as here, it scored a deserved success. Secondly, we heard a new Symphony in F by Taubert, which was played with great virtuosity by the orchestra under him and also given in one of the Leipzig Gewandhaus concerts.[100]

It is a natural and inexpensive annual demand from the musical public, a German one at that, not to let slip the chance of hearing the instrumental works of the great German masters Mozart, Haydn and Beethoven in the most perfect performance possible. ... Unfortunately with nine, at most twelve concerts, it is impossible to perform all their overtures and symphonies. This winter we did not hear any of Beethoven's overtures or his first and last symphonies, nothing at all by Schubert, Gade or Schumann; and as for Mendelssohn, whose third symphony we have not heard at all, just one of his well-known overtures. As it happens, a work by Gade was performed for the first time, namely his overture *Im Hochland*, conducted by his compatriot, the dance composer [Hans Christian] Lumbye [1810–74], in the Kroll Theatre.[101]

---

[98] *AMZ*, Vol. 48 No. 12, 25 March 1846, col. 215.
[99] Karl Möser was a violinist and conductor, leader of his own string quartet, Hofdirektor at Berlin from 1840, and conducted the first Berlin performance of Beethoven's ninth symphony in 1826.
[100] On 19 March 1846.
[101] The Kroll Theatre was opened two years earlier in 1844.

However, we have yet another issue with the royal orchestra's symphony-soirées that needs to be addressed. Because almost always all the seats in the hall are sold, the orchestra cannot give free tickets to young composers, for it is not sustainable to reduce the takings destined for the widows and orphans.[102] Moreover, as far as we know, entry to rehearsals is also denied to young musicians and budding composers of instrumental music, for whom therefore all opportunity to hear the best performances of classical German instrumental music in Berlin is denied. In our opinion, Berlin has gradually become big enough to sustain and make a profit from a second instrumental music association, giving a dozen winter Subscription Concerts. With no great trouble, one could assemble a good orchestra of about 48–60 players, but it would be harder to find an excellent conductor. If Ferdinand Hiller were not already doing something similar in Dresden, we would suggest this plan to him. Because it would be difficult to count on the public already subscribed to the current symphony concerts, it would be necessary to build a new audience for such a contemporary concert society, which is not at all problematic providing he is a significant musician and a real conductor. The duty of this body must be to establish concerts here following the model of Leipzig and Paris, and if possible, with due consideration to the works of living composers. ... [Schubert's] great Symphony in C has until now been performed just once in Berlin; solely because it did not appeal immediately to the Classically minded subscribers to the symphony-soirées, nor to the even more Classically minded city critic, it has become *ad acta*.[103] If it had been possible to blacken this beautiful work as a posthumous one by Beethoven, all those classical know-alls would have protested vehemently; it would have taken a place among the rest of his masterpieces. *Jurare in verba magistri*[104] remains a matter of course with these classicists.[105]

Six years later, in 1852, the reception in the press of a series of winter concerts in Berlin retaining the name 'Symphony-Soirées', founded and conducted by Taubert, must have made dispiriting reading for any would-be symphonist. A withering report dismissed the series as merely a rendezvous for the world of elegance and asserted that there was nothing encouraging in a choice of repertoire that went no further than satisfying the audience's musical taste (or rather the lack of it). The proven instrumental works of Beethoven and Cherubini were taken for granted, while there was generally nothing more than acceptance for those of Mozart and 'the naïve sounds of Haydn'. There was enthusiasm for established instrumental works by Weber, fanaticism for anything in that field by Mendelssohn, but a decidedly antagonistic response from the public to anything new, despite many reports of enthusiastic applause between movements. The

---

[102] They benefited from the proceeds raised at the concerts.
[103] *Ad acta* means filed away.
[104] *Jurare in verba magistri* means to accept opinion on authority.
[105] *AMZ*, Vol. 48 No. 25, 24 June 1846, cols 426–9.

only way to attract an audience to concerts seems to have been by feeding its need for an undemanding well-established repertoire by familiar names among dead composers.[106]

After Félicien David's innovative *ode-symphonique*, it was another Frenchman, Henri Litolff (1818–91), who came up with a new hybrid, this time a blend of concerto and symphony. Although born in London of mixed French–Scottish descent, he became a citizen of Braunschweig in 1849 but lived in Paris from 1858 until his death. The score of his *concerto-symphonique* No. 2 Op. 22 was published by the Berlin firm of Schlesinger in 1846 and reviewed soon after.

> Once again another description, a new title for a larger composition for piano and orchestra; in the past one differentiated between concertos and symphonies, now both are fused into one, as the title implies. Viewed objectively, only the title is new, the essence remains the same. All large piano concertos, from the founder of the genre (Mozart) to the present day, have symphonic characteristics. The piano, even when taking pride of place, works symphonically together with the other instruments. If we consider the title *concerto-symphonique*, it implies as much as it did before, a symphony written for a concert. But the composer did not mean this. He wanted to do something different but failed. He should have written four movements, like a symphony; in other words with a *scherzo*, not three like concertos of old. This outward appearance is not enough, but because without them we would have only concert pieces [*Konzertstücke*], preferable though they are in their concise (rather than spread) form, they do not make an attractive proposition for imitation.[107]

The five *concerti-symphonique* (the first of which is lost) are essentially symphonies with piano *obbligato*. The fourth (1867) has the four movements preferred by this reviewer and ironically the added movement, the *scherzo*, is the only piece of music by which the name (other than as a music publisher) of Litolff is known today.

The 1840s was a decade littered with unpublished symphonies, their composers so disillusioned by failure, their works proved to be their only attempt at the genre. One such young man was Julius Emil Leonhard (1810–83), a pianist and pedagogue based first at Munich then at Dresden, who conducted his only symphony at the Gewandhaus on 10 December 1846 from manuscript score and parts. Despite some generally helpful comments from the writer, one can only feel for the composer who must have sensed the *caveats* signposted fairly early on in the review. What one deduces from his colourful advice to Leonhard is that the symphony was satisfactory but dull. Needless to say, it never made it into print.

---

[106] *NZfM*, Vol. 36 No. 3, 16 January 1852, 32.
[107] *AMZ*, Vol. 48 No. 30, 29 July 1846, col. 501.

Mr Leonhard, the composer of the symphony and which he himself conducted, has previously not only won the prize for a sonata but also deserved it. This was the most significant misfortune a young man can encounter on his artistic road! First, because his fellow competitors will be very angry, not with themselves for having been beaten but with him because he beat them and woe betide if one of them were a critic! Second, because consequent demands are no more arrogantly made than when made of a prize-winner. He simply cannot do anything well but has to achieve even better. The symphony has all the good qualities: thematic work, fluently finished form, interesting and clear scoring, melodic ideas, skilful part-writing. In short it is a well-constructed and finely fashioned symphony. The composer is accordingly on the right artistic path, though currently he is only in the most moderate zone, where one is warm, but not yet in the hot zone, where one catches fire. His thoughts satisfy but do not yet reach that point of enthusiasm where they arouse and sweep away the listener. Hot blood must run through the veins of the symphony of our time, all feelings and emotions must be felt in a tropical glow. Let Mr Leonhard press onwards into that hotter climate, for he has the power to do so. But what leads him there? The objective. For his next such work, he should conjure up a powerful picture from his imagination of Earth, viewed from Hell or Heaven, fix the image long and hard in its clearest form, then draw it stroke by stroke and paint it with glittering and glowing colours. Only thus will he achieve greater individuality and true originality. He who looks at a powerful objective will find that the great prototypes will disappear from view. The planet Saturn has seven satellites. The planet Mendelssohn has more and Mr Leonhard cannot definitely be counted among them, even though he sometimes appears to circle that orbit. If he encircles an objective, he will become a planet. Eventually, after a couple of years, he will bring out not an earlier symphony but a new one. Do not rest nor be complacent in what you have done but surge ahead restlessly and progressively for what remains to be done; that is the main ingredient of genuine talent and while we take Mr Leonhard for as much, we remind him of his duty. The public responded to all movements of the symphony with warm and deserved applause, and the orchestra played with love and customary art under the composer's direction.[108]

Leonhard and any aspiring fellow-symphonists of the day had some tough competition. Just two weeks after this symphony was scrutinised, a review of the published full score of Mendelssohn's violin concerto appeared, in which it was pointed out that

for the most part the interest of a concert-going public in our time is shown towards more important orchestral music, namely the symphony. The symphony

---

[108] *AMZ*, Vol. 48 No. 50, 16 December 1846, cols 847–8.

at the present time is the main work in an evening concert, placing the rest of the programme, in terms of value and effect, below or at best on the same level.[109]

In the 1840s, the public's interest was primarily focussed on new symphonies by Mendelssohn and Schumann. Their reputations were long established, their profiles high, having already made names for themselves in non-symphonic genres. Both found themselves caught between two extremes. On the one hand they had to cope with the stresses and strains placed upon their respective states of health, the consequences of physical exhaustion in Mendelssohn's case and mental instability in Schumann's. This they did in their different ways. On the other hand they had in common a symphonic journey to make. Living in close proximity at Leipzig, they dealt with these two problems with varying success. Chopin and Liszt faced the same dilemma, but the former stuck more or less exclusively to solo piano music, while the latter took another route and invented a new genre during the 1850s, which became the symphonic poem.

Of course, such problems also confronted those with lesser talent, but how they were dealt with, either by those of the best or by those of more modest ability, tends to emerge during this decade. In at least three of his symphonies (Nos 3, 5 and 9), Beethoven has a message for humanity, which he conveys by creatively excavating the bedrock of tradition. Unfortunately, like lemmings to the edge of a cliff, many of the lesser lights tried to send the same message by the same means but by a creative process that diluted its impact because it relied upon devices rapidly becoming clichés through overuse, a state of affairs that continued for the next quarter-century. We find excessive preference for certain keys, D minor, C minor and its relative E♭ major, themes unimaginatively constructed around the *arpeggio*, sequences of phrases too weak to sustain repetition and continual resort to the stock-in-trade diminished seventh for melodramatic effect. A generation earlier, Spohr, as we have seen in the previous chapter, remained wedded to Mozart and relied upon an historical mimicry of tradition reflected in the titles he gave his symphonies from the fourth onwards. On the whole, Mendelssohn steered clear of such potentially choppy waters. He opted for the sunnier climes of A major or the cloudier A minor in his two best symphonic essays, while the essence of his music remained embedded in the Classicism in which it was steeped but into which mix he added a splash of Romanticism. Schumann sought solutions other than those chosen by Spohr and Mendelssohn but still felt compelled to take Beethoven as the point of departure. Schumann's published second (in C major) had two performances, both under Mendelssohn at the Leipzig Gewandhaus within 11 days on 5 and 16 November 1846, and, given the composer's reputation, its first hearing was eagerly awaited. Nevertheless the opportunity was also taken by the reviewer to air more general thoughts on the condition of the symphony in 1846:

---

[109] *AMZ*, Vol. 48 No. 52, 30 December 1846, col. 876.

It is a momentous occasion when a new work in the highest artistic genre of instrumental music appears, namely the symphony, and when it does so from the pen of one of the most gifted musical spirits, it becomes an occasion of the highest significance for the world of music. It is a testimony to the artistic attitude and creative powers of our times. The genuine artist does not write at random or on the spur of the moment but rather expresses in music the content of his inner self and, aesthetically speaking, in the form and means he considers best.

With few exceptions, the recent period depicts in the symphony the high points of the state of the soul. That which is humorous, lovely and graceful, the world of calmer feelings recedes into the background and the rushing river of excited passion flows more and more powerfully into the foreground. Schumann's new symphony reflects this aspect of our time. The first and *scherzo* movements show it in its totality, the *finale* in the wild, stormy passion, while even the short *Adagio* gives us no peace. Although we cannot but admire the rising fire of emotion in the composer, we regret that he releases it so continually and without restraint.[110]

As far as the symphony is concerned, to describe the 1840s as 'a period depicting the highpoints of the state of the soul' is, even with the benefit of hindsight, surely an overstatement. Nevertheless, one cleverly crafted symphony deserving of mention was written towards the end of the decade by the German-speaking Swiss, Franz Xaver Schnyder von Wartensee (1786–1868), who worked for 30 years (1817–47) in Frankfurt, where he was encouraged by his contemporary, Spohr. Schnyder wrote three symphonies, the second of which includes a clever *pastiche* of Haydn.[111] His third was written between September and December 1848 and bears the name 'Military' (appropriate for that year of heady, if ultimately failed, revolution).[112] Schnyder was a symphonist whose style shows both independence of spirit and quirky eccentricity, even though both its harmonic language and phrasing shapes remain firmly wedded to the early nineteenth century. We know that the third symphony was performed at Frankfurt on 18 January 1850 at a Frankfurt Museum concert conducted by Franz Josef Messer (1811–60), Karl Guhr's successor from 1848 until his death. Although the *finale* alone was heard the following year in Bern, it took a further 90 years before Hermann Scherchen (1891–1966) revived it at Geneva.[113]

---

[110] *AMZ, Vol. 48* No. 47, 25 November 1846, col. 785.

[111] It bears the title *Erinnerung an Haydn* and was written in 1835. In the year of his death (1868) he also wrote a children's symphony for strings and eight toy instruments.

[112] Symphony No. 3 is on Sterling label CDS 1073–2, recorded in 2007 by the Württembergische Philharmonie conducted by the author.

[113] On 24 December 1939 in the Victoria Hall, Geneva. Foreword to the full score by Bärenreiter in *Schweizerische Musikdenkmäler Vol. 9* (ed. Peter Otto Schneider) (Basel, 1973), vii.

It contains many striking features and surprises from the very first bar of the slow introduction (Ex. 3.23). A rising (strings) and falling (winds) gathering of two diminished sevenths is presented in unusual order, with wide intervals of sixths or sevenths rather than piling minor thirds atop each other. The effect sounds years ahead of its time. There is an even greater surprise later in the first movement when the full orchestra pauses, after which a solo double bass plays a cadenza under which is written the instruction, 'Here the double bass becomes sentimental' (Ex. 3.24). It is a parody of the cello/bass recitative in the opening of the *finale* in Beethoven's ninth. Schnyder's prowess as a contrapuntist is impressive in the development section of the first movement, where, for 30 bars, we hear a canon between violins at the octave followed two bars later by violas, cellos and basses in augmentation, with clarinets and bassoons providing harmony in four parts (Ex. 3.25). The slow movement too has its surprises, although not initially, for the first 139 bars are unremarkable and largely confined to a prettily scored thematic dialogue between strings and winds (Ex. 3.26). We then encounter a complete change of mood and style when, switching from minor to major, this material is turned into a brisk march (Ex. 3.27), according to the symphony's military theme. As if following the *scherzo-trio* construction, this march has an attached section marked trio (Ex. 3.28), in which instrumental family groups again engage in dialogue but with a prevalent dotted rhythm and quietly throughout to give dynamic contrast.[114] The movement recapitulates all preceding material, back through the march to a reprise of the opening, giving it a pyramidal ABCBA structure.

Example 3.23   Schnyder von Wartensee: Symphony No. 3. First movement, opening

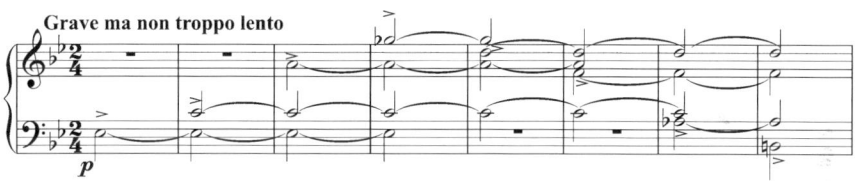

Example 3.24   Schnyder von Wartensee: Symphony No. 3. First movement, double bass solo

---

[114] It is actually marked *forte*, but a relentlessly loud section is unwanted and a dynamic contrast surely required.

Example 3.25   Schnyder von Wartensee: Symphony No. 3. First movement, canon in augmentation

Example 3.26   Schnyder von Wartensee: Symphony No. 3. Second movement, opening

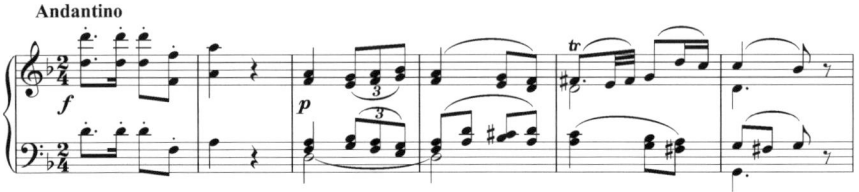

Example 3.27   Schnyder von Wartensee: Symphony No. 3. Second movement, March

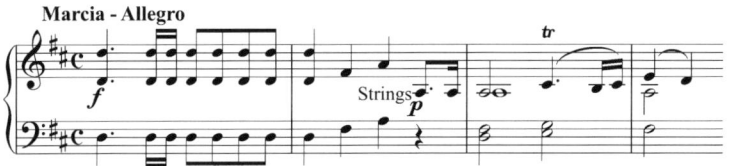

Example 3.28   Schnyder von Wartensee: Symphony No. 3. Second movement, Trio

The *scherzo* begins with an eight-bar military-style motif, followed by a theme of nine notes (Ex. 3.29) based on a rising arpeggio, which is passed around virtually the entire orchestra.[115] Much is made of the rhythmic distortions brought about by tied notes across bar-lines (Ex. 3.30) over a persistent pedal. In the second half, which without modulation begins with a switch from F to D♭, we

---

[115] The tempo of the *scherzo* is determined by the speed that this motto (Ex. 3.29) can be played by the first horn!

find the rising *arpeggio* is now inverted. Schnyder thinks nothing of disturbing otherwise predictable four-bar paragraphs by occasionally slipping in one of three or five. By so doing, he shifts the balance and keeps the aural senses of the listener on their toes. The trio is a typical *Ländler* (Ex. 3.31) at a markedly slower one-in-a-bar, with exaggerated 2+1 phrasing of three crotchets in the bar. Even this is suddenly thrown into disarray three bars into the second half, when, without warning, the music changes from triple to duple time and lurches from E♭ to A *via* an enharmonic change (D♭/C♯) and once again we are back in military mode (Ex. 3.32). Before the trio ends, there is a clever bridge passage leading to a restatement of the *Ländler* (Ex. 3.33).

Example 3.29   Schnyder von Wartensee: Symphony No. 3. Third movement, Scherzo, opening

Example 3.30   Schnyder von Wartensee: Symphony No. 3. Third movement, second theme

Example 3.31   Schnyder von Wartensee: Symphony No. 3. Third movement, Trio section

Example 3.32   Schnyder von Wartensee: Symphony No. 3. Third movement, Scherzo, enharmonic transition

Example 3.33   Schnyder von Wartensee: Symphony No. 3. Scherzo, transition to recapitulation

The *finale*, based on a two-bar fanfare for two trumpets and drums (Ex. 3.34), is a straightforward *rondo*, but towards the end Schnyder becomes more inventive, particularly in his harmony. One of the episodes resolves on to a chord of A major, but the recapitulation of the two-bar brass and timpani fanfare, instead of waiting for it to conclude, sets off before the transition to B♭. The fanfare seems to have started two bars too soon, for the discord sits uncomfortably with the predominantly classical style of the symphony (Ex. 3.35). Interspersed between restatements of the fanfare are cheerful melodies, mostly in strings and solo winds, that could have come from his contemporary Rossini.[116] We also hear extended passages of dialogue between strings and winds played *staccato* and *pianissimo*, the effect of which is charming and witty. Two surprises are reserved for the faster coda. The first is the addition of a piccolo just for the last 50 bars of the work (an inconsiderately delayed contribution from the player's point of view), and the second is a brief, quiet restatement (Ex. 3.36) of the opening chord clusters by the strings. Military colour is provided not only by plenty of *arpeggio* fanfares played by the pairs of horns and/or trumpets with drums but also by the percussion instruments consisting of triangle, bass drum, cymbals and a bell tree described in the score as a Chinese pavilion or Turkish crescent, an ornate pole carrying rows of cup-shaped bells once used in marching bands. Despite Schnyder's eccentricities, his style, like Haydn's before him, is an amalgam of the conservative and the progressive. It is a style that is notable for its creative freshness of melody, harmony, rhythm and form, and rarely, if at all, found in the symphonies by Mendelssohn or the contemporaneous ones by Schumann. His occasionally novel orchestration might well have been influenced by the excursions Berlioz undertook in 1830. With no hint of modesty, Schnyder mentions his own 'freshness and imaginative innovation' in an autobiographical sketch, and the music does sound as striking and inventive today as it must have done 160 years ago.[117]

---

[116] Although Rossini was six years younger than Schnyder, they both died in the same year, 1868. At least two of Schnyder's themes were recycled from Rossini's operas, which were written 20 years earlier.

[117] *Einige Blätter aus meinem Tagebuch* in *Neue Alpenrosen* 1848, quoted in *MGG* Vol. 11 (Kassel, 1989), col. 1923.

Example 3.34   Schnyder von Wartensee: Symphony No. 3. Rondo finale, opening

Example 3.35   Schnyder von Wartensee: Symphony No. 3. Finale, episodic transition

Example 3.36   Schnyder von Wartensee: Symphony No. 3. Finale recalls first movement opening

Schnyder closes a decade in which hope for the symphony was sustained not only by Mendelssohn and Schumann but also by Spohr, Kalliwoda and Lachner, with Verhulst and Gade as 'honorary German symphonists'. It is ironic that the analysis of Gade's first symphony written in 1843, reproduced earlier in this chapter and which begins, 'The domain of the symphony is of the greatest importance for the *German* musician' [my italics], then goes on to eulogise one of the best new symphonies of the period, written by a Dane. Justification for such an accolade would be that Gade received a German musical education, to which topic we now turn.

Chapter 4
Leipzig, its Gewandhaus and Conservatoire

This incessant whirl of symphony music[1]

It was in the 1840s that music education in Germany took a quantum leap forward, the implications of which were spread far and wide within and without the country's borders. Leipzig became the city where huge advances were made, drawing young musicians like a magnet from far and wide, educating them and sending them out into German towns and cities or back to the foreign parts whence they had come. The question arises, however, as to whether its influence was brought to bear in a positive way on developing the symphonic form, or negatively, thereby stultifying it. Leipzig's dominating position was to last virtually until the end of the nineteenth century and so the chronology of this chapter will necessarily move on and take a longer-term and wider geographical view before resuming the decade-by-decade approach to the study of the symphony in Germany.

During the seventeenth and eighteenth centuries it was *de rigueur* for those who could afford it to undertake the Grand Tour, a term coined by Richard Lessels.[2] Having crossed the Channel, travellers from Britain would usually go straight to Paris by coach and horse, after which their journey would continue further south over the Alps to Switzerland and Italy. Their aim was to improve their ability to speak foreign languages and to widen their knowledge of, or acquaint themselves with, architecture, geography and culture, in particular the visual and aural arts. Painting and music were high on their agenda. By the middle of the nineteenth century, the Industrial Revolution and the advent of railways had transformed such travelling as it became comparatively safe and easy. If nothing else, the legacy of the Grand Tour was the word 'tourist'. In 1867 the 32-year-old Mark Twain told 'the Gentle Reader [that he] will never, never know what a consummate ass he can become, until he goes abroad. I speak now, of course, in the supposition that the Gentle Reader has not been abroad, and therefore is not already a consummate ass'.[3]

Without palaces, gardens and art galleries, nor vistas of the sea in warm climes, Germany was not generally on the traveller's itinerary, although its Austro-Hungarian neighbour's capital Vienna must have gone some way to meet what Paris and Rome had to offer in terms of architecture and music, and it did have the advantage of being on the route to the south. Nevertheless Germany attracted

---

[1] Constance Bache, *Brother Musicians: reminiscences of Edward and Walter Bache* (London, 1901), 31.
[2] Richard Lessels, *A Voyage to Italy* (London, 1670).
[3] *The Innocents Abroad* (Hartford, CT, 1869), 233.

musicians and of its major cities Leipzig stood out as a centre of performance and learning. 'Germany is the country of philosophy and of music', wrote Francis Hueffer.[4] From Britain and elsewhere, many fledgling musicians went there to study, to work or to visit, for by the middle of the century Leipzig had become renowned throughout Europe and America for its orchestra, its concerts, its music in church, as well as a centre for music journalism, music publishing and music education. Unlike Weimar or Dresden, Leipzig was a city that owed no allegiance to the whims and fancies of a ducal or royal court. Instead it was run by its merchant middle class and celebrated twice per year with an international trade and book fair, which attracted huge numbers of visitors. Since 1409 the city had a university that, by the mid-nineteenth century, had attained a considerable reputation and could claim such renowned alumni as Klopstock (1746), Lessing (1746), Goethe (1765), Wagner (1831) and Nietzsche (1865). Bach had been Cantor at the St Thomas School and Director of Music at the Thomaskirche for 27 years (1723–50), but it was only from the mid-1830s that the true significance of his music was realised thanks to the efforts of Mendelssohn.[5]

Mendelssohn was appointed music director and conductor of the Leipzig Gewandhaus orchestra in 1835.[6] The dual nature of the post was significant and unique on this occasion; it could be offered as such only because, coincidentally in that year, the leader of the orchestra, Heinrich Matthäi, died and the conductor August Pohlenz retired through ill-health. Hitherto it had been the leader's responsibility to direct instrumental concerts from the violin, leaving the director to conduct just choral works. Mendelssohn's first five years were devoted to the Gewandhaus, but from 1840 until his death seven years later that connection was loosened (but never broken) for a variety of reasons. His was a restless nature, while he also had little patience for bureaucrats and any of their pedantry. He came to Leipzig from Düsseldorf, but after five years and at the height of his success he was temporarily lured away to Berlin to take up a specially created post based around a medium-sized choir of boys and men. Yet despite periods away, during which others stood in for him, he always kept himself fully involved and informed of all musical matters in Leipzig.[7] Mendelssohn conducted concerts at the Gewandhaus between the autumn and spring, leaving himself free during the other half of the year to conduct and perform at concerts elsewhere. In Germany

---

[4] 'Arthur Schopenhauer', *Fortnightly Review*, December 1876 in Francis Hueffer, *Musical Studies: a series of contributions* (Edinburgh, 1880), 85.

[5] The first performance at the city's concert hall (the Gewandhaus or Drapers' Hall) of any music by Bach was his concerto for three pianos played by Clara Schumann, Louis Rakemann and Mendelssohn on 9 November 1835.

[6] Established in 1781, its music directors before Mendelssohn were Johann Adam Hiller (1781–85), Johann Gottfried Schicht (1785–1810), Johann Philip Christian Schulz (1810–27), August Pohlenz (1827–35).

[7] His deputies or appointees, such as Gade, David, Rietz and, briefly, Hiller, were his musical followers.

(in particular at Frankfurt and Berlin) he conducted summer choral events, such as the Niederrheinisches Musikfest (Lower Rhenish Music Festival) at Aachen or Düsseldorf and in England at the Birmingham Triennial Festival. Ferdinand Hiller substituted for him for the Leipzig season of 1843–44, but he was not a success. Mendelssohn, on hearing his own *Scottish* symphony under him, felt that orchestral standards had slipped.[8] Worse still, Hiller was upstaged during his season by the highly successful debuts of three future Leipzig music directors, Niels Gade and Julius Rietz conducting their own symphonies and Carl Reinecke as pianist on the same programme as the popular young violinist Joseph Joachim, who was making a return visit.[9] Mendelssohn became Leipzig's adopted son, and his influence would last way beyond his death.[10] Vienna could justifiably lay claim to the title of capital of the musical world during the 50 years from 1780 to 1830, thanks to the first Viennese school of Haydn, Mozart, Beethoven and Schubert. However, once these celebrated resident composers were dead by 1828, Vienna could not boast any such line-up again until the last two decades of the century when Brahms, Bruckner and Mahler had made it their home.[11] In the intervening half-century 1830–80 Leipzig wore the crown, even though the focus of its fame, Mendelssohn, was dead before even half that period had elapsed.

Mendelssohn's arrival in Leipzig in 1835 had an immediate impact on the city's music-making.[12] Having dispensed with the former duality of the post, he took on all musical duties and generally conducted everything from memory. He was both demanding of accuracy and precise in detail when he rehearsed. Standards improved significantly at once, a fact not lost on his discerning musical audiences. He also had a canny talent for gathering good musicians around him, such as the pianists Ignaz Moscheles and Clara Schumann, while soon after his appointment to the Gewandhaus orchestra he was reunited with an old friend, the violinist and conductor Ferdinand David, when both attended the funeral of Mendelssohn's father in Berlin.[13] Mendelssohn used the occasion to persuade David to become his right-hand man in Leipzig and to lead the orchestra.[14] The directors of the Gewandhaus presented Mendelssohn to Leipzig's music lovers and supporters as a composer, conductor, versatile performer (pianist, violinist and violist), and a

[8] The concert was on 22 February 1844.
[9] Dörffel, 105–7; Todd, 471.
[10] Richard Wagner was born there in 1813, but following brief periods in several cities after his studies he chose Dresden instead as his domicile in 1842, until he was forced into exile in Switzerland in 1848.
[11] Of these seven composers, only Schubert was actually born in Vienna.
[12] Leipzig first heard music by Mendelssohn on 1 February 1827 (two days before his nineteenth birthday), when his Symphony No. 1 in C minor Op. 11 was played. In the two years leading to his appointment 1833–35, three of his overtures were performed, *A Midsummer Night's Dream* (1833), *Hebrides* and *Calm Sea and Prosperous Voyage* (1834). Such was their popularity that they were played annually for years.
[13] The orphaned David had been brought up by Mendelssohn's family.
[14] David would remain in the post for 37 years from 1836 until his death in 1873.

brilliant administrator. 'At the Gewandhaus he drew largely upon classic and early nineteenth century German repertoire, and thereby reinforced the canonization of an increasingly familiar musical tradition', according to R Larry Todd.[15] His first concert, on 4 October 1835 marking the start of the winter season, began with his own overture *Calm Sea and Prosperous Voyage*. His choice of symphonies for this initial season was a mix of the predictable and the enterprising, which laid down a template for the style of programming in future seasons. There were those of Haydn, Mozart (the last four) and Beethoven (all but the first), all staple fare, but Georges Onslow's in A (on 29 October) showed that contemporary works would continue to be heard in Gewandhaus concerts. Onslow wrote four symphonies, all of which were played at Leipzig between 1831 and 1853, the year of his death, No. 1 eight times, No. 2 five times, and Nos 3 and 4 once each.[16] Mendelssohn's four predecessors had established a tradition for programming new symphonies, whether by past or contemporary composers. Pohlenz had included those by Spohr (Nos 3 and 4), Moscheles and the 20-year-old Wagner.[17] In most seasons two or three were performed, but exceptionally in the one before Mendelssohn took over there were six.[18]

The 46 new symphonies performed during Mendelssohn's tenure as music director were:[19]

1835–36: (1) Onslow
1836–37: (5) Reissiger, Hetsch, Molique, Franz Lachner, Joseph Strauss[20]
1837–38: (2) Täglichsbeck, Burgmüller
1838–39: (5) Spohr, Möhring, Lachner, Dobrzyński, Schubert[21]
1839–40: (4) Lindblad, Kittl, Schneider, Kalliwoda
1840–41: (5) Spohr, Lachner, Kalliwoda, Maurer, Schumann[22]
1841–42: (6) David, Hermann, Spohr, F. Müller, C.G. Müller, Mendelssohn[23]
1842–43: (4) Gade, Hesse, Kittl, Pape
1843–44: (4) Rietz, Gade, Drobisch, Kalliwoda

---

[15] *Mendelssohn: a Life in Music*, 314.
[16] *Grove* (editions 1–5) dismisses Onslow's symphonies as 'soon forgotten', *New Grove* edition 6 as 'displaying faults, conventionally good orchestration but often repeats a pattern monotonously', while *New Grove* edition 7 makes no comment, observing only that No. 4 was written for the 1847 Lower Rhenish Music Festival.
[17] Wagner's Symphony in C on 10 January 1833; but Pohlenz had already conducted an overture by him on 23 February 1832.
[18] Spohr (No. 4 *Die Weihe der Töne*), Adolf Hesse (No. 3), J.W. Kalliwoda (No. 4), C.G. Müller (No. 3), Georges Onslow (No. 3) and Franz Lachner (No. 1).
[19] See Dörffel.
[20] Those by Lachner and Strauss were the prize-winning works at Vienna described in Chapter 3.
[21] Schubert No. 9 in C *Great*.
[22] Schumann No. 1 in B♭ *Spring*.
[23] Mendelssohn No. 3 in A minor *Scottish*.

1844–45: (3) Hesse, Markull, Lührss
1845–46: (2) Rosenhain, Taubert
1846–47: (5) Leonhard, Rietz, Helsted, Pape, Schumann[24]

Mendelssohn wrote from Leipzig to Ignaz Moscheles in London on 4 April 1839, reporting some of the new works played in the 1838–39 season:

> We recently [12 March] played a most remarkable and interesting symphony by Franz Schubert. It is without doubt one of the best works we have lately heard. Throughout bright, fascinating and original, it stands quite at the head of his instrumental works. Spohr's symphony [No. 5, 25 October 1838], which we performed before, I suppose you will give it at the Philharmonic [Society]. Lachner's [No. 6] I liked but little; the others liked it less. David can tell you about these.[25]

After Mendelssohn's death in 1847, the post of music director at the Gewandhaus was held twice by Julius Rietz, from 1848 to 1852 and from 1854 to 1860. Ferdinand David conducted the first half of the 1852–53 season and Niels Gade led the second half of 10 concerts beginning in the New Year of 1853 and the whole of the 1853–54 season. All three faithfully adhered to the programme structure preferred by Mendelssohn – a familiar overture, a popular operatic aria, an instrumental concerto, three songs, three short solo pieces, and finally a symphony.[26] A triumvirate of Moritz Hauptmann (Cantor at the Thomaskirche), Rietz and David rigorously examined all new compositions submitted for performance.[27] They were then played through before a final decision was taken whether or not to include them in a concert.

During the period 1848–60 there were 31 new symphonies by 23 composers in the subscription series programmes:[28]

1848–49: (3) David, Hiller, Spohr
1849–50: (4) Lührss, Gouvy, Spindler, Mendelssohn[29]
1850–51: (4) Gade, Spohr, Taubert, Walter

---

[24] Schumann No. 2 in C.
[25] *Letters of Felix Mendelssohn to Ignaz and Charlotte Moscheles* (trans. Felix Moscheles) (London, 1888), 191.
[26] Dörffel, 143.
[27] For the 1852–53 season alone there were 24 new symphonies submitted for consideration. Ibid., 145.
[28] None was played in the season 1856–57, while Schumann's *Rhenish* was part of an Extra Concert and not part of the subscription series. Performance dates are listed in Chapter 5.
[29] Mendelssohn Symphony No. 4 in A *Italian* on 1 November 1849.

1851–52: (3) Goltermann, Hermann,[30] Schumann[31]
1852–53: (3) Gade, Kufferath, Lachner
1853–54: (4) Gouvy, Pott, Ulrich, Schumann[32]
1854–55: (3) Hiller, Rubinstein, Dietrich
1855–56: (3) Gouvy, Taubert, Rietz
1857–58: (3) Gade, Rubinstein, Wüerst
1858–59: (1) Reinecke
1859–60: (1) Veit

Carl Reinecke followed Rietz for 35 years, 1860–95, of which this book covers the period 1860–76, to the year preceding the Leipzig premiere of Brahms's first symphony. Once again 31 symphonies were played, this time by 22 composers, of whom 19 were alive at the time of performance.[33]

1860–61: (1) Jadassohn
1863–64: (2) Jadassohn, Volkmann
1864–65: (4) Burgmüller, Abert, Bargiel, Gade
1865–66: (1) Reinecke
1866–67: (3) Naumann, Rheinberger, Schubert[34]
1868–69: (3) Raff, Bruch, Mendelssohn[35]
1869–70: (2) Dietrich, Vierling
1870–71: (2) Bruch, Svendsen
1871–72: (2) Abert, Gade
1872–73: (2) Raff, Grimm
1873–74: (2) Raff, Breunung
1874–75: (3) Raff, Reinecke, Gernsheim
1875–76: (2) Jadassohn, Goetz
1876–77: (2) Raff, Brahms[36]

An overwhelming proportion of the new repertoire was devoted to the music of German composers, but this was also true of other genres such as overtures, concertos and symphonic poems. It was also the case that, either by public demand or because Mendelssohn and his successors thought they merited repetition, novelties were sometimes played again in later concerts (thus excluding more new ones), for in many ways it was (and remains today) harder for a composer

---

[30] Friedrich Valentin Hermann was the orchestra's principal violist 1846–78.
[31] Schumann Symphony No. 3 *Rhenish* on 8 December 1851.
[32] Schumann revised version of Symphony No. 4 in D minor on 27 October 1853.
[33] The three exceptions were Schubert, Mendelssohn and Norbert Burgmüller. There were no new symphonies played in the seasons 1861–62, 1862–63 and 1867–68.
[34] Schubert Symphony No. 8 *Unfinished* on 13 December 1866.
[35] Mendelssohn Symphony No. 5 *Reformation* on 29 October 1868.
[36] The Leipzig premiere of Brahms's Symphony No. 1 took place on 18 January 1877.

to achieve a second performance rather than the premiere itself.[37] The series of Subscription Concerts was supplemented by so-called Extra Concerts promoted by a visiting performer or composer (e.g. Franz Liszt, Clara Schumann, Ole Bull, Anton Rubinstein) and Historic Concerts (Mendelssohn's brainchild), which were either themed entirely to music of one past master or mixed with that by his contemporaries.[38] Concerts were given regularly for the benefit of the poor and for the orchestra's pension fund, while anniversary concerts either marked the births or deaths of great composers or were held *in memoriam* to mark the recent passing of royalty, a composer or performer, aristocrat or town dignitary associated with Leipzig. Together with David, Mendelssohn established a new series of chamber music events called Morning Conversation Concerts from February 1836, which proved so popular, they had to be moved from the foyer into the main hall of the Gewandhaus. Apart from a handful of foreign composers who were included in the subscription series, the works of non-German composers tended to be found in these extra themed concerts. These 'approved' foreigners included the Dane Gade, the Swedes Svendsen and Lindblad, the French-born Onslow and the Russian Rubinstein, but in each case a connection can be made to Mendelssohn, whether to his hallowed circle while he was still alive or as an apostle in the next generation. Such was Mendelssohn's influence in Leipzig that, as Todd observes, his 'sole performance of Wagner's music [conducting the overture to *Tannhäuser* on 12 February 1846] reinforced a general antipathy towards the Dresden Kapellmeister, a rejection Wagner later did not hesitate to ascribe to Mendelssohn's influence'.[39] On the other hand, from 1841 Mendelssohn promoted the music of Schumann, whose reception in the city had been slow in coming, possibly due to the public's negative response to his conducting, which was, according to Gerald Abraham, 'passive and ineffectual'.[40] His marriage in September 1840 to the pianist Clara Wieck (a popular soloist in Leipzig) appeared to soften his public image, while the brief period he spent as a member of the teaching faculty in the new Conservatoire also meant a closer involvement in the city's musical life.

In the field of music education, Paris had established its Conservatoire in 1795, followed by Vienna in 1808, Prague in 1812, London's Royal Academy of Music in 1822 and Brussels in 1833. Some insight into preparation and performance opportunities offered by at least two of these Conservatoires to its composition

---

[37] This may account for the almost 50 per cent drop in the performances of new symphonies 1835–77.

[38] The four consecutive concerts, on 15 and 22 February and 1 and 8 March 1838, were devoted respectively to the music of Bach, Handel and Gluck; Haydn, Cimarosa, Naumann and Righini; Mozart, Salieri, Méhul and Romberg; Abt Vogler, Beethoven and Weber. The next series was in 1841, when the minor composers were omitted from the four concerts on 21 and 28 January and 4 and 11 February, the first pairing Bach and Handel, the rest respectively given to Haydn, Mozart and Beethoven. See Dörffel, 91 and 98.

[39] Todd, 511.

[40] 'Robert Schumann' in *New Grove* edition 6 (1980), 841.

students in the 1830s can be found. We are told that, at the Royal Academy of Music, Cipriani Potter took an exceptional place among the British composers of his day by devoting himself chiefly to instrumental composition and by basing his works on such forms; and he was certainly the first who had the opportunity, through his connection with the Academy, to set any appreciable number of English students on the same path. Concerted instrumental music, whether for the orchestra or the chamber, became the daily study of many Academy boys.[41]

The Belgian writer, pedagogue and composer François-Joseph Fétis visited on a fact-finding mission and, of the student composers, described how

> these young persons enjoy the inestimable advantage of having their compositions performed by a complete orchestra on the Tuesday and Saturday of every week. This practical instruction seems to me to be the best that is received in the Academy. ... The practices are directed by Mr Potter, who resided for a long time in Vienna and received instruction from Beethoven, whose style he imitates in his compositions. Mr Potter is an excellent musician and in every respect qualified for the office which he fills. These practices were very interesting. I was present at several of them and was always satisfied with what I heard.[42]

Sterndale Bennett was the star composition pupil at the time Fétis made his observations, but before he became a pupil of Potter he studied for a year with the older and more old-fashioned Dr William Crotch. This meant that

> Bennett was now allowed to take a sudden leap from Chants to Symphonies, the first of which, in the key of E flat, was finished on 6 April 1832, a week before the composer's sixteenth birthday. This work is not quite dead yet, for the opening subject was used much later for an eight-part motet. ... The symphony was played at the Academy concert in the following June. ... His grandfather could now read in the Report of the Committee that "Bennett had composed a Symphony, performed at the last concert, which had done him the greatest credit".[43]

Another account of student training made after visiting a new Conservatoire was written by Edward Holmes, who visited Prague in 1830:

> The Conservatorio [sic] of Prague furnishes Germany, Russia and France with some of the best of their singers and players, and it is the principal assistance to the cultivation of good music in the city. Every year the numbers of the pupils are thinned – the elder young men are drafted off to different orchestras, the young women to different operatic establishments. ... In a garden ... I found

[41] J.R. Sterndale Bennett, *The Life of William Sterndale Bennett* (London, 1907), 16.
[42] Ibid., 17.
[43] Ibid., 26.

groups of young men chatting away their leisure before the commencement of the afternoon's practice: it did not seem to have tinged their countenances or conversation with melancholy, that music and the perfecting of sinfonias was the serious business of their lives. On certain days in the week all individual *blasting* and *bowing* ceases, and the young men play in concert. The composition given this afternoon was Mozart's *Jupiter* sinfonia, and it was played with a precision and degree of execution that astonished me.[44]

The offer to Mendelssohn of a post at Berlin was, in its initial stages, purely hypothetical, so he accepted it in principle if not in fact. He was able to stall any move from Leipzig for some time, retain his post there and, during the three years 1840–43, develop his ideas for a Conservatoire. The city's varied concert life became an added draw to those Germans and foreigners attracted to the new Conservatoire; and this popularity lasted well beyond Mendelssohn's death until the last years of the nineteenth century, by which time cities such as Berlin with its Philharmonic Orchestra or Cologne with its Gürzenich Orchestra equalled if not superseded it. One could have argued that, if so many composers had studied with one or both of their parents or were sent to private teachers such as town organists, the need for music schools was questionable. Mendelssohn felt very differently and said so in a letter to Johann Paul von Falkenstein, a Leipzig ministerial representative at the Saxon court in Dresden.[45] Mendelssohn knew that Heinrich Blümner, the recently deceased uncle of Falkenstein's wife, had left money for the establishment of 'an institution dedicated to art or science'.[46] The composer was hopeful that a music school would be funded from this legacy. In his long letter, Mendelssohn raised concerns that too many pianists and not enough orchestral players were being produced by private instruction and that these latter students then struggled to pay for lessons. There was also a need to provide an outlet for teachers to practise their profession, making 'a public institution at this time as important for them as for their students'.[47] Mendelssohn's case for a Conservatoire in Leipzig was based on the University's crucial role at the hub of the city's intellectual life, to which adding a music college would provide a similar focus for what he termed 'public amusement'.[48] Meanwhile the lives of students at the Conservatoire would be further enriched by attendance at rehearsals for the Gewandhaus concerts and by the fine musical heritage of the Thomaskirche.[49]

---

[44] Edward Holmes, *A Ramble among the Musicians of Germany by a Musical Professor* (London, 1828; 2nd edition, 1830), 179–80.
[45] 8 April 1840, quoted in L.M. Phillips Jnr., *The Leipzig Conservatory 1843–1881* (PhD dissertation, Indiana University, 1979), 77–9.
[46] Ibid., 77.
[47] Ibid., 78.
[48] Ibid.
[49] Ibid.

The wheels of bureaucracy proceeded to grind slowly, but two years later, on 23 November 1842, Mendelssohn reported to Karl Klingemann, a friend in London, that his bid had been successful; Blümner's bequest of 20,000 Thalers was secured and a Conservatoire would be built.[50] The need for a national infrastructure for formal musical training at specialised public institutions throughout Germany's states had been mooted as far back as 1810.[51] A short-lived (1812–16) venture was tried in Stuttgart and several other places, but all of them were small-scale, parochial schemes to identify and train local musicians for courts, theatres or music societies as and when they were required. Mendelssohn, on the other hand, proposed not only a national institution based in Leipzig but also a broader scheme to attract foreigners as well as Germans, with stipends made available to those in financially straitened circumstances. Despite its close ties to the Gewandhaus orchestra (both institutions' boards had several directors in common and pupils' concerts were given in its hall), the Conservatoire was not perceived by the concert-giving organisation as a hothouse for rearing prospective players but rather as a means of providing opportunities for students to observe music being prepared and played at the highest level by permitting them to attend rehearsals. It took a year to organise the Conservatoire's premises, staff and students.

Mendelssohn was overworked in the season of 1843 because 'the second half of the winter 1842–43 was especially rich in musical events'.[52] On 9 March the Gewandhaus orchestra celebrated its centenary with a gruelling jubilee concert, the first half consisting of works written by four of its past musical directors, a concert master and two Cantors at the Thomaskirche.[53] The second half was a performance of Beethoven's ninth symphony under Mendelssohn. Berlioz had visited the previous month to conduct a concert of his own works on 4 February, including the *Symphonie fantastique*, which Mendelssohn undertook to prepare before his arrival in the city. Then, on 23 April, Mendelssohn conducted a concert of orchestral and choral music by Bach to mark the unveiling of his statue. During this flurry of activity, the Leipzig Conservatoire was officially opened on 2 April 1843.[54] From the 68 applications, 42 were selected as students; four of them were foreigners, two from Holland, and one each from England and America, though the two (unnamed) English-speakers lasted only briefly.[55] As student numbers built up through the century (3,462 had attended by 1881), it became clear that, from beyond Germany's borders, students, in particular from England, America and

---

[50] Ibid., 81–2.

[51] *AMZ* No. 12 (1810), quoted in Phillips, 32 and 33.

[52] Dörffel, 103.

[53] J.F. Doles, J.A. Hiller, J.G. Schicht, Mendelssohn, Concertmeister Matthäi, and Cantors Bach and Hauptmann.

[54] *NZfM* No. 19 (1843), quoted in Phillips, 89.

[55] Phillips lists the names of all students on pp. 90 and 91. He also surmises that the two English-speakers may have left because of their inadequate command of the German language.

Scandinavia, were being drawn to Leipzig's Conservatoire and that Mendelssohn's dominating presence both there and at the Gewandhaus was probably the reason. However, the students' names include very few recognisable today, whereas others, whose names are familiar and went to Leipzig, would appear to have done so privately and without formally enrolling at the Conservatoire.[56] Even after Mendelssohn's death, it seems to have been enough just to be in the city both to absorb his posthumous influence and to enjoy the musical events on offer. Neither was Leipzig ungrateful for Mendelssohn's contribution to its musical life, for the University awarded him an honorary doctorate on 20 March 1836 and the city made him a freeman on 17 April 1843.

From the observations penned by Fétis in the early 1830s, we know what the Royal Academy of Music in London was able to offer an apprentice composer in terms of practical opportunities to try out a new work.[57] What could Leipzig offer? Did Mendelssohn teach beyond the standard rubric of form and analysis that appeared to be the bedrock of his and his colleagues' thinking? Were composition classes simply a succession of harmony exercises written in the style of past master X, or a range of counterpoint tests from simple to complex fugues in the style of past master Y? Was the successful writing of a symphony or a five-part fugue considered to be the crowning achievement for the students on its three-year course? The American music educationalist Lowell Mason has left a description by a Bostonian ('Mr J.P.') of the opportunities offered to students at the Leipzig Conservatoire as it was in 1852, nine years after its establishment and five after Mendelssohn's death.[58] For any would-be composer among the applicants, it is hard to understand why the course, as described in the Conservatoire's prospectus, would have been considered as an attractive proposition.

> The first year is devoted to Simple Harmony; the second to Harmony and Simple Counterpoint; and the third to Harmony, Double Counterpoint and Fugue. The study of *Composition* and *Musical Form* [Lowell's italics] constitutes a separate branch, being under the charge of a different instructor. It comprises all the different forms of vocal and instrumental composition, with the analysis of classical works. There are also exercises in playing from score and the art of conducting an orchestra.[59]

---

[56] Karl Whistling, *Statistik des Königlichen Conservatorium der Musik zu Leipzig 1843–1883: aus Anlass des vierzigjährigen Jubiläums der Anstalt* (Leipzig, 1883), quoted in Phillips, 203ff.

[57] See page 132.

[58] J.P. was James Cutler Dean Parker, student number 351 registered in 1851. See Phillips, 87.

[59] Lowell Mason, *Musical Letters from Abroad*, 29 March 1852 (New York, 1854, repr. 1967), 72–6.

The teachers at the Conservatoire when it opened in 1843 were Mendelssohn for singing, piano and composition, and his appointees Schumann for piano and composition, Hauptmann for harmony and counterpoint, David for violin, Henriette Bünau-Grabau for singing, Carl Ferdinand Becker for organ, Moritz Klengel for violin, Ernst Friedrich Wenzel for second-study pianists, and Louis Plaidy, who, like Mendelssohn, taught first-study pianists. Hauptmann taught four times weekly, Klengel twice, otherwise the rest were required to teach three times per week.[60] However, there were some variations in further listings: for example, by the end of the year (December 1843) Hiller and Schumann appeared as teachers 'in the exercise' of composition. In August 1846 Mendelssohn is listed as a composition teacher, Gade as an instructor in harmony and instrumentation, while Hauptmann began his 22-year stint as a teacher of harmony and counterpoint.[61] All sorts of contrapuntal techniques (fugues in particular) were now obligatory components in symphonies, the more so since the reawakening if not discovery of Bach's music in the 1830s and 1840s. What Mendelssohn began, Hauptmann (who also occupied Bach's former post as Cantor at the Thomaskirche) continued in his rigorous teaching at the Conservatoire.

Despite being *ipso facto* director of the Conservatoire, Mendelssohn declined the title, fearing it would rank him above his teaching colleagues. Yet despite this reluctance to be seen as *primus inter pares*, he nevertheless left a philosophical legacy to which his colleagues and their successors rigidly adhered for the rest of the century. As he himself put it in his original proposal to von Falkenstein, each teacher would 'teach from a unified viewpoint' that he himself would formulate and cast in tablets of stone.[62] As to instruction in composition, it would appear to have been limited to the production of songs, instrumental and chamber works, or, for orchestra, nothing larger than overtures, with emphasis on the rules and regulations of traditional harmony and counterpoint as well as the study of the classical repertoire as a template for original work. Mendelssohn was often the absentee teacher, particularly after the second semester when he was being drawn further into negotiations with Berlin as the choir there took shape and the post crystallised into something viable. Nevertheless his name remained associated with the Leipzig Conservatoire and its growing prestige. His international reputation was well established, particularly in England where he had taken London and then the provinces by storm, all greatly helped by the admiration and approval shown him by, first, King William IV and Queen Adelaide, then Queen Victoria and her consort Prince Albert. It was small wonder that English students of both sexes and from teenagers to adults were soon flocking to Leipzig.

Lowell Mason was highly impressed by what he saw and read of the Leipzig Conservatoire and considered it a model for establishing one in his own country:

---

[60] *NZfM* No. 18 (1843), quoted in Phillips, 87.
[61] Phillips, 128.
[62] Ibid., 77–9.

When young Americans, having good natural talent, favourable early musical associations and a sufficient preparatory education, shall devote themselves like Mr P[arker] to the thorough study of musical science and art, we may look for the rapid progress and success of music in our land, and may hope to realize some of the advantages for which it was designed.[63]

He then went on to describe a concert given by pupils of the Conservatoire on 1 April 1852:

Last evening the saloon of the Gewandhaus was crowded to listen to the pupils of the Conservatory. Concerts are occasionally given, perhaps once a quarter or once in six months, under the direction of the professors, in which the pupils give specimens of their proficiency in the composition and in the performance of music, vocal and instrumental. ... Tickets are not sold but given away by the teachers and pupils to their friends. The orchestra at such times is in part made up of the pupils, deficiencies being supplied by professors employed for the occasion; of course they have an efficient band. David and Dreyschock were at the head of the violins. Moscheles conducted the piano pieces; David conducted the violin concertos; Reitz [sic] conducted the songs; Richter conducted the chorus music and the respective authors themselves conducted the overtures. There were two original overtures performed, [one] composed by W. Frederic Nicolai of Leyden, Holland, [the other] by Heinrich von Sahr of Dresden, Saxony. Both of these overtures were highly creditable to the young men, and were well received; the last perhaps being the most meritorious production.[64]

Clearly either the composition students were not guaranteed a performance of either a symphony or even movements from one they had written, or it was simply the case that none had been written. There were nevertheless at least two exceptions who studied at Leipzig but whose respective futures lay in conducting rather than composing, namely Otto Dessoff (1851–53) and (with further detail to come in Chapter 5) Hermann Levi (1855–58). They both conducted their compositions in their graduation examinations, but perhaps it was the manifestly high standard of their conducting abilities that secured these apparently rare performing opportunities.

Mendelssohn could have had London's Royal Academy of Music in mind as a prototype when planning Leipzig's Conservatoire, for he was present at Sterndale Bennett's performance of his own piano concerto at one of the pupils' concerts. It was held at the Hanover Square Rooms on 26 June 1833. Mendelssohn invited Bennett to Leipzig, famously not as a pupil but 'to be my friend'.[65] Between 1837 and 1857 at least one of his works was played every season except two (1844 and

---

[63] 29 March 1852, Mason, 72.
[64] 2 April 1852, Mason, 92–3.
[65] Sterndale Bennett, 30.

1852), though none of his four symphonies was ever played there.[66] Stanford, in his centennial review of Bennett, took a typically cynical view of what the Englishman encountered in Leipzig between the autumn of 1836 and the spring of 1837. 'As novelties, Bennett now heard symphonies and overtures of contemporary German composers: Hetsch, Hiller, Lachner, Lindpaintner, Molique, Müller, Reissiger, Rosenhain, Joseph Strauss. There can indeed be little ground for thinking that the music thus presented to him gave him any fresh direction to his own thought as a composer.'[67]

Another English composer making his way in the 1830s was George Macfarren (1813–87), whose career was in many ways similar to Bennett's. They were both students at the Royal Academy of Music and, though three years older, Macfarren eventually followed Bennett as its director and to the professorship of music at Cambridge on Bennett's death in 1875. Macfarren did not study at Leipzig, however, nor did he make the Grand Tour that might have taken him there; but in his seven years at the Royal Academy of Music (1829–36) he made full use of opportunities to have his music performed under its auspices and he did have contact with Mendelssohn in a way that merits passing mention. Nicholas Temperley praises Macfarren as 'the only English composer of his generation to persevere in writing symphonies, undaunted by their almost inevitable failure to command public attention'.[68] The German appetite for the genre would no doubt have motivated foreigners such as Bennett and Macfarren to seek performances there, but in order for a work to enter the concert repertoire, they quickly learned that a composer probably needed to be working or studying in the country.[69] In short, Bennett and Macfarren were two British musicians drawn to Leipzig prior to the opening of the Conservatoire in 1843 after both had just completed years of postgraduate study in London. Unfortunately, however, Mendelssohn had mixed success with having either young man's music played at the Gewandhaus.

It may be true that Bennett seemed to give up on the symphony (the piano concerto, with himself as soloist, was a more certain way of promoting his own music) while Macfarren persisted for a further 10 years, yet despite their differing approaches there is a common denominator linking both composers. Macfarren wrote eight symphonies between 1828 and 1845, while Bennett had written four (a fifth is probably lost) between 1832 and 1835. Then for both men there is a gap of virtually the same number of years, 29 for Macfarren until 1874 and 28 for Bennett until 1863, whereupon they returned to the genre and in their maturity wrote one further symphony, (a growing list consisting of Lachner, Kittl, Schneider

---

[66] The works played were the overtures *The Naiades*, *The Wood Nymphs* (specially written for the Gewandhaus in 1839) and *Parisina*, two piano concertos (Nos 3 and 4), a Caprice and a song.

[67] C.V. Stanford, 'William Sterndale Bennett (1816–75)' in *The Musical Quarterly* Vol. 2 No. 4 (October 1916), 635–6.

[68] *New Grove*, edition 6, 425.

[69] See Mendelssohn's letter to Macfarren (footnote 74).

and Rosenhain in Germany), albeit with the gap reduced to more like a dozen years. Both Macfarren and Bennett studied under Cipriani Potter, whose teaching methods were based on a plan:

> A most significant and completely comprehensive word, to represent the principles of design in musical art, ... in the arrangement of ideas, in the conduct of keys, in the juxtaposition of one musical phrase with another, the distribution of rhythm, and the whole musical structure; ... it makes music really into an art instead of an accident. ... It seems probable that Potter, after his continental experience and the advice given him by Beethoven ['you must study counterpoint'] would, in his position at the Royal Academy of Music, insist on the importance of contrapuntal training. Under Potter's training [Macfarren] made such great advancement in composition that a Symphony in C by him was considered worthy of performance at an Academy concert in September 1830. Another (D minor, at the Academy on 3 December 1831) was followed by one of his most important early works (F minor, 27 October 1834) as the initial piece at the first concert of a most useful society then recently founded, the Society of British Musicians.[70]

The *Athenaeum* reviewed this last concert and expressed itself satisfied with the performance:

> We were pleased and interested with Mr Macfarren's symphony – both from the youth of the composer, and the enthusiasm and originality discernible throughout his work – it gives good promise of excellence; the trio of the minuet in particular struck us as full of fine bold fancy, and the conclusion to the *finale* was at once clever and animating. We are not, at this instant, able to remember any work of similar length from the pen of a native writer which has given us so much pleasure.[71]

For the sake of the reader without a score, Macfarren's biographer Banister identified some of the critic's favourite moments: 'The trio here alluded to is for horns *obbligati*, with interruptions by the full orchestra. The "conclusion to the *finale*" is a coda in fugal style. The whole symphony is marked by the freshness and vigour of youth, ably and soundly trained in the study of the best models.'[72] Mendelssohn too was impressed by Macfarren's seventh symphony, which dates from 1839–40 and is in the unusual key of C♯ minor.[73] There were high hopes of

---

[70] Henry C. Banister, *George Alexander Macfarren* (London, 1891), 22–6.
[71] *Athenaeum* 2 November 1834, quoted in Banister, 28.
[72] Banister, 28.
[73] Examples of the key of C♯ minor in the symphonic literature are hard to find, other than those that come later by Mahler (No. 5), Prokofiev (No. 7) and Bloch. Macfarren is

a performance during the Gewandhaus season of 1842–43, but Mendelssohn was forced to disappoint Macfarren:

> I tried to bring out the symphony in one of our concerts but, as I suspected when I first wrote to you, there was some opposition from the directors, merely because there had been four new symphonies in the course of the last two months [by Hesse, Kittl, Pape and Gade] and they did so much that I was obliged to postpone it until the beginning of the next season, although it was half copied already. I am sorry you feel disappointed by the delay but it was not in my power to help it. Meanwhile I must repeat what I said in my first letter – if you *had* an overture I am sure it would be a better beginning for the public and these concerts than a symphony. Ask Bennett, who knows the place and will certainly concur in this opinion. So if you could accordingly let us have an overture *before* the symphony, I am sure the last would be much better understood and received by the public, even if there had not been such a quantity of new native symphonies beforehand, as there had been this year. ... As for those good friends of yours who think, as you say, that English music is a thing which cannot be endured in Germany and that a work of yours here would be like an appearance of two moons – pray ask them to wait a few months before they repeat an opinion equally creditable to us and to you, or pray tell them in my name that they are all sadly mistaken and that the event will soon prove them to be so.[74]

Macfarren seems to have followed Mendelssohn's advice, for his overture *Chevy Chace* was performed at the Gewandhaus on 26 October 1843. The composer was not present to hear the performance, but he received an extremely positive response from Mendelssohn, including the promise of programming more of his music. He mentions in particular this symphony (No. 7 in C♯ minor), though as he was about to leave Leipzig for Berlin for the rest of the season, Macfarren might well have had reason to feel concerned that Mendelssohn would not be there to press his case.

> I must tell you that your overture went very well, and was most cordially and unanimously received by the public; that the amateurs hailed it as a work which promised them a great many treats to come and which gave them such a treat already in itself; that the orchestra played it with true delight and enthusiasm; in short, that it is sure to be a favourite with all of them. ... I left the whole of your music with the concert directors, who will forward it back to you after the end of the season and have promised me they will bring out at least one of your

---

more likely to have had Beethoven's Piano Sonata No. 14 Op. 27 No. 2 (*Moonlight*) or String Quartet Op. 131 in mind.

[74] Mendelssohn to Macfarren, 2 April 1843, quoted in Banister, 87–8.

other works, if not several in the course of this winter; most probably it will be the symphony.⁷⁵

In fact the performance of the *Chevy Chace* overture on 26 October 1843 was the only occasion on which music by Macfarren was heard in Leipzig during the period under discussion to 1877.⁷⁶ Macfarren may well have had cause for complaint that Mendelssohn did not or could not always deliver his hopes or make good his promises. This may explain Macfarren's highly charged and very bitter description of Mendelssohn's character, which formed part of the biographical entry he wrote for the *Imperial Dictionary of Universal Biography* many years later in 1870: 'The foible of his character was his thirst for good opinion, which led him indiscriminately to conciliate everyone whose judgement could receive attention; thus his testimonials are of little credit, and his complimentary letters are not always utterances of his true opinion.'⁷⁷ The fate of the seventh symphony in England was hardly encouraging for Macfarren either. It took another two years before the Philharmonic Society put it on at a concert on 9 June 1845 under Moscheles, but the performance was 'discreditably indifferent, and the reception by the more conservative portion of the (at that time) very conservative audience worse than apathetic, ill-mannered and hostile'.⁷⁸

We now turn to the post-Mendelssohn era in Leipzig and to other musicians who chose to study there, some registered at the Conservatoire, the rest living and studying privately. The 20-year-old American pianist William Mason (third son of Lowell) studied there for just six months, between September 1849 and March 1850 (piano with Moscheles, harmony and counterpoint with Moritz Hauptmann, and instrumentation with Ernst Friedrich Richter), and was initially overwhelmed by what he found in the city:

> I well remember the feeling of awe mingled with interest with which I looked upon every German whom I met in the streets of Leipsic on my first arrival in that famously musical city. I looked on even the labouring-men, the peasants as well as those in higher positions, as being Mozarts and Beethovens and the idea gained such ascendancy that I felt my own inferiority and metaphorically held down my head. This feeling, however, was not of long duration, and changed in the course of a month or two on account of what happened at a concert of the Euterpe Society which I attended.⁷⁹

---

⁷⁵ Mendelssohn to Macfarren, 20 November 1843, quoted in Banister, 41.
⁷⁶ Dörffel, *Statistik*, 36.
⁷⁷ Banister, 75.
⁷⁸ Ibid., 88.
⁷⁹ William Mason, *Memories of a Musical Life* (London, 1901), 34–5. At that concert Mason considered a solo clarinet work, 'inferior kind of music ... out of place in the classical atmosphere of a symphony concert [especially as it] turned out to be the most popular piece of the evening' – ibid., 35–6.

Too late to study with Mendelssohn, Francis Edward Bache (1833–58) became a pupil of Sterndale Bennett for four years (1849–53) and then went to Leipzig to study with Hauptmann. At the time there were high hopes for Bache, especially from the *Athenaeum*, which was clearly still awaiting its English musical Messiah: 'To judge from this essay, we have met with no Englishman more likely to give us the English composer for whom we have so long been waiting than Mr Bache, for whose future appearances we shall watch with interest.'[80] Constance Bache, writing reminiscences of her brothers Edward and Walter in 1901, began her chapter on Edward's Leipzig years with a paean of praise to the city: 'Leipzig! That magic name! At the time of which I am writing it was the Mecca of every young musical aspirant, the Parnassus of his ambition. It was just in the zenith of its fame, i.e. under the aegis of Mendelssohn's great name.'[81] Edward Bache did not quite see it his sister's way when he arrived there in the autumn of 1853. Birmingham born, he had received initial instruction in counterpoint from the city's organist James Stimpson before moving south to London, where he studied with Bennett. Once in Leipzig and after a couple of lessons with Hauptmann, he revised his plan, deciding that the way forward was to perfect his studies with a weekly lesson in counterpoint rather than to study composition. He imbibed the musical life, including sharing the company of the visiting Berlioz and Liszt, and formed a friendship with fellow-student Francesco Berger, the future long-lived (1834–1933) and long-serving (1884–1911) secretary of London's Philharmonic Society. After five months, however, Edward was writing, 'I thought I would go to Berlin and hear something there and also get out of this incessant whirl of symphony music'.[82] His views of the benefits of a German musical education soon crystallised during his stay in Leipzig:

> I should say now, if I knew any lad twelve or thirteen years old of great musical genius, "Go to Germany till fifteen years old to learn mechanical grammar wherewith to express your ideas fluently and correctly; go to Italy afterwards to study principles of art as distinguished from details of execution".[83]

Bache wanted at all costs to avoid the career path Sterndale Bennett was taking, both a sensible and prescient move on Bache's part as it was teaching and administration that probably did more to impede Bennett's progress as a composer:

> At all events I want to avoid the professor's life in London. ... I feel more and more how bad a place is England for artistic development in music, at all events;

---

[80] *Athenaeum* 19 June 1852 quoted in Bache, 11. The music referred to is 'an *Allegro* of a manuscript piano concerto', probably the first movement of his Concerto Op. 18 completed at Leipzig in 1856.
[81] Bache, 18.
[82] Ibid., 31.
[83] Ibid., 45.

money is the ruin of young artists there, who find teaching etc far too profitable to be neglected in favour of continued artistic improvement.[84]

Edward Bache died of tuberculosis aged only 25 in August 1858, just weeks after his 16-year-old brother Walter was sent to Leipzig. Constance described some of the Leipzig pedagogues as 'becoming possibly just a little bit fossilized; they tacked on to the tail of Beethoven, of Czerny, of Mendelssohn, whereas a new gospel was beginning to be preached, which they looked upon as dangerous and visionary'.[85] Walter, who became a concert pianist, was a strong supporter of Liszt and spent most of his life promoting his music in Britain. His audition at Leipzig was in October 1858 before Hauptmann, Moscheles and David, and one of his earliest friendships formed there was with 'a new pupil here from the Royal Academy named Sullivan, whom I like very much. He cannot play well but has written some things which I think show great talent'.[86] In his third year Bache reported that he had begun composition lessons with Carl Reinecke, now in charge at the Gewandhaus, but regrettably gave no details of their structure.[87] We do, however, have an interesting insight provided by a source unidentified beyond being 'a musician of high standing'.[88] He was one of the group of English music students in Leipzig about 1860, a group that included Sullivan, Franklin Taylor, Carl Rosa and John Francis Barnett together with his three cousins Domenico Dragonetti Barnett, Rosamunde Liszt Barnett and Clara Kathinka Barnett. Because Walter's letters home were full of accounts of frivolity and japes, one could well take the view that he had done nothing but amuse himself during his time there until his Damascene conversion to Liszt; indeed that 'musician of high standing' confirmed to Constance Bache that 40 years earlier 'in Leipzig nobody was compelled to work, there being no particular supervision'.[89] Walter Bache himself described one of the staff as 'quite an old man now; his lessons do not do any good at all and I think they only keep him because his name looks well in the prospectuses'.[90]

After the death of Mendelssohn, it was Hauptmann who drew students to Leipzig with his reputation for the teaching of counterpoint. Barnett, who would become known principally for his cantata *The Ancient Mariner* written for the 1867 Birmingham Festival, began with private study with Hauptmann before enrolling in 1858 together with Walter Bache and Sullivan. His teachers at the Conservatoire were Hauptmann, Moscheles and Plaidy, but 'I think in many respects the greatest advantage I enjoyed was studying with Julius Rietz, who was a wonderful master

---

[84] Ibid., 80.
[85] Ibid., 131–2.
[86] Ibid., 132.
[87] Letter dated 22 October 1860.
[88] Bache, 144.
[89] Ibid., 145.
[90] Ibid., 133.

for enabling the student to give finish and conciseness to his compositions'.[91] Sullivan was recommended to Moscheles by Sir George Smart with the words 'composition is what he shines most in'.[92] Moscheles's reply gives an indication of what Smart's protégé would encounter at the Leipzig Conservatoire,

> which, having been founded by Mendelssohn, is still administered after his intention. Pianoforte and violin players have to learn the truly beautiful in the classics. You know who are the teachers; Hauptmann for counterpoint, Richter for organ, Rietz for instrumentation and composition. Although Leipzig only *tolerates* the "music of the future", the taste here is not for being so rigid as *only* to like the music of Sebastian Bach's deep learning and antiquated manner. We like our young composers to find a *juste milieu* and develop elements fit for every school of art. ... The course of lessons will be arranged entirely according to the ability and speciality of the pupil. ... As you tell me Sullivan has a peculiar talent for composition, it stands to reason that his chief time will be devoted to this branch.[93]

Sullivan's three years were used to the full and he was given plenty of opportunity to conduct, culminating in his final examination on 6 April 1861, a public concert in which students either performed or had their works performed and in which he conducted six movements from his incidental music to Shakespeare's *The Tempest*. This was conceivably a tribute to Mendelssohn and his *Midsummer Night's Dream* as Sullivan bade farewell to Leipzig, though he returned to conduct his overture *In Memoriam* in a concert at the Gewandhaus on 17 October 1867.[94] Response was mixed: one review dismissed it as offering 'too little that is original for us Germans', although another acknowledged that it gave 'an impression of music of true feeling ... while maintaining the customary shape of an overture, it is fresh in its avoidance of dull formality and displays a psychological consistency in conception and disposition'.[95] Sullivan's only symphony (in E *The Irish*) had been played for the first time at Crystal Palace under August Manns (10 March 1866), then a month later at St James's Hall under Alfred Mellon (11 April) and Sullivan himself (11 July). It would get a private read-through in Leipzig in October 1867 but no public performance. A review of the Crystal Palace premiere is worth quoting from *The Times*. Written almost resentfully that Sullivan is the darling of musical society and needs taking down a peg or two, it also harbours both grudging respect and an acknowledgement that his is a talent to watch:

---

[91] John Francis Barnett, *Musical Reminiscences and Impressions* (London, 1906), 36.
[92] Arthur Jacobs, *Arthur Sullivan* (2nd edition, Aldershot, 1992), 20.
[93] Moscheles to Smart trans. Carl Klingemann, quoted in Jacobs, 20–21.
[94] Percy Young, *Sir Arthur Sullivan* (London, 1971), 57.
[95] *Leipziger Allgemeine musikalische Zeitung* (henceforth *LAMZ*), Vol. 2 No. 43, 23 October 1867, col. 346 quoted in Young, 57.

> The Symphony ... is not only by far the most noticeable composition that has proceeded from Mr Sullivan's pen, but the best musical work, if judged only by the largeness of its form and the number of beautiful thoughts it contains, for a long time produced by an English composer. ... Mr Sullivan should abjure Mendelssohn, even Beethoven, and above all Schumann, for a year and a day. ... Not that Mr Sullivan has been conquered but that he must conquer; and the best way to do this is to study the most legitimate and natural models, in the works of Haydn and Mozart, trusting to himself to the rest. ... The works of Haydn and Mozart in one sense, Bach and Handel in another, should be the text books of every young composer, who, ungifted with the genius of a Beethoven, is incapable of declaring himself, like Beethoven, independent of all precedents. Meanwhile Mr Sullivan, who, though young, is already shrewd enough to have steered clear of that dangerous quicksand Spohr, the most mannered of all mannerists, has composed a first symphony, which, or we are greatly mistaken, will for some time hence, engage the attention of the musical world, and lead to a second that may possibly fix it for at least a generation.[96]

A second symphony from Sullivan was not forthcoming, but a future more prolific writer of them from Britain was Frederic Cowen, who enrolled at the Conservatoire in 1865 and whose composition teacher was Reinecke.

> He belonged to the old school, and did not encourage modern innovations but on the whole he was an excellent master. ... At the time I was in Leipzig, Schumann had superseded Mendelssohn in the students' affections; he was their great apostle and the model on which they based all their early compositions. I wrote a string quartet while there, of which two movements were a mixture of Mozart and Mendelssohn; but I too, soon caught the prevailing epidemic and the remainder of the work was as near an imitation of Schumann as I could arrive at.[97]

Fellow students of Cowen, who registered from Britain in 1865, were Charles Swinnerton Heap (organist and chorus master in Birmingham), the pianist and composer Oscar Beringer from Norwood in south London, and the Czech composer Zdenko Fibich.[98] Already there in 1863 was Johan Svendsen, while before him another Norwegian, Grieg, had registered in 1858.[99] There had been a constant flow of Scandinavian students from the very opening of the Conservatoire, when Pauline Solberg came from Bergen in Norway as student number 44.[100] It was not uncommon for students to go to Leipzig in their early to mid-teen years. Cowen

---

[96] Press review (by J.W. Davison?) quoted in Young, 41.
[97] Frederic Cowen, *My Art and My Friends* (London, 1913), 22.
[98] Phillips, 274–5.
[99] Ibid., 263 and 272.
[100] Ibid., 248.

was only 13 when he went, while Grieg was a very homesick 15-year-old. It was the Norwegian violinist Ole Bull who urged Grieg's parents to send him to Leipzig and receive a systematic course of study at the Conservatoire, something that he, Bull, felt he had sadly lacked at the start of his career. Grieg, however, was as disappointed as many others who had gone before or who would come after him, though the city's musical life based at the Gewandhaus and the Opera more than made up for the quality or nature of the tuition he received. 'It was fortunate for me', he recalled, 'that in Leipzig I was able to hear so much fine music, especially orchestral and chamber music. This compensated for the training in composition that I failed to get at the Conservatoire. It developed my spirit and my musical judgement considerably'.[101] Grieg was an ardent admirer of Schumann's music, but, as Cowen points out, it was only in favour at the Conservatoire from the mid-1860s despite Ernst Wenzel (Grieg's piano teacher) having been a close personal friend of Schumann. While Grieg had cause to be grateful to Leipzig for providing so many satisfying musical experiences during his four years there 1858–62, the city did not reciprocate by showing any interest in his music, which caused him much bitterness: 'Leipzig, in spite of its Conservatoire and its University, never was and never will be a cultured city. The inhabitants of the city are by nature altogether too bourgeois and philistine for that.'[102] To the end of his life he retained negative memories, probably tainted by the passage of time, even if there may well have been cause for complaint:

> In contrast to Svendsen, I must say that I left the Leipzig Conservatoire just as dumb as I was when I was there. I had learned a bit to be sure, but my own individuality was still a closed book for me.[103]
> How I envy you your technique, which each day I miss more and more. And it isn't just my own fault either; it is primarily the fault of that damned Leipzig Conservatoire where I learned *absolutely nothing*.[104]
> How I hate this Conservatoire in Leipzig.[105]
> I would have found it completely reasonable if neither the director nor the teachers at the Conservatoire had taken any interest in me, for I didn't accomplish anything during those three [sic] years that would create any expectation for the future. If, then, in these glimpses of the Conservatoire, I have had to criticise various things about both the institution and the people within it, I must hasten to add that I take it for granted that it was due primarily to my own nature that I

---

[101] Edvard Grieg, 'Min förste suksess' (1903) (*Artikler og taler*, ed. Gaukstad, 1957), quoted in Finn Benestad and Dag Schjelderup-Ebbe, *Edvard Grieg: The Man and the Artist* (Gloucester, 1988), 30.
[102] Letter to Gerhard Schjelderup (undated), ibid., 31.
[103] Letter to Aimar Grönvold, 25 April 1881, ibid., 32.
[104] Letter to Julius Röntgen, 30 October 1884, ibid.
[105] Letter to Johan Halvorsen, 6 December 1901, ibid.

left the Conservatoire about as stupid as I was when I entered it. I was a dreamer with no desire for competition.[106]

Johann Svendsen (mentioned above by Grieg) had a much more successful time in Leipzig, where he studied from the end of 1863 to the spring of 1867.[107] Reinecke was his composition teacher, though his career path was undecided at the start when his prospects as a concert violinist were thwarted by a hand injury. Unlike other composition students, Svendsen forged ahead regardless of whether he received Reinecke's approval or not and produced a string octet, string quintet and his first symphony all during his student years, so even his strictly conservative and sceptical teacher was forced to concede that 'these works were written with great skill, ... rarely have I met a student who has developed as quickly as Svendsen'.[108] The first movement of the symphony was performed, together with the octet, under Svendsen's baton at a graduation concert on 14 May 1866 and received a generally favourable reception, while the remaining three movements were performed a year later at a similar event on 29 May 1867. Its clarity of form and wealth of ideas were praised, as well as its composer's evident skills in orchestral scoring, and by the 1870s Svendsen's music was being performed in modest amounts at the Gewandhaus.[109]

In 1914 Stanford looked back to 1874 and the lot of a young English composer for whom only London's Royal Academy of Music (headed by its conservative director, Sterndale Bennett) was a place of study: 'The serious student of composition therefore had both for tuition and experience to betake himself abroad; and the centre which was most attractive was Leipzig.'[110] Stanford lists many reasons why Leipzig exerted such a pull, including its concert and opera performances as well as a self-perpetuating tradition orchestrated by an 'apostolical succession of Englishmen who had gone there'.[111] Its geographical location put Berlin, Weimar and Dresden within comparative easy reach, though in 1874 Berlin's Hochschule was only just beginning to build its reputation thanks to Joachim's appointment as director. Like Mendelssohn before him in Leipzig, Joachim would surround himself with quality staff such as Clara Schumann, Julius Stockhausen and Ernst Rudorff, while elsewhere in the city Hans von Bülow began to build the Philharmonic Orchestra into a formidable unit. Weimar was dominated by Liszt and his piano students, while Dresden was an operatic centre with no teaching magnet save the elderly Julius Rietz, once of Leipzig.

---

[106] Grieg, 'Min förste suksess' (1903), ibid.

[107] Phillips, 272.

[108] Finn Benestad and Dag Schjelderup-Ebbe, *Johan Svendsen: The Man, the Maestro, the Music* (trans. W.H. Halverson) (Columbus, 1995), 46.

[109] The first two symphonies, a violin concerto, a cello concerto, the octet and a coronation march, were given single performances between 1870 and 1877.

[110] C.V. Stanford, *Pages from an Unwritten Diary* (London, 1914), 142.

[111] Ibid., 142.

When Stanford studied privately in Leipzig rather than as a registered student at the Conservatoire, Reinecke was both conductor of the Gewandhaus concerts and, following the Mendelssohn tradition, also principal professor of composition at the Conservatoire. The administrative director at the Conservatoire was a former lawyer Conrad Schleinitz (1802–81), one of the members of the founding directorate in 1843, intimate of Mendelssohn, and chairman from 1849; only with his death in 1881 was the umbilical chord of Mendelssohn's direct influence finally cut. In Stanford's day (1874), Hauptmann, David, Dreyschock, Plaidy and Moscheles were dead, so Reinecke, Jadassohn and Richter became the leading pedagogical lights. Opera was never a strong suit in Leipzig during the Mendelssohn years or immediately thereafter, but by the 1870s this was no longer the case and Stanford heard a wide repertoire of works throughout the two years he spent in the city, probably a more interesting experience for him than the few new symphonies played at the Gewandhaus, which were more or less limited to those of Joseph Joachim Raff. Completely dissatisfied with his experience of Reinecke's training methods, Stanford moved from Leipzig to Berlin and continued his studies with Friedrich Kiel (1821–85), with whom he was far more content. Unlike Cowen, Stanford had no kind words for his composition lessons with Reinecke:

> Of all the dry musicians I have ever known, he was the most desiccated. He had not a good word for any contemporary composer, even for those of his own kidney. ... He enjoyed himself hugely when he was expounding and writing canons and had a fairly good idea of teaching them. His composition training had no method about it whatever. He occasionally made an astute criticism and that was all. He never gave a pupil a chance of hearing his own work, the only really valuable means of training, and the better the music, the less he inclined to encourage it. He was in fact the embodiment of the typical "Philister".[112]

Leipzig's fame and reputation as a musical centre in the nineteenth century was therefore built upon Mendelssohn's activities there between 1835 and his death in 1847, 12 years (except for one season away in Berlin) during which time he raised both the standards of orchestral playing and chamber music at the Gewandhaus and founded the Conservatoire. In 1828 Edward Holmes had not only described the activities of the new Conservatoire in Prague but also a very different pre-Mendelssohn 'Leipsic' where Pohlenz had just (1827) succeeded Schulz at the Gewandhaus the year before.[113] Holmes makes no mention of the Gewandhaus but starts with a description of music at the Thomaskirche, and writes favourably about the city's opera house. At the time, the most celebrated musician in the city, according to Holmes's account, seems to have been Karl Traugott Queisser, active there as a famed trombonist between 1821 and 1843. Holmes also mentions Cantor Weinlich at the Thomasschule but not that one of his private composition

---

[112] Stanford, *Pages from an Unwritten Diary*, 156–7.
[113] Holmes, 246–59.

pupils was Wagner. Nor does he mention Mendelssohn, probably because his first symphony was the only music to have been heard there by 1828. Within seven years, however, the musical life of the city would begin to be transformed until the end of the century. It became a beacon that enticed not only the composers discussed here but also Elgar (whose financial circumstances precluded study there), Parry (who then opted instead for lessons in London with Eduard Dannreuther, himself a Leipzig pupil of Moscheles in 1859), Delius (who studied there with Reinecke, Jadassohn and Hans Sitt 1886–88), Percy Pitt, Ethel Smyth, Maude Valerie White and Janáček. What the students and the public were fed at the Gewandhaus in the 50 years 1830–80 was a diet of orchestral music dominated by Beethoven, Haydn, Mozart, Weber, Mendelssohn, Schumann and Spohr, while of Liszt and Wagner there was little (none in Mendelssohn's day). Max Bruch studied for four years in his native Cologne with Hiller and Reinecke; he then spent 1858–59 in Leipzig, where, as a 20-year-old composer, he was soon absorbed into the circle of Rietz, Moscheles, David and Hauptmann. Bruch's first two symphonies will be discussed in Chapter 6. From among those of this next generation, Percy Pitt wrote as follows of his musical education at the Conservatoire in 1886:

> It was not at the time all it might have been. The school was living on its reputation. It was quite as happy-go-lucky as its students; nor did the professors seem to mind very much whether one worked or not as long as fees were paid. ... Composers had their chances at the bi-weekly orchestral practices. There was a possibility of having one's works tried out before a "real" audience at Bonorand's restaurant in the Rosenthal Park outside the city.[114]

It would seem, therefore, that many young musicians who went to Leipzig to study composition after 1835 became more or less disillusioned, although students of the violin and piano under David and Moscheles respectively appear to have been more satisfied. Hauptmann seems to have been consistently admired, but if one strayed from the path laid down by Mendelssohn, it was, with the possible of exception of Svendsen, hard for a student to satisfy those in charge of the Conservatoire. Tuition in composition was part of the study of form, with emphasis laid upon the completion of technical exercises slavishly following styles of the previous hundred years. Score reading was given high priority; Mendelssohn was insistent upon accuracy. 'Es steht nicht da!' was his immediate reaction to any errant note brought into a chord by an incompetent score-reader.[115] Opportunity for performance of orchestral compositions by students was limited when compared to London's Royal Academy of Music, although concerts did take place in the Gewandhaus with section leaders from the professorial staff and with gaps in the orchestra filled by Gewandhaus players. As we have seen, the musical life of cities in Germany was often influenced, even dominated, by a composer or performer

---

[114] Daniel Chamier, *Percy Pitt of Covent Garden and the BBC* (London, 1938), 31–3.
[115] 'It's not there' – W.S. Rockstro, *Mendelssohn* (London, 1884), quoted in Phillips, 111.

with a strong personality – Liszt in Weimar, Wagner followed by Schumann in Dresden, Hiller in Cologne, Spohr in Kassel, Joachim in Berlin, Mendelssohn in Leipzig –, and like a magnet, the cities themselves then often attracted their supporters to cult proportions. The problem was that, where other German cities could thrive on the presence in their midst of a living composer, Leipzig relied on the enduring reputation of a dead one. As new music drifted and developed further and further away from Mendelssohn and the Classicism that he represented, so the attraction of Leipzig to a youthful would-be composer waned and became nothing more than a matter of musical history.[116] By the end of the nineteenth century this was a city whose concert hall and Conservatoire were living on their past. As far as the German symphony was concerned, Leipzig was part of the problem, not the solution.

---

[116] While opera is beyond the remit of this book, it should be noted that Leipzig's opera house was far more progressive in its repertoire than its concert hall. It was perhaps no coincidence that Mendelssohn wrote no opera. By the end of the 1880s conductors such as Nikisch and his assistant Mahler were at work there, so here at least a student's horizons were not limited.

Chapter 5
The German Symphony in the 1850s

> The creation of a symphony nowadays [1855] is a rock on which, with only a few exceptions, most composers suffer a complete shipwreck.[1]

The criteria required for a new symphony to impress an audience enough to demand repetition became more crucial as its very direction drifted aimlessly through the central decade of the nineteenth century. By the mid-1840s Mendelssohn had shown the way with object lessons in orchestration, while by the same point a decade later Schumann had made some innovative moves in symphonic construction. Together these two represented the best of the active German symphonists of the day, but neither composer did much more than stir the ingredients of the symphonic pot on their culinary journey. Although each was indisputably and in his own way a musician of significance and influence, they were also merely the mid-point signposts on the genre's road linking Beethoven to Brahms. They were not alone, for, as we have seen, there were worthy symphonies by composers such as Spohr, Kalliwoda, Lachner and Burgmüller. Such works played a greater part than indicating a direction, indeed they actually progressed the genre to a greater or lesser degree down the symphonic path. Nevertheless the paucity of successful composers active during the 1850s is striking compared to the two preceding decades and for this there are several reasons. Mendelssohn's unexpectedly premature death had already removed the first of the three most influential figures before the decade even began; the growing illness and insanity of Schumann followed by his death in 1856 carried off the second; while the last to die was Spohr in 1859. On the other hand, on one side of a great divide now forming between conservatives based at Leipzig and progressives based at Weimar, we find Liszt, whose symphonic poems were all written and performed during the decade. To trace the origins of this schism and put it into context, we must go back 20 years to the 1830s, when Romanticism was burgeoning and composers of any hue (whether Mendelssohn and Schumann or Chopin, Berlioz and Liszt) were all seemingly on the same revolutionary side, though for some it was a case of yesterday's revolutionaries becoming today's conservatives. No better example of the converse can be found than Beethoven, the classical composer turned revolutionary progressive, whose music neither dated nor became conservative with the passage of time. On the contrary, the late piano sonatas and string quartets are as tough for today's audiences and performers as they were almost two centuries ago.

---

[1] Emil Klitzsch in *NZfM*, Vol. 42 No. 26 (22 June 1855), 273.

Mendelssohn died in 1847, Chopin in 1849; Schumann had been forced to resign his editorship of *NZfM* when he moved to Düsseldorf in 1844, losing control of a vital conduit for disseminating his views, while Berlioz in the 1850s was constantly seeking a platform for his music. Only Liszt soldiered on with his struggle to secure performances of his music. Gradually he accrued allies, among them his piano pupils, the next generation of keyboard virtuosi, some of them composers. There were his supporters in the musical press, Franz Brendel (Schumann's successor as editor of *NZfM* in Leipzig for 23 years until his death in 1868), Richard Pohl (in Weimar) and Hans von Bronsart (writing anti-Hiller diatribes in *Das Echo*), but the vastly influential Eduard Hanslick (1825–1904), who took the side of the classical traditionalists, stood up to them all and gave as good as he got. This schism in the press defined two schools of composers, each taking a position on one side or the other of the divide. Many of them were wary of causing offence, so they trod a safe path during the decade of the 1850s. This situation continued to the end of the century with Bruckner a prime example of a composer who proved to be easy prey of a critic such as Hanslick, who was for 40 years (1855–95) the chief music critic of the Vienna-based *Neue Freie Presse*. In 1854 Liszt founded the New Weimar Association, which served as a counterweight to the loosely organised Leipzig-based conservative institutions of Gewandhaus and Conservatoire. Even the Saxon capital of Dresden eventually buried the hatchet with Leipzig and, in order to defeat the Weimar progressives, joined forces when one of Mendelssohn's torch bearers, Julius Rietz, took over in 1860. There were also some strange players in the drama who were either wandering between the two camps (Ferdinand David), crossing over and back (Joseph Joachim), or withdrawing from the fray to take a neutral stance (Joachim Raff). Most composers eventually had to be pragmatic and go whichever way the wind blew. Performance and publication of their music was paramount, whatever the cost, for whereas Mendelssohn and Schumann could afford a varying degree of success as symphonists, thanks to their highly successful achievements in other musical genres, most could not.

The issue of the symphonic poem seems to have been the principal inhibitor of classical symphonic production during the 1850s. Colours had to be nailed to the mast, especially after Hanslick's attacks in *Vom musikalischen Schönen* in 1854, followed by further onslaughts on Liszt's *Faust* symphony in 1857 and his (then six) tone poems in 1858. Wagner gave his support in 1857 in an 'Open letter on Liszt's symphonic poems'. Four years earlier, we find the 20-year-old Brahms has entered the fray, at a time when his career was undergoing critical development. He did himself no favours, however, by sleeping through a private performance of Liszt playing his own B minor piano sonata, after which Brahms's alleged exhaustion miraculously vanished as Liszt sight-read the young man's untidy original manuscript of his own Scherzo Op. 4, in the distinctly uncomfortable key of E♭ minor to great acclaim from the assembled company at Liszt's Altenburg home. This occurred in June 1853, after which Brahms went on to spend that autumn with the Schumanns and was hailed by Robert as music's Messiah in a letter to Joachim. This sequence of events led in turn to Schumann's article 'Neue Bahnen' in *NZfM*, which placed an uncomfortably heavy burden of expectation on the young man's shoulders.[2] After Schumann's death, his widow Clara took his place, making a formidable trio with Brahms and Joachim against the New German School. The so-called War of the Romantics was underway.

We take leave of Schumann as a symphonist at the start of the 1850s. Alfred Einstein summarised the importance of Schumann's fourth symphony (1841, revised 1851) thus when he wrote, 'We stand here before a new form of the symphony'.[3] Schumann picked up and developed Kittl's double trio structure in the symphonic *scherzo* in his first (1841) and second symphonies (1846) and in his third piano trio (1851). He also created a principle of thematic unity overarching all the movements in a symphony, namely in his fourth. Its originality therefore lay in its unity, achieved not only by being through-composed, without breaks between its four movements, but also by the use of a *leitmotif* right at the start, which recurs in every movement in some shape or form. Beethoven, in his search for symphonic unity, used a spectacular and uniquely dramatic device, when he recapitulated all the main themes of his ninth symphony in the introduction to its *finale*; Berlioz used an *idée fixe* throughout his *Symphonie fantastique*; but Schumann's fourth is not programmatic (only the first and third symphonies carry titles that steer the listener to Spring and Rhineland imagery respectively). When it comes to his influence on other composers, however, his symphonies (particularly the second and fourth, which were singled out for their unity in construction) took up to 20 years to filter through, the best-known composer to respond being Max Bruch. One aspect of Schumann's style did catch on sooner, however, and that was his predilection for syncopation, soon copied and developed by many composers, particularly in their *scherzo* movements. However, it was the symphonies of Mendelssohn and Spohr that influenced the next generation of symphonists rather than those of Schumann.

After 12 years, and as Schumann departs, it is Franz Lachner who returns in 1851 with his symphonic postscript, his eighth (G minor) and last, given at Leipzig for the first time on 20 January 1853. During the intervening years, Lachner's themes responded more and more to other influences, mainly those of Mendelssohn, Schumann and Schubert, their music now not only more frequently played but with some of the scores readily accessible in the public domain. At 50 bars the slow introduction to Lachner's eighth is substantial, but the orchestration is so dense that the thematic material has to be doubled to penetrate the textures of the accompaniment. In his fifth symphony, *quasi-recitativo* passages from the oboe (see Ex. 2.82, page 62) interrupt the start of the *Allegro* like Beethoven's ninth, but here in the eighth it is the violas who take a gentler approach with what is clearly a vocal line and this already from the second bar (Ex. 5.1). Characteristics of this viola motif (with its upward direction, intermittent triadic intervals and

---

[2] 'New paths'. *NZfM*, Vol. 39 No. 18, 28 October 1853, 185–6.
[3] *Music in the Romantic Era* (London, 1947), 131.

feminine ending) feature in the main theme of the movement when it appears in augmentation played by cellos, basses and bassoons at the start of the *Allegro maestoso* (Ex. 5.2). Lachner's second subject (Ex. 5.3) is typical; it is a theme shaped in two four-bar phrases, a safely familiar feminine construct bringing calm after the *Sturm und Drang* of the principal theme. The first of several fugues (in this case a double fugue) is also based on this theme. The transition to the development is characterised by a passage for solo flute, then oboe, in a dialogue with a more aggressive full orchestral response, recalling the slow movement of Beethoven's fourth piano concerto (see also Lachner's fifth symphony, p. 61, Ex. 2.82). Just before the coda, it is the solo bassoon (an instrument that, in its high register, Lachner favours on more than one occasion in his symphonies) that is given not only a cadenza but also two *ritardandi*, an unusual instruction, as it was in his fifth symphony, for there are only one or two other instances of the music slowing down in the eighth (Ex. 5.4).

Example 5.1   Lachner: Symphony No. 8. First movement, introduction

Example 5.2   Lachner: Symphony No. 8. First movement, principal theme

Example 5.3   Lachner: Symphony No. 8. First movement, second subject

Example 5.4   Lachner: Symphony No. 8. First movement, bassoon cadenza

The start of the slow movement shows little change in style since his earlier symphonies. After a somewhat functional 12-bar introduction, there follows a lengthy passage (briefly strengthened by chords from two each of horns and bassoons) for violas and cellos (both *divisi*) and *pizzicato* double basses (the start of the slow movement of the fifth symphony was also for strings alone but shorter). The shape of the phrasing may appear four-square with cadential half- or full closes every fourth bar, but the music is beautiful and the line of the phrasing tenderly sustained, with strong reminiscences of Schubert, in particular his string quintet (Ex. 5.5), a work already alluded to in Kalliwoda's Symphony No. 6 (see page 39) and Lachner's own Symphony No. 1 (see page 57–8). The movement then proceeds in a more inspired and imaginative way to present the thematic material in variation form, such as running semiquaver patterns in the *pizzicato* strings (Ex. 5.6), the same (but now *arco*) accompanying solo horn (Ex. 5.7), then oboe. It is followed immediately by an extended 38-bar florid passage for solo flute accompanied by just violins and *divisi* violas (Ex. 5.8) until cellos and basses join *pizzicato* for the last bars. Here Lachner broadens and explores his use of orchestral colour and produces music of sustained fine quality. The rollicking *scherzo* (Ex. 5.9) is unashamed Mendelssohn until its second section, where it all stops for a four-part fugue based on the principal material. It is, however, the trio (Ex. 5.10) that is a sheer delight and arguably contains some of the best music in the symphony, even though the shadows of Mendelssohn and Schumann (the first trio from the second symphony) continue to loom large, although the possibility that both composers might themselves have been inspired by Lachner's existing seven symphonies cannot itself be ruled out. Accompanied only by violas, cellos and basses, Lachner's trio is wholly and appropriately for three flutes, with the piccolo having to swap to third flute in an impossible change during a silent *fermata* in the last bar of the *scherzo*. Coming after the elaborate flute solo in the slow movement, it may be deduced that Lachner must have had a fine principal flute in his Munich orchestra. Having scaled the heights with this third movement, the *finale* is something of an anticlimax despite material that might have been penned by Schumann (Ex. 5.11). Lachner's beat-bound bass lines do tend to plod relentlessly on their way, while middle-voice accompanying figures sound commonplace and too predictable in shape and form. This *rondo* may seem humdrum, but it is based on an attractive melody; and while it receives merely token contrapuntal treatment in augmentation (Ex. 5.12), Lachner leaves the best of the symphony to last and sure enough it occurs midway through this finale, when, by a series of complex chromatic sequences and unexpected side-steps, the music undertakes a tortuous journey of 14 bars from G minor to G♭ major, the most inventive foray into chromaticism to be found in the work (Ex. 5.13).

Example 5.5   Lachner: Symphony No. 8. Second movement, bars 13–20

Example 5.6   Lachner: Symphony No. 8. Second movement, variation

Example 5.7   Lachner: Symphony No. 8. Second movement, variation

Example 5.8   Lachner: Symphony No. 8. Second movement, flute solo variation

Example 5.9   Lachner: Symphony No. 8. Third movement, Scherzo

Example 5.10   Lachner: Symphony No. 8. Third movement, Trio

Example 5.11   Lachner: Symphony No. 8. Rondo finale, opening

Example 5.12   Lachner: Symphony No. 8. Rondo finale, theme in augmentation

Example 5.13   Lachner: Symphony No. 8. Rondo finale, chromatic modulation

What, if anything, had Lachner learned in the intervening 12 years between the seventh and eighth symphonies? Steinbeck finds passages of Lisztian thematic transformation, if too blatantly set out.[4] In Liszt's music (by 1851 his orchestral music consisted of the six symphonic poems *Ce qu'on entend sur la montagne, Tasso, Les préludes, Orpheus, Prometheus* and *Mazeppa*) we find regular development with elements growing out of what has gone before. Lachner, on the other hand, laid everything out in paratactic rows (i.e. in phrases following one another with random connection); nothing emerges, instead everything is placed in orderly fashion side by side. Lachner was simply not up to the symphonic task and never really felt comfortable in the genre. His symphonies seem to have run their course at a relatively early stage; he probably peaked with his sixth in 1837, considering Schumann's description of him at that time as 'the most talented and knowledgeable among south-German composers'.[5]

Lachner's eighth in 1851 does not seem to have added much in the way of new ingredients to the mix. Instead, after another gap, this time of 10 years and for another 20 thereafter, he spearheaded a revival of the orchestral suite and produced seven of them. They succeeded because they were shorter, easier to digest and intellectually undemanding of an audience, while Lachner himself seemed more comfortable in a compositional process that used the template of a prescribed form. Occasionally (such as in the central movement, variations and march of the first Suite Op. 113) a movement takes on symphonic proportions (the other three movements here total less than half the work), but generally they are brief and bear familiar titles such as chaconne, prelude, minuet, scherzo, intermezzo, mazurka and waltz, and, but for the *Ball* suite, always give this Simon Sechter-trained composer the opportunity to include at least one fugue in either the first or last movement (Kretschmar acknowledged him as a master of the form – 'his fugues are fresh, powerful, free and full of effect')[6]. As we shall see, Robert Volkmann turned from the symphony to the serenade (Brahms would make the opposite

---

[4] Steinbeck, 133–44.
[5] South-German, i.e. Munich-based. *NZfM*, Vol. 11 No. 5, 16 July 1836, 18.
[6] Kretschmar, Vol. I part ii, 556.

journey), but in the next decade (from 1861) Lachner turned from the symphony to the suite and wrote works that were instantly popular, not only throughout German concert halls but also abroad. Soon after he started to enjoy success with them, his brother Vincenz wrote to the publisher Franz Schott criticising classical symphonies for no longer having the capacity to impress, while new ones were dismissed as music that would not endure. Vincenz felt that, in the suite, his brother had found a milder alternative to the profound demands made upon the listener by Beethoven's symphonies:

> As far as I know, the first suite was indeed performed in Frankfurt and soon every concert organisation will have to perform it, because we are done with symphonies. Unending performances of Beethoven's are just not on, while the other, older ones no longer have any impact. Today's [1863] musical generation does not want to be shaken and stirred to the core. The newer symphonies will not survive (I prophesy Raff's *Prize* Symphony [1861] will share the same fate) and so, given today's obsession with being bent on change, it was a happy thought my brother had of turning to a form from the past, and dressing the old, yet still viable suite in today's style of orchestration.[7]

Another afterthought (after a similar gap of a dozen years of symphonic silence) was Jacques Rosenhain's third symphony (in F *Frühlingsklänge* or 'Sounds of spring'), written in 1856, first performed in Paris under Pasdeloup in 1858 and repeated in Brussels under Fétis the following year. Anton Schindler described a performance of it at Frankfurt under Rosenhain:

> The work has nothing in common with the artificial products of so many other composers of symphonies. Mr Rosenhain characterises his work as *Sounds of Spring*, which suits it perfectly. Strong thematic development, pleasing and occasionally beautiful motifs freshly spun in all four movements reveal an expert craftsman, who, with assured skill, achieves his goal without any scholastic stiffness. The connoisseur can truly enjoy the freedom with which this composer moves, while keeping to the rules. Rosenhain directed his work himself and was fully supported by the orchestra. The auditorium might have preferred to hear a more nerve-shattering opus but nevertheless these artistic "sounds of spring" were not allowed to pass us by without respectful applause.[8]

Another report of the same performance described, with more than a touch of irony, its depiction of silence through the medium of sound:

---

[7] 24 April 1863, quoted in Robert Pascall, 'Lachner spricht echten Suitenton' in Steinbeck, 145.

[8] *Leipziger musikalischen Zeitung* n.d., quoted in Kratt-Harveng, 25.

> We can only be thankful that the management of the museum gave us the third symphony by this talented artist, for in it we got to know a work that merits the highest appreciation. The impression it gave was devoid of all pretensions, clear and simple in Haydn's style. It pleased the listener by depicting the silence of idyllic country life in a work in which one might well while away the time by being absorbed in one's own thoughts.[9]

The three Silesian (Breslau) Franck brothers were extremely well connected. Albert (1809–95), a bookseller and music publisher, was befriended by Chopin, Stephen Heller and Hallé when he moved to Paris; Hermann (1802–55), a renowned musicologist, was acquainted with Goethe, Heine and Wagner; and Eduard (1817–93) became a private composition pupil of Mendelssohn in 1834, aged 17. According to Paul and Andreas Feuchte (Eduard Franck's direct descendants and joint biographers), two of his symphonies are extant, one of which remains unpublished (B♭ Op. 52) but is known to have been performed at Cologne on 26 January 1858.[10] The only one in print (A major Op. 47) was possibly completed in Rome in 1845 but only published in 1882.[11] Two other symphonies (in A minor and G minor) have disappeared without trace, but performances are known to have taken place on 30 November 1846 in Berlin and on 15 May 1852 (in an early incomplete version) and officially on 12 February 1856 in Cologne respectively.[12] Franck's Op. 47 bears the hallmarks of his mid-century times, Mendelssohn, Schumann and Gade being obvious influences, and his chamber music in particular is worthy of revival.[13] Performances of the Symphony in A major are known to have taken place on 9 or 10 May 1882 in Berlin and, later that year, on 26 October under Wilhelm Taubert. Emil Krause discussed the work briefly when reviewing some of Franck's music when it was published in the spring of 1883:[14]

> The symphony is laid out on a large scale and works because of the natural flow of its musical thought and especially its detailed and fine skill in orchestration. The weightiest are the outer movements, while in the middle there is a very beautiful and moving *Adagio* followed by a lively *scherzo* in due contrast. The formal structure of the symphony, as well as its varied motivic content and unified tonal colour effects, all invest the work with especial interest.[15]

---

[9] *Frankfurter Zeitung* n.d., quoted in Kratt-Harveng, 25.

[10] Paul and Andreas Feuchte, *Die Komponisten Eduard Franck und Richard Franck* (Stuttgart, 1993; repr. Leipzig, 2010), 136.

[11] Feuchte, 2nd edn, 128.

[12] Ibid., 150–51.

[13] Wilhelm Altmann in *Cobbett's Cyclopedic Survey of Chamber Music*, 2 vols, Vol. 1 (London, 1929), 429.

[14] Feuchte, 2nd edn, 127–9.

[15] Emil Krause, *Musikalisches Centralblatt*, Leipzig, Vol. 3 No. 15, 12 April 1883, 168ff. quoted in Feuchte, 296–7.

Hoping for further performances, Franck's music tended to lie in his desk drawer only to be published years later, by which time his style was old-fashioned. The A major symphony is a highly attractive work. The hymn-like first movement, from its very start, includes some cruelly stratospheric writing for the first and third horns (Ex. 5.14), a stylistic feature repeated, but this time with the bassoon playing a high-lying, lovely melody (Ex. 5.15), at the start of the second. As with Lachner's eighth, the *scherzo* is the best movement in the symphony, a masterly exercise in syncopation, playing havoc with the ear while attempting to focus the rhythmic patterns within the triple pulse structure (Ex. 5.16). This may have had in mind the hemiolas in the *finale* of Schumann's piano concerto (Ex. 5.17). Even better is the brilliantly constructed trio to which it is coupled, the whole movement a canon on a beautiful melody, two bars separating solo oboe and solo cello (Ex. 5.18), and which, after the repeat of the *scherzo*, reappears for a brief coda, the melody now redistributed between first violins and violas, then between oboe, bassoon, flute and cello. This movement is a gem, but regrettably the *finale* has nothing like such quality. This is Schumann-style music largely textured by endless repeated quaver 'scrubbing' in the strings, a clichéd attempt (by a pianist–composer to whom such patterns were commonplace) to create a sustained, powerful sound effect but which is never one to endear itself to orchestral players. The movement's best feature is once again syncopation, its $^6_4$ metre sounding either as 3×2 or as 2×3 beats and further complicated by tied notes across strong beats.

Example 5.14   Franck: Symphony in A. First movement, opening

Example 5.15   Franck: Symphony in A. Second movement, opening

Example 5.16   Franck: Symphony in A. Third movement, Scherzo

Example 5.17   Schumann: Piano concerto. First movement, second subject

Example 5.18   Franck: Symphony in A. Third movement, Trio, oboe and cello in canon

It is unclear whether or not the words 'componirt 1883' on the title page of the manuscript of Franck's Symphony in B♭ or the date 22 January 1883 at the end, refer to the date of composition or a revision. Like the Symphony in A, the music reads and sounds much earlier and could therefore be a reworking of one in the same key performed under Hiller at Cologne on 26 January 1858. While in places the harmony is more chromatic than the A major symphony, there are stylish similarities between them: a simple chordal first movement; a rollicking *scherzo* in 6/8 (Ex. 5.19) that, at the horns–bassoons fanfare (Ex. 5.20), may well have had Kittl's *Jagd* symphony in mind (Ex. 3.2); and a poignant

Adagio (Ex. 5.21) with hints of the future Bruckner in its melodic intensity, broad phrasing, slow tempo and more advanced harmonic language (Ex. 5.22). The symphony has a better *finale* despite the now-clichéd horn calls (Ex. 5.23). If this symphony really was written in 1883, when Brahms already had two in the repertoire, then it is seriously old-fashioned, except for the *Adagio*, which is more than a match for music written in that year.

Example 5.19   Franck: Symphony in B♭. Second movement, Scherzo

Example 5.20   Franck: Symphony in B♭. Second movement, Scherzo

Example 5.21   Franck: Symphony in B♭. Third movement, opening

Example 5.22   Franck: Symphony in B♭. Third movement, chromatic variation

Example 5.23   Franck: Symphony in B♭. Finale

A good barometer for assessing the condition of the German symphony during the 1850s is a study of the programmes of Leipzig's Gewandhaus concerts, for our purposes beginning at the death of Mendelssohn and ending with the departure of his successor Julius Rietz, in other words from 1848 to 1860. It makes uninspiring reading, and if it was not the 'dead time' that Dahlhaus would have us believe, it was certainly a period when the patient had become seriously ill. Dörffel lists 31 new symphonies performed during those 12 years.[16] It would appear that a certain lack of appetite for them developed there in the latter half of the decade, or Rietz got cold feet, for 22 were played there for the first time 1848–54 but only nine 1855–60:

Leipzig's musical infrastructure was in turmoil during the 1850s. Its leaders were becoming more and more obsessed with their struggle against the New German School, in particular Liszt, three of whose symphonic poems (Nos 10, 11 and 12) were first played during the second half of the decade. Paradoxically, even Leipzig's own operatic activities appeared to defy the city's musical hierarchy, when, like a Trojan horse, Wagner's operas insinuated themselves for the first time into the repertoire from 1853 with productions of *Tannhäuser* and, the following year, *Lohengrin*. This must have taxed the undermanned 56-strong opera orchestra, which had to have seven six-hour rehearsals on its own for *Tannhäuser*.[17]

---

[16] Performance dates from Dörffel, 146.

[17] Johannes Forner, *Die Gewandhauskonzerte zu Leipzig (1781–1981)* (Leipzig, 1981), 98.

Table 5.1   Programmes of Leipzig's Gewandhaus concerts

Gade (3)[18]	(16 January 1851)	(3 March 1853)	(22 October 1857)
Gouvy (3)[19]	(24 January 1850)	(26 January 1854)	(27 November 1856)
Hiller (2)[20]	(15 March 1849)	(15 February 1855)	
Rubinstein (2)[21]	(16 November 1854)	(12 November 1857)	
Spohr (2)[22]	(14 December 1848)	(24 October 1850)	
Taubert (2)[23]	(6 February 1851)	(28 February 1856)	
David[24]	(19 October 1848)		
Dietrich[25]	(14 December 1854)		
Goltermann[26]	(11 December 1851)		
Hermann[27]	(29 January 1852)		
Kufferath[28]	(25 November 1852)		
Lachner[29]	(20 January 1853)		
Lührss[30]	(10 January 1850)		
Mendelssohn[31]	(1 November 1849)		
Pott[32]	(15 December 1853)		

[18] Symphony Nos 4, 5 and 6. The fifth included the first use of a piano *obbligato* part in a symphony.

[19] Louis-Théodore Gouvy (1819–98). Rhenish composer, but lived in Paris 1846–95; he wrote six symphonies, mostly in the style of Mendelssohn.

[20] Ferdinand Hiller (1811–85). Symphony in E minor Op. 67 *Es muss doch Frühling werden* and the unpublished *Im Freien*.

[21] Anton Rubinstein (1829–94). Symphony No. 2 Op. 42 *Ocean* and No. 1 in F Op. 40 respectively.

[22] Symphony Nos 8 and 9.

[23] Wilhelm Taubert (1811–91). Symphony No. 2 in B minor and No. 3 in C minor respectively.

[24] Symphony marking Goethe's centenary and based on his poem 'Verschiedene Empfindungen an einem Platze'.

[25] Albert Dietrich (1829–1908). Noted friend of Schumann and later Brahms. This unpublished symphony is lost.

[26] Georg Goltermann (1824–98). Concert cellist, later music director at Frankfurt Opera.

[27] Friedrich Hermann (1828–1907). Violist and composer.

[28] Ferdinand Kufferath (1818–96). Rhenish musician, lived in Brussels from 1844. His only symphony remains unpublished.

[29] Symphony No. 8 in G minor Op. 100.

[30] Carl Lührss (1824–82). Composer and pedagogue in Berlin. See page 89 for a review of his earlier symphony played in 1845.

[31] This is the posthumous premiere of No. 4 *Italian*. From his death in 1847 to 1860 three symphonies by Mendelssohn were played: No. 2 (3), No. 3 (10) and No. 4 (6), No. 3 retaining its popularity.

[32] August Pott (1806–83), music director at Oldenburg (1832–61).

Table 5.1 continued

Reinecke[33]	(2 December 1858)
Rietz[34]	(18 October 1855)
Schumann[35]	(27 October 1853)
Spindler[36]	(13 December 1849)
Ulrich[37]	(9 March 1854)
Veit[38]	(20 October 1859)
Walter[39]	(6 March 1851)
Wüerst[40]	(10 December 1857)

Meanwhile, the Gewandhaus and the Conservatoire reacted to Mendelssohn's death and the arrival of Liszt and Wagner by withdrawing deep into their shells for the next 30 years, if not for a further 15 until Artur Nikisch took over from Carl Reinecke in 1895 and threw off the shackles as the new century dawned. What became paramount for the guardians of the Mendelssohn Grail was the protection of his cultural legacy. Gade, Rietz and David between them led the musical life until 1860, when Reinecke took over for 35 years. Julius Rietz was at the helm for the bulk of the decade of the 1850s, after which, in 1860, he held a similar post at Dresden, thus stunting any rivalry or competition with its fellow Saxon city Leipzig. Indeed by going to Dresden until his death in 1877, Rietz preserved the tradition of another illustrious forbear, Weber, who had held the post there. In both cities, musical conservatism and a strict adherence to continuity were the first priorities, even if progress in musical culture became a victim of stagnation. As Antje Pieper, in her study of Leipzig's nineteenth-century musical life, has pointed out, 'rather than the artist acquiring independence from previous

---

[33] Symphony No. 1 in A in its first version (revised in 1863 and published in 1864 as Op. 79).

[34] No. 3, which was played six times to 1877, while Nos 1 and 2 received performances between 1844 and 1851.

[35] The definitive version of No. 2 in D minor (1841) published as No. 4, then played every year during the decade except 1855.

[36] Fritz Spindler (1817–1905). Saxon pianist and composer, pedagogue at Dresden.

[37] Hugo Ulrich (1827–72). Silesian composer, wrote three symphonies.

[38] Wenzel Veit (1806–64). Bohemian composer, whose only symphony (E minor, 1859) 'was a notable milestone in the development of the Czech symphonic style' according to Adrienne Simpson in New Grove edition 6, 592.

[39] August Walter (1821–96). Composer from Stuttgart, who became music director at Basel.

[40] Richard Wüerst (1824–81). Prussian pedagogue, critic and composer at Berlin, who wrote three symphonies.

artistic epochs, it was precisely the study of previous masters that produced the contemporary artist'.[41]

Among the composers listed above is the Gewandhaus orchestra's principal violist Friedrich Hermann, whose symphony was performed from the manuscript in 1852, another example of the orchestra encouraging one of its own to compose.[42] It is mentioned in another of Lowell Mason's reports to America. His comments about Hermann's work were prefaced by a summary of the concert as 'inferior to the general average'. The symphony still took centre stage in a programme as 'a principal point of attraction', but on this occasion Hermann's symphony replaced the usual one by Mozart, Beethoven or Mendelssohn, which was hardly to his advantage.

> It did not meet with a very warm reception, though sufficiently so to afford good encouragement to the author and his friends. There is always so much caution and incredulity and sometimes suspicion, envy and jealousy abroad, that the path to fame, even to true merit, is rough and beset with difficulties. ... There were undoubtedly fine points indicating talent, taste and judgement. Its themes were concise and clear and there seemed to be a considerable degree of the effusion of genuine feeling, without dry detail, commonplace thoughts, or tedious repetitions. ... The thoughts were easy, natural and chaste but yet never so striking as to call forth a rapturous or involuntary exclamation of delight or applause. The interest too was well-sustained through the four movements and although we suppose that the critics will not allow to this symphony a higher place than mediocrity, yet the young author may be well contented with the award bestowed, return to his study and try again.[43]

The secret weapon at the disposal of Leipzig's musical hierarchy in its struggle against Liszt was Brahms, but even that became a case of missed opportunity. Schumann's description in the press of Brahms as music's Messiah was his last public utterance; four months later, on 27 February 1854, he made his first suicide attempt. Brahms had first appeared as both pianist and composer at the Gewandhaus on 17 December 1853 in chamber music by Mendelssohn and Mozart, and played his own C major sonata and E♭ minor *scherzo*. The concert was a great success. To show her support and, by implication, confirm that of her incarcerated husband, Clara Schumann played the *Andante* and *scherzo* from Brahms's Sonata Op. 5 on 23 October 1854, while on 10 January 1856 Brahms himself returned to play Beethoven's fourth piano concerto and two solo pieces by Schumann. Brahms then played his own first piano concerto on 27 January 1859

---

[41] *Music and the Making of Middle-Class Culture: A Comparative History of 19th Century Leipzig and Birmingham* (Basingstoke, 2008), 76.

[42] Christian Gottlieb Müller, a violinist, also had several works played; see Chapter 3, footnote 49.

[43] Lowell Mason, 33–4.

under Rietz. This was a work that had preoccupied him for much of the 1850s, first as a sonata for two pianos (movements 1–3, February to April 1854), then with its first movement orchestrated as a symphony (summer 1854) and finally as a concerto for piano (and mention of it will recur). Meanwhile the premiere had been five days earlier in Hanover, but this he had treated as a dress rehearsal for Leipzig, where, and despite high hopes, it proved to be an unmitigated disaster. First, his appearance as a pianist followed in the wake of virtuosic displays by Liszt, von Bülow, Bronsart and Dreyschock, all of them in a league way above and beyond him, but even as a composer Brahms fared no better. The piano concerto, with its troubled genesis, to be or not to be a symphony, was not understood. 'The fiasco with the piano concerto illustrated the situation perfectly; the fundamentally bourgeois public wanted above all to enjoy, not be overwhelmed by problems.'[44] Brahms conducted his A major serenade there on 26 November 1860, but it was another flop (the public was bewildered by a work without violins) and he did not return to Leipzig for 14 years. This was after the triumph of the *German Requiem*, when, in February 1874, he played and conducted there in three concerts in a week. By then these unsuccessful visits to Leipzig in the mid-1850s would nevertheless prove crucial in the genesis of his first symphony two decades later.

Of the 23 composers on the Leipzig list who between them produced 31 new symphonies in the 1850s, several, such as Spohr and Lachner, were coming to the end of their creative lives, while Gade, having peaked with his fourth, continued with his fifth and sixth on his way to an eventual eight. There were of course composers from beyond Germany's borders, such as the Russian Rubinstein, whose *Ocean* symphony had its vogue, while the French were having, what was for them, a relative harvest of plenty (if lightweight) symphonies, one from Bizet, and two each from Saint-Saëns and Gounod, which, apart from one performance years later of the second by Saint-Saëns, did not secure a foothold in the Gewandhaus programmes.[45] There were, however, three German symphonies written in the 1850s that did gain favour with the concert-going public, largely because their composers were held in the highest esteem not just in Leipzig but throughout Germany and because they held high-profile positions within the German musical hierarchy. They were Rietz, Hiller and Reinecke.

A study (based on reports in *Die Signale*) of the most performed symphonic novelties in Germany 1850–75, lists those that received three and more performances in the season. Apart from the season 1851–52, in which *no* symphony achieved that target, Gade's Symphony No. 4 took first place every season in the first half of the decade, generally with four hearings. In 1855–56 it was Rietz's Symphony No. 3, which was also heard four times. That year, three composers took joint second place with three hearings, namely Hiller (in E minor), Gade (No. 3) and Raff. This last was Raff's now lost symphony of

---

[44] Johannes Forner, *Johannes Brahms in Leipzig: Geschichte einer Beziehung* (Leipzig, 1987), 27.

[45] Symphony No. 2 in A minor on 20 February 1879, conducted by the composer.

1854, another post-Berlioz and Schumann example in five movements (*Allegro appassionato*, *Andante*, March, *Scherzo*, Fugue) first heard on 20 April 1855 at Weimar, then twice (the second by ducal command) at Wiesbaden early in 1856.[46] Interestingly Liszt's *Les Préludes* takes first place in 1856–57, after which Rubinstein and Gade share the honours to the end of the decade, with Rietz once again holding second place to five performances of Rubinstein's *Ocean* symphony, with four in 1859–60, but by the mid-1860s it has disappeared from the repertoire.

In 1834 Julius Rietz (1812–77) went to Düsseldorf to assist Mendelssohn, who had recognised his conducting talent. He took over as music director when Mendelssohn went to Leipzig and remained for a dozen years before himself moving to Leipzig (Opera and Conservatoire) in 1847. After Mendelssohn's death and Gade's brief tenure as music director, Rietz held the post with the Gewandhaus orchestra for 10 years in two stints (1848–52 and 1854–60) before finally moving to Dresden. Among his pupils at the Conservatoire were future composers Woldemar Bargiel and Felix Draeseke as well as the conductors Hermann Levi and Otto Dessoff. It was not usual for conducting lessons *per se* to be given at the Conservatoire; instead they were an added supplement to composition or instrumental study. Dessoff, with a career as a conductor ahead of him, also composed. The first movement of a symphony (now lost) was performed at the Leipzig Conservatoire as part of his final examination on 16 November 1853 and again a month later on 18 December at one of the Gewandhaus Conversation Concerts in the presence of the King of Saxony, on both occasions conducted by its composer. Conductors of the day were primarily known as either composers or instrumentalists, including Rietz, who began his career as a cellist in the Royal Theatre in Berlin and encountered Mendelssohn through his older brother Eduard (1802–32).[47] His reputation at Leipzig was largely based on the success of his opera *Der Korsar* on 21 December 1850. Rietz was criticised, usually by Franz Brendel in the *NZfM*, for his conservative programmes, dominated as they were by the Viennese classics, Mendelssohn, Schumann and their followers. On the other hand, he commended Rietz for taking what he acknowledged was a remarkably bold step when he invited Liszt to conduct and von Bülow to play in a concert at the Gewandhaus on 26 February 1857. Rietz conducted the first half, Liszt the second and the programme was as follows:

---

[46] Helene Raff (1864–1942), the composer's daughter and biographer, *Joseph Joachim Raff: ein Lebensbild* Deutsche Musikbücherei Vol. 42 (Regensburg, 1925), 135–6, 140. Grotjahn, 225, mistakenly identifies Raff's symphony as No. 1, but this was not begun until 1859.

[47] Eduard Rietz led the first Berlin performance of *St Matthew Passion* under his friend Mendelssohn. After his premature death at 30, Mendelssohn took the younger Julius under his wing.

Overture: *Hermann und Dorothea*	Schumann
Prayer (*Genoveva*)	Schumann
Adagio and *Rondo* for violin	Vieuxtemps (soloist: Jacob Grün)
[Interval]	
Symphonic poem: *Les Préludes*	Liszt
Duet (*Der fliegende Holländer*)	Wagner
Piano concerto No. 1	Liszt (soloist: Hans von Bülow)
Symphonic poem: *Mazeppa*	Liszt

Brendel described the concert as 'epoch-making, a turning point of significance in the annals of Leipzig's musical life'.[48] A week later Liszt conducted *Tannhäuser* at the Leipzig Opera, so for those Conservatoire pupils who dared to follow the New German School, this was a heady experience, but, as it turned out, somewhat of a 'Prague Spring', for Rietz made no further concessions apart from conducting Liszt's second piano concerto on 16 January 1858. Levi, taken on as a conducting pupil by Rietz while studying piano and composition, was one such youngster whose head was threatening to turn; and a letter from Rietz to his pupil's father, in response to concerns raised by son to father (and forwarded to Rietz) as to whether or not he should complete his course at the Conservatoire, is revealing. He warned of the dangers facing 'young musicians of our time', of how they could be drawn 'by zealous propaganda' into a 'wild, ugly, unruly, inartistic musical atmosphere' and that it took 'strength of character to withstand it'. He believed that Levi junior 'had not yet won through the struggle, that he was not yet clear where the next step would take him, and that his work, as well as containing much that was good and beautiful, also had much that was dark, crude and pessimistic in outlook'. His answer to the question whether Levi should go elsewhere to study was an emphatic 'No. Let us keep your son'.[49] Levi stayed on and completed his final examinations in March 1858, when he accompanied a fellow pupil singing three of his songs, played Beethoven's Piano Sonata Op. 111, and conducted his own Symphony in three movements. These were public events, occasionally attended by royalty and reviewed in the musical press. His symphony demonstrated 'signs of talent and good study, a deep grasp of form and content, all of which was unexpected. Most original was the third movement, whereas the first was highly reminiscent of Schumann'.[50]

Rietz's occupation of the post of music director at the Gewandhaus was an uneasy one. His name had not been among the first choices as Mendelssohn's successor; preferred were the likes of Gade, Sterndale Bennett, Hiller, Kufferath, Lührss, even Schumann.[51] There was also the matter of his conducting post at the

---

[48] *NZfM*, Vol. 10 No. 46, 6 March 1857, 101ff.
[49] Julius Rietz to Dr Benedikt Levi, 1 March 1857, quoted in Frithjof Haas, *Zwischen Brahms und Wagner: der Dirigent Hermann Levi* (Zurich, 1995), 35.
[50] *NZfM*, Vol. 14 No. 48, 2 April 1858, 154.
[51] Dörffel, 139.

Leipzig opera, which put enormous pressure on his workload in the first four-year period at the Gewandhaus. This eased for his second six-year stint in charge of concerts because he resigned from the opera house, but throughout both he was also on the staff at the Conservatoire. Important also was Rietz's relationship with Ferdinand David, a strong-willed musician passionately loyal to Mendelssohn's memory but who found in Rietz a like-minded devotee and so gave him his support. While we have seen that Rietz promoted new symphonies in the first half of the 1850s, if less so in the second, he also used his post to promote his own music. During his tenure he premiered concertos he had written for the violin, the clarinet and the cello, other solo instrumental pieces and his new third symphony.[52] Thanks to Mendelssohn, much of his music was already established in the Gewandhaus repertoire, the most popular being his Concert Overture in A Op. 7, of which 23 performances were given between 1840 and his death in 1877 as well as other overtures and medium-scale choral works. He wrote three symphonies, all of which were performed at the Gewandhaus.[53] The third became popular, was probably published in 1856, its final Leipzig performance given *in memoriam* following the composer's death at Dresden a month earlier.[54] It was dedicated to Moritz Hauptmann 'with love and respect'. Dörffel refers to its 'characteristically musical sensitivity, clarity of thought and compactly finished form'.[55]

The oboe introduces a charming melody above sustained chordal blocks (Ex. 5.24), but the second subject, played by the woodwinds, is more adventurous in its chromaticism (Ex. 5.25). The second movement, in a style occupying territory somewhere between *scherzo* and minuet, contrasts two themes. The first (Ex. 5.26) is lightly textured; the strings play *saltato* (with a springing bow) among ornamental trills and, with carefully judged *ritardandi*, create subtle changes of tempo. The second theme (Ex. 5.27), played by winds over a horn pedal, is more fragmented, the phrases broken by brief rests to create *espressivo* sighs. Like a set of variations following a theme, the music becomes increasingly busy, the note values faster and with frequent changes between minor and major modes. The slow movement (Ex. 5.28) has warmth of line in the first violins above a dense texture of the other strings and again (and particularly with the quaver pulse of the $\frac{3}{8}$ time signature) note values increase to what appears very complex figurations of 32nd and 64th notes. The *finale* (a brisk *rondo*) is an anticlimax, its material uninspiring, sounding merely like a complex technical exercise, which provides neither player nor listener rewarding or memorable moments. It is an uneven work; and once its creator was no longer alive, it vanished from the repertoire,

---

[52] According to Dörffel (145), 24 new symphonies were submitted for consideration in the 1852–53 season.

[53] No. 1 Op. 13 (8 February 1844, 20 January 1848, 30 January 1858), No. 2 Op. 23 (14 January 1847), No. 3 (18 October 1855, 30 October 1856, 28 January 1858, 16 February 1860, 19 December 1867, 11 October 1877).

[54] British Library holding (shelf mark e.286.a) states Leipzig [1856].

[55] Dörffel, 145.

despite being described at least on one occasion as 'confirming my opinion that it occupies one of the top places among the orchestral works of modern times'.[56] Rietz's obituary in the *Musical Times* emphasised the connection he had with both Mendelssohn (personally) and Weber (as one of his successors at Dresden) and that with his death, literally days before retirement, 'a link has been severed which still connected us with a great epoch in the history of the art, ... none could have been found more qualified to perpetuate the influence they had exercised'. With the benefit of a quarter-century hindsight following the third symphony, his compositions were 'characterised less by vigorous originality than by a classical refinement of taste and true musician-like workmanship, and [they] will ... always be heard with pleasure'.[57] Unfortunately that did not prove to be the case.

Example 5.24   Rietz: Symphony No. 3. First movement, opening

Example 5.25   Rietz: Symphony No. 3. First movement, second subject

---

[56]   *Die Signale*, Vol. 14 No. 45 (1856), 516.
[57]   Almost all Rietz's musical autographs were destroyed in Dresden in 1945. See Matthias Wiegandt in *Vergessene Symphonik?*, 40, footnote 12.

Example 5.26   Rietz: Symphony No. 3. Second movement, quasi
                Minuet, opening

Example 5.27   Rietz: Symphony No. 3. Second movement, quasi Trio

Example 5.28   Rietz: Symphony No. 3. Third movement, theme

Throughout his life, Ferdinand Hiller (1811–85), a pupil of both Spohr and Mendelssohn, alone exerted as much influence throughout pre- and post-unified Germany as those in control at the Leipzig Gewandhaus, when it came to securing posts for conductors. He seemed to relish the political intrigues that raged here, there and everywhere; he had his favourites but would drop them immediately at any hint of slight or provocation. As a progressive in his youth, he enjoyed the company of Berlioz, Chopin and Liszt, while his experience was considerably broadened by living and working in Paris and Italy. For the year 1843–44, his conducting career took him to Leipzig to replace the overworked and exhausted Mendelssohn, but the two fell out when Mendelssohn declared himself alarmed 'at the deterioration of the orchestra under Hiller's leadership'.[58] Hiller then went to Dresden, followed later by a move to Düsseldorf as Rietz's successor, from where it was an easy move to Cologne, where he took over from Heinrich Dorn. There he remained for 35 years almost until his death. He treated that post very much as he would have operated had he been in charge at Leipzig, in other words establishing a Conservatoire in the city and running the Gürzenich concerts on the lines of those at the Gewandhaus. It follows, therefore, that Hiller used his post as a power base from which to perform his symphonies, five of them (but it is not known how many different ones are meant) given between 1849 and 1858.[59] As he grew older, so his musical politics and style veered to the conservative camp. Among his pupils were Max Bruch and Friedrich Gernsheim. He was a frequent conductor at the Lower Rhine (choral) festivals (11 at Cologne between 1853 and 1883) but fell out with Liszt, who was preferred over him to conduct the 35th festival at Aachen in 1857.[60] These festivals gave Hiller the opportunity to write large-scale choral works; his five operas failed, but one of his symphonies enjoyed fair success, while another three remained unpublished and are no longer extant. Two were written between 1829 and 1834; his Symphony in G *Im Freien* ('Outdoors') was performed in London under Hiller on 28 June 1852 at a Philharmonic Society concert. Its resemblance to Beethoven's *Pastoral* was obvious, its movements bearing the titles 'In the fields', 'In the valley', 'In the wood' and 'On the mountain'. 'He has equalled his happiest inspiration', the *Musical Times* reported. 'It will readily be acknowledged that the new symphony is a valuable addition to the class of music to which it belongs. ... It was very flatteringly received by the audience.'[61]

Hiller's only published symphony was that in E minor Op. 67, written about 1849 and published by Schott in Mainz about 1860.[62] Rebecca Grotjahn divides symphonic novelties into two categories, those with an initial steep curve of success followed by a short shelf-life and those that took a while to achieve success, became fashionable, and held a more constant place in concert programmes.[63] One such

[58] Todd, *Mendelssohn*, 471.

[59] An index of all performances of symphonies played at concerts given by the Cologne Concert Association between 1840 and 1868 appeared in *AMZ*, Vol. 4 No. 13, 31 March 1869, 100–102.

[60] After Liszt played his first piano concerto, Hiller whistled on his latch key as a signal for his claque to bang their seats in protest. Walker, 419.

[61] *Musical Times*, Vol. 5 No. 99, 1 August 1852, 45.

[62] Exact dates are unknown. Clara [and Robert] Schumann from Dresden: 'We have heard many good things of your new symphony.' Dated 11 April; Sietz suggests 1848, so it could be Op. 67. Reinhold Sietz, *Aus Ferdinand Hillers Briefwechsel (1826–1861)*, Beiträge zur Rheinischen Musikgeschichte Vol. 28 (Cologne, 1958), 75.

[63] Grotjahn, 221–3.

symphony from the latter group was Hiller's Op. 67, which had 21 performances between 1850 and 1875.[64] Grotjahn suggests that some concert managements may have performed it out of respect for, if not fear of, its composer, whose influence was not to be underestimated.[65] The score carries a motto on the title page, 'Es muss doch Frühling werden' ('Spring must surely come'), which ends the first and last stanzas of a poem called *Hoffnung* by Emanuel Geibel (1815–84). The title's *cri de coeur* is resolved in the *finale*, though not before passing through the adversity of dark and wintry gloom of E minor to emerge triumphant into the spring sunshine of E major. The slow second movement is in C major; and though the *scherzo* is in the minor mode of A, its character is cheerful. Neither is the motto in any way a musical *leitmotif* that one encounters throughout the work; rather, as Selmar Bagge described it in his analysis on the symphony's publication in 1865, it is a poetical–musical illustration of the struggle between winter and spring and the final victorious outcome by the latter. Bagge had some positive words, 'pleasant, thoughtful and charming' for the first three movements, but, in his view, the *finale* did not live up to the expectation of the title. There were too many signs of the usual suspects, Mendelssohn, Schumann and Gade, as well as undefined 'other elements', to make it original. He found its best feature was its instrumentation, but there were also moments that certainly pleased, particularly the *scherzo* and trio. Some of the *finale* was likened to Wagner, although Bagge hailed Hiller as an Odysseus resisting that New German's siren call by lashing himself to the Classical–Romantic mast. In his view, the work enriched the symphonic repertoire and would sound impressive in a large hall such as the Redoutensaal in Vienna, for he had already heard a performance in the summer of 1864 at the Lower Rhine Music Festival in Cologne's Gürzenich.[66] Liszt conducted it at Weimar on 14 January 1852.[67] He also wrote to its composer that he was looking forward to hearing it under his direction at the same Festival to be held at Düsseldorf in 1855.[68]

The two subjects in the first movement make a stark contrast. The opening ('menacing winter' according to Bagge) is marked a fiery *con fuoco* and has the energy and rhythmic shape yet to be encountered (1888) in *Don Juan* by Richard Strauss (Ex. 5.29), while the second subject is a total contrast with the chorale-like woodwinds (Ex. 5.30), varied immediately by the strings and a florid accompaniment. Both examples have in common a unifying five-note semiquaver motif (Ex. 5.29 bar 3, Ex. 5.30 bars 4 and 8). The development is mainly based

---

[64] It held joint 17th place in the 20 most often performed new symphonies (novelties) in the period 1850–75, as reported in *Die Signale*. Grotjahn, 215–16.

[65] Ibid., 223–4.

[66] *Allgemeine musikalische Zeitung neue Folge* ('new series'; henceforth *AMZ (nF)*), Vol. 3 No. 32, 9 August 1865, cols 521–8.

[67] Walker, 287.

[68] 'Je suis charmé d'entendre exécuter sous votre direction "Es muss doch Frühling werden"' – Sietz, 107.

upon the opening interval of the rising seventh and groups of four semiquavers. Textures tend towards excessive density at loud dynamics, while persistent dotted rhythms create a sense of melodrama. The *Adagio* has moments of beauty (Ex. 5.31), but why the cellos' parallel fifths at the start remind Bagge of the opening of Beethoven's *Waldstein* piano sonata Op. 53 is a mystery; the key and intervals may be the same, but we hear none of Beethoven's agitated quavers. If anything, the score bears more similarity to a slow movement from a late sonata or string quartet, as the variations and accompaniments become increasingly more complex (Ex. 5.32) and challenging for the strings.

Example 5.29   Hiller: Symphony in E minor. First movement, opening

Example 5.30   Hiller: Symphony in E minor. First movement, second subject

Example 5.31   Hiller: Symphony in E minor. Second movement, main theme

Example 5.32   Hiller: Symphony in E minor. Second movement, variation

The *scherzo* (Ex. 5.33) is pure Mendelssohn: shimmering strings, *pizzicato* or *staccato* fairy footsteps and puckish interjections from the solo clarinet, further evidence of the impact his incidental music to *A Midsummer Night's Dream* made on so many composers who followed in his wake. Its trio (Ex. 5.34) juxtaposes the *scherzo*'s *pizzicato* theme in the strings against woodwind and horn chords tied across the barlines. The repeat of the *scherzo* is shorter by 110 bars, and written out because there are some subtle changes of scoring, including at the start the third horn's tricky doubling of the violins' *pizzicato* descending and ascending *arpeggio* passage (Ex. 5.33 bars 1–5), followed by another statement by bassoon doubling the violas. Hiller briefly revisits the trio in the 32-bar coda, while the final bars (Ex. 5.35) make a witty sign-off. All too predictably the *finale* disappoints. There is much huffing and puffing from the outset in loud *unisono* scoring and dense homophonous textures of the first subject (Ex. 5.36), followed by a second that takes the extreme opposite in its leanness (Ex. 5.37). Hiller takes no risks; and, apart from three passages of half a dozen bars each in $\frac{6}{8}$ rather than $\frac{9}{8}$, there is nothing out of the ordinary in this movement, including its virtual lack of counterpoint and chromatic harmony. Spring may have come by the *finale*, but it was hardly worth the wait. Hiller's obituary in the *Musical Times*, written in 1885, two years after the death of Wagner, sums him up as

> essentially a master of the classical school, [who] could write music faultless in construction and marked by all possible technical skill. His works, however, lacked the qualities by means of which genius gives vitality to its creations. They were often "dry" – [a] fatal fault, for which nothing can atone. Nevertheless, they showed distinguished merits, which musicians, at least, could recognise and appreciate. Hiller, in the records of his art, will stand high among the *dii minores*, and even within the shadow of the throne of genius – not the loftiest place, but one worth gaining.[69]

---

[69] *Musical Times*, Vol. 26 No. 508, 1 June 1885, 337.

Example 5.33   Hiller: Symphony in E minor. Third movement, Scherzo

Example 5.34   Hiller: Symphony in E minor. Third movement, Trio

Example 5.35   Hiller: Symphony in E minor. Third movement, Coda

Example 5.36   Hiller: Symphony in E minor. Finale, opening

Example 5.37   Hiller: Symphony in E minor. Finale, second theme

Hiller was a fine pianist, but so was Rietz's successor at Leipzig, Carl Reinecke (1824–1910). He was renowned in particular for his playing of the concertos of Mozart and Beethoven. Initially his career was that of a touring concert pianist, but once established at Leipzig, where, like Hiller in Cologne, he stayed in the post for 35 years from 1860, he also became an eminent pedagogue. Of the 288 published works bearing his name, most were salon pieces for piano, many of them specifically written for children; indeed in his autobiography he accurately predicted that his music would not endure for long, 'perhaps with the exception of those pieces which I have written for the young'.⁷⁰ Reinecke seems to have gone through several periods of self-doubt in his twenties, and he consigned at least one symphony to the fire. Unfortunately it is far from clear whether symphonies referred to in his memoirs are one and the same or different, as keys are not always identified. A symphony written in 1848 was lost, though Reinecke recalled that he used 'its *scherzo*, which had stayed fairly secure in my memory, in my Symphony in A Op. 79'.⁷¹ This latter work was written in 1858, when he was music director at Barmen, today a district of Wuppertal. The lost symphony may have been performed during his two-year stay at Bremen 1849–51, for he recalled that 'as one who had never been tried and tested as an orchestral composer I was to be envied, because the management of private concerts accepted my Symphony in A minor, first begun in Copenhagen. It was performed on 5 February 1850'.⁷² His next sojourn was for three years at Cologne, 1851–54. There he wrote,

> among other larger works by me, a symphony, an overture *Hamlet* and a concert overture. The symphony was performed in Cologne, Schumann conducted the overtures in Dresden. … All three works no longer exist. In a moment of huge, pessimistic self-doubt, I must have destroyed them; at least I do remember that later I took one of the main ideas from the symphony, which had stayed with me, and adapted it for my piano quintet Op. 83.⁷³

None of these symphonies was printed until 1864, when a final version of No. 1 Op. 79 was published by Breitkopf & Härtel (Leipzig).⁷⁴ It was his concert overture *Dame Kobold* Op. 51 that brought him to the public's attention as a composer at Barmen (20 January 1855), after which Rietz conducted it at a Gewandhaus concert on 12 October 1856 and again a year later.⁷⁵ His recollections refer briefly to what became his first published symphony:

> From time to time I travelled to Leipzig [from Barmen], not only to hear a Gewandhaus concert but also to study the orchestra's excellent achievements. I did not want to run the all-too-easy risk of self-satisfaction with the average standard of my orchestra. On one such occasion, Rietz conducted my A major symphony on 2 December 1858, written in Barmen, and it still gives me pleasure today [1902] to read this [1864] review. "First of all, if we question the historical context of this symphony, where it belongs, the answer must be that it neither follows dogmatically the classical symphonic models of the Viennese masters,

---

⁷⁰ Reinecke, 187.
⁷¹ Ibid., 69.
⁷² Ibid., 75.
⁷³ Ibid., 86.
⁷⁴ Ibid., 101–2.
⁷⁵ Dörffel, Statistik, 53. Rietz also had initial success with his concert overture Op. 7 at the same venue on 13 February 1840.

nor, which appears obvious in Reinecke's case, is it in any way influenced by current aims, that music, even at the cost of its own essence, must either express a worded content or serve as an illustration of an historical personality.[76] But in certain details in the means of musical expression, he does occasionally show his dependence upon the newer masters, Schubert, Mendelssohn and Schumann, without following blindly in the footsteps of any one of them. He is not moved by the great breadth and many repetitions of Schubert, his themes do not have the lyricism of Mendelssohn, nor is he tempted to copy the mannerisms of Schumann's new harmonic relationships or incomprehensible rhythmic distortions. As a result, we believe he is able to express a certain independence and do not want this to cast the smallest demerit upon him". This judgement weakens once and for all the stereotypical assertion that I imitated Mendelssohn and Schumann too much.[77]

This review concludes that a symphony needs to withstand the passage of time and therefore have certain basic ingredients, such as counterpoint, but that on the whole this work has enough interesting material to give food for thought and to please the public and critical musicians alike. Selmar Bagge had reviewed a performance of it a year earlier on 23 October 1863 and greeted the chance of hearing a new work in the symphonic genre with relief ('a real comfort'), even if it was one that was conceived with Beethoven as its model. He described a very warm reception from a grateful public and praised it to the skies, singling out its content, scoring, logical construction and melodious themes. Nevertheless Bagge, who had an aversion to both chromatic harmony and loud, brassy (in other words Wagnerian) orchestration, criticised each movement in turn but without objectivity and merely reflected his own personal taste. What precluded greater success for Reinecke's first symphony, which is a good work, was the first performance a month later on 12 November 1863 of Volkmann's first symphony, which is a far better one.

Paradoxically Reinecke was satisfied that the review of this symphony had distanced him from the influences of Mendelssohn and Schumann (he should also have mentioned Gade), whereas in fact it was precisely those three composers who seemed to inspire him to produce his best music. One should also mention his influence in turn upon the 20-year-old Bruch, who by 1858 had left Cologne (where, among others, Reinecke taught him) and made the obligatory move to Leipzig. There he continued with lessons from Reinecke, whose slow introduction to his first symphony (Ex. 5.38) has resonances in Bruch's own first a decade later in 1868. The main material for Reinecke's opening movement is a rather mundane first subject (Ex. 5.39) recalling Schumann's in D minor, but a much more attractive

---

[76] Ironically Reinecke's second symphony Op. 134 (1875) would be a portrait of the tenth-century Norwegian king Haakon Jarl.

[77] Reinecke, 101–2.

second (Ex. 5.40) follows, played quietly by the strings. His scoring is often too typical of nineteenth-century reinforcement of sound by recourse to doubling winds and strings, in this instance oboe and violins, but he also creates an unusually novel effect by bringing forward accents, quaver by quaver in successive bars in a passage for cellos (Ex. 5.41). The *Andante* introduces trombones for the first time (they feature only in the second and fourth movements to fill out textures) and the cellos are divided (Ex. 5.42). Later, however, this melody is given full rein in a solo trio of horn, violin and upper cellos, under which more complex rhythmic accompaniments (Beethoven) are kept discreetly in the background (Ex. 5.43).

Example 5.38   Reinecke: Symphony No. 1. First movement, slow introduction

Example 5.39   Reinecke: Symphony No. 1. First movement, first subject

Example 5.40   Reinecke: Symphony No. 1. First movement, second subject

Example 5.41   Reinecke: Symphony No. 1. Shifting accents for lower strings

Example 5.42   Reinecke: Symphony No. 1. Second movement, opening

Example 5.43   Reinecke: Symphony No. 1. Second movement, variation

The C major *scherzo* could be an Irish jig, or a Scottish reel with its drone-like bare fifths, but there is also a clever distortion of the rhythm here. For eight bars, the accented first beats (*sfp*) sound to the ear like an anacrusis or upbeat, but, just as the listener has got used to hearing that pattern, in the second group of four bars the composer confuses the ear by switching the accent to the second beat of the bar (Ex. 5.44).[78] The trio (Ex. 5.45) is slower and dreamy, with muted, divided first violins drifting in thirds above sustained fifths and *pizzicato* chords, the cellos once again divided to give a fuller texture. Shortly before the movement ends, there is a brief *cadenza* for solo clarinet (Ex. 5.46) followed by a quiet signing-off by the orchestra. This six-bar phrase then reappears immediately as the introduction to the *finale* (Ex. 5.47), again in the clarinet, the first two bars totally alone, which was probably a first for a symphonic *finale*. What follows is regrettably another anticlimax due to material that is superficial and largely unmemorable. A conductor seeking to revive or even premiere this and other such symphonies may be tempted by the positives, even excellence, of the first three movements but is likely to be repeatedly disappointed by a weak *finale*.

---

[78]   The *scherzo* in Franck's Symphony in A plays the same trick. See Ex. 5.16.

Example 5.44   Reinecke: Symphony No. 1. Third movement, Scherzo

Example 5.45   Reinecke: Symphony No. 1. Third movement, Trio

Example 5.46   Reinecke: Symphony No. 1. Third movement, Coda with quasi cadenza for clarinet

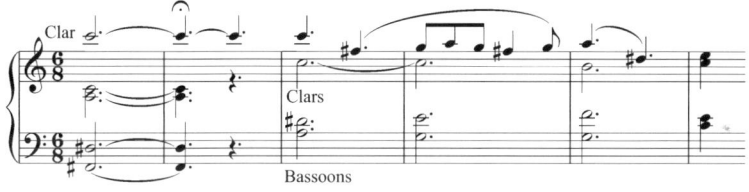

Example 5.47   Reinecke: Symphony No. 1. Third movement Cadenza linking to Finale

Elsewhere there were more symphonies to be heard on occasion, but they acquired neither popularity with audiences nor public awareness beyond the place where their composer lived and worked. Written by conductors, these works reflect the relative insignificance of the provincial posts that their composers held and, of course, they were never published. Among them were symphonies by Ferdinand Breunung (Aachen), Theodor Schneider (Chemnitz), Max Seifriz (Löwenberg) and Leopold Damrosch (Breslau), all of whose works were primarily intended for performance in their concert seasons, in effect written to order (*Gebrauchsmusik*) as demanded of them by their aristocratic or civic paymasters.[79]

The decade of the 1850s proved to be neither memorable nor significant as far as symphonies were concerned. The best emerged right at its start, Schumann's *Rhenish*, after which Rietz, Hiller and Reinecke managed at least to keep the genre alive, albeit with uneven works. The next 15 years, however, would prove far more productive as the green shoots of symphonic change and development began to appear.

---

[79]   Grotjahn, 217.

Chapter 6
The German Symphony in the 1860s

Ours is a poor time for new symphonies.[1]

Despite the pessimism of the quote above, by the end of the 1860s symphonic green shoots were beginning to show and to take a firmer hold than those sporadic instances that had marked the previous three decades. By 1869 Joachim Raff had produced his first two, Max Bruch his first, shortly followed by Albert Dietrich (we must discount all three men's youthful attempts if only because they are no longer extant). It is also clear that composers, having reached a mature age (their 30s or 40s), were then prepared to take the symphonic path. What is more, they did so despite their awareness of all Liszt's symphonic poems and his *Faust* symphony, works that had dominated the previous decade and were now being promoted by his followers as a viable alternative to the strict Classical format. In the orchestral field, Brahms had written just two serenades and the first piano concerto by 1860, while his attempts at a first symphony over two decades were neither ready for public consumption nor available for scrutiny by most of his colleagues. With the premieres of two of Wagner's operas (*Die Meistersinger* and *Tristan und Isolde*) and his first music drama (*Das Rheingold*) in the second half of the decade, German music was generally beginning to wake up.[2] Meanwhile Volkmann, Raff and Bruch, as guardians of the symphonic flame, were its principal movers and shakers. Farther east, composers of symphonies in the 1860s include at least four Russians with their first essays in the genre – Balakirev, Borodin, Rimsky-Korsakov and Tchaikovsky – while in 1863 Rubinstein was revising his *Ocean* symphony. Dvořák wrote his first two in 1865, but neither (nor indeed the next three) has found a secure place in the repertoire, while in England the first stirrings of a revival came with Sterndale Bennett's eighth (1863–64, revised 1867). British and Scandinavian composers who had studied at Leipzig now contributed symphonies, Sullivan with his *Irish* in 1863 (first performed 1869), the year Frederic Cowen wrote the first of his six. The ever-productive Gade, whose seventh appeared in 1865, was now joined by fellow Scandinavians Grieg (1863) and Svendsen (1865–67).

The repercussions of events in Germany after the revolution between July 1848 and February 1849 were reflected in the emigration figures a dozen years later. Although the industrial revolution elsewhere (particularly North America) had become an attractive prospect to those seeking to better themselves, emigration from Germany had dwindled to 50,000 by 1848, half that earlier in the decade.

---

[1] *Die Signale*, Vol. 26 No. 15, 21 February 1868, 229.
[2] *Tristan und Isolde* (1865), *Die Meistersinger* (1868) and *Das Rheingold* (1869).

After 1848 [emigration] soared once more, running at a steady average of more than 250,000 a year throughout the 1850s. These emigrants were the best of their race – the adventurous, the independent, men who might have made Germany a free and civilized country. They, the best Germans, showed their opinion of Germany by leaving it for ever.[3]

One of the consequences of the failure of liberal organisations to consolidate their initial success in the summer of 1848 was the rise of nationalism, which took hold during the 1850s and 1860s. 'As it grew in the nineteenth century, music was both a mirror and a lamp; it reflected the development of nations and it illuminated and heated that development from within.'[4] At least one musician, Wagner, did return, and although German Romantic music before him was not explicitly nationalistic, in other ways it fitted in with the general Romantic current, which was distinctly nationalist.

Liberalism and conservatism occupied a secondary place in the minds of the leaders of thought, and either could have marched hand in hand with nationalism, but the battle fought in German history between 1848 and 1871 would decide which it was to be. From intoxicated youth to sober old age, nationalism was in the air.[5]

Mention has frequently been made of symphonists whose names have barely survived but whose works merit mention for keeping the genre alive, even if they impressed only fleetingly in their own day. Georg Vierling (1820–1901), Johann Joseph Abert (1832–1915), Woldemar Bargiel (1828–97) and Carl Reinthaler (1822–96), who all enjoyed short-lived recognition, are four such composers. Georg Vierling's Symphony in C was performed at Leipzig (9 December 1869), having had its premiere in Berlin a year earlier (14 December 1868).[6] This work was briefly *à la mode* in 1869 and 1870, but its Classical roots (it has the spirit of Beethoven's eighth) and conventional format did not offer much in the way of progress. At the time, Vierling was approaching his 50th year, so his 'slow but logically developing nature, the result of the maturity of his years, brought to the symphony the best, most fully developed artistic production, bearing the stamp of complete mastery of all the material'.[7] This same reviewer's optimism that, as it had made such a good impression on its first hearing and with so many orchestras in Germany, the symphony would soon be published, was regrettably misplaced.

---

[3] A.J.P. Taylor, *The Course of German History* (London, 1945), 94.

[4] Tim Blanning, *The Triumph of Music: The Rise of Composers, Musicians and their Art* (Cambridge, MA, 2008), 298.

[5] Marshall Dill, *Germany: A Modern History* (Ann Arbor, MI, 1961), 102.

[6] Georg Vierling was based in Berlin. He composed choral works but also one symphony.

[7] *LAMZ*, Vol. 3 No. 49, 2 December 1868, col. 390.

Robert Eitner, writing in a Berlin music paper, prefaced his analysis of Vierling's symphony with flowery language for the symphonic challenge in Germany in 1869, but nevertheless they were familiar words that could have been written at any time during the previous 30 years. If it took a Raphael to paint the hardest yet most beautiful of challenges, namely a Madonna, similarly it took a Beethoven to write a symphony. Many were called, but few were chosen. Eitner, who believed that melody in a symphony should only be present in diluted quantities, observed that most composers found the task too daunting, so they took the safer path of the symphonic poem or the formulaic, shorter, less challenging suite or serenade. Eitner took a strange view of the symphony, misjudged the future of this one by Vierling, praised Mendelssohn's *Scottish* to excess, and implied that counterpoint is a feature of Schubert's ninth, which is not the case, as Tovey points out:[8]

> Vierling's genuine artistic temperament has kept him on the straight and narrow as he scaled the rocky heights of Parnassus with a symphony written in the best fashion, and which is now sent out into the world to fight its own battle for survival, like so many other important ones. No musical work of art offers so little substance to material pleasure as the symphony, and the reason lies in the form itself ... for the symphony is the embodiment of contrapuntal craftsmanship and not the outpouring of sentimental, melodic feeling. There is only one such work of art that, to a greater extent, gives more emphasis to the melodic element and that is Mendelssohn's A minor symphony; I say in part, for to do so from beginning to end would be out of the question else, like many others, it would have fallen into oblivion long ago. The greatest melodist, Franz Schubert himself, restrained his powers of invention in his C major symphony and, with true artistic instinct, created a beautiful symmetry between both melody and counterpoint.[9]

Similarly we find that Johann Joseph Abert's *Columbus* symphony (1864) had a limited shelf-life.[10] His problem would become Raff's, that neither public nor critic could place him in either the 'programmatic' or the 'abstract' camp, because this symphony was built on a programme within a Classical structure. Ironically, given its title, it lacked the instinct to rise to the challenge of exploring new territory that drove Columbus himself, although, to be fair to the composer, the subject matter is more a portrait of the sea and the relationship between a sailor and the elements than it is of the man himself.[11] Abert was a pupil of Johann Kittl

---

[8] 'By good luck almost unique in Schubert's short career, he lost interest in this project before he had written nine bars of it ... the dingy little fugue subject was struck out before the answer had well begun.' See D.F. Tovey, *Essays in Musical Analysis* Vol. 1 'Symphonies' (London, 1935), 211.

[9] *Neue Berliner Musikzeitung*, Vol. 23 No. 49, 2 December 1869, 390.

[10] Johann Joseph Abert was a Bohemian-born composer based at Stuttgart.

[11] Its full title is 'A musical portrait of the sea in the form of a symphony'.

at Prague, and wrote seven symphonies between 1851 and 1894, three of them with programmatic titles and all of them written in deference to Beethoven.[12]

Woldemar Bargiel, half-brother of Clara Schumann, studied in Leipzig's heyday of the 1840s, after which (in 1859) Hiller called him to Cologne as a theory teacher until he went to Rotterdam in 1865. His final move (in 1874) was to the Music Academy in Berlin as one of the leaders of the composition class. His one symphony (in C Op. 30, written in 1864) is an attractive, eclectic work with Haydn, Mozart and Beethoven as its role models. In its first movement we hear the persistent rhythm of the last-named's *Egmont* overture or the first-movement motto of his fifth symphony, while the *Andante*, with its divided cello melody, recalls his brother-in-law Schumann's fourth. We then go back to a pre-*scherzo Menuetto* in which, after its double bar, horns quote the four-note opening of the last movement of Mozart's *Jupiter* symphony, while the trio is based on the traditional horn call (see also Ex. 2.68, the trio in Burgmüller's second symphony orchestrated by Schumann). The *Allegro molto* finally brings the work more up to date, its interplay within instrumental families, syncopations and repeats made the more effective by switching between major and minor modes, giving an occasional anticipatory glimpse of Brahms, whom Bargiel befriended. The Symphony in C was published in 1866, but its scoring was revised in 1880. While acknowledging that 'themes and figures met elsewhere could be heard', it was nevertheless praised by two critics after its first performance for 'avoiding banality and [for] adhering to classical principles in the great scheme of the symphonic style'.[13] 'His themes have focus, their development is of the highest quality; in short he is a fine contrapuntist and musician. The orchestra played it with virtuosity and evident love, the public gave it a friendly reception but the composer deserved even greater recognition.'[14]

One suspects that the public, rather than the critic, got it right. Bargiel finds a place in Fuller Maitland's series *Masters of Contemporary Music* written at the end of the century, though it bodes ill to read the view that yesterday's revolutionary is today's reactionary: 'It is always the followers of the innovators, never the innovators themselves, who undergo this transition from living enthusiasms to dry-as-dust formulae.' In this instance Bargiel admired Beethoven and then Schumann, but this adulation 'during his early life gradually changed into a more or less cold and academic habit of mind and work'. Maitland identified teaching as having been an immediate blight upon his career prospects as a composer, for his 'own compositions have failed to make a very deep or permanent mark upon the art of his time'. Of the symphony itself, Fuller Maitland took the view that it 'suffers from a certain triviality in the thematic material, and a want of originality in its treatment. The working out of his subjects seems often to be done in an almost perfunctory way, as if from a sense of duty to the composer's pupils, rather

---

[12] Hermann Abert, *Johann Joseph Abert: sein Leben und seine Werke* (Leipzig, 1916), 163–88.
[13] Leipzig, 23 March 1865.
[14] *AMZ (nF)*, Vol. 3 No. 13, 29 March 1865, cols 221–2.

than in obedience to any impulse of genius'.[15] This is an interesting development, for symphonies that formerly ticked the boxes for competition judges were now doing so for a composer's own pupils.

The year 1863 was a significant turning point as far as the fortunes of the symphony were concerned. In June of that year, as a preamble to a review of Carl Reinthaler's Symphony in D Op. 12, this critic described how matters currently stood for the genre:

> Has the symphony made "progress" since Beethoven? Has the form of this genre been extended – as far as content is concerned, has something greater or more meaningful been created in the same way that one can say that Beethoven did in relation to Mozart? All things considered and taking into account all the subjectively new and therefore epoch-making compositions of Schubert, Mendelssohn and Schumann, the answer must be "No". Has music experienced any kind of transformation thanks to these three composers, as a result of which it is impossible to return to the sounds and means of expression of those former masters whom Beethoven, in his earliest symphonies, had to follow? This is really the burning question of today and one has to doubt the fate of every work that attempts to resist historical facts. Our whole way of feeling and musical style has changed at the same time. The expert scorns neither the idyllic nor the robust, expressed so perfectly and beautifully in earlier musical works; in fact he even prefers it to the vague or exciting romanticism of our time – but only where it emerges through new thinking and means of expression does it seem to him, after all that he has experienced, to lay claim to greater inner feeling. Where this is not the case we have epigonism, of which Mendelssohn and Schumann are unjustly accused as a way of thanking them for producing something really new and at the same time beautiful and significant. How can you tell the difference between what is really new and what is merely pale imitation? The answer is that the former gives rise to a school whereas the latter remains a dead end. So, Mendelssohn and Schumann established schools, for little is written these days that does not seem influenced in many ways by the methods of one or both of these composers. We must count [Reinthaler's] symphony as belonging to the latter category. Its roots lie in Beethoven's D major symphony [No. 2] and in his first creative period; its branches and leaves have little inner relationship with the music of the present day and only in some external details, particularly orchestration, do they reveal a more modern composer.[16]

Despite this dismissal, Reinthaler's symphony was generally welcomed by the press. It ruffled no feathers. While the content of the first movement (as pointed out by the critic above) clearly models itself on Beethoven's early second symphony (Ex. 6.1) in its clean-cut lines, the *Andante* (Ex. 6.2) is music of charming lyricism: both the *scherzo* and trio (Exx 6.3 and 6.4) make a feature of the rhythmic patterns

---

[15] See John A. Fuller Maitland, *Masters of German Music* (London, 1894), 210–15.
[16] *AMZ (nF)*, Vol. 1 No. 23, 3 June 1863, cols 401–2.

in the bass line, while the *finale* (Exx 6.5 and 6.6) is a simple slow–quick coupling, the textures thickly scored for full orchestra, the lower strings busy from the start. The addition of trombones and piccolo in this last movement was considered superfluous, giving nothing more than an overpowering, strident quality, merely for the sake of effect. This did not, however, detract elsewhere from purity of sound and lively rhythms, which pleased the public at a time when new works capable of making such a positive impression were lacking. As this dearth meant forever hearing the old favourites, so Reinthaler's work, which made no serious demands upon player or listener, was accepted without question in concert halls. In January 1872 the composer conducted it at Bremen, where he was the city's music director, and it received an ovation from both public and orchestra. Its 'plastic clarity of form, easy graceful handling of the finest details and masterly scoring, has earned the work a place among modern symphonic compositions and therefore will hopefully continue to be heard at other artistic venues in Germany'.[17]

Example 6.1   Reinthaler: Symphony in D. First movement, opening

Example 6.2   Reinthaler: Symphony in D. Second movement, opening

[17]   *AMZ*, Vol. 7 No. 8, 21 February 1872, col. 132.

Example 6.3   Reinthaler: Symphony in D. Third movement, Scherzo

Example 6.4   Reinthaler: Symphony in D. Third movement, Trio

Example 6.5   Reinthaler: Symphony in D. Finale, slow introduction

Example 6.6   Reinthaler: Symphony in D. Finale

While the four composers Vierling, Abert, Bargiel and Reinthaler have remained in relative obscurity for the past century and a half, from among German composers of symphonies during the 1860s, another four stand head and shoulders above the rest, namely Robert Volkmann, Max Bruch, Joseph Joachim Raff and Albert Dietrich.

Robert Volkmann (1815–1883) was born near Meissen in Saxony and his musical education was received largely in Leipzig during the latter part of the 1830s, just at the time when Mendelssohn was exerting enormous influence over young composers who studied there. It was also where Volkmann met Schumann, whose music he admired, but it was to Pesth in Austro-Hungary that he moved in 1841. He achieved only moderate success as a composer until his Piano Trio in B♭ minor (1850) was taken up by both Liszt and Hans von Bülow. As a result his reputation spread further afield, though it was the elusive but final acceptance by nearby Vienna that confirmed his status as a composer. In 1854 he moved there, but he could never assimilate himself into the city's infamous web of musical–political intrigues and by 1858 he had returned to Pesth, where he remained for the rest of his life. He was fortunate in being taken up by the publisher Gustav Heckenast, who provided him with a salaried contract for 13 years between 1857 and 1870 when the firm closed. It was possibly the end of this association that caused a waning of Volkmann's creative powers, for he produced little music during the last 15 years of his life and instead became professor of harmony and counterpoint at the Music Academy in Budapest, newly founded by Liszt and Erkel. As a composer, Volkmann managed to steer a safe passage through the treacherous waters of musical thought in post-1850 Germany; and despite his decision to join the Classical traditionalists, his music was admired by Wagner, while Liszt too was very encouraging. Volkmann also became a close friend of Brahms, who spoke highly of his orchestral music where it mattered in Vienna, while Volkmann reciprocated in Pesth, where he was an equally influential figure in the city's musical life for a quarter of a century. Apart from failed attempts in opera or oratorio, Volkmann's musical output covers most genres, but it was in the 1860s that he wrote his two symphonies. The first even appeared in miniature score about 1910, a reflection on the greater and longer-lasting renown that his name enjoyed during the last century, at least until the First World War.[18] Volkmann's obituary described him as 'one of the most genuine and reliable composers of our day, whose name will live forever as long as his Symphony in D minor ... [is] counted among music's treasures'.[19]

Volkmann's two symphonies were written in 1862 (No. 1 in D minor) and 1864 (No. 2 in B♭ major) respectively, and in both he followed the established format of the last three decades of the eighteenth century. Kretschmar notes that the first movement of the first symphony has 'a direct spiritual relationship to [Beethoven's] powerful ninth'.[20] The opening five-note motto (Ex. 6.7) is found throughout the first movement, its character defined by several elements, namely orchestration (full strings), harmony (unison), articulation (accents on all articulated notes), playing style (*pesante*), dynamics (*forte*), and typical *Sturm und Drang* indications such as *Allegro* (tempo) and *patetico* (mood). This last designation appears in Beethoven's Piano Sonata Op. 13 (*Pathétique*, 1799) and Tchaikovsky's sixth symphony (1893). More striking still is the similarity to the eight-note motto that starts Borodin's second symphony (1869–76) (Ex. 6.8). Borodin could well have heard the Russian premiere of Volkmann's symphony in Moscow in 1864. There are moments in Volkmann's fine first symphony (the second is decidedly

---

[18] Eulenburg Editions (Leipzig) lists his overture to *Richard III* (part of incidental music to the play), the Serenade for Strings in D minor, several chamber works and Symphony No. 1 in D minor Op. 44.

[19] E.W. Fritsch in *Musikalisches Wochenblatt*, Vol. XIV No. 46, Leipzig, 8 November 1883, 573.

[20] Kretschmar, Vol. I part ii, 605.

weaker and was accordingly less successful) that clearly influenced other emerging composers during the 1860s, such as the pedal point that occurs at the appearance of the first subject following the 24-bar introduction. Volkmann establishes one in the cellos and basses for 35 bars (Ex. 6.9); and despite some uneasy clashes in places, its harmonic language is admirably uncompromising as well as unexpected (Exx 6.10 and 6.11). Another pedal point of similar length (36 bars) occurs, after Volkmann's symphony was written, at the conclusion of the third movement of the *German Requiem*. However, it is a device that Brahms had used before, for 10 bars at the start of his Piano Concerto No. 1 in D minor Op. 15 (1854–58, published 1861) and for 27 bars in the opening movement of his Serenade No. 1 in D minor Op. 11 (1858), in all of which works coincidentally the pedal sits on the tonic D. Volkmann likes the device, for he also lays one on the dominant C under the thematic material of the second subject (Ex. 6.12). Although not marked as such, the implication is that the tempo would become more measured at this point, particularly given the subsequent return of the motto marked *tempo primo*. This is also the case in the development, where the syncopation would become frenetic unless a slightly broader speed is adopted (Ex. 6.13). The similarity to the emerging symphonies by Bruckner is striking in two features. The first is the rhythmic shape (2 + 3 crotchets) of Volkmann's first subject in its third bar, which, albeit in a more rugged and muscular context rather than *con espressione*, Bruckner came to make his own. The second is the *tremolando* accompaniment in the strings. Both feature in Bruckner's fourth symphony (1874–81) (Ex. 6.14), by which time Volkmann's first symphony was frequently played. During the 1860s, the music of Volkmann, Bruckner and Brahms was heard in Austro-Germany, though performances of Bruckner's works were comparatively rare and received with more scepticism than those by either Volkmann or Brahms. Bruckner uses the terraced dynamics of piston-selected organ stops in his orchestration, while Volkmann has no such starting point. Bruckner's sense of architecture drives the inner rhythmic energy and pulse of his music; Volkmann achieves this only sporadically. The strength of this first movement lies in its sense of drama; there are hints of the overture to Mozart's *Don Giovanni*, also in D minor. Volkmann, at the recapitulation of the opening motto, adds timpani to full brass but extends its roll by three beats, while Mozart does so (bass instruments) by a beat in the second bar of the overture. General weaknesses tend to lie in Volkmann's overkill of the *arpeggio* and passage work that borders on the pedestrian, but the counterpoint in the coda makes a welcome relief and there are some extraordinary harmonic sequences to sustain the listener's attention in the opening movement.

Example 6.7   Volkmann: Symphony No. 1. First movement, opening

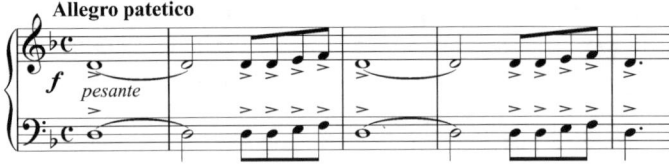

Example 6.8   Borodin: Symphony No. 2. First movement, opening

Example 6.9   Volkmann: Symphony No. 1. First movement, pedal point

Example 6.10   Volkmann: Symphony No. 1. First movement, bars 71–4

Example 6.11   Volkmann: Symphony No. 1. First movement, bars 80–83

Example 6.12   Volkmann: Symphony No. 1. First movement, second pedal point

Example 6.13   Volkmann: Symphony No. 1. First movement, development, bars 122–8

Example 6.14   Bruckner: Symphony No. 4. First movement, rhythmic motif

After a brief introduction for bassoon and strings in the slow movement, we hear a remarkable 41-bar *cantando* passage for clarinet (ending with a mini-cadenza) accompanied by a tread of *pizzicato* crotchets (Ex. 6.15), like the *Romanze* in Schumann's fourth symphony (yet another in D minor). As far as melody is concerned, Volkmann is not in the same league as his near-contemporary Bruch, who would probably have scored it above a featherbed of soft string texture and so avoid Volkmann's arid miscalculation in choosing *pizzicato*. If homage to Schumann was in Volkmann's mind (Ex. 6.16), Brahms made a better fist of it

20 years later in his third symphony (Ex. 6.17). Developing the strings' opening bars, Volkmann avoids totally enfeebling the movement with sentimentality by introducing a second theme, more agitated, textures gradually thickening, leading to a Beethoven-style climax. There follows an effective winding-down over 28 bars (Ex. 6.18) of chromatic progression with an internal pedal C on an *ostinato* for a pair of horns, which must have impressed Kretschmar, who went into raptures in describing it as 'an exceptionally mysterious moment, like Siegmund's depth of despair in the first act of *Die Walküre* when he calls ['Nothung!'] to his fellow Wälsungen'.[21] As the emotional intensity subsides, the two themes are redistributed within the orchestra, accompanied by more elaborate rhythmic shapes.

Example 6.15   Volkmann: Symphony No. 1. Second movement, introduction

Example 6.16   Schumann: Symphony No. 4. Second movement, opening

Example 6.17   Brahms: Symphony No. 3. Second movement, opening

[21] Ibid., Vol. I part ii, 606.

Example 6.18   Volkmann Symphony No. 1. Second movement, pedal point

The third movement is a conventional *scherzo* followed by a slower trio in the major key, the whole repeated with a faster coda. Its time signature of 3/2 has a precedent in 'Seid umschlungen, Millionen' (the *finale* of Beethoven's ninth), but the similarity lies only in the contrapuntal nature of its treatment. Volkmann follows the examples of Franck and Reinecke with the syncopated rhythmic shape of his main theme with its three-note anacrusis, strong first-beat accent and final *sforzando* (Ex. 6.19). Kretschmar refers to the contrapuntal version of the main theme as 'reliving the spirit and method of the old North German School'.[22] Tovey also points out 'one of the finest pieces of ecclesiastical polyphony since Bach', namely Schumann's *Rhenish*, in which the fourth movement doubles the speed at bar 23 to a 3/2 time signature.[23] The marking *cantando* returns in the trio's expressive, rising chromatic *Ländler*-style theme, one that, in its repeated motivic rhythm, also echoes the *Rhenish scherzo* (Exx 6.20 and 6.21). As a contrapuntist Volkmann rises to all challenges, while the fragmentation of his instrumental textures and his ability to dismantle and then reconstruct the rhythmic elements produces the best music of the symphony. Before long, such subtle shifts in rhythm will appear in Brahms's *Liebeslieder Walzer* (1868).

Example 6.19   Volkmann Symphony No. 1. Third movement, Scherzo

---

[22] Ibid., Vol. I part ii, 607.
[23] Tovey, Vol. 2 'Symphonies', 55.

Example 6.20   Volkmann Symphony No. 1. Third movement, Trio

Example 6.21   Schumann: Symphony No. 3. Third movement, Scherzo

The last movement is a jubilant affair recalling the explosive start of the *finale* of the *Rhenish*, its fully scored chordal energy driven hard by accents and *staccato* articulation (Ex. 6.22), after which Volkmann soon embarks on a variety of impressive contrapuntal exercises. There is a muscular drive to the instrumental scoring and textures, but the music's overall rhythmic structure has a lack of clarity, in which a sense of pulse is neutralised. Notably there are passages that hint at the later Brahms. Particularly striking is the similarity to Volkmann's first symphony in the development of the first movement of Brahms's fourth, both sharing similar accented canonic patterns (Exx 6.23 and 6.24). Once again, the final *Presto* has a distinctly Russian flavour, though this time the music anticipates Tchaikovsky's fourth rather more than anything by Borodin.

Example 6.22   Volkmann: Symphony No. 1. Finale, opening

Example 6.23   Brahms: Symphony No. 4. First movement, development

Example 6.24   Volkmann: Symphony No. 1. Finale, development (canon)

Matthias Falke estimates that Volkmann's first symphony was performed about twice per month for its first 12 years (1863–75) and ranks 12th among the 20 most oft-performed symphonies in the period 1850–75, despite its composition being only midway.[24] Bagge, writing from Leipzig, described its first performance on 12 November 1863 as expertly 'conducted with heart and soul by Reinecke as if he himself had written it'. He was also delighted that, with one work, 'which sustained its weight of pathos by the simplest of musical means', Volkmann had fulfilled hopes that he would become one of the most significant composers of the period.[25] A week later he resumed his praise of this 'new symphony, universally applauded by conductor, leader, the whole orchestra and the critics representing the various periodicals', so we can perhaps assume that this was discerning rather than indiscriminate applause. He concluded:

> Volkmann's symphony is a product of Beethoven and Schumann, with an added splash of Berlioz's manner [its energy?]. On the whole we regard it, despite all its weaknesses, as one of the most significant works of the present day. We see in this symphony as a whole, and repeat, that it manifests required greatness of style without becoming tasteless in more than just a few passages. It does not swim in a fog of nice-sounding homophony, nor does it consist of worn-out harmonic material, but it is complex in its counterpoint and everywhere has the self-contained unity of form of the masters – and must therefore be regarded, compared to variously dubious, sickly or weak compositions of our day, as an effective antidote.[26]

Volkmann's first symphony is undoubtedly a persuasive work, written at a time when composers could be forgiven for their noticeable reluctance to produce new symphonies. For years the press had been discouraging; in fact it is puzzling that critics took such an attitude with a new symphony, while at the same time approving it. They were good at dampening spirits, as this review of Volkmann's published second symphony shows, although it is admittedly an inferior work compared to his first:

---

[24]   Falke, 159.
[25]   *AMZ (nF)*, Vol. 1 No. 47, 18 November 1863, cols 798–9.
[26]   *AMZ (nF)*, Vol. 1 No. 48, 25 November 1863, col. 805ff.

A new symphony by Volkmann, after the first in D minor, should make us really curious. Is he not one of the few among our current artistic generation who dares to write a symphony, whereas other people, if they write for orchestra at all, are content to produce suites and serenades and suchlike? Is it not strange that a composer living in Hungary, far from his native Saxon homeland, can succeed in such a difficult task and thereby uphold the honour and dignity of orchestral music? ... We are convinced that, in Beethoven, the symphony reached its high point in spiritual and technical quality. Yet it pleases us when the best talents of today test their wings even in this difficult form and at least manage to create something interesting and pretty.[27]

Volkmann may have been put off by this review, for this second symphony proved to be his last, after which he turned to composing the very suites and serenades so disparaged by the writer. The patronising attitude of the press to new symphonies is symptomatic of the pessimism that prevailed during the 1850s and persisted through much of the decade of the 1860s, until Brahms's first finally appeared in 1876. 'One can imagine how Reinthaler and Volkmann must have felt, having the symphonic deck not only stacked against them in this way but shuffled in their very faces.'[28] Volkmann's first symphony was immediately popular with the public and, although adjudged here as the first of four significant new symphonies by emerging German composers in the 1860s, it should also be remembered that Reinecke's first symphony (1858, described earlier) was revised in 1863 and published in 1864, effectively becoming a fifth. It too went on to enjoy great popularity and was performed throughout the country. However, the next man of the moment with a first symphony that immediately scored a success was Joseph Joachim Raff (1822–82). In 1875, with six symphonies published and a further five to come, Ebenezer Prout described Raff as one of three first-rate German composers who stood head and shoulders above their fellow countrymen, the other two being Wagner and Brahms. Prout dismissed most new symphonies written at this time as heard once, then consigned to oblivion.

The best point that strikes the student of these symphonies is their individuality. They possess, it is true, that family likeness which shows them to be productions of the same brain ... [Raff's] ideas are by no means of equal merit but at all events the well never runs dry and inexhaustible fluency seems to be one of the composer's striking characteristics ... I have no hesitation in saying that since Beethoven nobody has equalled Raff in the absolute mastery of thematic treatment. By his skill in this respect, he frequently succeeds in constructing an interesting movement out of the most unpromising material; and when, in addition, he has been happy in the choice of themes, he produces music worthy

---

[27] *LAMZ*, Vol. 2 No. 10, 6 March 1867, 80.
[28] Walter Frisch, *Brahms: The Four Symphonies* (New Haven, CT, 2003), 12.

to rank with the masterpieces of our art. No less remarkable ... is his complete command of counterpoint.[29]

By the end of the century (18 years after Raff's death) the wheel had turned full circle and most opinions of Raff were uncomplimentary. One was more equivocal and concluded that, 'if Raff in the last analysis lacked genius, its stern simplicity and perfect coherence, he nevertheless ... wrote with so much spontaneity and sensuous beauty and decked out his ideas in so attractive a garment, that he must be admitted to an honourable place among those composers who fall just short of the highest rank'.[30] Raff's music had a good reception in England, despite Shaw's dismissive description of him as 'a cuckoo composer of nineteenth century music'.[31] Parry, writing in 1889, gave an honest appraisal of his symphonic output:

> The ease and speed with which he wrote and the readiness with which he could call up a certain kind of genial and often very attractive ideas, both interfered with the concentration necessary for developing a closely-knit and compact work of art. His ideas are clearly defined and very intelligible and have much poetical sentiment; and these facts, together with a very notable mastery of orchestral resource and feeling for colour, have ensured his works great success; but there is too little self-restraint and concentration both in the general outline and in the statement of details and too little self-criticism in the choice of subject-matter to admit the works to the highest rank among symphonies. In the broadest outlines he generally conformed to the principles of the earlier masters, distributing his *Allegros*, slow movements, *scherzos* and *finales*, according to precedent. And, allowing for the laxity above referred to, the models which he followed in the internal structure of the movements are the familiar types of Haydn, Mozart and Beethoven. His *finales* are usually the most irregular, at times amounting almost to fantasias; but even this, as already described, is in conformity with tendencies which are noticeable even in the golden age of symphonic art. Taken as a whole, Raff's work in the department of symphony is the best representative of a characteristic class of composition of modern times – the class in which the actual ideas and general colour and sentiment are nearly everything, while their development and the value of the artistic side of structure are reduced to a minimum.[32]

---

[29] See Ebenezer Prout, 'Raff's symphonies' in *The Academy*, Vol. 7, 10 April 1875, 386–8.
[30] Daniel Gregory Mason, *Raff, Masters in Music* Vol. 1 part 6 (Boston, MA, 1903), 11.
[31] George Bernard Shaw, *Shaw's Music* (ed. Dan H. Laurence), 3 vols, Vol. 1 (London, 1981), 269.
[32] Parry, 40.

Franz Gehring credited Raff with a 'conscientious striving towards a very high ideal', and believed that 'in the whole of his published symphonies the slow movements are, without a single exception, of extreme melodic beauty, although weak from a symphonic point of view'. At the other extreme, 'the *scherzo*s are as a rule weak, and the *finale*s without exception boisterous and indeed vulgar. Writing here, as ever, for an uneducated public, Raff has forgotten that for a symphony to descend from a high tone is for it to be unworthy of the name'.[33]

Raff's career was blighted by bad luck and compromise. Mendelssohn was so impressed by his musicianship that he negotiated the publication of some piano compositions for him; but no sooner had Raff made plans to study with him, than they were forestalled by Mendelssohn's unexpected death in 1847. Three years later, Raff had completely switched his musical allegiance and went to Weimar to become Liszt's secretary, copyist and orchestrator, in particular of the early symphonic poems, but this relationship proved short lived. A book written in 1853, in which he was critical of Wagner, eventually alienated him from many composers, performers and critics, and it took many years to restore his reputation and reassess his significance, particularly regarding his contribution to the genre of the symphony.[34] He was criticised about the programmatic elements contained in some of his 11 symphonies, for only Nos 2 and 4 have no motto, title or literary programme. He therefore seemed to fall between two stools and finally pleased nobody. Ultimately he was dismissed as a *Vielschreiber*, for having written too many works like Reinecke, whose opus numbers also exceed two hundred.[35] According to the singer and conductor Georg Henschel, Brahms said of Raff, 'He isn't happy unless he composes for a certain number of hours each day and on top of that he writes out his orchestral parts himself'.[36] The unpublished five-movement symphony (1854) (see pages 168–9) no longer exists, but its last two movements were reshaped for his first orchestral suite (1863). Raff's 11 symphonies bear opus numbers from 96 to 214, so he already had much published music to his credit by the time he began writing them. That was in 1859, when marriage took him to Wiesbaden, where he lived until 1877, then to Frankfurt to head the Hoch Conservatoire until his death five years later. He was not an epigone but an eclectic, who was one of the most skilled German symphonists at work in the third quarter of the nineteenth century.

Raff was 37 when he began his first symphony *An das Vaterland* ('To the Fatherland') in the late summer of 1859, after the Treaty of Villafranca was signed between Austria and France, ending the Second Italian War of Independence, and it took most of the following year to complete the work. Despite falling midway between the failed upheavals of 1848 and unification in 1871, it does not share

---

[33] Franz Gehring, 'Raff' in *Grove* edition 4, Vol. 4, 64–5.

[34] Joseph Joachim Raff, *Die Wagnerfrage* (Braunschweig, 1854).

[35] Like *Kleinmeister*, another derogatory term in German was *Vielschreiber*, this one applied to prolific composers with high opus numbers to their credit.

[36] Avins, 754.

the patriotism of Wagner's *Kaisermarsch*, nor the political fervour of Brahms's *Triumphlied*, Bruch's *Das Lied vom deutschen Kaiser* or Raff's own *Deutschlands Auferstehung* ('Germany's resurrection'), despite the overt message of the symphony's preface and its movement headings. Like Lachner's fifth (1835), it already existed when it was entered in a symphony competition at Vienna in April 1861. From 32 entries, Raff's and one by Albert Becker (in G minor, composed 1858) were chosen for performance, whereupon Raff's was proclaimed the winner.[37] It was a bold move to have five movements once again, after the models of Beethoven, Berlioz, Schumann and Raff's own lost work. The possible question of whether or not its inspiration was driven by patriotism is undermined by the late addition of descriptions prefacing the movements, which were made public only the day before the competition. This happened because one of the judges complained about Raff's use of Gustav Reichardt's (1825) melody 'Was ist des Deutschen Vaterland?', composed for the (1813) poem by Ernst Moritz Arndt and still popular in 1861.[38] Only then did Raff add his descriptions to the score, which Hiller confirmed were not made known to him or his fellow judges. Raff's daughter Helene revealed more in her biography of her father:

> The first three movements are supposed to show German life and existence, the fourth describes German disunity and, alluding to Reichardt's melody, Raff himself added: "Here the composer felt himself permitted the use of a motif (not original) as a symbol". The fifth movement begins with a lament on the destiny of greater Germany and then proceeds to develop prophetic visions of future unity and majesty.[39]

Although it would be contrary to Raff's wishes to do so, ignoring the prefaces as set out in the first symphony would improve it at least as far as the fourth movement and Reichardt's tune, for at this point, with the brass section in full cry, it can justly stand accused of bombast. Yet seen in the context of pre-unified Germany, one can understand the call for national union of the greater states of Germany (Prussia, Swabia, the Rhineland, Bavaria, even Switzerland and Austria), and its strong anti-French tone. More than any music by Wagner, which would be hijacked by the Nazis for their own political purposes 50 years later, the way Raff sets Reichardt's melody (even without the help of Arndt's text) conjures up images

---

[37] The judges were the critic Wilhelm Ambros, the conductor Vincenz Lachner and the composers Hiller, Reinecke and Volkmann. Among many artists and critics who attended the second rehearsal was Brahms. The manuscript of Becker's symphony is in Northwestern University Music Library Collection, Evanston, Illinois, USA and bears many coloured pencil markings by a conductor.
[38] Gustav Reichardt (1797–1884); Ernst Moritz Arndt (1769–1860).
[39] Helene Raff, 160–61.

of marching jackboots and the sound of massed male voices.[40] Study of Raff's first symphony identifies significant compositional procedures in the opening bars,

> the most of important of which is a collection of motivic fragments, which, by remaining fragmentary, coalesce into any number of variant forms without ever assuming a primary shape. ... The exposition of the first movement contains, within its 209 bars, at least eight different motivic bits and pieces that are subjected to numerous transformations and combinatorial mutations before beginning the formal development itself. ... The opening fragments do not settle into their ultimate form until the very end of the symphony, thus anticipating not only César Franck by nearly two decades, but also any number of twentieth-century composers and the general technique of perpetual evolution and resolution through ultimate arrival.[41]

The two main themes are very different in character: first there is the optimistic heroism of Liszt in the opening flourish of the first subject (Ex. 6.25), followed by a more introspective second theme (Ex. 6.26). In the development the first subject is treated as a canon simultaneously in augmentation and double augmentation, after which Raff's remarkable contrapuntal skills are tested even further by the intervention of strongly marked fugal episodes (Ex. 6.27).

Example 6.25   Raff: Symphony No. 1. First movement, first subject

---

[40] Each verse begins and ends with the same lines. As an example, this is the first verse:
Was ist des Deutschen Vaterland?
Ist's Preussenland? Ist's Schwabenland?
Ist's wo am Rhein die Rebe blüht?
Ist's wo am Belt die Möwe zieht?
O nein, nein, nein!
Sein Vaterland muss grösser sein!
Sein Vaterland muss grösser sein!
(Note: Rebe is a grape, Möwe a seagull, and Belt is the strait between the main Danish islands of Zealand and Funen.)

[41] Foreword to the score of Raff's Symphony No. 1 published by Musikproduktion Jürgen Höflich (Munich, 2007).

Example 6.26   Raff: Symphony No. 1. First movement, second subject

Example 6.27   Raff: Symphony No. 1. First movement, fugal development

The *scherzo* has an exciting build-up from the initial solo call to the full quartet of French horns (Ex. 6.28) reminiscent of Weber, but, unlike Mendelssohn, Raff uses a heavier hand in this mercurial gallop (Ex. 6.29). It leads seamlessly into the trio, a calmer section predominantly for woodwinds, their melody in thirds doubled (Brahms-style) at the octave for 56 bars (Ex. 6.30) and punctuated by answers from the *pizzicato* strings, giving this movement a bucolic quality.

Example 6.28   Raff: Symphony No. 1. Scherzo, introductory fanfare for horns

Example 6.29   Raff: Symphony No. 1. Second movement, Scherzo

Example 6.30   Raff: Symphony No. 1. Second movement, Trio

Once again images of 'German men [hunting] in a German forest, to the fresh sounds of folksong as [the listener] walks the blessed fields with joyful girls and boys' are best left to one side. In the third movement we hear Raff at his best (Ex.

6.31), lyrical, long-breathed lines and impassioned climaxes recalling the beauties of the slow movement in Beethoven's ninth. Raff wears his heart on his sleeve. There is no holding back as he peppers the score liberally with instructions such as *espressivo cantando*, *espressivo largamente*, *con gran espressione* and *radolcente* (*sic*, from *raddolcire*, meaning to calm down). At heightened climaxes in the first movement there is a call for *vibrato* from the violins, printed twice in the full score (Ex. 6.32), and for the solo cello in the *Larghetto* (Ex. 6.33). Criticism of Raff's music as lacking emotion, or of being shallow because of an obsession with blending old forms, traditions and genres with a programmatic content, is completely without foundation. In many ways, the music benefits precisely from such imposed discipline and logical structure, though it does not follow that his symphonic movements are always sufficiently concise and there are meandering passages that could leave themselves open to the possibility of judicious cuts.[42] On the other hand, this slow movement has an emotional intensity, which, in its intimate moments, is beautifully scored for a solo instrument such as the viola and has both appealing directness and gentle poignancy.[43]

And so to the fourth movement, which in retrospect gave the work its title, and in which, according to the composer's preface, we are expected to hear signs of German disunity dispersed in short motifs, phrases and rhythmic elements, eventually pulled together as Reichardt's uniting theme emerges after several false starts from clarinets, bassoons, violas and cellos. Without wishing to suggest a conspiracy theory at work, panel judge Vincenz Lachner did not appear to recognise this three-note anacrusis from his own brother Franz's *finale* of his fifth symphony, the winning entry for the same competition back in 1835 and the similarity of their main themes (compare Exx 6.34 and 2.80, and Exx 6.35 and 2.83). Raff, through his Weimar association, was an admirer of Berlioz (they met in 1855); and not only does the movement begin with the rhythmic energy of one of the Frenchman's overtures, there also seems to be a subtle quote from the *finale* of the *Symphonie fantastique*. Where Berlioz uses the French horn, Raff uses oboe and clarinet, but in both works the phrase is played over quiet drum rolls (Exx. 6.36 and 6.37). Raff keeps his audience in suspense with snatches of the three-note anacrusis and a 20-bar timpani roll until the arrival of German unity (Ex. 6.35), followed immediately (Ex. 6.38) by a restatement from the brass heavyweights, accompanied by busy strings in passage work recalling the opening of the symphony (Ex. 6.25) and so arrive full circle.

---

[42] Such criticism was evident from the outset in *AMZ* and other German music journals, then taken up by English ones.

[43] Compare the *canto popolare* in Elgar's *In the South* (1904). Raff's music may have impressed Elgar, and also Richard Strauss (*Aus Italien*, 1886 and the *Alpine* Symphony, 1915).

Example 6.31   Raff: Symphony No. 1. Third movement

Example 6.32   Raff: Symphony No. 1. First movement, vibrato in the violins

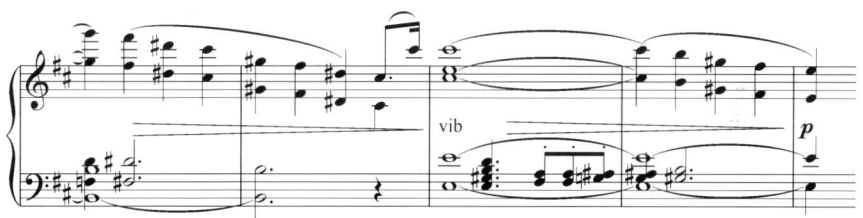

Example 6.33   Raff: Symphony No. 1. Third movement, vibrato for solo cello

Example 6.34   Raff: Symphony No. 1. Fourth movement, main motif

Example 6.35   Raff: Symphony No. 1. Fourth movement, main theme

Example 6.36   Raff: Symphony No. 1. Fourth movement, hints of Berlioz

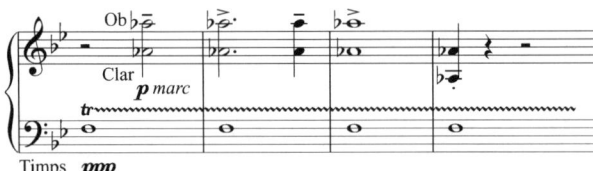

Example 6.37   Berlioz: *Symphonie fantastique*. Finale, introduction

Example 6.38   Raff: Symphony No. 1. Fourth movement, letter B, main theme in the brass

The fourth movement ends too abruptly and could easily have been elided into the *finale*. In three distinct sections divided by linking episodes, it begins with a funeral march led by cellos (Ex. 6.39), then a brass-led chorale (the Gods enter Valhalla followed by a march of Elgarian pomp and circumstance) (Ex. 6.40), while the last could be the *finale* to an early German Romantic opera by Weber, Marschner or Lortzing (Ex. 6.41). Raff's music is bursting with thematic ideas in this, his longest symphony, lasting 70 minutes. A thread-gathering exercise concludes the work with reference to motifs from the first movement and ending with Reichardt's melody. It is remarkable how, apart from a final acceleration in the coda, in many of the 10 symphonies that follow, Raff (like Lachner before him) rarely changes tempo with a *ritardando* nor interrupts with a *fermata*.[44]

Example 6.39   Raff: Symphony No. 1. Finale, opening Funeral March

Example 6.40   Raff: Symphony No. 1. Finale, brass chorale March

Example 6.41   Raff: Symphony No. 1. Finale, main theme

Following Beethoven's example, Raff produces more concise symphonies as a reaction to the longer ones; his second, fourth and sixth are markedly shorter and more compact than the odd-numbered, programmatic first, third and fifth. The second (1866) is an open-hearted, sunny symphony in the bright key of C major, its air of confidence and optimism (perhaps reflecting his competition success) marked by simple triadic thematic ideas dominated by a horn call (Ex. 6.42). The second subject, on the other hand, has lyrical warmth (Brahms) in its setting for strings. The movement follows conventional classical format with a thrilling blaze of brass and timpani to end; Raff certainly knew how to rouse his audience. The slow movement is more introspective, its simple, beautiful melody (Ex. 6.43)

---

[44]   See Chapter 2, page 65.

colourfully scored as each variation develops, the quiet ones displaying Raff's contrapuntal skills. It is in the loud ones, however, that the music is trapped in its own lengthy four-square melody, while ponderous accompaniments and lumpy rhythms (double dots played *ff*) threaten to assault the ear. The swift tempo of the *scherzo* (Ex. 6.44), its cello/bass drone and constantly shifting woodwind accents in the playfully tricky Trio make a brilliant movement, and it is fair to say that Raff writes fine scherzos throughout his symphonic canon.

Example 6.42   Raff: Symphony No. 2. First movement, opening

Example 6.43   Raff: Symphony No. 2. Second movement, opening

Example 6.44   Raff: Symphony No. 2. Third movement, Scherzo

The *finale* has a dramatically loud, octave-driven slow introduction in the manner of Beethoven, somewhat pompous for the jolly, boisterous *Allegro* that follows. Harmonic exploration is not at the heart of Raff's music here; we are always in touching distance of the tonic key, but it is worth pointing out that the technique that Raff adopts of dispersing and reassembling thematic and harmonic shapes, anticipates 'virtually everything we know to be the essence of Tchaikovsky's mature style'. Indeed we know that Tchaikovsky thought highly of Raff, as a symphonist, from when, in 1886, he used his name with which to beat that '"untalented s***! [Brahms]. Why, Raff is a giant by comparison with him" [and later] confirmed his admiration by contributing to Raff's memorial fund'.[45] Nothing demonstrates more flagrantly the connection between the two men than a melody in Raff's tenth symphony, first heard in 1881.[46] It is in its slow movement Elegy (bars 73–6) that we find, first on the bassoon (Ex. 6.45) then the oboe, an ear-opening anticipation of the famous horn solo (Ex. 6.46) in the *Andante* of Tchaikovsky's fifth symphony to come seven years later. Clearly guilty of theft, the Russian took only the second half of Raff's original melody, but, given their mutual admiration, did no worse than follow the precedent, as we have seen, of Borodin's plundering of Volkmann's first symphony at the start of his own second. One would not dream of calling Tchaikovsky an epigone of Raff, or even a plagiarist; somehow in the totality of Tchaikovsky's ultimate achievement with his fifth symphony we view such an accusation as a mark of respect for Raff, whose music clearly must be reassessed.

Example 6.45   Raff: Symphony No. 10. Third movement

Example 6.46   Tchaikovsky: Symphony No. 5. Second movement

In the case of Lachner, there was a gap of 12 years from 1839 to 1851 between his seventh and eighth symphonies and therefore they were described over two chapters. However, because Raff continued to write symphonies without a break and despite having to stray across to the next half-decade, two more of Raff's canon will be dealt with at this point. When first played and published in 1872, his fourth symphony became one of his most successful, although later the third and fifth overshadowed the rest of his symphonic *oeuvre*. This is a pity, because the fourth is a fine work. Written during the Franco-Prussian War, it has a mood of uncertainty (the war's outcome?) at the start (Ex. 6.47), but soon shows a more positive one in the chattering woodwinds' persistent rhythmic articulations

---

[45] Tchaikovsky's diaries, 101 quoted in David Brown, *Tchaikovsky: The Final Years 1885–1893* Vol. 4 (London, 1991), 83.
[46] Symphony No. 10 *Zur Herbstzeit*, 'Autumn' in the season's cycle (Nos 8–11), its revised form in the new slow movement.

(Ex. 6.48).[47] Raff is by now a mature tunesmith and a master of orchestration, with a distinct flavour of folk music rather than overblown nationalism in the melodic simplicity of his music. After a warning E♭ from winds and horns, the duple-time *scherzo* in the symphony bursts forth with powerful energy; and while woodwinds continue their chatter, the strings charge ahead (Ex. 6.49). There is a striking resemblance here to the *scherzo* in Bruch's first symphony (1868) (see Ex. 6.62).

Example 6.47   Raff: Symphony No. 4. First movement, first subject

Example 6.48   Raff: Symphony No. 4. First movement, second subject

Example 6.49   Raff: Symphony No. 4. Second movement, Scherzo

---

[47] 'Dorabella' in Elgar's variations (1899)?

As in the second symphony, the slow movement has a 16-bar melody that is effectively a *chaconne* with 11 variations (Ex. 6.50).[48] In handling variation form, Raff has Beethoven's seventh symphony in his sights, particularly in the grandiose seventh variation, but his presence is felt much more in the introduction to the *finale*. Here a reference to the opening phrase of the work is rejected by the cellos in a *recitativo*, like the beginning of the ninth's *finale* (Ex. 6.51, bars 1–17). This quasi-vocal feature has now been encountered three times, namely in Burgmüller's second, Schnyder von Wartensee's third and now Raff's fourth. Apart from another brief recall of that opening melody before the thrilling coda, Raff refrains from rejecting material from the subsequent movements but instead launches into the *finale* with a duo for flute and oboe bearing the characteristic rhythm and style of a hornpipe (Ex. 6.51 *Vivace*). The coda's excitement lies in its ever-accelerating tempi (*un poco più mosso* followed by *ancora più mosso*), another comparative rarity in Raff's music as already mentioned. The fourth symphony was premiered in Wiesbaden on 8 February 1872 under Wilhelm Jahn, at Frankfurt under Karl Müller on 25 October, and at Leipzig on 31 October under Raff himself.

Example 6.50   Raff: Symphony No. 4. Third movement, theme

Example 6.51   Raff: Symphony No. 4. Finale, introduction

[48] Modelled on Bach's from the *Partita* in D minor for solo violin, BWV1004.

The years 1871–76 were Raff's most productive, with five symphonies.[49] His sixth (D minor Op. 189) was written in the summer of 1873, but, like the fourth's disappearance into the shadow of the third (*Im Walde*), it was overwhelmed by the fifth (*Lenore*). Though not programmatic, the sixth bears an allegorical motto on the title page, describing the struggle of an artist's life, but this one is not as dramatic as Berlioz's *Episode de la vie d'un artiste*, his subtitle for the *Symphonie fantastique*. Raff's consists of three almost alliterative pairings, 'Gelebt, gestrebt; Gelitten, gestritten; Gestorben, umworben'.[50] Leichtling perceives the sixth symphony as constructed from four *scherzo* movements, that there is no slow movement as such, rather a swift-moving funeral march, and that Raff himself saw this work as his most original. 'This is partially borne out by such clues as "the novel construction of the first movement", the "vivid modern cast of the funeral march", the "connection of the last part to the first movement".'[51] With each successive symphony by Raff we encounter music that could have been conceived for set pieces in a ballet. In this instance, the 'oompah' passages in the duple-time *scherzo* could have been a *Trepak* as found in the second act *divertissement* of Tchaikovsky's *Nutcracker* ballet, again linking the two composers. There are also passages taken at breakneck speed that test any principal flute, recalling not only more Berlioz (*Queen Mab scherzo*) but also Mendelssohn (his *scherzo* from *A Midsummer Night's Dream*). It obviously impressed the critics, but then Raff's *scherzo*s usually did and with justification. Whilst reviewers generally dismissed the *scherzo* genre as 'the lightest of all forms', this one also contained counterpoint and surprisingly their praise of it did not please the composer:

> The Berlin papers, with their enthusiasm for a *scherzo*, are only partly correct as this piece was written with the most refined contrapuntal art, proof once and for all that this "lightest of all forms" has a significantly greater capacity than one had thought. Uniquely, the value of this symphony lies mostly in the way the content was determined (which the gentlemen never want to understand), through the relationship of the last part to the first and the way this was laid out.[52]

In Raff's entry in Grove, we read of 'unattractive eclecticism and mixture of styles'.[53] This is too harsh. He has a highly attractive style, which mixes folk tunes, ballet and nationalism, and he is a master of orchestral scoring. However, when it comes to his unashamed borrowings, the view taken in the article is not harsh enough. The third movement of the sixth symphony depicts, as in the *Eroica*, the

---

[49] Helene Raff, 191.
[50] 'Lived, aspired; suffered, strove; died, renowned'.
[51] Avrohom Leichtling's Foreword to the score of Raff's Symphony No. 6 published by Musikproduktion Jürgen Höflich (Munich, 2007).
[52] To his wife Doris, after the Berlin premiere under Wilhelm Taubert on 21 October 1874, quoted in Helene Raff, 200.
[53] Horst Leuchtmann in *Grove* edition 6 (London, 1980), Vol. 15, 534.

lengthy passage of a funeral cortège building to a shattering climax, while at the start of the *finale*, we find, with no explanation (or apology), that Raff blatantly plagiarises, almost note for accented note, the same striking passage that begins Schnyder von Wartensee's third symphony, written a quarter of a century earlier (Exx 6.52 and 6.53).[54]

Example 6.52   Schnyder von Wartensee: Symphony No. 3. First movement, introduction

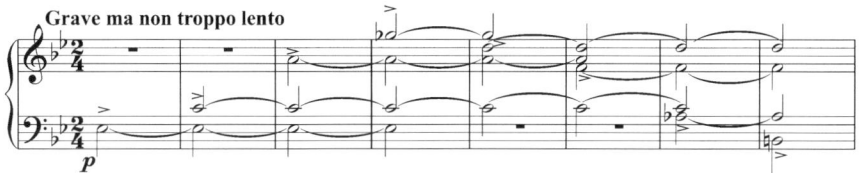

Example 6.53   Raff: Symphony No. 6. Finale, opening

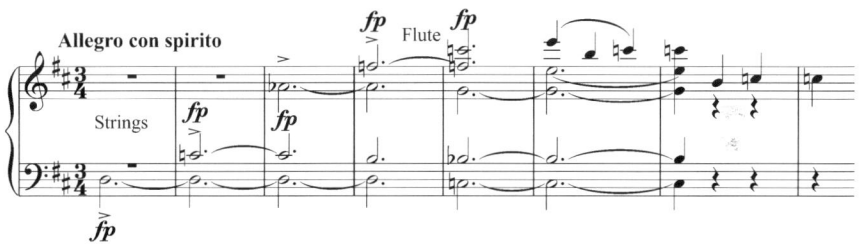

Neither should the accusation of having 'a penchant for salon music, making him susceptible to triviality and sometimes vulgarity' be allowed to stand, at least in the context of his symphonies, for his melodies are more than skin-deep in conception and, far from common-place, highly engaging.[55] Raff decoded the motto of the sixth symphony to Hans von Bülow:

> The struggle itself is nothing less than against negation (suffering and strife) but the artist, rather than fighting with a cudgel or a newspaper article, uses the soul's ideas developed in new manifestations to inspire him. These I wanted to depict as the sublime in the first movement, the humorous in the second, a death knell for the fallen in the third, while the fourth, in no way an apotheosis in the normal sense, instead begins joyously after suffering for the departed, until

---

[54] The common denominator here may be Frankfurt, where Schnyder died in 1868 and Raff in 1882; this is hard to prove, however, as there are no documented performances of Schnyder's symphony between 1851 and 1939.

[55] *Grove 6*, Vol. 15, 534.

humming voices arrive confirming he was not so bad, and the ideas he followed in life were at last praised with daring acclamation.[56]

Is this how Raff saw himself as an artist and, moreover, was that his perception of the fate of his music after his death? There do seem to have been various pockets of resistance, judging by reports of the reception of his symphonies. By his death in 1882, Leipzig had heard his second, third, fourth, fifth and seventh symphonies, but each was played only once. The Leipzig critic at the first performance of his second symphony (the first time one by Raff was played there) suggested that judicious pruning would help the work and the audience, which, being one of the shorter symphonies, did not bode well for the longer ones.[57] Frankfurt's reviewer was very pleased with the fourth when it was performed there at the end of 1872, though curiously it was for its immediate predecessor, which had already been acclaimed by the concert-going public, that he had some harsh words:

> Raff had the tact, or the wisdom, to withdraw the advertised *Im Walde* symphony and instead substitute his newest in G minor. ... We are heartily grateful to him ... that he has given us nothing other than beautiful music, for here, as in all other works by this tireless composer, craftsmanship comes to the fore. The work has such positive characteristics that one might prognosticate it a future, because he has basically stuck to the established classical format.[58]

Farther to the north, in Hamburg, the reviewer of a concert there in February 1875 took the opposite view:

> As much as the *Lenore* symphony roused our delighted applause, so this newly heard work could only engender scant excitement. The motto seems to indicate that Raff has much to tell us and to complain about, but this is not the case. The high opus number by this composer, who in his younger years was much too lavish with his talent, weighs heavily upon this work, for Raff seems to have written himself out. Already the first movement passes by relatively meaninglessly; a wild dance like a Hungarian *Czardas* forms the second and is very effective and attractive, if aesthetically not quite convincing. Suddenly we hear a finely scored but long funeral march and we really have arrived at "died" from the motto, which leaves "renowned'; this is depicted in a somewhat long-winded *Allegro-Finale*. May the composer not produce such routine work again without the spark of inspiration![59]

---

[56] Raff to von Bülow 13 April 1875 in Theodor Müller-Reuter, *Lexicon der deutschen Konzertliteratur* (Leipzig, 1909), 388–9.
[57] *AMZ*, Vol. 4 No. 5, 3 February 1869, col. 39.
[58] *AMZ*, Vol. 7 No. 50, 11 December 1872, col. 804.
[59] *AMZ*, Vol. 10 No. 9, 3 March 1875, col. 141.

If Raff was ahead in the symphonic field for the 1860s and half the 1870s (with competition from others from about 1868), why did his music get such a mixed reception in the concert hall and musical press during his lifetime and then suffer virtual oblivion after his death in 1882? The main reason must be attributed to his vacillation when choosing between the New German and Classical camps. The problem was exacerbated because he *had* been in the former and never joined the latter. By his own choice, he could not, nor would not be pigeon-holed, but the music profession in Germany has always persisted with such labelling.[60] The New Germans (in particular Liszt on a personal level) were more forgiving, but they could afford to be because they were not writing symphonies. Wagner had put paid to that idea by pronouncing its death knell and none of his followers would dare contradict him. Raff did not join the circle that formed around Brahms led by the Viennese critic Eduard Hanslick. Neither was he asked to sign the 1860 Manifesto (Erklärung), drawn up by Brahms and Joachim, which railed against the New Germans and Liszt at Weimar, either when it was prematurely released to the press or when other signatories belatedly joined.[61] Had he been approached, he might have refused despite falling out with Weimar, for many of his symphonies bear the hallmark of the programmatic symphonic poem, within the structure and form of the non-programmatic genre. He did not join the ultra-conservatives based at Leipzig and led by Reinecke, who operated according to the Gospel of Mendelssohn, neither was he a follower of Rietz in the Schumann mould at Dresden, nor was he an acolyte of Hiller at Cologne.

Raff was, therefore, in all senses unique. Rather than relating to any specific programme, most of his symphonies are essays in impressions and feelings, but if they were considered evidence of radical tendencies, then Brahms and his *Tragic* overture must stand similarly accused. Raff seems to have been a rootless square peg in any of the available round holes. Despite living through Germany's most turbulent years yet and despite *An das Vaterland*, he created no Nationalist school, the seeds of which were growing fast elsewhere in Moscow and Prague. For the New Germans he was too reactionary, for the Classicists he was too revolutionary; effectively he was frozen out and became a lone wolf. Ironically his closest musical ally was a man who, by domestic circumstances and not musical philosophy, had also opted to change allegiance. That was Hans von Bülow, but he was primarily a conductor and pianist, not a composer. As far as Raff was concerned, no School was created out of which any disciple could carry his torch. Perhaps that might have happened had he not died from overwork and exhaustion after just five years as head of the Hoch Conservatoire in Frankfurt. He was considered an eclectic and a *Vielschreiber*. While it is true that he studied the music of the previous two centuries and honed his contrapuntal skills by arranging Bach and editing Beethoven, this had been common practice for 30 years and, however formulaic

---

[60] As opera singers in Germany will confirm when discussing their vocal *Fach* even today.
[61] *Berliner Musik-Zeitung Echo*, May 1860.

in essence, it enhanced rather than devalued his symphonies. He excelled at orchestration and largely avoided Germanic dense textures. His melodic inventiveness was boundless, his pacing of tension finely judged. Unlike Brahms, Raff took few risks (though more than Bruch would): his harmonic language never developed and showed no sign that all but the first of his 11 symphonies were written post-*Tristan* (i.e. after 1865). His problems were rooted in a misplaced sense of focus. Instead of producing musical ideas that first captured and then held the attention of his listener, he was too pedantically obsessed with the technique of developing and treating those same ideas, only to find himself restrained within a formulaic straitjacket. He was the best of the symphonists between Beethoven and Brahms in the post-Mendelssohn and Schumann years (1851–76), yet from that very same lofty position his failings seem to have become more exaggerated. As the ultra-conservative Woldemar Bargiel told his half-sister Clara Schumann,

> I am sorry that [as far as his music is concerned] I can no longer feel any sympathy for him. He has learned much, writes brilliantly for orchestra and has great contrapuntal skills but nevertheless everything remains cold and hollow. ... The man is puzzling to me musically. He produces ideas and melodies that appear as if they should tear the soul from the body but one is left with the conviction that their inventor felt absolutely nothing for them; and on top of that, there is this most modern harmonic impurity![62]

Raff (and indeed Lachner) is omitted from the list of 17 composers chosen by Fuller Maitland for his book *Masters of German Music* and that is unjustified, though the reason is probably no more sinister than that he selected only living composers when he wrote it in 1894.[63] One who was selected was Max Bruch.[64] Among the myriad lost 'youth' symphonies of the nineteenth century is one written in 1852 by the 14-year-old Bruch when, as the winner of the Frankfurt-based Mozart Foundation award, he was studying privately with Hiller in Cologne.[65] Two other symphonies, written in 1853 and 1861 respectively, have also not

---

[62] Letter dated 11 January 1879 in Berthold Litzmann, *Clara Schumann: ein Kunstlerleben* 3 vols, Vol. III (Leipzig, 1909), 393.

[63] His selection varies from the obvious to the surprising. While Brahms, Bruch, Goldmark and Rheinberger have their own chapters, Kirchner, Reinecke, Bargiel, Joachim, Clara Schumann, von Herzogenberg, Hofmann, Bruckner, Draeseke, Nicodé, Richard Strauss, Sommer and Kistler are dealt with in groups totalling four chapters.

[64] Max Bruch (1838–1920). Christopher Fifield, *Max Bruch: His Life and Works* (London, 1988, repr. 2005).

[65] The Foundation charged Hiller with 'raising the Mozart-pupil to be an honest musician and composer' – ibid., 21. Bruch's prize-winning string quartet (1852) was discovered in Frankfurt in 2012 and published (ed. Fifield) by Fr. Hofmeister (FH 2994) in 2014. See Ulrike Kienzle, *Neue Töne braucht das Land: die Frankfurter Mozart Stiftung im Wandel der Geschichte 1838–2013* (Frankfurt, 2013), 105–29.

survived.⁶⁶ The first that has, was written in the summer of 1868 and published as Op. 28. By then Bruch had already made his name with chamber music, opera, songs, short choral works and the first violin concerto, on which work alone his fame will forever rest. Writing in such diverse genres was deliberate in order to broaden his experience, but it also brought him success and substantial fame within Germany, in particular the opera *Die Loreley* (Mannheim 1863) and the male-voice cantata *Frithjof* (Aachen 1864). The 1860s were significant years for Bruch in ways he could not possibly have foreseen. The decade not only shaped his career as a professional musician but also established his style for 60 years until his death, by which time changes had outrun him. Indeed he made no attempt to move with the times in the post-*Tristan* era, and his last music (two string quintets and a string octet, 1918–20) could have been written half a century earlier.⁶⁷ Bruch's harmonic language is that of Spohr, Mendelssohn and Schumann, while his resistance to the New Germans remained consistent and unchanging throughout his life. Encouraged by success, Bruch sought a conducting post to consolidate his fame and to programme performances of his own music. In 1865 he was appointed to Coblenz and two years later he moved to Sondershausen (1867–70), both towns fortunate to have the patronage of music-loving royalty. Bruch's concerts at Coblenz attracted musicians including Clara Schumann (who spoke highly of him to Brahms) and Hermann Levi, who encouraged him to write more instrumental music, in particular a violin concerto followed by a symphony. Bruch was a complex and difficult man, broke friendships as fast as he made them, and, as his music was performed less, grew increasingly bitter and disillusioned as time passed him by. While prepared to accept technical advice from colleagues, he was also quick to discard it. While Brahms was enjoying growing success, Bruch felt his admirers deserting him for the composer he himself acknowledged was far greater, so it was sheer bad luck that in 1868, the year of his G minor violin concerto followed by his first symphony, Brahms scored a triumph with the six-movement version (the seventh added the following year) of his *German Requiem*.

Bruch's Symphony No. 1 in E♭ was first performed at Sondershausen on 26 July 1868 under his direction from manuscript score and parts.⁶⁸ Five days before the premiere, a press announcement shows that what turned out to be the first version of the symphony was actually a work in five movements rather than the conventional four.⁶⁹ Another performance took place there three weeks later, the

---

⁶⁶ 15 August 1853: 'Bruch came to me with ... a symphony. [On] 8 September he brought [it] back improved' – Fifield, *Max Bruch*, 21.

⁶⁷ By then (1920) Stravinsky's *Le sacre du printemps* was already seven years old and Schoenberg's *Pierrot Lunaire* eight.

⁶⁸ Haas, *Brahms und Wagner*, 115, incorrectly cites the premiere of Bruch's first symphony as under Levi's direction at Karlsruhe on 20 February 1869 in one of the city's museum concerts.

⁶⁹ *Der Deutsche*, No. 87, 21 July 1868.

press previewing identical details.[70] However, by the time of a third performance (also in Sondershausen, almost a year later on 6 June 1869) it carried the opus number 28, probably indicating that the work had now been published. In this final form the second movement Intermezzo was discarded, but some confusion remains, for contrary to the contents list on the title page, at the point in the score where the *Finale* actually begins is printed 'IV *Finale*'.

21 July 1868	6 June 1869
I *Allegro maestoso*	I *Allegro maestoso*
II Intermezzo (*Andante con moto*)	II *Scherzo*
III *Scherzo*	III *Grave* und *Finale*
IV *Grave*	
V *Allegro guerriero* (*Finale*)	

The version played today is effectively a symphony in three movements, in which the slow movement acts as a substantial slow introduction to the *finale*, but originally, by structuring it in five movements, Bruch was probably following the example of Schumann's *Rhenish*, which also has an 'extra' preceding movement linked to its *finale*. Despite its description as a separate movement, it remained linked by a soft drum roll, not an unprecedented device as linking movements with a sustained note had just occurred in Bruch's own violin concerto following Mendelssohn's example. In June 2001, while guest-conducting in Sondershausen, the author discovered the symphony's discarded Intermezzo movement in the library of the orchestra (still called, as it was in Bruch's day, Das Lohorchester).[71] The material, in a copyist's hand, consists of a *Directionstimme* (the orchestral leader's violin part with instrumental cues), parts for strings, double winds, four horns, two trumpets and timpani, and totals 191 bars. It is in the relatively unusual key of B major, its median D♯ an enharmonic switch from the symphony's tonic key of E♭ major, which was a key relationship favoured by Schubert and later by Bruckner. At the time, Bruch was immersed in Schumann's symphonies, having conducted all four during his tenure at Sondershausen including the *Rhenish* on 12 July 1868, just two weeks before he conducted his own, and again on 13 May 1869, three weeks before the definitive version was first performed.[72]

Bruch was a Rhinelander with a deep love for the river, which is often reflected by the character of his music rather than by any specific motto or programme, but

---

[70] *Der Deutsche*, No. 97, 16 August 1868.

[71] The parts are stamped 'Fürstliche Hofkapelle Sondershausen'. The origin of the name Das Lohorchester lies in the local tanning industry, in which Loh is part of the burning process.

[72] Christopher Fifield, 'Max Bruch and Sondershausen' in *Max Bruch in Sondershausen (1867–1870)* (ed. P. Larsen) (Göttingen, 2004), 69–110.

there remains a possible link between the symphony's key of E♭ and the river. Not only Schumann but also Wagner, an unlikely bed-fellow, depicted the river Rhine in the opening of *Das Rheingold* in that key on a tonic pedal for 136 bars at this very time (premiered in 1869, albeit against his wishes). Although Bruch disliked Wagner's music intensely, he acknowledged his genius as 'a brilliant man, who strives with great energy and exceptional talent for undoubtedly the wrong goals'. He even included orchestral excerpts of operas from *Rienzi* to *Die Meistersinger* in his Sondershausen concerts.[73] In 1870, Bruch planned to use the discarded Intermezzo in a third symphony. 'Many sketches for the third symphony (in E major, including the Intermezzo in B major from the first symphony) are already lying around.'[74] This symphony was not completed until the Symphony Society of New York commissioned it 10 years later but with no sign of the Intermezzo when it was first performed there on 17 December 1882.[75] The key of the Intermezzo would have made its inclusion logical in this later symphony, but clearly Bruch found no place for it anywhere. He performed it at Sondershausen on 15 August 1869, the only time it was played on its own.[76] The Intermezzo may have been 'lying around' well before Bruch composed the rest of the symphony, but it may also have had a role to play afterwards, in 1872, when Bruch was writing his secular oratorio *Odysseus*, the third movement of which is *Odysseus and the Sirens*. At the start, the men's chorus of Odysseus's companions is in D, the key of the middle section of the Intermezzo (bars 49–110), while from their first appearance at bar 77, the female chorus of Sirens' music is in B and in $^6_4$ time, like the start of the Intermezzo, which was 'lying around' when *Odysseus* was being written. All three keys, B, D and E♭ majors, play as significant a role in this chorus as they do throughout the symphony. When Bruch left Sondershausen, the copied material for the Intermezzo parts remained but not the manuscript score. The author has compiled one, edited parts, and conducted it in its original place in the symphony.[77] There are no reports of the Sondershausen performances of the symphony in the music journals of the day (and therefore no mention of the disappearance of its Intermezzo), no doubt because space was limited and the town considered too insignificant in German music-making. The timing was also unfortunate, for much newsprint was currently being devoted to the premiere just over a month earlier (on 21 June 1868) at Munich of Wagner's *Die Meistersinger*.[78]

The rhythmic and harmonic elements that predominate in the 30-bar introduction in the first movement share characteristics with Wagner's prelude

---

[73] Letter to Rudolf von Beckerath, 9 April 1870, in Fifield, *Max Bruch*, 116.
[74] Bruch to Rudolf von Beckerath, 2 August 1870, quoted in Petra Riederer-Sitte (ed.), *Max Bruch: Briefe an Laura und Rudolf von Beckerath* (Essen, 1997), 95.
[75] It was published in 1887 by Breitkopf & Härtel as Op. 51.
[76] Fifield, 'Max Bruch and Sondershausen', 99.
[77] London, 17 May 2008.
[78] 21 June 1868 at Munich. On 5 July Bruch conducted the prelude to Wagner's new opera at Sondershausen. Fifield, 'Max Bruch and Sondershausen', 89.

to *Das Rheingold*, but whether Bruch would have known that work in 1868 is unclear. He might have seen, or even had the vocal score, published in 1861, but the full score, completed in 1854, was not printed until 1873 and the 1869 Munich first performances followed the premiere of his symphony. The prelude was not an orchestral extract for concert performance. Nor do we encounter any sign of chromatic harmony: Bruch's material is tonic–dominant bound, its shape, so typical of thematic material in nineteenth-century symphonies, locked in to the ascending or descending *arpeggio* format (Ex. 6.54). Bruch then produces a wistful tune typically scored for clarinet, a favoured alto-register instrument (Ex. 6.55), while its reply in the strings uses the same duplet-plus-triplet rhythmic pattern found in Volkmann's first symphony (1862), which Bruch had studied and conducted at Sondershausen (compare Exx 6.56 and 6.09).[79] Bruch, like Raff, was becoming more of an eclectic in his style following the flash of brilliance he brought to the moods of restrained simplicity and emotional intensity, which lie at the core of the G minor violin concerto.

Example 6.54   Bruch: Symphony No. 1. First movement, first subject

Example 6.55   Bruch: Symphony No. 1. First movement, second subject

Example 6.56   Bruch: Symphony No. 1. First movement, second subject, strings

The question remains why the Intermezzo was rejected. Like the prelude to *Die Loreley*, it is a charming, tuneful but understated, almost functional work,

---

[79] 23 August 1868, ibid., 92.

which does little to prepare its audience for what follows. It falls between two stools, too long as an introduction and too short as a movement.[80] Its lighter scoring with refreshingly more translucent textures is chamber music, making an uneasy juxtaposition with the movements surrounding it, while its simplicity is a reflection of its immaturity. In short, it seems out of place.[81] If, with rocking woodwinds and flowing violins at the start (Ex. 6.57), we are back in the realms of river imagery, this was depicted more vividly in the first movement, where we find the turbulence of a rushing river in a three-part passage for strings (Ex. 6.58). Bruch constructs this florid principal theme around the *arpeggio* and scores it richly for bassoons, horns, violas and clarinets (Ex. 6.59), while the second theme (Ex. 6.60) has folk-like charm, all of which lie at the heart of Bruch's creative process and melodic invention. Unusually (because he invariably prefers the middle or alto register) we find textures written at a higher *tessitura* in a passage consisting of syncopated chords and a quick ebb and flow of dynamic changes in the strings over a pedal, thus giving a novel touch of colour (Ex. 6.61).

Example 6.57   Bruch: Symphony No. 1. Second movement, Intermezzo, opening

Example 6.58   Bruch: Symphony No. 1. First movement, development

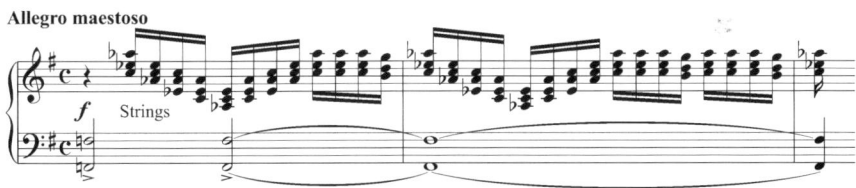

---

[80] In 1868 the second trumpeter marked his part 6½ minutes. My performance 140 years later was faster by a mere 27 seconds!

[81] Twenty years later Mahler's first symphony had a similarly inappropriate Intermezzo movement *Blumine*, which, like Bruch, he withdrew after just three performances.

Example 6.59   Bruch: Symphony No. 1. Second movement, first subject

Example 6.60   Bruch: Symphony No. 1. Second movement, second subject

Example 6.61   Bruch: Symphony No. 1. Second movement, syncopation

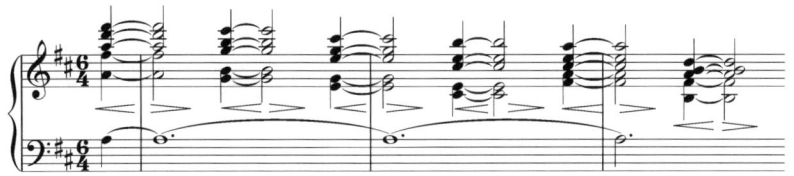

As frequently noted, in the 50-year period under discussion composers were invariably most successful in the *scherzo* movements of their symphonies and Bruch's here is no exception. It is full of excitement and packed with energy in the relentlessly driven *ostinato* of its quavers, whether in the strings or woodwind and horns (Ex. 6.62). It powers along with no contrast in mood or change of tempo between *scherzo* and trio, just a sudden change of mode from minor to major to stunning effect. Relentlessly the woodwinds fire staccato quavers as an accompaniment to a rich melody in *unisono* strings (Ex. 6.63), later swapping the two allocations around. Four years later, as we have seen, Raff followed Bruch's example.[82] The *scherzo* in his fourth symphony begins with similar string patter but builds canonically (Ex. 6.49); however, with the trio, the mood softens, unlike Bruch's. Since Beethoven's late chamber music, scherzos, although retaining their character, were not necessarily in triple time and could be second or third in the order of movements. A point of orchestral colour passes unnoticed to the ear (but not to the eye) in an eight-bar passage during which the timpani play *pp* an open fifth of G and D.[83] Three years earlier, in the second movement of Brahms's *German Requiem*, the timpani play *pianissimo* repeated fourths (F and B♭), possibly the

---

[82] Also compare the scherzo of Raff's fourth symphony to the *finale* of Lachner's first symphony (1827) (see page 59, Ex.2.77).

[83] Beginning ninth bar of letter E. Even more bizarre is the very same fifth *pp* on G/D at *only* the fifth and seventh bars of B in the *scherzo* of the *Scottish Fantasy*. Its relevance in

first example of simultaneously played notes for timpani since Beethoven and Berlioz. Kretschmar summarises Bruch's *scherzo* as 'a broadly effective and very popular work, which has several points of similarity with the encampment scene in Rheinberger's *Wallenstein* [1866]'.[84] Apart from bustling *tempi*, it is not easy to find much in common between the two, but it is perhaps more than a coincidence that Rheinberger's movement was often played as a symphonic extract and Bruch conducted it twice at Sondershausen a year later.[85] A final word on the *scherzo* comes from Brahms, who, after the first Vienna performance on 20 February 1870, reported that it 'in particular received quite unusual applause, which not only the piece but also the splendidly stirring performance deserved'.[86]

Example 6.62   Bruch: Symphony No. 1. Third movement, Scherzo

Example 6.63   Bruch: Symphony No. 1. Third movement, Trio

The third movement *Grave* (Ex. 6.64) anticipates by a dozen years the opening of his own *Scottish Fantasy* Op. 46 (1880) (Ex. 6.65), with which it shares the relatively unusual key of E♭ minor and the same sombre mood. According to Kretschmar,

> All the motifs in this movement are doom-laden, while in the middle, a reference is made [by the violas] to the restless [clarinet] motif [Ex. 6.55] from the first movement.[87] Without a break, this slow movement leads into the *finale*, which,

---

a 'Scottish' work is arguably stronger than in the symphony but must be deemed ineffective at such a quiet dynamic.

[84]   *Wallensteins Lager*, the third movement of his Symphony Op. 10 (1867).
[85]   22 August and 26 September 1869. Fifield, 'Max Bruch and Sondershausen', 99 and 101.
[86]   Brahms to Bruch, Vienna 21 February 1870, quoted in Fifield, *Max Bruch*, 87.
[87]   It does not give a cyclical shape by placing it here rather than in the *Finale*, but maybe that was not Bruch's intention.

like Mendelssohn's *Scottish* symphony, is made semi-programmatic by the indication *Allegro guerriero* [Ex. 6.66]. In the poetic context of the symphony, this *finale* rescues it with a happy ending, its musical form constructed and modelled like a march in which a lively theme is contrasted, if somewhat monotonously, with a sentimental one.[88]

Kretschmar's 'sentimental [theme]' sits above three distinct rhythms, producing a restless effect despite the intention of the composer's *tranquillo* (Ex. 6.67), while his two words 'somewhat monotonously' lie at the heart of the *finale*'s weakness. For a composer who hated the piano ('that unmelodious keyboard thing, that dull rattle-trap'), the material is far more suited to that instrument than to the strings, for whom perpetual triplets in the inner parts, dotted rhythms and an overdose of *arpeggios* threaten to make the work dull as well as tiring to play.[89] Composers did themselves no favours by exhausting their string players in striving to achieve the impossible. The result was rarely worth the effort, a notable exception being the *ostinato* of triplet quavers that dominates the *finale* of Schubert's ninth symphony, a work that Bruch also conducted at Sondershausen.[90]

Example 6.64   Bruch: Symphony No. 1. Fourth movement, opening

Example 6.65   Bruch: Scottish Fantasy. First movement, opening

---

[88] Kretschmar, Vol. I part ii, 609.
[89] Bruch to his publisher Fritz Simrock in 1875 and 1883. He wanted 'a grand *auto da fé* of 10–20,000 pianos, so that this nineteenth-century epidemic, if not wiped out, might at least be reduced to manageable proportions'. Quoted in Fifield, *Max Bruch*, 24.
[90] 4 July 1869. Fifield, 'Max Bruch and Sondershausen', 96.

Example 6.66 Bruch: Symphony No. 1. Finale, opening

Example 6.67 Bruch: Symphony No. 1. Finale, second subject

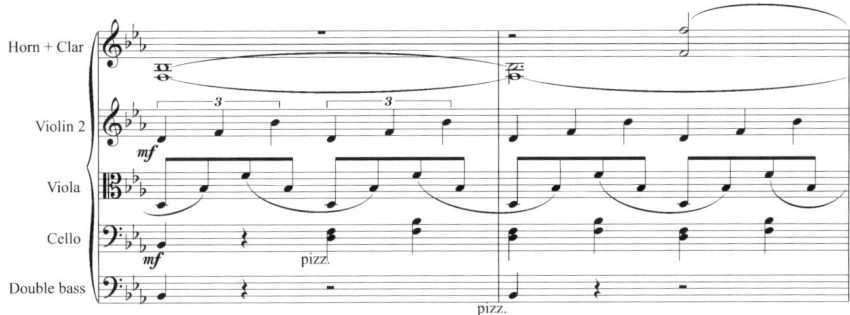

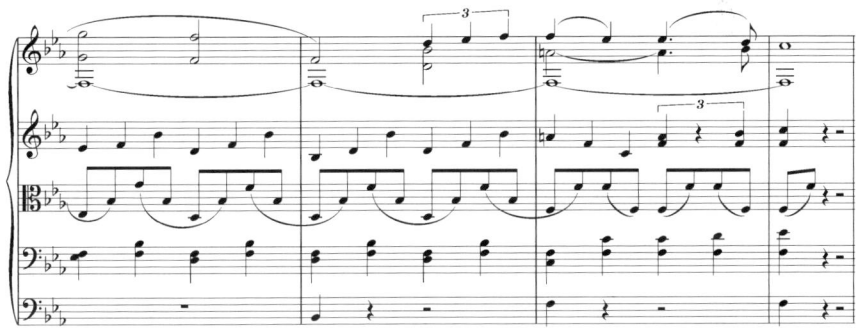

Bruch dedicated his first symphony to Brahms,

> before asking you beforehand and hoping that you will not accept it less amicably as a result. Inasmuch as I decorate my work with your name, dear Brahms, I wish you to know how highly I regard your gifts and your achievements. … It would be understandable and forgivable if you, who for years have pursued your own way so energetically, were to have little interest in the labours of your artistic colleagues. It pleases me the more that you so clearly proved just the opposite to me in Cologne at Whitsun; your lively interest, your sincere, warmly expressed pleasure in my symphony gave me an especial happiness and, already

then, awakened in me the wish. So I ask you once again, dear Brahms, to accept the dedication of the symphony as it is meant.[91]

Brahms's response was a mixture of surprise, pleasure and gratitude, although one can never be quite sure from his letters to what extent such feelings were expressed with a hint of sarcasm or a touch of irony. Bruch was certainly not an intimate friend, nor was he one of the inner circle despite their mutual friends, such as Joachim. Brahms's response certainly lacks sincerity in some places:

> It can hardly have been your intention to surprise me on Christmas Eve. I came home … and found your letter, which was the loveliest festive present, one announced in great seriousness and I think and feel nothing but the most vivid joy and heartfelt thanks. I must, however, wait for the score (because of the holiday), but meanwhile memory and imagination help me by playing, as best they can, trumpets and drums in E♭ as well as certain appropriate melodies.[92]

In the late 1860s, Brahms was in the ascendancy thanks to his *German Requiem*, of which Bruch was a sincere admirer: 'I am especially moved to say this to you at this time: your powerful *Requiem* lies before me, excellent through and through, greatly conceived, deeply felt and it brings me an artistic joy which I have not known in a long time.'[93] In a letter to his former teacher Hiller, Bruch again showed his high regard for Brahms and his *Requiem*, which he had heard with Joachim and Clara Schumann at Bremen on Good Friday 1868:

> The work is very greatly conceived and deeply felt. It makes a meaningful impression on not only artists but also the public. It appears that Brahms has achieved something here which had failed him hitherto. Nevertheless I believe that one will feel more respect and awe for this work of his, rather than love. I am frank enough to say that a powerful ravishing melody is preferable to the most beautiful imitations and contrapuntal tight-rope walk.[94]

There are interesting points here, including some that may also account for the return to daylight of the genre of the symphony after 40 years. Many composers, such as Kalliwoda, Lachner and Raff, did indeed walk a 'contrapuntal tight-rope', often to satisfy teachers or competition judges, but these ingredients then went on to become part of the symphonic furniture. Once embedded in the genre, they may have posed a challenge to a composer, but any victory thus gained may not necessarily have given equal satisfaction to an audience, then or now. Brahms, it is true, does include complex counterpoint in his *Requiem*, no doubt in

---

[91] Bruch to Brahms, 22 December 1868, quoted in Fifield, *Max Bruch*, 86.
[92] Brahms to Bruch, 25 December 1868, in ibid., 86.
[93] Bruch to Brahms, 22 December 1868, in ibid., 86.
[94] Bruch to Hiller, 26 April 1868, in ibid., 87.

deference to his polyphonic ancestors in whom he showed considerable interest, but 'Ihr habt nun Traurigkeit' can hardly be found guilty of lacking 'a powerful ravishing melody'.[95]

The success of Bruch's first symphony appears to have been considerable. Twenty years later, even at the time when it was competing with all four by Brahms, Kretschmar described it as 'one of the best known symphonies in recent times'.[96] A lengthy analysis appeared in the press.[97] It stated that the good reviews that had appeared were, on the whole, borne out by the evidence of the full score, though it also amply illustrated how opinions could be so repeatedly diverse.[98] Performances of the symphony, mostly conducted by Bruch, were plentiful enough in the next two years; and once the season was over, he had from October to May to freelance with it elsewhere. 'I will journey forth to introduce the symphony to several places in the world.'[99] What followed was not exactly a world tour, but to cities within Germany:

Leipzig	22 October 1868
Bremen	December 1868 (private concert)
Oldenburg	4 December 1868
Hamburg	22 January 1869
Crefeld	February 1869
Cologne	16 February 1869
Karlsruhe	20 February 1869 (conducted by Levi)
Dresden	1869
Mannheim	date unknown
Lübeck	date unknown
Leipzig	January 1870

Reaction was mixed. On hearing it at Leipzig, Eduard Bernsdorf recalled a remark by Gluck to the young Ignaz Pleyel on how to thin out instrumental texture: 'My young friend, clearly you've already thoroughly learned how to put notes down on paper; now you still have to learn how to remove them again.' Bernsdorf found Bruch's scoring too dense, the harmonic and instrumental outlines of the music (apart from the *scherzo*) shrouded in excessive detail. As to his style, he identified clear signs of Schumann and Gade with Mendelssohn in the *scherzo*, but generally Bruch did not have his own characteristic imprint. He concluded that, while it did not stand on the threshold of being a masterpiece, the symphony

---

[95] The fifth movement for soprano solo, added after his mother's death.
[96] Kretschmar, Vol. I part ii, 609.
[97] By Friedrich Chrysander in *AMZ*, Vol. 4 No. 9, 3 March 1869, 67–9.
[98] In November 1868 it was published by Cranz of Bremen; the score cost seven Thalers, the orchestral parts eight. There was also a version available for piano (four hands).
[99] Bruch to Laura von Beckerath, 27 June 1868, in Riederer-Sitte, 71. The season actually ended on 27 September.

nevertheless contained enough elements and features to indicate a promising future, perhaps after concentrating more on writing smaller-scale instrumental compositions. Despite his criticisms, the performance of the symphony (which he acknowledged was 'not easy throughout') was praised, and he noted that the good-sized audience applauded generously after each movement.[100]

The concert at Oldenburg on 4 December 1868 shows that the city's music director, Brahms's friend Albert Dietrich, was in a position to compile his programmes with impunity, as this one included three works by living German composers.[101] We do not know the size of the audience, but one might surmise that, had it been small, some comment might have been made in a press always happy to carp and criticise. A work each by Schumann (his Overture, Scherzo and Finale Op. 52) and Beethoven (his overture *Coriolan*) may have been included to keep the audience happy, though Schumann's was (and still is) not so familiar. The critic sent by *AMZ* seems to have taken against Bruch's podium manner, which apparently lacked modesty or restraint and, as he himself acknowledged, may then have coloured his impression of the symphony. Published in the next issue was an anonymous, spirited defence of Bruch. According to the writer (who, it would be refreshing to think, may have been an orchestral player), Bruch's 'personal manner both in rehearsal and when conducting [the concert] was that of a cultured man, devoid of any arrogance'. While he found excessive the composer's use of colour, creating an over-theatrical impression (particularly in the *finale*), he praised him as a melodist, singling out the masterly build-up throughout the first movement and the moving warmth of the *Grave*.[102] The critic at the second Leipzig performance praised the work as one that 'will rank quite rightly among the best of those currently in the genre'.[103] Bruch's sideswipe at the Cologne public about the forthcoming performance there of the symphony is not surprising, for already at this time his bitterness towards the city of his birth was being fed by what was becoming a lifelong obsession as the prospects of becoming music director there receded. 'It goes without saying that I will conduct the symphony in Cologne on 16 February [1869]. I am not looking forward to it very much, because I know in advance that it will not be understood.'[104] After the performance he wrote a somewhat pathetic letter to his former teacher Hiller, clearly seeking his master's approval:

> We spoke about much, only you said nothing at all about the symphony. I must therefore assume that it totally displeased you. If that was so, then between our current musical thinking and feeling a gulf has now obviously occurred, which

---

[100] *Die Signale*, Vol. 26 No. 47, 29 October 1868, 946.
[101] *Salve regina* Op. 11 by Friedrich Gernsheim, two Lieder for women's chorus Op. 16 by Franz Wüllner, and Bruch's Symphony No. 1 Op. 28.
[102] *AMZ*, Vol. 4 No. 2, 13 January 1869, col. 15.
[103] *Musikalisches Wochenblatt*, Vol. 1 No. 5, 28 January 1870, p. 74, col. 2.
[104] Bruch to Rudolf von Beckerath, 10 January 1869, quoted in Riederer-Sitte, 75.

appears to be difficult to bridge. Do not, for God's sake, think that I wish only to be praised. I know full well the value of open discussion between artists. I do not delude myself that the symphony is perfect – one could take another point of view of the dramatic development in the *finale* – but neither do I believe that it deserves to be silently ignored. Many of my artistic colleagues (including Joachim, Brahms, David, Dietrich, Reinecke, to say nothing of my close friends) acknowledge substantial progress in this symphony since all my early works, in particular the aspect of thematic material and the use of polyphonic elements. I know full well that some things in it give full scope for discussion. It would have been so interesting after the performance to have heard the opinion of such an honoured and important master as you. The opportunity offered itself, for we sat next to one another and were often engaged in conversation but you said nothing and so I can only take it that you had so much in your heart against it, you did not wish to distress me by saying as much.[105]

Bruch's music follows a cautiously predictable path, trying not to disturb too many established symphonic formulae, though he had no such qualms about doing just that in two movements of his first two violin concertos.[106] The apparent success of the first symphony encouraged him to write a second, which he completed during the summer of 1870, towards the end of his time at Sondershausen.[107] He had five rehearsals for it before its first performance on 4 September, Joachim having undertaken to bow the string parts. Reinecke then invited the composer to conduct it himself at Leipzig, where it was poorly received. Bruch thought it was because the symphony was in three movements. 'A *scherzo* does not fit into the construction of this symphony,' he wrote defiantly to Hermann Levi, 'so there is none, to the great annoyance of the Leipzig public, who always want to dance on a freshly-dug grave.'[108] Omitting a *scherzo* was probably unwise, as that movement in new symphonies was invariably the most popular with the public. All three movements are in sonata form, which runs the risk of structural monotony, but the central *Adagio* is beautiful, with some lovely solos in the orchestra's alto register (upper cello, viola, clarinet and horn). Once again the last two movements are linked, but after 18 bars we come to the main theme of the *finale*, one that poses a fascinating question. Could it have circulated thereafter for six years from 1870, only to invite comparison with the famous quasi-Beethoven melody in the *finale* of Brahms's first symphony? In this particular instance (Ex. 6.68), while it is only the first four notes and their note values that are identical, the anacrusis and interval of a rising fourth, its rich resolution upon and setting around a single C *sul* G, the

---

[105] Bruch to Hiller, 25 May 1869, in Fifield, *Max Bruch*, 88–9.
[106] The first movement of the first is a *Vorspiel*, while the second movement of the second is a *recitativo*.
[107] Symphony No. 2 in F minor Op. 36. The eight new works between the two symphonies were all choral or vocal.
[108] Bruch to Levi, 29 November 1870, in Fifield, *Max Bruch*, 110.

phrasing, the character and mood do all inevitably invite such comparison. Was this one of those symphonies (others will arise) that helped to propel Brahms on his way down the symphonic path he had shunned since 1854?

Example 6.68   Bruch: Symphony No. 2. Finale, principal theme

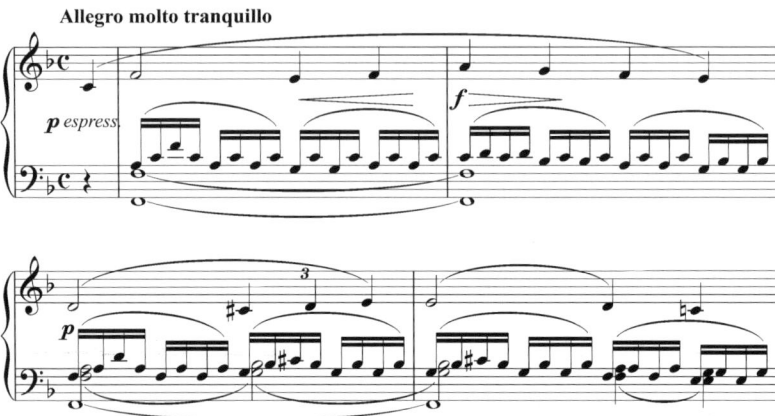

On the sensitive subject of plagiarism, even the act of Raff's blatant plundering of Schnyder's third for the *finale* of his sixth or of Tchaikovsky's quotation of Raff's tenth for his fifth should be interpreted as no more than marks of respect. Whatever the motive (and bearing in mind statistical or mathematical probabilities, it must be a given that themes will inevitably have both intervals and rhythms in common), there is a definable symphonic language forming here, creating a template or mould into which thematic shapes, harmonic progressions, instrumental scoring and a division of orchestral labour in the search for new textures gather momentum through the 25 years between Schumann's last and Brahms's first symphonies. While it is also likely that Bruch and then Brahms were doffing their respective hats to Beethoven, it was Brahms, not Bruch, who was burdened with von Bülow's sobriquet 'Beethoven's tenth'. While wearing the mantle of the alliterative 'third B' following Bach and Beethoven, it was Brahms and not Bruch who had greatness thrust upon him.

Bruch's strengths lie in his gift of melody, with folksong the primary source. In 1870, he wrote a potted history of his life, followed by some personal reflections:[109]

> Like all German musicians, after I had written anything and everything possible,
> I sought out my path like a mule in the mist. After *Loreley* I finally asked myself,

---

[109] The lengthy article appeared in *Musikalisches Wochenblatt* in three weekly instalments during November 1870.

where does the ever-flowing beauty of a so-called classical work lie?[110] ... I acknowledged that true melody is what is lacking in modern music ... and now I do not hesitate to study genuine melody at its source. Since 1862, I have preoccupied myself exclusively with folksong. Today I still believe that the melodic beauty of genuine folksong is only rarely achieved in creative works of art but everyone should refresh themselves at this source.[111]

In a postscript he acknowledged that this focus on melody alone, without the infusion of polyphony, was at the root of the problem but that in the first movement of the symphony he had successfully integrated both elements so that the emphasis was properly balanced.

Another in the Brahms circle, Albert Dietrich (1829–1908), had been an intimate friend since the early 1850s. Best remembered for the FAE sonata, a collaborative effort between Schumann, Brahms and Dietrich as a gift for Joachim in 1853, that same year Dietrich was named as one of the 12 Apostles for the Messiah Brahms in Schumann's article 'Neue Bahnen'.[112] Like Raff, he wrote a symphony in 1854, which was performed at Leipzig on 14 December that year, but neither score nor parts have survived.[113] He spent the years 1855–60 at Bonn, before moving to Oldenburg, where he was music director for 30 years (1861–91), and where his second symphony was premiered on 19 February 1869. Upon retirement he moved to Berlin and joined Bruch as a professor of composition at the Academy of Arts. Acknowledged as 'an excellent conductor and fine pianist', Oldenburg's musical diet benefited from his contacts with musicians such as Bruch and by his membership of the close-knit Brahms circle.[114] Newspapers announcing the imminent performance of Dietrich's new symphony there also noted the presence of Brahms and Clara Schumann, who had played the *Liebeslieder Walzer*. At the start of his time in Oldenburg, Dietrich observed to Clara that 'the majority of the town's populace, despite its apparent cool reserve, had a warm regard for music and its performers'.[115]

Dietrich's Symphony in D minor Op. 20 is conventionally scored but with two horns, where four might have been wiser given the rest of the brass section of two trumpets and three trombones. A pattern emerges in this study of unearthed symphonies composed during the mid-years of the nineteenth century, namely the expectation that builds through three movements only to fall inevitably at the final hurdle because of uninspired material and the way it is handled. Too many

---

[110] *Die Loreley* Op. 16 was Bruch's first full-length opera, premiered at Mannheim in 1863.
[111] Bruch to von Beckerath, 16 October 1870, in Fifield, *Max Bruch*, 120–26.
[112] The others were Joachim, Naumann, Norman, Bargiel, Kirchner, Schäffer, Wilsing, Gade, Franz, Mangold and Heller.
[113] Dörffel, Statistik, 15.
[114] *LAMZ*, Vol. 3 No. 8, 19 February 1868, 61.
[115] Albert Dietrich to Clara Schumann, 26 December 1861, in Litzmann, Vol. 3, 114.

of them suffer the anticlimax of a weak *finale*. The audience needed to leave with the best music ringing in its ears, but in Dietrich's case the material in the *finale* is comparatively dull and unmemorable after three far finer movements. The usual influences appear for the usual reasons, namely Dietrich's musical education and early established loyalties. In the first movement we have from the very start (as in Volkmann's first) a *unisono* motto theme in the *Sturm und Drang* of D minor (Ex. 6.69) but with a more elaborate and complex structure (for example, the sonata form's exposition itself contains another sonata form). Next is a beautiful slow movement whose opening recalls the murmuring brook of Beethoven's sixth. It is soon joined by a hauntingly tranquil horn theme like the 'Alpine' horn theme to come in Brahms's first (Ex. 6.70). In three distinct sections, the middle one (in $\frac{9}{8}$ compound triple time, the outer ones in $\frac{6}{8}$ compound duple time) brings the music to a searing climax (Ex. 6.71).

Example 6.69   Dietrich: Symphony in D minor. Opening motto theme

Example 6.70   Dietrich: Symphony in D minor. Second movement, horn theme

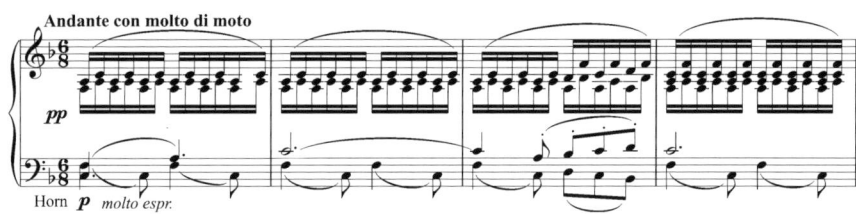

Example 6.71   Dietrich: Symphony in D minor. Second movement, climax

The attractive *scherzo* abounds in hemiolas, confusing the listener by being written in a fast one-in-a-bar $\frac{3}{4}$ but that, when heard in two-bar groupings, sound in a steadier $\frac{3}{2}$ (Ex. 6.72).[116] Following the precedent of first Kittl then Schumann,

---

[116] See also Exx 3.11, 3.12, 5.16, 5.17 and 7.36.

it has two trios, the first in duple time led by active strings with a light touch (Ex. 6.73), the second a delightful *Ländler* waltz for pairs of horns and (in the absence of a second pair) bassoons (Ex. 6.74), in which the horn call features prominently. The *finale* revisits the opening, this time in the major mode. Its mundanely four-square shape is not helped by a new second half to the original phrase, a dogged rhythm that overstays its welcome (bars 2–3 in Ex. 6.75). The overall impression of the symphony is of the omnipresence of Schumann and Mendelssohn, although in the second subject of the first movement (Ex. 6.76) and at the climax of the second (Ex. 6.71), we can begin to discern some signs of Brahms. Even Bruch appears at one point in the first movement (compare Exx 6.56 and 6.77).[117] On the other hand, the rhythm here of two-plus-three crotchets could well have been Volkmann's influence at work on either composer.

Example 6.72   Dietrich: Symphony in D minor. Third movement, Scherzo

Example 6.73   Dietrich: Symphony in D minor. Third movement, first trio

Example 6.74   Dietrich: Symphony in D minor. Third movement, second trio

---

[117] Dietrich was an admirer and programmed an early performance of Bruch's first symphony on 4 December 1868 at Oldenburg.

Example 6.75   Dietrich: Symphony in D minor. Finale

Example 6.76   Dietrich: Symphony in D minor. First movement, second subject

Example 6.77   Dietrich: Symphony in D minor. First movement, see also 6.56 (Bruch)

Dietrich's symphony was liked by the public and considered 'a significant and splendid orchestral work for which one could justifiably predict an auspicious horoscope' by one critic.[118] He noted that it shared the contemporary trend for rich scoring in instrumental music (although one rather than two pairs of horns would appear to contradict that observation) but that its success was also due to the quality of the colour and treatment of the musical content, again hard to justify in view of the weakness of the *finale*. Less favourably received was the *Andante* because it was too melodious, again an odd response in view of the public's insatiable appetite for melody then and now. Oldenburg's concert hall was thought

---

[118]   *AMZ*, Vol. 4 No. 10, 10 March 1869, col. 79.

too small for the work; instead it required a more spacious arena such as Leipzig. It was played there for the first time on 28 October 1869 and seems to have aroused great interest, although, according to a review, it would have been even greater had it been shorter. Except for some smaller details and matters of taste, the work was singled out for considerable praise; nevertheless some very pertinent issues were also raised. The critic got to the heart of the symphonic problem that arose thanks to Beethoven and suggested that the solution lay in what happened after Schumann:

> Again and again the question arises: has the composer, who has proven himself truly poetic, high class and inclined to a Romantic artistic nature, really chosen the appropriate form for his talent? Would it not be shown in even more favourable light in a more concise, directly dramatic form? If anything can confirm this supposition, it is the second and third movements with their respective fascinating lyricism and dramatic life. ... Again and again the question arises with the newest symphonies from several composers: after Beethoven and Schumann, can we find anything more outstanding, and especially novel? Can real progress still be achieved in this form, for it is the form that is spent, not so much the content? It was lucky instinct ... that took Liszt down the route of the much more concise symphonic poem. Why do more of our most gifted composers not have the courage or the inclination to follow him along this more grateful, easier and modern path? Returning to the impression of [Dietrich's symphony], it pleases us to confirm that an unusual warmth and respectful reception was given to it by our reserved Gewandhaus auditorium. The composer, who conducted with watchful eye, earned not only applause after each movement, but also at the end received two lively recalls. May such a wonderful success and its fresh excitement bring him further achievements.[119]

Another composer who bridged the decade and produced two of his four extant symphonies between the late 1860s and mid-1870s was Felix Draeseke (1835–1913). At 17, he entered the Leipzig Conservatoire to study under Moscheles (piano), Brendel (musicology) and Rietz (composition), but his anti-establishment writings for Brendel's *Neue Zeitschrift für Musik* eventually brought about his expulsion. Instead he took private lessons with Rietz, though more significant was his encounter with the playing and conducting of Hans von Bülow in Berlin in 1853. At this period, having met and heard Liszt conduct *Lohengrin* at Weimar, Draeseke gave himself wholly to the New German School and began to compose. In the summer of 1859 he visited Wagner in Lucerne and showed him his opera *König Sigurd*; and although he was engrossed in the completion of *Tristan*, Wagner found time to compliment the young man. As Raff left Liszt's circle at Weimar, so Draeseke joined it and found a natural home. Liszt was enormously impressed by *König Sigurd* and wanted it staged, but Peter Cornelius's *Der Barbier von Bagdad* took precedence and was given its premiere on 15 December 1858, during

---

[119] *NZfM*, Vol. 65 No. 45, 5 November 1869, 383.

which anti-Liszt demonstrations took place and he resigned his post as music director. Draeseke therefore lost his champion at Weimar and the opera remained unpublished. Draeseke was inspired by poetry, sagas and Germany's heroic past, but his setting of Kleist's ode *Germania* caused a scandal at Weimar in 1861 and the following year an overture was withdrawn from a celebratory concert after its royal dedicatee heard a rehearsal. Draeseke completely lost his self-confidence, destroyed his juvenilia, and left Germany in 1862 for self-imposed exile in Switzerland, where he became a piano teacher.

By 1876, however, he was unable to sustain a living in Switzerland and moved back to Germany thanks to a substantial inheritance. In Dresden he managed to subsist on this until he accepted a teaching post at the Conservatoire in 1884, followed by a professorship in 1892. Meanwhile, his inspiration as a composer was reawakened and he continued to work on the oratorio trilogy that occupied him for much of his life, *Christus-Mysterium*, first performed in its entirety at Berlin in 1912. His three operas were published and performed as well as his four symphonies, various symphonic preludes or poems, and concertos for violin and piano, all largely thanks to conductors such as Franz Wüllner, Ernst von Schuch and Artur Nikisch. The years in exile caused a profound rethinking in Draeseke's musical outlook. He suffered from depression, lost much of his radical zeal and developed very conservative views, fiercely opposing the 'musical decadence' of Strauss by 1906 in his book *Die Konfusion in der Musik*, despite having admired *Don Juan* just 10 years earlier. Though he never lost his regard for Liszt and Wagner (*Christus-Mysterium* was a sacred response to the *Ring*), it was thanks to Wagner's championing of Beethoven that Draeseke turned to Classical form with its contrapuntal rules.[120]

Allegedly among the destroyed works of his juvenilia is his Symphony in C, performed just once at the Ducal Court Theatre in Draeseke's hometown of Coburg under its conductor Ernst Lampert (1818–79). This took place on 11 November 1856, when it was sandwiched between two short operettas, *Er sucht seine Braut* by Johann Otto Prechtler (1813–81) and *Die Unglücklichen* by August von Kozebue (1761–1819). While neither score nor parts have survived, there is a review by Brendel that appeared in the *Leipziger Musikzeitung* and is reproduced in Roeder's biography of Draeseke.[121] Despite the lack of firm evidence, this early symphony of 1854–56 would appear to indicate the style he developed, judging by its two immediate successors. His four extant symphonies (1868–72, 1870–76, 1877–86, 1912) took a path that would seem to link Schumann with Bruckner rather than with Brahms. As far as it is possible to ascertain from Brendel's review of the *Jugendsinfonie*, it and the next two symphonies explore a route that, with the benefit of hindsight, lead to his crowning achievement of the third (*Symphonia*

---

[120] See Krueck, *The Symphonies of Felix Draeseke*.
[121] Erich Roeder, *Felix Draeseke: der Lebens- und Leidensweg eines deutschen Meisters* 2 vols (Dresden and Berlin, 1932–37).

tragica), which was completed and first performed in 1886, a decade after the scope of this study.

Brendel's review introduced Draeseke as an accomplished critic and writer but also drew attention to the large audience present because of his growing reputation as a composer. The performance was a success and 'this result is all the more welcome ... as he belongs to our direction', meaning a follower of the New German School.[122]

> For the most part the symphony is written in customary form and is not programme music; nevertheless it is not composed according to routine. Hence in place of the usual scherzo, there is a march, ... totally original and harmonically interesting with its two trios which follow immediately. In the middle of the turbulence the *Adagio* enters as a sort of resting point. A series of modulations and ill-prepared transitions disturb the quiet which can be sought in an *Adagio* and prevent the listener from achieving full pleasure. There is too much change here, the succession of tonalities too quick, the melodic periods too short-lived and because of these the architecture of the work suffers. The closing movement is magnificently laid out, though somewhat broadly developed. The composer may have intended to repeat the thought which inspired him, however we miss the necessary brevity in which this had to take place and can, for example, point to the three final *crescendi* which follow *f* to *fff* on top of one another and declare them unjustified.[123]

As in the case of most of Draeseke's predecessors and his contemporary symphonists, the model of Beethoven's introduction to the *finale* to the ninth was the prototype for achieving unity through diversity of form. In a move of 'total originality', the young man took a further leaf from the book of a past master by adding two trios to a march rather than, as Schumann had done in his second symphony, adding them to a conventional *scherzo*. How frustrating also to read in Brendel's review that this particular march was 'harmonically interesting', as in what way and to what extent will never be known. Brendel had a complaint about the orchestration, singling out in particular the handling of the brass. While we do not know the precise details of the *Jugendsinfonie*'s scoring, Draeseke's first symphony, begun a dozen years later, has a comparatively light brass section without trombones but with four horns and three trumpets, thus producing much lighter textures in the lower registers, possibly in response to that criticism. Their function in the second symphony is also not the answer, for he adds a pair of trombones that largely play an octave apart and merely serve to reinforce the cello and bass lines. Only in his third symphony (1886) does Draeseke treat the trio of

---

[122] 'Dies Resultat ist um so erfreulicher ... als Felix Draeseke unserer Richtung angehört' – *Leipziger Musikzeitung* quoted in and translated by Krueck, 31.

[123] Ibid., 144–5.

heavy brass conventionally as an independent group and achieve a denser inner texture and the full panoply of instrumental colour.

In his first symphony there are other elements that subsequently entered Draeseke's symphonic language and that may have been tried and tested in his *Jugendsinfonie*. Recapitulations that traditionally conclude movements constructed in sonata form have themselves acquired developmental characteristics in the first symphony. Indeed the *Sonata-Allegro* of the first movement and the fourth movement *finale* both have recapitulations that, if put together, almost equal the length of their respective exposition and development sections. In Draeseke's first symphony, instead of a motto theme, it is the interval of a fourth that predominates (Exx 6.78 and 6.79). The first movement contains a complexity of thematic elements, later extracted and used individually as material for the rest of the work. Draeseke is, therefore, prepared for changes, but they remain subject to the restraints of Classical procedure. This is a composer who pushes the boundaries of structure and explores new harmonic paths (Ex. 6.80). It is quite unlike the music of his exact contemporary Bruch, whose first two symphonies were first performed in 1868 and 1870 respectively, during the four-year gestation period 1868–72 it took Draeseke to produce his first. Rather than a fugue, he uses sequences or the canon (Ex. 6.81) as a contrapuntal device. The sprightly *scherzo* is unusually in duple time and lacks a trio (Bruch's second symphony lacked both). Once again it starts with the motto interval of a fourth (Ex. 6.82) and frequently teases the audience with unexpected twists and turns, dislocated accents, silent bars (a general pause or GP) that herald a new section, and sudden *ff* outbursts on timpani. The tautly constructed but passionate slow movement is manifestly on a definable route to the complex *Adagios* of both Bruckner and Mahler (Ex. 6.83). After such a fleeting scherzo (its marking *Presto leggiero* says it all) and now with a tempo indication of *Adagio molto*, it lasts 15–20 minutes and lies at the heart of the work. Krueck puts it on the 'finest' level between Schumann (his second) and Bruckner (his seventh). 'In the climaxes the music attains gripping passion, a passion which is both heroic and poignant'.[124] However, for all its spirited energy and speedy excitement, the finale takes us no further beyond where the *Adagio* had left us but instead appears mundane in the wake of such originality and emotional depth. While, in Krueck's view, it is harmonically more enterprising than the first movement, this finale is 'something of a problem' and 'dangerously related' to those in Mendelssohn's fourth (*Italian*) and Schumann's second (Ex. 6.84).[125] Perhaps Elisabeth's 'Dich, teure Halle' from Wagner's *Tannhäuser* might also have been somewhere at the back of Draeseke's mind.

---

[124] Ibid., 53.

[125] Ibid., 57–8. Krueck identifies the finales of both works; but regarding the *Italian*, he surely means the start of the first movement.

Example 6.78   Draeseke: Symphony No. 1. First movement, Introduction

Example 6.79   Draeseke: Symphony No. 1. First movement, first subject

Example 6.80   Draeseke: Symphony No. 1. First movement, development

Example 6.81   Draeseke: Symphony No. 1. First movement, development

Example 6.82   Draeseke: Symphony No. 1. Second movement, Scherzo

Example 6.83   Draeseke: Symphony No. 1. Third movement, opening

Example 6.84   Draeseke: Symphony No. 1. Fourth movement, opening

Just three months before Brahms's first symphony was premiered (4 November 1876), Draeseke produced his second on 10 June. Although he had started work on it some six years earlier in 1870, even before his first was completed, his ever-worsening tinnitus, teaching commitments in the Swiss cities of Lausanne and Geneva, broken engagement and the death of his father all contributed to delay and postponement. It took a further two years before the symphony received its premiere under Ernst von Schuch in Dresden on 15 February 1878. Schuch was one of several conductors who had a high regard for Draeseke's music and did their best to promote performances wherever they could.[126]

Draeseke's second symphony takes a different path to that of its immediate predecessor, albeit that in both cases unity through diversity is the chosen goal. Here the composer adopts the principle of thematic metamorphosis. According to Krueck, 'the three main ideas of the first movements are taken and modified to serve as the basis for the following movements; the main theme of the first movement (Ex. 6.85) becomes the material for the second movement, the subsidiary theme (Ex. 6.86) that of the scherzo and the feminine subject (Ex. 6.87), the rondo theme of the finale'.[127] The opening of the symphony is infused with the electrifying energy and élan of, first, the *ff* chordal start to Beethoven's *Eroica* followed by the rhythmic shape and melodic outline of the theme of *Don Juan* by Richard Strauss at the start of his symphonic tone poem over a decade later (1888).[128] The slow movement is an *Allegretto marziale* in D minor with a tread of low-lying open fifths (Ex. 6.88) recalling Burgmüller's second symphony and its uncanny resemblance to Schubert's ninth (see Exx 2.62 and 2.63), although Draeseke's sombre melodic interjections above this pedal look ahead to Mahler (his first

---

[126]   Schuch also conducted the premiere of the third symphony on 13 January 1888. Artur Nikisch did his best to promote Draeseke's music, as had Julius Rietz followed by Hans von Bülow in the 1880s. Krueck wrongly identifies Bülow as Hans Richter, ibid., 11, 62–3. See Frithjof Haas, *Hans von Bülow: Leben und Wirken* (Wilhelmshaven, 2002), 249, 289.

[127]   Krueck, 63–4.

[128]   By 1906 Draeseke had no time for Strauss's music and wrote an article (also published as a pamphlet) entitled *Die Konfusion in der* Musik in which he severely criticised the opera *Salome* in the *Neue Stuttgarter Musikzeitung*, October 1906. The pamphlet was published by Grüninger, Stuttgart. See Krueck, 13, 142. The opening of Hiller's 1850 symphony is even more strikingly similar to Strauss's tone poem. See Ex. 5.29.

symphony) rather than back to Schubert. This slow movement lies at the heart of the work; but contrary to the first symphony, emotions do not run so high. It has two contrasting episodes. The first is in D major and is introduced by martial fanfares played by a trio of trumpets (another premonition of Mahler, whose reveille calls were said to originate in his local barracks) (Ex. 6.89).[129] The second section is in B♭ major with a simple and idyllic pastoral style. Draeseke's mastery of scoring has matured in this second symphony, and by the end of this second movement his palette of instrumental colour and his exploration of orchestral effects has significantly grown. The most extraordinary example (considering this was the period 1860–70s) occurs at the very end of the movement where (over a recall of the *ostinato* drone of fifths) the texture has become diaphanous as instruments are shed, leaving a final harmonic D to just the first violins, a highly unusual call upon a section rather than a solo instrument (Ex. 6.90).

The scherzo of the second symphony has little of the high quality found in the first, which, despite its brevity, was published alone and given separate performances in response to popular demand. Nevertheless interest lies in other areas of this one in the second symphony. It opens at a leisurely pace (*Allegro comodo*) but with the strict instruction that it should not be played faster than the first movement (*Nicht schneller als der erste Satz*), its forthright statement *unisono* of the material having shattered the somewhat eerie mood left by the march that has faded away at the end of the second movement (Ex. 6.91). This scherzo material has a retrospective connection to the second theme of the first movement; in other words, through the process of thematic metamorphosis Ex. 6.86 has become Ex. 6.91. Its trio (Ex. 6.92) is both calm and intimate. It bears the hallmark of chamber music and is unusually a little faster than the scherzo in which it is embedded. Draeseke frequently uses the word *pochettino* – a very little – as a subtle but vital ingredient of tempo variation in his symphonies. The scherzo returns with modifications until a blaze of brass fanfares gradually builds to a full orchestral climax (Ex. 6.93), followed by a shortened reminiscence of the trio but this time with not even a *pochettino* change of tempo. Like the end of the first movement, the conclusion of the scherzo is marked by a translucent texture in the scoring with quiet *pizzicato* chords preceding a *fermata*, followed by another general pause before a headlong four-bar rush (*presto)* for the full orchestra in conclusion (Ex. 6.94).

The joyful mood at the end of the scherzo continues at the start of the finale, a *rondo* with episodes that twist and turn, recalling what has gone before in other movements. The start is first *unisono* followed by chords with simultaneously diverging chromatic ascents and descents until it reaches the home key of F major. A pair of high-lying flutes produces a *staccato ostinato* under which the clarinet plays the principal *rondo* theme, a quirky tune, its phrases starting

---

[129] The vocabulary of Draeseke's detailed instructions in the score and trumpet parts includes the word 'schmetternd' (blaring) at this point (see Ex. 6.89). This was a term that Mahler would frequently use.

with the ubiquitous interval of a fourth and including the imaginative addition of three single strokes on a triangle at alternate bars to colour and highlight this somewhat impish melody. This is ostensibly a recall, not of an earlier movement in this symphony but rather of the scherzo in the first symphony (Exx 6.95 and 6.82). A restatement then inverts the distribution, for now it is the two clarinets who accompany the flute. After a series of explosive outbursts, a lyrical, even melancholic subject (Ex. 6.96) appears, again to be taken a tiny (*pochettino*) bit slower (*un pochettino rit* and *un pochettino più largo* are just two bars apart and are typical of Draeseke's very subtle gradations of tempo adjustment). The return of the *rondo* theme followed by yet another general pause leads into a fugue in which only the strings participate (Ex. 6.97), the rest of the orchestra interjecting fragments of accompaniment in places.

Example 6.85   Draeseke: Symphony No. 2. First movement, first theme

Example 6.86   Draeseke: Symphony No. 2. First movement, second theme

Example 6.87   Draeseke: Symphony No. 2. First movement, third theme

Example 6.88   Draeseke: Symphony No. 2. Second movement, opening, March

Example 6.89   Draeseke: Symphony No. 2. Second movement, first episode

Example 6.90   Draeseke: Symphony No. 2. Second movement, final bars

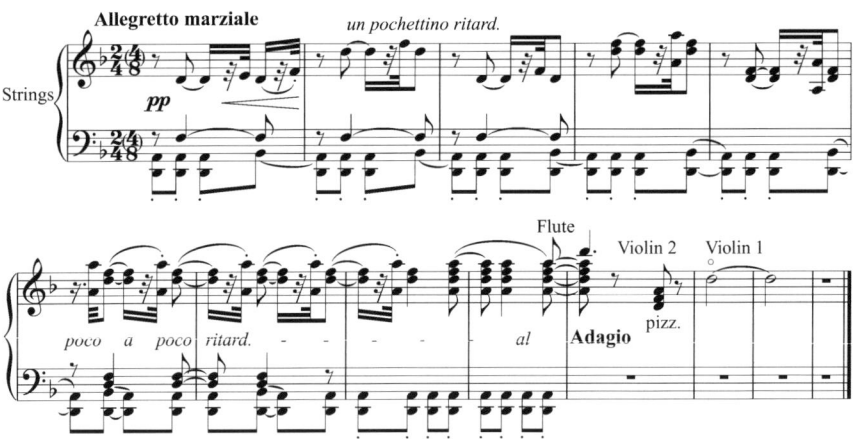

Example 6.91   Draeseke: Symphony No. 2. Third movement, Scherzo, opening

Example 6.92   Draeseke: Symphony No. 2. Third movement, Trio

Example 6.93   Draeseke: Symphony No. 2. Third movement, Scherzo climax

Example 6.94   Draeseke: Symphony No. 2. Third movement, Scherzo, conclusion

Example 6.95   Draeseke: Symphony No. 2. Fourth movement, Rondo, opening

Example 6.96   Draeseke: Symphony No. 2. Fourth movement, second theme

Example 6.97   Draeseke: Symphony No. 2. Fourth movement, fugue subject

Whereas Liszt brought thematic unity to his symphonic poems and the *Faust* symphony (1855) some years before Draeseke even set off down that road, the younger composer managed to avoid his mentor's meanderings and instead produced tauter results thanks to the thematic metamorphosis that provided the bricks and mortar to bind together the symphony's movements. Draeseke went on to even greater success, culminating in the more mature and significant third and fourth symphonies, *Symphonia tragica* and *Symphonia comica* during the 1880s and in 1912 respectively. Krueck is unequivocal in his praise of the second symphony, as indeed he is of all Draeseke's four symphonies, and his study of the them often reflects his frustration at the lack of any public performances:[130]

> Draeseke's F major symphony is not just a good symphony, it is a great one and deserves at least equal the attention which its successor, the *Symphonia tragica* warrants – perhaps even more so, since the second symphony has never received even the minimum of recognition earned by its sister. [It] represents Draeseke at a peak of inspiration; it has all the melodic sweep and rhythmic verve which kept the symphonies of Brahms, Bruckner, Dvořák and Tchaikovsky part of the standard repertoire. It has a compactness of structure which demonstrates the highest technical ability. Its freedom of line and developmental methods exhibits an uncommon mastery of contrapuntal elements. Its orchestration points the way to Richard Strauss and the New German School of the early twentieth century. In short, it is the supple, vital work of a great master and woe be to him who would

---

[130] All four were recorded by cpo in 1997–8 and reissued in 2013. See Discography.

compromise its greatness by placing it on the level of the better works of a Bruch or Goldmark or Raff. The F major symphony is the product of a superior musical mentality, of a unique personality and it must be judged anew.[131]

Draeseke's symphonies do not establish a style others could readily imitate, which is proof positive of his originality. His music has a unique quality and the results prove far ahead of their time. Just how far is illustrated by comparing his second symphony with the first by his exact contemporary, Bruch. With signs of Beethoven, Mendelssohn and Schumann all over Bruch's work, it also shows just how advanced Draeseke's symphonic thought was. Their shared year of composition, 1868, was, after all, three years post-*Tristan*. Krueck concedes that 'Draeseke's progress as a symphonist is akin to Bruckner, though in actual sound they have little in common'.[132] Such a comparison can readily be drawn but only after Bruckner has produced his later symphonies, such as the eighth and then with Draeseke's third, but this applies far less to the early symphonies of both men. As the unacknowledged leading symphonist of his day, in the late 1860s to mid-1870s Draeseke cuts a very solitary figure.

---

[131] Krueck (page unnumbered; this quote is printed between 85 and 86).
[132] Ibid., 20.

Chapter 7

The German Symphony 1870–1876

A true symphony must improve on hearing.[1]

Like Albert Dietrich, the composer and conductor Friedrich Gernsheim (1839–1916) was close to Brahms. According to his biographer Karl Holl, his teacher Christian Hauff took the view that 'music is a large flowering garden laid down and cared for by our great composers until Haydn. Then Mozart came and built a house in the garden, while Beethoven built a tower upon the house, [an act] which nothing can surpass'.[2] This view summarises the symphonic pessimism of the day. At 13, Gernsheim was the youngest pupil at the Leipzig Conservatoire, saw the first staging there of *Tannhäuser*, and was 'carried away' by a concert performance of parts of *Lohengrin* conducted by Julius Rietz on 17 January 1853.[3] Before he was 15 he graduated, but such precocity was hardly encouraging. According to Holl, he was 'a composer of whose future development there was little to detect at this time', confirming the indifferent methods of teaching composition at that institution described in Chapter 4.[4] He was present in Paris on 30 April 1855 at the premiere of Berlioz's *Te Deum* under the composer's direction. By 1859, he had 'performed a four-movement symphony', but nothing survives of this work or its performance history.[5] The French capital was still under the huge influence of Habeneck, who had died in 1849 after almost 50 years spent shaping orchestral growth and activity there, an achievement that in turn may have inspired Mendelssohn's pioneering work at Leipzig.[6] It was Habeneck who almost single-handedly established Beethoven's music in Paris, so Gernsheim, a German and former Leipzig student abroad, felt at home in its musical climate that, by the end of the 1850s, had expanded the German repertoire with symphonies by Schubert, Mendelssohn and Schumann.[7] French symphonies would probably have included

---

[1] Eugen d'Albert to Marie Joshua (19 January 1882), quoted in Christopher Fifield, *True Artist and True Friend: A Biography of Hans Richter* (Oxford, 1993), 178.
[2] Karl Holl, *Friedrich Gernsheim: Leben, Erscheinung und Werk* (Leipzig, 1928), 9.
[3] Ibid., 20.
[4] Ibid., 21.
[5] Ibid., 28.
[6] François-Antoine Habeneck (1781–1849) attempted to conduct the first performance of Schubert's 'Great' C major symphony in Paris in 1842 but was defeated by the resistance of the players.
[7] As Frosch says in Goethe's *Faust* (Part 1): 'I praise my Leipzig! It is a little Paris and educates its people.'

those by Gounod and Saint-Saëns, written in the 1850s but in the classical Austro-German form.

At the heart of Gernsheim's music lay its personal melodic language, unlike his contemporary Bruch, whose melodic inspiration was folksong. The 65-year-old Rossini gave the 18-year-old teenager Gernsheim a 'Parisian blessing', advising him that 'the essential ingredient of music is melody'.[8] At winter Saturday soirées in Paris, Gernsheim befriended influential musical figures, among them Liszt and Anton Rubinstein, and in 1859 he renewed a childhood friendship with Hermann Levi, who would play a large part in shaping Gernsheim's conducting career. That year he also met Wagner but soon withdrew from his circle despite Franz Wüllner's advice, 'Do not give your opponents the excuse to say that you are avoiding Bayreuth [Wagner] because inwardly you fear him and therefore do not want to get to know him'.[9] In 1860, Gernsheim and Bruch made plans to move together to Mannheim, but Gernsheim went instead to Saarbrücken, where Levi had recommended him as his own successor. There he was introduced to the music of Brahms by Henriette Gouvy, in whose house it was enthusiastically studied and played, including the newly published orchestral serenades and the sextet.[10] In the spring of 1862 Gernsheim and Brahms met for the first time at Hiller's house.[11] Three years later Gernsheim was appointed to the Cologne Conservatoire, where Engelbert Humperdinck and Julius Buths became his pupils.[12] Brahms and Gernsheim next met in 1868 at Bonn, the former bringing the proofs of his *German Requiem* with him.[13] Gernsheim immediately resolved to conduct it in Cologne, but musical politics decreed that it should be Hiller, who had no particular feeling for the work and conducted only four movements (Nos 1, 2, 4 and 6) on 16 February 1869.[14] A year later Gernsheim, by now a close friend of Brahms, performed it in November 1870 during the Franco-Prussian war in memory of the fallen, and again in March 1871 but this time 'for the benefit of the survivors'.[15] Their surviving correspondence, consisting of only nine letters or postcards written between 1870 and 1884, makes no mention of symphonies. In June 1874 Gernsheim moved to Rotterdam, where he conducted concerts and the German Opera.[16] His two immediate predecessors had been Levi (1861–64) and

---

[8] Holl, 29.
[9] Ibid., 110.
[10] Ibid., 41.
[11] L. Schmidt (ed.), *Johannes Brahms im Briefwechsel mit Friedrich Gernsheim* (Berlin, 1910), 205.
[12] In 1901 Buths was conductor of the first successful performance of Elgar's *Dream of Gerontius*, which took place at the Lower Rhine Music Festival in Düsseldorf.
[13] Schmidt (ed.), 205.
[14] For a report on the performance see Bruch's letter (25 February 1869) to Brahms in *Johannes Brahms im Briefwechsel mit Max Bruch* (ed. W. Altmann) (Berlin, 1908), 93.
[15] Florence May, *The Life of Brahms* 2 vols, Vol. 2 (London, 1905), 414.
[16] He was appointed by the *Maatschappij tot Bevordering van Toonkunst* (Society for the Promotion of Music).

Bargiel (1865–74). As in any similar German post, he was able to programme his own music, which in turn spurred him on to finish the first of his four symphonies.[17] At a concert in the winter of 1875 it was enthusiastically received by the Dutch public and repeated in Leipzig's Gewandhaus, Cologne's Gürzenich and at the Academy in Munich, while the publisher Simrock printed it (No. 1 in G minor, Op. 32). Gernsheim therefore played a prominent role in the ever-growing Brahms circle, which by now included Max Bruch (in Sondershausen), Albert Dietrich (in Oldenburg), Julius Otto Grimm (in Münster) and Hermann Levi (in Karlsruhe). All were conductors able to perform their own music and that of their contemporaries, including symphonies.[18] At the sixth Gewandhaus concert in Leipzig on 25 November 1875, Gernsheim conducted his first symphony, but although it is a passionate work, it seems to have left this particular critic unimpressed:

> Gernsheim's work is noble, stylised, fully formed and of extensive construction. While an absence of dramatic energy and originality leaves much to be desired (now and then the composer struggles with his own lack of high-flying flight of fancy, very much the territory of Beethoven or Schubert), it seeks instead to replace this with a permeating broad sense of tone. The symphony was given an excellent performance and acknowledged as such by the public, though by no means did it get an enthusiastic reception.[19]

As if following a conductor's schedule more typical of a century later, Gernsheim was in Munich just two days later. Here the symphony fared better at the hands of its reviewer; but considering that the journey from Leipzig must have taken most of the intervening day, how much time could have been given to rehearsing this unfamiliar work?

> Already the first movement fascinates with its original, skilfully inventive treatment of the main theme, after which there is a contrasting *cantilena* played by the French horn. An excellent *Larghetto* is throughout moving, tenderly ingenious and especially rich in sound, though it might have been more effective in a shorter version as it lacks contrast. The *scherzo* is fully mischievous in mood with attractive, folksy content in the trio. The *finale* is also rich in beautiful, original ideas, though so rich in *cantilena* that its character suffers somewhat. The work arises from the study of Classical form and, apart from the somewhat superficial main theme, possesses an abundance of beautiful details, which, at first hearing, pass one by too fleetingly. The instrumental treatment reveals a very talented hand, which initially treats the strings as carrying the orchestral weight but tries to do so in an especially original way with a partiality for powerful tone and striking

---

[17] Gernsheim wrote four symphonies; they were first performed in 1875, 1882, 1887 and 1895 respectively.
[18] Hiller was a generation older, his style more influenced by Spohr.
[19] *AMZ*, Vol. 10 No. 50, 15 December 1875, col. 796.

climax. As conductor Mr Gernsheim was the attentive ruler of his hardworking, accurate orchestral subjects and earned merited, rich appreciation.[20]

While Gernsheim's style retains many familiar devices, the *unisono, arpeggio*-based start (Ex. 7.1), pedal points and melodies in thirds doubled at the octave, his instrumentation, thematic shapes, accompaniments and orchestral textures owe much to Bruch (his first violin concerto and the first two symphonies) and Brahms (his first piano concerto and the two serenades). The strong orchestral statement of the first theme, characterised by the Munich critic as 'carrying the orchestral weight', recalls both mood and key of the first *ritornello* in the opening movement of Bruch's concerto. In the orchestral texture, Gernsheim establishes a division of labour between highly active strings (his idiosyncratic touch of orchestral colour is a simplified double bass line independent of cellos) accompanying sustained unison winds, with occasional brass punctuation in the middle to glue the outer sections together. When the winds eventually split into thirds over three octaves, we are not only drawn to Brahms but further to Dvořák's cello concerto (Ex. 7.2).

Hard on its heels we hear the second subject with its familiar melodic outline (French horn) from the *finale* of the *Eroica* symphony (Ex. 7.3). When Gernsheim breaks free from block scoring and instead fragments his textures with instrumental solos, the result is more expressive, even when such moments serve as no more than a transition (Ex. 7.4). He eschews long development; nevertheless its promising start degenerates into repetitive rhythmic patterns, the whole punctuated by the brass on upbeat chords. Holl describes this lamely as 'full of strange melismatic and harmonic features', but if truth be told it simply lacks ideas and threatens to become dull.[21] However, Gernsheim's key relationships are cleverly neutralised by unison passages and disguised by chromatic sideslips, misleading the listener to take unexpected paths. The coda, beginning with 22 bars over a pedal D (second violins), followed by a tattoo of repeated D triplets from the timpani, is surely Gernsheim showing his high regard for Brahms's *German Requiem*, in which the final 36 bars of the third movement are also played over a pedal D.

---

[20]   *AMZ*, Vol. 10 No. 52, 29 December 1875, col. 825.
[21]   See Holl, 165–7, at 165.

Example 7.1 Gernsheim: Symphony No. 1. First movement, opening

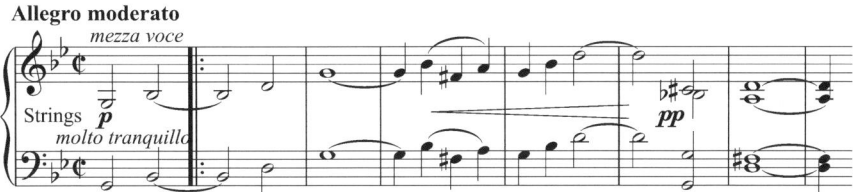

Example 7.2 Gernsheim: Symphony No. 1. First movement, first subject

Example 7.3   Gernsheim: Symphony No. 1. First movement, second subject

Example 7.4   Gernsheim: Symphony No. 1. First movement, transition on pedal

Bruch's first violin concerto was frequently played from 1868 and Gernsheim may well have acknowledged his friend's masterpiece in his own slow movement, for both works have stylistic similarities including a *cantilena* in 3/8 time, while Gernsheim's first five notes from the clarinet and French horn (Ex. 7.5) and later a more elaborate version of this simple melody (Ex. 7.6) are notably Bruch-like. As just noted in the case of Bruch's second symphony, such phrases appear to be more green shoots of the melody that could have pointed Brahms to the grand theme in the *finale* of his first symphony. The critic at Munich described Gernsheim's *Larghetto* as 'lacking contrast', but this is the one constituent that it has in abundance, with its unusual but well-defined structure of four sections and alternating time signatures (3/8 and 4/4). The model for the *scherzo* (Ex. 7.7) could be any one of three Beethoven symphonies, a reminiscence that by now was becoming expected by critics and public alike, while the *Ländler* melody of the trio is an amalgam of Beethoven and pure Schubert (Ex. 7.8). Its coda speeds to an exciting conclusion, for 'Gernsheim's natural temperament and masterly skill raises *scherzos* (also in his chamber music) above the general level of other symphonic movements'.[22]

---

[22]   Ibid., 166.

Example 7.5   Gernsheim: Symphony No. 1. Second movement, main theme

Example 7.6   Gernsheim: Symphony No. 1. Second movement, thematic elaboration

Example 7.7   Gernsheim: Symphony No. 1. Third movement, Scherzo

Example 7.8   Gernsheim: Symphony No. 1. Third movement, Trio

Gernsheim's predilection for pedal points continues in the *finale*, the main theme accompanied by violas and cellos in gently rocking triplet quavers (Ex. 7.9), like the second theme in the *finale* of Bruch's first symphony (Ex. 6.67). Gernsheim's second subject (Ex. 7.10) is rather too much like the first, but what is more interesting is the bridge passage that links them. It contains two elements that will be heard again in the *finale* of the first symphony of Brahms; however, where Gernsheim places the contrasting rhythmic patterns one after the other (Ex. 7.11), the more innovative Brahms combines them (Ex. 7.12). As the *finale* progresses, such 'Brahms moments' become easier to spot. More and more, they become a wake-up call that the long-awaited first symphony is just a year away and a reminder too that, where Gernsheim is at his most imaginative, he and Brahms can be perceived as ploughing parallel furrows.

Gernsheim now proceeds to develop the material he has laid out. The first theme (Ex. 7.9) *molto dolce*, having initially focussed on quiet dynamics, now assumes and develops a shimmering *tremolando* quality in tone colour (Ex. 7.13), after which he draws the ear to two elements (Ex. 7.11). They have even more Brahms (Ex. 7.12) about them in their persistent articulations of punctuated rhythmic passion led by violins and violas over a wide compass, cellos and basses on a four-bar pedal, while winds engage in a rising semiquaver dialogue (Ex. 7.14). Here we sense the inadequacy of instruments incapable of dealing with the sheer power of the music, already noticeable some two decades earlier in Brahms's first piano concerto, itself a frustrated symphony. Similarly we find a bridge passage (Ex. 7.15) leading to the coda that has a rhythmic kinship (*sforzando* punctuation) with a two-bar passage (Ex. 7.16) in the *finale* of Brahms's violin concerto still to come two years later in 1877. Gernsheim's coda starts energetically with a wide range of dynamics and a carefully graduated increase of tempo, but the effect is lost in an anticlimax of ubiquitous rising *arpeggios*. The *finale* is a case of missed opportunity, for Gernsheim gave himself no chance with such a lame resort to convention at the end. Holl singles out his slow movements and finales as forming 'the weak side of his symphonic output' and that as a composer/conductor 'his musical steadfastness of purpose is externally applied', not 'internally motivated'.²³ On the other hand, he credits the composer with an ability to 'express the symphonic idea' thanks to his 'constant dealings with an excellent symphonic orchestra'.²⁴ Despite the fact that Gernsheim's first symphony is inconsistent in quality and that it only intermittently shows inspirational originality, there are nevertheless clear signs of the beneficial effect that his career as a conductor was having upon the practical application of his technique as a composer and orchestrator, a talent that not all composer–conductors could be assumed to possess.²⁵

Example 7.9   Gernsheim: Symphony No. 1. Fourth movement, first subject

Example 7.10   Gernsheim: Symphony No. 1. Fourth movement, second subject

---

²³ Ibid., 185.
²⁴ Ibid.
²⁵ Others that did include Mendelssohn, Lachner, Gade, Rietz, Reinecke, Bruch, Raff and Dietrich.

Example 7.11 Gernsheim: Symphony No. 1. Fourth movement, bridge passage

Example 7.12 Brahms: Symphony No. 1. Fourth movement, bridge passage

Example 7.13 Gernsheim: Symphony No. 1. Fourth movement, first subject developed

Example 7.14 Gernsheim: Symphony No. 1. Fourth movement, development

Example 7.15 Gernsheim: Symphony No. 1. Fourth movement, bridge passage to coda

Example 7.16 Brahms: Violin concerto. Finale, bars 141–3

A new symphony to appear just before Brahms revealed his first at Karlsruhe on 4 November 1876 was the second written by Hermann Goetz (1840–76), a German who lived in Switzerland from the age of 23 until his death at 36. He had written an earlier symphony (E minor) in 1866, which was played once at Basel (3 March 1867).[26] His second (F major Op. 9) was finished in Zürich on 14 June 1873 and prefaced with a motto by Schiller, 'You must flee from life's tumult into the sacred, silent rooms of the heart'.[27] The symphony was submitted to another competition, this time set up by the Leipzig Gewandhaus in October 1873 for performance that winter season and the jury was chaired by Carl Reinecke. This proved rather embarrassing for him judging by a surviving and somewhat indiscreet letter, which made no attempt to conceal the fact that he clearly favoured Goetz's composition but was in a minority on the panel and therefore compelled to announce Ferdinand Breunung from Aachen as the successful candidate. Reinecke softened the blow as much as he could; Goetz's symphony was at least one of the three shortlisted and rehearsed by the orchestra from the 'very many' submitted:

> Whether [Breunung's] will find favour with the public is now another matter. I do not have to tell you how much I would have liked to write to you with more pleasant news; it would have given me the utmost joy to have performed your

---

[26] Only the first part of the first movement survives in a four-hand piano version at the Bavarian State Library.

[27] 'In des Herzens heilig stille Räume, musst Du fliehen aus dem Lebens Drang.'

symphony. Naturally I have to maintain a fully impartial position and you also know that three other gentlemen, who had votes, sat alongside me.[28]

Once over his disappointment, Goetz came to feel that Leipzig had done him a favour by giving him the opportunity to revise the symphony. Its original version was first performed at Mannheim on 25 December 1874 under Ernst Frank; but after revisions to the third and fourth movements, Friedrich Hegar conducted it on 9 March 1875 at Zürich. It was published by Kistner in 1875 and Reinecke conducted it at Leipzig on 27 January 1876, by which time Goetz was famous for his opera *Der Widerspänstigen Zähmung* (*The Taming of the Shrew*). 'Think of it!', he wrote. 'My F major symphony was received with the liveliest applause at the concert for the pension fund, ... and, what is more, in the Gewandhaus, where for decades every new symphony always fails'.[29]

The choice of Schiller's words as a motto puzzled a critic at the premiere. Apart from the slow third movement, he detected 'a fundamentally fresh and joyful sound', far removed from so serious a sentiment, while its *finale* had 'a triumphant, exuberantly healthy lust for life', ironic words to describe music by a man who, like Mozart, Schubert, Weber and Burgmüller before him, would be dead by his mid-thirties. The writer assured his readers that this was not

> an admonition, for its inner thoughts emerge freshly and the treatment of the orchestra is again in the nature of those lively, flowering thoughts. How far the spiritual influence of Wagner, Gounod, Meyerbeer and in part also Mendelssohn is detectable, could not be discussed in such a limited space.[30]

This was a strange selection of bedfellows, for (*pace* Mendelssohn) with symphonies they were hardly in their natural habitat, while reference to Wagner's influence when stripped of its operatic or New German context was rare. He concluded with a pertinent summary, 'the symphony is a child of its time, but a really fresh, spirited, well-behaved child that one would like to have'. The part he least liked was the main section of the intermezzo, which he likened to *Dinorah* (hence the reference to Meyerbeer), 'which crumbled here somewhat and where the instrumentation is often affected and not always noble or beautiful'.[31] Its success at Leipzig was confirmed by a second performance there at the end of the same year, on 21 December 1876.

In November 1876 the printed full score was reviewed and the symphony praised for 'its skilled structure, form, thematic control of modulation and fluent

---

[28] Reinecke to Goetz, 12 January 1874, quoted in Marek Bobéth, *Hermann Goetz: Leben und Werk* (Winterthur, 1996), 438. Breunung's Symphony in E♭ was performed three days later at Leipzig on 15 January 1874.

[29] Hermann Goetz to Ludwig Abel, 2 February 1876, in Bobéth, 442.

[30] *AMZ*, Vol. 11 No. 6, 9 February 1876, cols 92–3.

[31] Ibid.

instrumentation, above all a freshness and unanimity of sound, which works laudably'. The writer urged his readers to 'look to the score at the intermezzo, which is like making an interesting journey, perhaps into a wood; there is certainly a wedding procession. The horn begins happily with a flourish and an echo returns it. Then there's the bustle of life, a charming humming, whispering, playfulness'. Taking a diametrically opposite view to that of his colleague 10 months earlier, he concludes that 'this intermezzo is a very beautiful part of the symphony'. The appeal of the slow movement lay in its serious mood, with plenty of references to sighs, suffering and sadness. However, as was usual when first assessing new symphonies, praise was anaesthetised by pedantry, as if purposely to deflate a composer's self-confidence. This could be criticism of length (cuts were almost always demanded) or of a lack of structural clarity, if, for example, the conventional signposts for the three sections of sonata form were not blatantly obvious. At such moments, the nineteenth-century music critic had clearly lost touch with the concert-going public, if not his average reader. This commentator also praised the 'fresh, flowing *finale*, which makes a good ending to the symphony, breathing life, desire and joy. Like a sparkling wine, which, even if it still has a few unfermented sections clinging to it, does not fail to make a positive effect'. Yet despite finding so many positives in the symphony, including the revelation of a significantly creative talent, the quality of its themes was adjudged to be lacking in sufficient depth. This superficiality, allegedly the result of note-spinning, was like a game of nice effects; and although always interesting, the work lacked loftier spiritual content and fell short of 'Parnassian heights'. Referring back to the premiere with the 'estimable' Reinecke at the helm, it was 'confident and enthusiastic and the large audience responded with much applause'. The critic finally sent the work out into the musical world 'with his best hopes, and the wish that the composer, who quickly made a name with his opera, would gain new admirers with the symphony'. However, he was still mystified by the relevance of the motto taken from Schiller and surmised that it was an after-thought by Goetz, rather than the spark of inspiration for the symphony.[32]

Goetz had indicated some suggestions on interpretation to Ernst Frank, conductor of the early performance at Mannheim, among them 'flexible tempi, therefore no rigorous observation of metronome marks' and the fact that the *finale* 'speaks for itself'.[33] A whiff of Raff's style appears in the attractive themes of the conventionally structured first movement (Exx 7.17 and 7.18). When Goetz originally wrote the symphony in 1873, Raff was working on his sixth; and even beyond the mutually shared key of F, one also detects the pastoral *Im Walde* in the various components of the intermezzo, such as the rustic horn call and its echo (Ex. 7.19) leading to a dance 'of almost folkloristic character' (Ex. 7.20).[34] The

---

[32] *AMZ*, Vol. 11 No. 46, 15 November 1876, cols 733–4. The performance described here was also of the premiere, despite its having taken place some nine months earlier.

[33] Goetz to Frank, 9 December 1874, quoted in Bobéth, 452.

[34] Bobéth, 443.

sounds of the countryside continue with a substantial cadenza of bird-calls on the flute (Ex. 7.21), leading to the meat of the sandwich (Ex. 7.21 * *a tempo*), a Schumann-like episode coloured by its shifting modality. The second theme (Ex. 7.22) consists of lush string chords surrounding a horn pedal, another step on the road to Brahms, who admired the symphony but we do not know when he first read or heard it.[35] After a brief return of the opening fanfare on the trumpet, both themes are worked in various keys and colours to reveal yet another motif in the strings, which has the rhythmic and intervallic shapes of Schumann (Ex. 7.23). At the end of the movement, the horn motif (doubled by flute and clarinet) combines with the major version of * *a tempo* in Ex. 7.21. This intermezzo bristles with ideas, but the vessel into which they are poured can barely cope with them all. Carl Goldmark (1830–1915) probably knew Goetz's music when he wrote his *Rustic Wedding* symphony three years later (1877), but it would be Mahler who eventually enlarged symphonic proportions to accommodate such a wealth of ideas.

Example 7.17   Goetz: Symphony No. 2. First movement, first subject

Example 7.18   Goetz: Symphony No. 2. First movement, second subject

Example 7.19   Goetz: Symphony No. 2. Second movement, Intermezzo, fanfare bars 1–7

---

[35] In a letter praising Robert Fuchs's Symphony No. 2, 'If I look around for a comparison, Goetz's symphony springs to mind'. Brahms to Simrock, 8 November 1884, quoted in Bobéth, 453.

Example 7.20   Goetz: Symphony No. 2. Second movement, Intermezzo, dance bars 8–12

Example 7.21   Goetz: Symphony No. 2. Second movement, Intermezzo, flute cadenza leading to main section

Example 7.22   Goetz: Symphony No. 2. Second movement, Intermezzo, trio

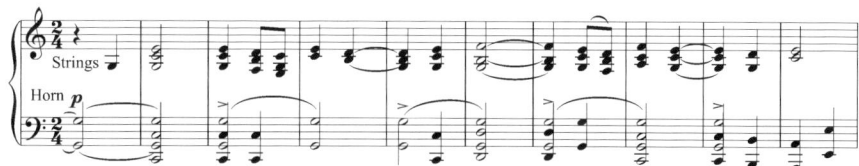

Example 7.23   Goetz: Symphony No. 2. Second movement, Intermezzo, coda

Goetz balances his thematic extravagance by going now to the opposite extreme and builds the third movement *Adagio* on a monothematic principle (Ex. 7.24), while the joyously impetuous *finale* plays safe and reverts to florid scales and *arpeggios* (Ex. 7.25), 'not to be considered from the standpoint of the first-movement form but in the grand style of a Rondo'.[36] Once again, its zest for life hardly reflects the desperate physical and psychological condition of this man, who, had he not died on 3 December 1876 just as his name was being feted throughout Germany, clearly would have wanted to develop traditional forms and, as Bobéth surmises, create new ones.

Example 7.24   Goetz: Symphony No.2. Third movement, opening

Example 7.25   Goetz: Symphony No.2. Fourth movement, finale, bars 5–7

In England, Goetz's symphony was a work that, for half a century, enjoyed a popular success. The Philharmonic Society performed it ('Goetz's fine symphony') in London on 5 May 1887 under Arthur Sullivan and on 28 May 1891 under Frederic Cowen.[37] More impressive though was Sir Dan Godfrey, who performed it at Bournemouth 17 times between the 1897–98 season and 1921.[38] After Manns performed it at Crystal Palace on 11 November 1893, Grove told the composer's widow Laura that 'the extraordinarily poetic beauty of the two middle movements and the force and spirit of the first and last, made an immense impression upon me'.[39] The *Musical Times* described it as 'delightful ... each successive hearing of [it] only enhances the regret inspired by the premature removal of its gifted composer'.[40] Having heard it in London on 22 November 1893, George Bernard Shaw lavished extravagant praise upon it, one suspects in order to tilt at the four windmills he names:

---

[36] Goetz to Frank, 16 March 1875, quoted in Bobéth, 453.
[37] Myles Birket Foster, *The History of the Philharmonic Society 1813–1912* (London, 1912), 408, 427.
[38] Stephen Lloyd, *Sir Dan Godfrey: Champion of British Composers* (London, 1995), 38.
[39] Sir George Grove to Laura Goetz, quoted in Bobéth, 453.
[40] *Musical Times*, Vol. 34 No. 610, 1 December 1893, 728, 1.

I suppose it is the only real symphony that has been composed since Beethoven died. ... Goetz alone among the modern symphonists is easily and unaffectedly successful from beginning to end. He has the charm of Schubert without his brainlessness, the refinement and inspiration of Mendelssohn without his limitation and timid gentility, Schumann's sense of harmonic expression without his laboriousness, shortcoming and dependence on external poetic stimulus; while as to unembarrassed mastery of the material of music, shewing itself in the Mozartian grace and responsiveness of his polyphony, he leaves all three of them simply nowhere. Brahms, who alone touches him in mere brute musical faculty, is a dolt by comparison to him. ... [It is] a masterpiece which places Goetz securely above all other German composers of the last hundred years, save only Mozart and Beethoven, Weber and Wagner.[41]

In Chapter 5, the relative paucity of symphonies written in the 1850s was noted; however, there is one from that decade that has great significance although it has to find a place here some 20 years later in the 1870s, because its existence was barely known until it was published in 1874. It has a complicated genesis. It was actually written and first played in 1852, albeit without a *finale*, and its composer was the Estonian-born Julius Otto Grimm (1827–1903). Six years older than Brahms, Grimm was to become one of his closest friends and, furthermore, he seems to play a vital part in the climax to the German symphonic revival. Having studied philology and philosophy, Grimm took a house tutor's post in St Petersburg, but music had always been his chosen career and with financial support from his sympathetic employer he studied at Leipzig from 7 March 1851 until 4 October 1852 under several of Mendelssohn's appointees.[42] His contemporaries included Robert Radecke (1830–1911), Theodor Kirchner (1823–1903), Dietrich, Bargiel and the 13-year-old Gernsheim. Grimm wrote one symphony, published in 1874 as Op. 19 in D minor, but any popularity he enjoyed during his lifetime rested almost entirely on his Suite for strings in canon form Op. 10. Two other suites, a march and the symphony constitute his total orchestral output. He spent the last 40 years of his working life (1860–1900) as music director in Münster.

According to the programme for a students' examination concert at Leipzig's Conservatoire on 19 June 1852, 'three movements from a Symphony in D minor by Julius Otto Grimm' were performed. While it is not possible to state categorically that one work is under discussion, given that both have the same key and that a funeral march is the second movement in each, it is highly likely that such a possibility is actually a probability. The reason for the absence of a *finale* must also be examined. The movements played in 1852 and listed in the full score when it was published in 1874 were as follows:

---

[41]   *Music in London 1890–1894* 3 vols, Vol. 3 (London, 1932), 94–5.
[42]   Franz Ludwig, *Julius Otto Grimm: ein Beitrag zur Geschichte der musikalischen Spätromantik* (Bielefeld, 1925), 13.

1852	1874
1. *Andante sostenuto, Allegro con fuoco*	1. *Sostenuto, Allegro*
2. *Tempo di Marcia funèbre*	2. *Trauermarsch*
3. *Scherzo: Allegro vivace*	3. *Scherzo: Presto*
	4. *Finale: Allegro vivace*

In 1855 Grimm moved to Göttingen as a teacher and choral conductor and on 18 February 1857 the symphony (possibly by now with a *finale*) was performed there. After this, nothing is heard of it until performances at Berlin (date unknown), Münster (9 November 1872) and at Leipzig's Gewandhaus on 16 January 1873 (under Grimm's direction but no review has been found) followed by publication the following year.[43] According to a review of the 1872 performance at Münster, the tempo indications on that occasion were the same as those printed in the full score two years later, apart from the *scherzo*, which was simply described as *Allegro*:

> The new grand symphony, still in manuscript, by our music director Grimm filled the second part of the programme. After one hearing, we liked the *scherzo* and the preceding funeral march, and these may be described as the most successful movements. The syncopation and *tempo rubato* in the *scherzo* are effective but in the first [movement] *Allegro* the strange use of *pizzicato* was new and surprising.[44] The scoring of the whole work (woodwinds, [trumpets], trombones, horns) appears powerful and solemn. To delve into finer detail without a second hearing or sight of the score is scarcely possible, so we reserve judgement on the symphony, which nevertheless can take its place alongside the newest works of Volkmann, Raff and Carl Reinecke and we want to return to it later, for hopefully Mr Grimm will give us the opportunity with a further hearing during the course of this winter. Meanwhile we recall the words of that magician Rossini after a performance of Spohr's *Faust*, "The man must be very rich and extravagant when spreading his ideas about. From one of his *finale*s, I would not hesitate to make at least three grand operas". May we make one request to Mr Grimm, namely that with overtures, symphonies and concertos – particularly new ones – the key should be printed in the programme; it would cause little inconvenience, and is of the greatest value to music lovers.[45]

---

[43] It was also played in the second half of a concert in Münster on 31 October 1885 to mark Grimm's silver jubilee as music director there. The movements listed in an advertisement were substantially as printed in the score: *Sostenuto, Allegro – Andante* (*Trauermarsch*) *– Scherzo – Finale.*

[44] There is only one passage of about 20 bars of *pizzicato* in the first movement and there is nothing out of the ordinary about it. The reviewer may have confused his technical terms and meant *ostinato*.

[45] *Münsterischer Anzeiger* 12 November 1872.

The word 'new', which began this review, could mean either a newly composed work or one that was new to Münster, which it was. In the printed score there is no obvious sign of its having been written in 1852, other than having tempo markings more or less identical with those listed in the Conservatoire programme. By now, however, there is an added fourth movement, namely a *Rondo*.[46] In 1925 Franz Ludwig identified 'a fourth movement, which appears to have kept Grimm occupied for long. As well as the printed *Rondo*, there is also another handwritten movement in sonata form with "IV" at the top, possibly conceived first; it has apparently been separated from a complete manuscript'.[47] Regrettably its whereabouts are unknown today, neither is it clear if it was played at Göttingen in 1857.[48] However, Ludwig saw it and by using quotes in short score, compared it to the *Rondo* that replaced it.[49] One other piece of anecdotal evidence may prove that, after disappearing for 16 years, the first three movements of Grimm's published symphony are the same as those of the incomplete one written back in 1852. In 1910 Gernsheim went to Dortmund and was met at the station by August Preising, formerly a pupil of Grimm, who had died seven years before. When the conversation turned to Grimm, Gernsheim asked his host what had happened to the symphony, 'which he was working on in [our] Leipzig time', whereupon he sang the two-bar motif that opens the first movement after the introduction (Ex. 7.28). It must have made an impression, if he could still sing it 58 years after hearing it at the Conservatoire.[50]

Why did Grimm's symphony disappear for 15 years? As music director in Münster he was in charge of various choral and orchestral societies and conducted what were called *Platzkonzerte*, like the *Lohkonzerte* that Bruch led in Sondershausen during his tenure there 1867–70. A commission set up in 1861 to assess Münster's concert requirements suggested 14 per year with a large orchestra (44), five with a smaller one (39) and one chamber music concert. The full orchestra consisted of 13 violins, six violas, three each of cellos and double basses, double woodwinds, horns and trumpets, a trombone and timpani, with extra piccolo, horns and trombones as required. A post was created for a leader, who was obliged to play six solos per season, so violin concertos tended to predominate the programmes.[51] Grimm was faced with a long uphill task raising playing standards,

---

[46] Full score, parts and a piano duet version were first advertised by Rieter-Biedermann in *AMZ*, Vol. 10 No. 5, 3 February 1875, col. 80. Curiously no review of the published score appeared in the paper. In 2007 Grimm's symphony was republished by Konsid Musikverlag, Mönchengladbach.

[47] Ludwig, 26.

[48] Despite help received from archives, orchestras and libraries at Göttingen, Münster and Berlin.

[49] Ludwig, 49.

[50] Ibid., 26.

[51] The first two leaders were Carl Bargheer (1861–66) followed by Richard Barth (1867–81), both pupils of Joachim. Barth (1850–1925) was (following an accident) a left-handed violinist, the teenage leader of Grimm's Münster orchestra and protégé conductor

but he set to it from the outset. He tried to perform Brahms's second serenade in 1861, but it had to be abandoned; it was 1869 before choral standards were high enough to do the *German Requiem*, while even the more straightforward *Triumphlied*, scheduled for 1873, took a further three years to come to fruition. By 1876 improvements were acknowledged in terms of precision and technique and he could invite soloists of the calibre of the singers Julius Stockhausen, Georg Henschel and Amalie Joachim, her violinist husband Joseph Joachim and pianists Brahms and Clara Schumann.[52] By concentrating totally on making Münster a viable performing centre, Grimm's own creative energies as a composer were distracted, while during those years of reconstruction and improvement the orchestra was simply not capable of playing his symphony.

Its introduction is slow, its sinister mood heavy with traces of Beethoven's ninth, but soon there emerges a brooding duplet-plus-triplet motto (Ex. 7.26), fragmented in the timpani, then passed around horns, trumpets and double basses until a midway climax. What seems to place the music years ahead of its 1850s origins is the following eruption of the motto rhythm (Ex. 7.27) in a broad, powerful, fully scored, unison statement over a pedal D at the *Allegro* (Ex. 7.28). It certainly anticipates Volkmann's first (D minor, 1863) and Bruckner, who uses a similar motif in his third symphony (D minor, 1873) (Ex. 7.29), after which this rhythm became his symphonic calling card. This conflict between duple and triple pulse within a bar is the primary characteristic of the movement and also forms part of the second subject, a simple, lyrical theme with the triplets now a *perpetuum mobile* occupying the middle of the texture (Ex. 7.30), becoming more rhythmically complex and harmonically chromatic over a grandly rising bass scale (Ex. 7.31), until it all reaches an apotheosis in one of those Mendelssohn-type unifying chorales, the duplets having won the day (Ex. 7.32).

Example 7.26   Grimm: Symphony in D minor. Duplet + triplet motto rhythm. First appearance (horns and timpani) at bars 31–2 in the Introduction

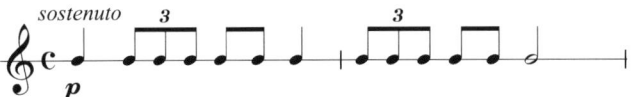

---

under his tutelage. He became music director in Hamburg on Brahms's recommendation and also edited the Brahms–Grimm correspondence.

[52]   *AMZ*, Vol. 11 No. 8, 23 February 1876, cols 124–5. Stockhausen had already sung Handel, Brahms and Schubert for Grimm at the concert on 9 November 1872 mentioned on page 268, the second half of which was given over to Grimm's symphony.

Example 7.27   Grimm: Symphony in D minor. First movement, motto rhythm

Example 7.28   Grimm: Symphony in D minor. First movement, motto rhythm with upper and lower pedal points on D

Example 7.29   Bruckner: Symphony No. 3. First movement, duplet + triplet motto rhythm

Example 7.30   Grimm: Symphony in D minor. First movement, second subject

Example 7.31   Grimm: Symphony in D minor. First movement, second subject

Example 7.32   Grimm: Symphony in D minor. First movement, second subject

The second movement is described as a funeral march, yet it has more optimism about it than befits such a description (Ex. 7.33). Its components are four-square, driven by *arpeggio*-constructed fanfares, while in the horns and trumpets the motto theme is heard once again (Ex. 7.34). The most interesting part of its ternary form lies in the chromatic harmony of the middle section reached by a move to D♭ after four repeated Fs by the third horn (Ex. 7.35), but the following repeat of the opening section provides only some variation of what has been heard before.

Example 7.33   Grimm: Symphony in D minor. Second movement, opening

Example 7.34   Grimm: Symphony in D minor. Second movement, motto rhythm

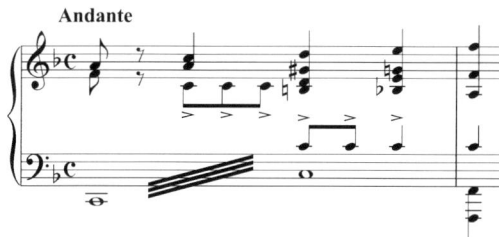

Example 7.35   Grimm: Symphony in D minor. Second movement, middle section

The fast *scherzo* (its quiet start again anticipating Bruckner) continues the duple–triple conflict but with a hemiola construct (Ex. 7.36). A similar effect

was achieved by Verhulst in the *scherzo* of his E minor symphony, first heard at the Leipzig Euterpe concerts in January 1842, four years before the *finale* of Schumann's piano concerto was performed (Exx 3.11 and 3.12), though whether, in 1852 (i.e. during Grimm's student days), Verhulst's work was still being played or whether he saw Schumann's score (published in Mainz in 1853) can only be speculated upon.[53] Eduard Franck's Symphony in A major (probably written 1845–55) is possibly a more likely model (Ex. 5.16), but Dietrich, as we have just seen, also achieved the same effect in his D minor symphony in 1869. Grimm's trio has charm despite its lean scoring. It is an attractively lopsided structure built upon three paragraphs of 12 bars rather than eight. The rondo-*finale* recalls the *scherzo* of Schumann's second symphony with its continual flurries of semiquavers (Ex. 7.37) and an accompaniment requiring a feather-light touch. By way of total contrast, it is followed by a calmer second subject melody of Schubertian simplicity (Ex. 7.38). Ludwig finds 'a striking metrical analogy between a majestic third theme and Brahms's later Rhapsody [for piano] Op. 119 [1892]' (Exx 7.39 and 7.40).[54] He then concludes with three examples (Exx 7.41–7.43), which he identifies as all we have from Grimm's discarded *finale* in sonata form and which he describes as 'quite different in character'.

> In its robust and brittle way it is more typical of Grimm. After three long, serious [*sic*] symphonic movements, the sparkling temperament and the contrasting rhythmic form of the printed rondo – already from an aesthetic point of view – is better in place. In itself it is remarkable, an energetic first theme [Ex. 7.41] that follows in the rhythmic wake of the first movement, a march-like second [Ex. 7.42] and a melodious coda related to this second theme [Ex. 7.43]. The development and recapitulation contain many details, but on the whole, the movement does not have the emotional tension that is demanded of the last movement of this symphony. This realisation prompted Grimm to compose the *rondo*.[55]

Example 7.36 Grimm: Symphony in D minor. Third movement, Scherzo

---

[53] Coincidentally Verhulst later introduced the aforementioned third symphony by Bruckner to Holland in 1885.
[54] Ludwig, 16.
[55] Ibid., 17–18.

Example 7.37   Grimm: Symphony in D minor. Rondo finale, opening theme

Example 7.38   Grimm: Symphony in D minor. Rondo finale, second theme

Example 7.39   Grimm: Symphony in D minor. Rondo finale, third theme

Example 7.40   Brahms: Rhapsody for piano Op. 119 No. 4. (see also Example 7.39)

Example 7.41   Grimm: Symphony in D minor. Discarded finale, first subject

Example 7.42   Grimm: Symphony in D minor. Discarded finale, second subject

Example 7.43   Grimm: Symphony in D minor. Discarded finale, coda

The three composers, Gernsheim, Goetz and Grimm, joining others already on the journey, took the route that led inexorably to Brahms just past the midway point of the decade of the 1870s. When we talk of the genesis of Brahms's first symphony, however, we are discussing neither spontaneous inspiration nor an easy pregnancy but rather a protracted gestation period of at least 15 years and a difficult birth followed by post-natal revisions. Once placed before the public, it became clear that it was 'an emphatic affirmation of the present vitality of the Beethovenian tradition'.[56] A purpose of this book has been to sketch the lives and musical activities of composers within the half-century under discussion and, above all, to bring to light some of the symphonies they wrote. In some cases it has been a matter of reviving reputations, while in others it has been one of revealing the very presence of the music in what has been hitherto portrayed as a symphonic dark age. What it has not been, however, is a search for evidence with which to accuse Brahms of symphonic plagiarism (indeed he was not born at the start nor does he feature until at least halfway through the period under discussion); rather, it has aimed to search for threads that, *via* his predecessors and then his contemporaries, connect by a natural process his first symphony to Beethoven's last a half-century earlier. It therefore raises the question, did symphonies written by German composers during these years eventually act as a catalyst to which Brahms's own creative powers responded or, to turn the process around, were they influenced by his pre-1876 orchestral music, with its readily identifiable language, instrumentation, melodic invention and structure? The third alternative to these two possibilities was a mixture of both, resulting in a two-way flow from which all parties benefited. Among Brahms's contemporaries most had tried their hand at symphonies early in their careers, but this juvenilia was often destroyed because of public failure, self-doubt, or following rejection by publishers. Leaving aside his early attempt at a first symphony, which eventually became the first piano concerto,

---

[56]   Robert Pascall, 'Brahms underway to the "1st Symphony": a hidden story of concept-development' in Ingrid Fuchs (ed.), *Festschrift Otto Biba zum 60. Geburtstag* (Tutzing, 2006), 405–23.

it was not in itself exceptional for Brahms finally to write his first symphony at the age of 43. From Table 7.1 we see that in the first half of the century the average age of a composer writing his first symphony was 26, after which it rose to almost 44 in the 25 years between Schumann's last and Brahms's first. Of the nine who produced a first symphony during the 13 years (1863–76) leading to Brahms, six were in their forties. On the other hand, in the years between Beethoven and Schumann there was none. The crushing weight of Beethoven's legacy and the many intimidating strictures in the press were clearly having a combined effect, although it is curious that there is a marked absence of calls for Brahms to produce his first symphony in reviews of his new music in other genres, or in analyses of a symphony freshly penned by another composer. In other words, when yet another new symphony had failed the litmus test of a review, it comes as a surprise to discover no hint, let alone a clarion call in the press, that Brahms would be the obvious man to show them how it should be done.

Hermann Kretschmar's writings on the subject reflect the nineteenth-century view of the symphony at the time of Brahms's death (1897) and, regarding his place in Beethoven's shadow, conclude that,

> among all the symphonists of our century, [he] is the most significant Beethovenian, as far as form and style are concerned. ... None, other than Brahms, can match Beethoven in the logic and economy of movement structure, the sustained high quality of material and its treatment and the elegant renunciation of the conventional.[57]

These, therefore, are some of the ingredients, most of which seem to have been consistently absent in their entirety from any symphony written between 1824 and 1876. Here is no place for another analysis of Brahms's first symphony, but speculation on what finally decided him to write it is another matter. In 1859 he told his friend Carl Bargheer, 'If you dare to write symphonies after Beethoven, they must look quite different'.[58] We know for certain that from 1862 it was, by the very nature of its absence, the problem of an introduction that held Brahms back, but it is possible that Grimm's symphony contained a solution, if not *the* solution. The time-lines of each man's symphony are virtually identical. It is the one work that appears to guide Brahms from his first attempts at writing a symphony in the mid-1850s to his final achievement in 1876, though why he waited as long as he did remains a matter of conjecture. What finally triggered its composition was possibly the higher standard of symphonic creativity that began in the late 1860s and continued to flower thereafter. Those composers were either at the fringes of the Brahms circle or deeply embedded at the heart of it and they were producing

---

[57] Kretschmar, Vol. I part ii, 632.
[58] Brahms to Carl Bargheer ?December 1859 in Carl Bargheer, *Erinnerungen an Johannes Brahms in Detmold 1857–1865* quoted in Max Kalbeck, *Johannes Brahms* 4 vols (Tutzing, 1904–14 reprint), Vol. I, 339.

Table 7.1   Average age of a composer writing his first symphony

Composer	Age	First Symphony
Beethoven	30	1800
Spohr	27	1811
Schubert	16	1813
Mendelssohn	15	1824
Kalliwoda	24	1825
Lachner	24	1827
Burgmüller	23	1833
Kittl	30	1836
Schumann	31	1841
Verhulst	25	1841
Gade	25	1842
Rietz	32	1844
Hiller	38	1849
Reinecke	34	1858
Raff	41	1863
Volkmann	47	1863
Reinthaler	41	1863
Bargiel	41	1866
Bruch	30	1868
Dietrich	40	1869
Draeseke	38	1873
Gernsheim	35	1874
Grimm	47	1874[59]

good, if uneven, symphonies. Although Grimm's solitary contribution has its roots in 1852, it only entered the public domain in 1874, so its provenance, connection and relevance to Brahms should be discussed here with the benefit of hindsight.

Grimm wrote his three-movement symphony at least 18 months before he met Brahms for the first time. This meeting took place in Leipzig on 17 November 1853 through Heinrich von Sahr, whose room in lodgings was on the same staircase as Grimm's. Brahms, in the city for talks with music publishers Breitkopf & Härtel, and Grimm immediately became lifelong friends.[60] The following year, Grimm journeyed to Hanover and, together with Brahms and Joachim, met the Schumanns. He then played a significant role in helping the 21-year-old Brahms reshape his sonata for two pianos (Grimm and Clara Schumann played it in public), *via* the eventually aborted first movement of a symphony, into its final format as the D minor piano concerto Op. 15. For Brahms this was a turbulent

---

[59]   Grimm was 25 when the first three movements of his symphony were played at Leipzig in 1852.

[60]   May, Vol. 1, 140.

period. He was coping badly with the 'greatness thrust upon him' by the tone and content of Schumann's article; and, possibly because of the latter's decline into madness and death, he published nothing between 1854 and 1860. It is also worth recalling that he heard Beethoven's ninth for the first time in 1854 at Cologne. It was an experience that, as has been pointed out repeatedly during the course of this book, was known not only to be revelatory and life-changing but also to shatter the confidence of even the most assured young composer from Schubert onwards, whether by being present at a performance or merely undertaking a study of the score.

Brahms's return to productivity was heralded by the publication of the two serenades, followed by the concerto.[61] As if to fill that six-year vacuum, he and Joachim exchanged counterpoint exercises to refine his technique. Much of 1857 was spent on the concerto; and although no mention of symphonies is made in any correspondence, it is significant that Brahms was in Göttingen on 12 February 1857, just six days before Grimm conducted his own symphony, and he may have stayed another week to hear it.[62]

We know, from Albert Dietrich's memoir of Brahms and a letter from Clara Schumann to Joachim, that Brahms had completed the first movement when he visited Münster am Stein in 1862.[63] However, we also know that it had no slow introduction at this point.[64] Brahms then seemed to postpone further activity on the symphony and concentrated instead on chamber music followed by the *German Requiem*. The next evidence (a letter to Clara quoting the famous 'Alpine theme' for the horn shortly after the start of the *finale*) occurred in 1868, by which time Bruch too was begging Brahms for a symphony.[65] Moving to the publication of Grimm's symphony in 1874, regrettably from the period January 1871 until October 1875 there are no surviving letters between him and Brahms, which crucially might have mentioned a final decision by Grimm to publish it, discussed details of its content or exchanged advice between the two. We have seen that it has some remarkable music for 1852, placing it ahead of its time, but whether Grimm wrote it then, updated his earlier style when preparing it for publication, or left it as first conceived is impossible to tell.

There is, however, a brief passage of 18 bars in Grimm's symphony that bears an uncanny resemblance to Brahms's introduction to his first symphony,

---

[61] The first serenade (in D Op. 11) is virtually an extended six-movement symphony, quoting others such as Haydn (104) and Beethoven (2), and fragments of material eventually used in his own first symphony (C minor, 1876).

[62] Brahms to Grimm, ed. Richard Barth, *Johannes Brahms im Briefwechsel mit J.O. Grimm* Vol. IV (Berlin, 1908), Letter XXX, 49.

[63] Münster am Stein is not to be confused with Münster, where Grimm was Music Director.

[64] Clara Schumann to Joseph Joachim, 1 July 1862. Kalbeck, Vol. III part i, 91–2.

[65] Brahms to Clara Schumann, 12 September 1868, in Frisch, *Brahms: The Four Symphonies*, 35.

namely the coda to the second movement funeral march (*Trauermarsch*). When we compare its first six bars to Brahms, we find that they have three features in common in terms of scoring and thematic distribution. First, the melody is spread over three octaves between first violins, second violins and violas (Grimm) or first violins, second violins and cellos (Brahms). Second, all eight woodwind instruments move in a mix of similar motion (Brahms) and/or contrary motion (Grimm) in pairs over a span of three octaves. Third, a pair of horns sustains an octave tonic pedal point, while timpani add support with a rhythmic tattoo on the tonic note (Grimm and Brahms). An insignificant difference is that Brahms sheds his trumpets after the first bar, while in Grimm's they shadow the timpani's funereal pulsating rhythm (Exx 7.44 and 7.45).

We do not know exactly when Brahms composed the introduction to his first symphony, but if he was involved in the preparation for publication of Grimm's symphony in 1874, then perhaps it was the coda to that work's funeral march that was the catalyst in helping him solve his own problem a year or two later. Perhaps Schumann's Messiah now had his John the Baptist. Brahms's first symphony had begun its journey in the 1850s with a backward glance at his symphonic progenitor, Beethoven. Then came Schumann, Lachner, Raff and Volkmann, while at the end of the journey, his inner circle awaited him – Bruch, Gernsheim, Dietrich and Grimm, one of whom may have prompted him to reveal his answer to the symphonic question. That person could have been Julius Otto Grimm.

Three years before his death in 1827, Beethoven's ninth symphony created not only a furore but also a shadow. Symphonists of the 1830s made no attempt to emerge from it and carry on where he had left off; indeed they more or less said as much in musical terms by imitating, if not quoting, the *finale*'s *recitativo* introduction in which Beethoven recapitulates the themes of all three previous movements, rejects each in turn and settles on a new one, adding the vocal and choral elements for good measure. During the 1840s it was first Mendelssohn, then Schumann who brought their own brands of innovation to the genre, although neither did so with consistency or total conviction. With their deaths, the 1850s became a low point when weak symphonists capitulated as Wagner transformed opera into music drama and Liszt the symphony into the symphonic poem. Meanwhile Brahms made his disastrous first attempts to enter the fray. Only in the 1860s did the tide turn with those composers whose musical language took on a more robust stance and who embraced the full panoply of the Romantic sound in both imaginative orchestration and greater flexibility in form. By the mid-1870s the symphony was set to rise like a phoenix from the ashes.

Are we faced with 'the usual army of disgruntled minor composers' when we haul them and their works from obscurity into the light of day and examine them?[66] There is a certain type of critical mentality that finds it necessary to belittle the achievements of others in order to further those of someone else. A correct balance needs to be struck and the reputations of many forgotten symphonists restored.

---

[66] Paul Henry Lang, *Music in Western Civilization* (New York, 1941), 895.

Example 7.44   Grimm: Symphony in D minor. Second movement, coda

Example 7.45   Brahms: Symphony No. 1. First movement, Introduction

Albeit at the cost of sometimes frustrating or tiresome encounters, detours into the byways of the past can ultimately be both rewarding and crucial. A sense of perspective and a grasp of how (or indeed if) lessons were learned are vital to the understanding of this history. There is a wealth of material that, if heard more often, would extend, broaden and ultimately enrich the established repertoire, not only in the field of recorded music where many specialist labels laudably already do take risks but also in the concert hall, where programmes are far too cautious and traditional, a situation that, in the light of this study, has frequently evoked the cry, '*plus ça change*'. Whether the symphony will finally die is a matter only time will tell, but meanwhile there is no question of once again falling into the trap of calling it a 'dead time'.[67]

During the course of the 50 years between Beethoven's ninth and Brahms's first, many symphonies of high quality fell short of expectation, more often than not in their finales. Even the best of them simply ran out of ideas. The '*finale* problem' was no figment of anyone's imagination and there were reasons for failure. Having heard the wonders of the ninth symphony, what was the public looking for? More of the same? One way to find out is to look at what they rejected and why they did so, even if it means accepting on trust that the press reflected public taste. First and foremost seems to have been the ideas themselves, which were weak in content. Then there was the treatment of material flawed by a lack of sustainable development or 'working through', and finally there were the unacceptable solutions of predictable formats and musical clichés. As we have seen, what was constantly expected were three non-negotiable qualities: originality, progress and consequent influence. As well as being comprehensible and tasteful to an audience, a new symphony had to have absolute mastery of form, evident skill in handling counterpoint, thematic material of worth, exemplary orchestration, a variety of effects and colour, and above all, that dramatic energy so typical of Beethoven. While few were called, most were found wanting. Wisely, Brahms watched, listened and waited, having stumbled at his first attempt. What finally emerged in 1876 was a work that fitted like a glove, meeting the demands of public and press alike, stamping its musical authority on the profession and fearlessly establishing from the outset and forever a topmost position in the repertoire of the concert hall. Not for Brahms was there a learning curve; there is no particular sense of growing maturity or increasing mastery between his first (1876) and fourth (1885) symphonies. In this he was unique. For sure, the symphony had finally emerged from Beethoven's shadow.

---

[67] Peter Maxwell Davies, Philip Glass, Arvo Pärt and Krzysztof Penderecki among others are still writing them.

Select Bibliography

Articles and Book Chapters

Brodbeck, David 'Brahms' in *The 19th Century Symphony* (ed. D. Kern Holoman) (New York, 1997), 224–70.
_____. 'The symphony after Beethoven after Dahlhaus' in *The Cambridge Companion to the Symphony* (ed. Julian Horton) (Cambridge, 2013), 61–95.
Brown, Clive 'The orchestra in Beethoven's Vienna' in *Early Music*, Vol. 16 No. 1 (February 1988), 4–20.
Fifield, Christopher 'Max Bruch and Sondershausen' in *Max Bruch in Sondershausen (1867–1870)* (ed. Peter Larsen) (Göttingen, 2004), 69–110.
Frisch, Walter '"Echt symphonisch": On the historical context of Brahms' symphonies' in *Brahms Studies 2* (ed. David Brodbeck) (Lincoln, NE, 1998), 124–30.
Grimm, Julius Otto 'Erinnerungen aus meinem Musikerleben' in *29. Jahresbericht des Westfälischen Provinzial-Vereins für Wissenschaft und Kunst für 1900/1901* (Münster, 1901), 151–60.
Hagels, Bert 'Nur neue Werke ohne Bedeutung? Die Sinfonie zwischen 1830 und 1860 im Spannungsfeld von Produktion und Rezeption' in *Aspekte historischer und systematischer Musikforschung*, Schriften zur Musikwissenschaft Vol. 5 (eds Christoph-Hellmut Mahling and Kristina Pfarr) (Mainz, 2002), 41–57.
Hepokoski, James 'Beethoven reception: the symphonic tradition' in *The Cambridge History of Nineteenth-Century Music* (ed. Jim Samson) (Cambridge, 2001), 424–59.
Jensen, Eric Frederick 'Norbert Burgmüller and Robert Schumann' in *The Musical Quarterly*, Vol. 74 No. 4 (1990), 550–65.
Kirby, F.E. 'The Germanic symphony of the nineteenth century: genre, form, instrumentation, expression' in *Journal of Musicological Research*, Vol. 14 (1995), 193–221.
Konrad, Ulrich 'Der Wiener Kompositionswettbewerb 1835 und Franz Lachners *Sinfonia passionata*: ein Beitrag zur Geschichte der Sinfonie nach Beethoven' in *Augsburger Jahrbuch für Musikwissenschaft*, Vol. 3 (1986), 209–39.
Kross, Siegfried 'Das "zweite Zeitalter der Symphonie" – Ideologie und Realität' in *Probleme der symphonischen Tradition im 19 Jahrhundert* (eds Siegfried Kross and Marie Luise Maintz) (Tutzing, 1990), 11–36.
Küster, Konrad 'Leipziger Perspektive' in *Aspekte historischer und systematischer Musikforschung*, Schriften zur Musikwissenschaft Vol. 5 (eds Christoph-Hellmut Mahling and Kristina Pfarr) (Mainz, 2002), 29–39.

Mason, Daniel Gregory *Raff, Masters in Music*, Vol. 1 No. 6 (June 1903), 1–48.
Musgrave, Michael 'Die erste Symphonie von Johannes Brahms – Stilistische und Strukturelle Synthese' in *Probleme der symphonischen Tradition im 19 Jahrhundert* (eds Siegfried Kross and Marie Luise Maintz) (Tutzing, 1990), 537–44.
_____. 'Brahms's first symphony: thematic coherence and its secret origins' in *Music Analysis*, Vol. 2 No. 2 (1983), 117–33.
Notley, Margaret 'Volksconcerte in Vienna and late nineteenth-century ideology of the symphony' in *Journal of the American Musicological Society*, Vol. 50 Nos 2–3 (1997), 421–53.
Pascall, Robert 'Lachner spricht echten Suitenton' in *Franz Lachner und seine Brüder Hofkapellmeister zwischen Schubert und Wagner* Kongressbericht Munich 2003 (eds Hartmut Schick and Stephan Hörner) (Tutzing, 2006), 145–81.
_____. 'Brahms und die Kleinmeister' in *Brahms und seine Zeit* (Symposion Hamburg, 1983), 199–209.
Pederson, Sanna 'On the task of the music historian: the myth of the symphony after Beethoven' in *repercussions*, Vol. 2 No. 2 (Autumn 1993), 5–30.
Rychnovsky, Ernst 'Ludwig Spohr und Friedrich Rochlitz: Ihre Beziehungen nach ungedruckten Briefen' in *Sammelbände der Internationalen Musik-Gesellschaft*, Vol. V (1903/4), 253–313.
Schönzeler, Hans-Hubert 'The Romantic Classicists' in *Of German Music* (London, 1976), 219–45.
Steinbeck, Wolfram 'Lachner und die Symphonie' in *Franz Lachner und seine Brüder Hofkapellmeister zwischen Schubert und Wagner* Kongressbericht Munich 2003 (Tutzing, 2006), 133–44.
_____. '"Krise" der Symphonie um 1850?' in *Aspekte historischer und systematischer Musikforschung*, Schriften zur Musikwissenschaft Vol. 5 (eds Christoph-Hellmut Mahling and Kristina Pfarr) (Mainz, 2002), 1–18.
Todd, R. Larry 'On quotation in Schumann's music' in *Schumann and his World* (Princeton, NJ, 1994), 80–112.
Vorwerk, Benno 'Norbert Burgmüller' in *Beiträge zur Geschichte des Niederrheins*, Vol. 4 (1889), 177.

Dissertations

Krueck, Alan *The Symphonies of Felix Draeseke* (PhD University of Zurich, 1967).
Mayer, Ludwig *Franz Lachner als Instrumental-Komponist* (PhD University of Munich, 1922).
Morris, Allan Scott *The Wellsprings of Neoclassicism in Music: The 19th century Suite and Serenade* (PhD University of Toronto, 1998).
Phillips, L.M. *The Leipzig Conservatory 1843–1881* (PhD Indiana University, 1979).

German Newspapers and Periodicals

Allgemeine Musikalische Zeitung (1830–48, 1869–76).
Allgemeine Musikalische Zeitung neue Folge (1863–65).
Berliner Musik-Zeitung Echo (May 1860).
Ein Centralorgan für Rheinland und Westfalen (1834).
Der Deutsche (No. 87 21 July 1868 and No. 97 16 August 1868).
Düsseldorfer Zeitung (1837, 1864).
Leipziger Allgemeine Musikalische Zeitung (1866–68).
Leipziger Nachrichten (1891).
Leipziger Tageblatt (November 1864).
Münsterischer Anzeiger (12 November 1872).
Musikalisches Wochenblatt (28 January and November 1870, 12 May 1882, 8 November 1883).
Neue Berliner Musikzeitung (8 December 1869).
Neue Zeitschrift für Musik (1836–58, 1869).
Die Signale für die Musikalische Welt (Nos 7, 11 1843, No. 14 1856, Nos 26, 47 1868).
Die Sonntagspost (25 November 1864).
Zeitschrift für Deutschlands Musik-Vereine und Dilettanten (1842).

English Newspapers and Periodicals

The Academy (April 1875).
Fortnightly Review (December 1876).
Musical Times (August 1852, June 1885, April 1903).
Musical World (No. 25 1850).

Books

Abert, Hermann *Johann Joseph Abert: sein Leben und seine Werke* (Leipzig, 1916).
Altmann, Wilhelm (ed.) *Johannes Brahms im Briefwechsel mit Max Bruch* (Berlin, 1908).
Avins, Styra *Johannes Brahms: Life and Letters* (Oxford, 1997).
Bache, Constance *Brother Musicians: reminiscences of Edward and Walter Bache* (London, 1901).
Balde, Ernst (pub.; author unknown) *Johann Friedrich Kittl* (Kassel, 1857).
Banister, Henry C. *George Alexander Macfarren* (London, 1891).
Barnett, John Francis *Musical Reminiscences and Impressions* (London, 1906).
Barth, Richard (ed.) *Johannes Brahms im Briefwechsel mit J.O. Grimm* Vol. IV (Berlin, 1908).

Benestad, Finn and Schjelderup-Ebbe, Dag *Johan Svendsen: The Man, the Maestro, the Music* (trans. W.H. Halverson) (Columbus, 1995).
_____. *Edvard Grieg: The Man and the Artist* (Gloucester, 1988).
Blanning, Tim *The Triumph of Music: The Rise of Composers, Musicians and their Art* (Cambridge, MA, 2008).
Bobéth, Marek *Hermann Goetz: Leben und Werk* (Winterthur, 1996).
Bonds, Mark Evan *A History of Music in Western Culture* (Upper Saddle River, NJ, 2003).
_____. *After Beethoven: Imperatives of Originality in the Symphony* (Cambridge, MA, 1996).
Brion, Marcel *Schumann and the Romantic Age* (trans. G. Sainsbury) (London, 1956).
Brown, Clive *Louis Spohr: A Critical Biography* (Cambridge, 1984).
Brown, David *Tchaikovsky: The Final Years 1885–1893* Vol. 4 (London, 1991).
Chamier, Daniel *Percy Pitt of Covent Garden and the BBC* (London, 1938).
Cobbett's Cyclopedic Survey of Chamber Music 2 vols (London, 1929).
Cowen, Frederic *My Art and My Friends* (London, 1913).
Creuzburg, Eberhard *Die Gewandhaus-Konzerte zu Leipzig 1781–1931* (Leipzig, 1931).
Csapó, Wilhelm von (ed.) *Franz Liszt's Briefe an Baron Anton Augusz, 1846–1878* (Budapest, 1911).
Dahlhaus, Carl *Nineteenth-Century Music* (Wiesbaden, 1980; trans. J. Bradford Robinson, Berkeley, CA, 1989).
Daverio, John *Crossing Paths: Schubert, Schumann and Brahms* (Oxford, 2002).
Deutsch, Otto Erich *Schubert: Memoirs by his Friends* (London, 1958).
Dill, Marshall *Germany: A Modern History* (Ann Arbor, MI, 1961).
Dörffel, Alfred *Geschichte der Gewandhausconcerte zu Leipzig 1781–1881* (Leipzig, 1884).
Eichner, Barbara *History in Mighty Sounds* (Woodbridge, 2012).
Einstein, Alfred *Music in the Romantic Era* (London, 1947).
Falke, Matthias *Die Symphonie zwischen Schumann und Brahms: Studien zu Max Bruch und Robert Volkmann* (Berlin, 2006).
Fétis, François-Joseph *Biographie universelle des musicians* (Brussels, 1835–44).
Feuchte, Paul and Andreas *Die Komponisten Eduard Franck und Richard Franck* (Stuttgart, 1993; repr. Leipzig, 2010).
Franck, Richard *Musikalische und unmusikalische Erinnerungen* (Heidelberg, [1928]).
Fifield, Christopher *True Artist and True Friend: A Biography of Hans Richter* (Oxford, 1993).
_____. *Max Bruch: Biographie eines Komponisten* (Zürich, 1990).
_____. *Max Bruch: His Life and Works* (London, 1988, repr. 2005).
Forner, Johannes *Johannes Brahms in Leipzig: Geschichte einer Beziehung* (Leipzig, 1987).
_____. *Die Gewandhauskonzerte zu Leipzig (1781–1981)* (Leipzig, 1981).

Frisch, Walter *Brahms: The Four Symphonies* (New Haven, CT, 2003).
_____. (ed.) *Brahms and His World* (Princeton, NJ, 1990, rev. 2009).
Gathy, August *Musikalisches Conversations-Lexicon* (Leipzig, 1835).
Graf, Max *Composer and Critic: 200 Years of Musical Criticism* (New York, 1946).
Grotjahn, Rebecca *Die Sinfonie im deutschen Kulturgebiet 1850–1875: ein Beitrag zur Gattungs- und Institutionengeschichte* (Sinzig, 1998).
Grove's Dictionary of Music and Musicians (London, 1899).
Haas, Frithjof *Hans von Bülow: Leben und Wirken* (Wilhelmshaven, 2002).
_____. *Zwischen Brahms und Wagner: der Dirigent Hermann Levi* (Zurich, 1995).
Hanslick, Eduard *Geschichte des Concertwesens in Wien* (Vienna, 1869).
Holl, Karl *Friedrich Gernsheim: Leben, Erscheinung und Werk* (Leipzig, 1928).
Holmes, Edward *A Ramble among the Musicians of Germany by a Musical Professor* (London, 1828, 2nd edition 1830).
Hueffer, Francis *Musical Studies: a series of contributions* (Edinburgh, 1880).
Hughes, Gervase *Sidelights on a Century of Music (1825–1924)* (London, 1969).
Jacobs, Arthur *Arthur Sullivan* (Aldershot, 1992).
Kalbeck, Max *Johannes Brahms* 4 vols (Tutzing, 1904–14 repr.).
Knapp, Raymond *Brahms and the Challenge of the Symphony* (New York, 1997).
Kratt-Harveng, Elise *Jacques Rosenhain, Komponist und Pianist: ein Lebensbild* (Baden-Baden, 1891).
Kreisig, Martin (ed.) *Robert Schumann: Gesammelte Werke über Musik und Musiker* 2 vols (Leipzig, 1914).
Kretschmar, Hermann *Führer durch den Konzertsaal: Sinfonie und Suite* (Leipzig, 1898).
Lang, Paul Henry *Music in Western Civilization* (New York, 1941).
Litzmann, Berthold *Clara Schumann: ein Kunstlerleben* 3 vols (Leipzig, 1909).
Ludwig, Franz *Julius Otto Grimm: ein Beitrag zur Geschichte der musikalischen Spätromantik* (Bielefeld, 1925).
Maitland, John Fuller *Masters of German Music* (London, 1894).
Mason, Lowell *Musical Letters from Abroad* (New York, 1854, repr. 1967).
Mason, William *Memories of a Musical Life* (London, 1901).
May, Florence *The Life of Brahms* 2 vols (London, 1905).
Mendel, Hermann *Musikalisches Conversations-Lexicon* Vol. 5 (Berlin, 1875).
Moscheles, Felix *Letters of Felix Mendelssohn to Ignaz and Charlotte Moscheles* (London, 1888).
Müller-Reuter, Theodor *Lexicon der deutschen Konzertliteratur* (Leipzig, 1909).
Musgrave, Michael *The Music of Brahms* (Oxford, 1994).
Die Musik in Geschichte und Gegenwart (Munich, 1989).
Neumann, William *Die Componisten der neueren Zeit* Biographien Vol. 41 (Kassel, 1856).
The New Grove Dictionary of Music and Musicians (20 vols, London, 1980; 29 vols, London, 2001).
Pieper, Antje *Music and the Making of Middle-Class Culture: A Comparative History of 19th Century Leipzig and Birmingham* (Basingstoke, 2008).

Pleasants, Henry (ed.) *The Musical World of Robert Schumann* (London, 1965).
Pratt, Waldo S. *The New Encyclopedia of Music and Musicians* (New York, 1944).
Raff, Helene *Joachim Raff: ein Lebensbild* Deutsche Musikbücherei Vol. 42 (Regensburg, 1925).
Reinecke, Carl *Erlebnisse und Bekenntnisse: Autobiographie eines Gewandhauskapellmeisters* (Leipzig, 1902, repr. 2005).
Richter, Alfred *Aus Leipzigs musikalischer Glanzzeit: Erinnerungen eines Musikers* (ed. Doris Mundus) (Leipzig, 2004).
Riederer-Sitte, Petra (ed.) *Max Bruch: Briefe an Laura und Rudolf von Beckerath* (Essen, 1997).
Riehl, W.H. *Musikalische Charakterköpfe* (Stuttgart, 1857).
Schilling, Gustav *Encyclopädie der gesammten musikalischen Wissenschaften der Tonkunst* (Stuttgart, 1838).
Schmidt, Leopold (ed.) *Johannes Brahms im Briefwechsel mit Friedrich Gernsheim* (Berlin, 1910).
Schumann, Robert *Tagebücher (1827–1838)* Vol. 1 (ed. Georg Eisman) (Leipzig, 1971).
_____. *On Music and Musicians* (ed. Konrad Wolff; trans. Paul Rosenfeld) (London, 1947).
_____. *Gesammelte Schriften über Musik und Musiker* 2 vols (ed. Martin Kreisig) (Leipzig, 1914).
_____. *Gesammelte Schriften über Musik und Musiker* 3 vols (ed. Heinrich Simon) (Leipzig, 1888).
Shattuck, Roger *The Banquet Years* (London, 1958).
Shaw, George Bernard *Shaw's Music* (ed. Dan H. Laurence) 3 vols (London, 1981).
_____. *Music in London 1890–1894* 3 vols (London, 1932).
Stanford, Charles Villiers *Pages from an Unwritten Diary* (London, 1914).
Sterndale Bennett, J.R. *The Life of William Sterndale Bennett* (London, 1907).
Strauss-Neméth, Laszló *Johann Wenzel Kalliwoda und die Musik am Hof von Donaueschingen* (Hildesheim, 2005).
Strunz, Karl *Johann Wenzel Kalliwoda (1801–1866)* (Vienna, 1910).
Taylor, A.J.P. *The Course of German History* (London, 1945).
Todd, R. Larry *Mendelssohn: A Life in Music* (Oxford, 2003).
Tovey, D.F. *Essays in Musical Analysis* Vols 1 and 2 'Symphonies' (London, 1935).
Wagner, Richard *Gesammelte Schriften und Dichtungen* Vol. 3 (2nd edition, Leipzig, 1887).
Walker, Alan *Franz Liszt: Vol. 2 the Weimar years (1848–1861)* (London, 1989).
Warrack, John *Carl Maria von Weber* (London, 1968).
Weber, Hildegard *Das 'Museum': 150 Jahre Frankfurter Konzertleben 1808–1958* (Frankfurt, 1958).
Weber, William *The Great Transformation of Musical Taste: Concert Programming from Haydn to Brahms* (Cambridge, 2008).
Weingartner, Felix *Die Symphonie nach Beethoven* (Leipzig, 1897).

Whistling, Karl *Statistik des Königlichen Conservatorium der Musik zu Leipzig 1843–1883: aus Anlass des vierzigjährigen Jubiläums der Anstalt* (Leipzig, 1883).

Wiegandt, Matthias *Vergessene Symphonik* Berliner Musikstudien Vol. 13 (Sinzig, 1997).

Williamson, D.G. *Bismarck and Germany 1862–1890* (London, 1986).

Young, Percy *Sir Arthur Sullivan* (London, 1971).

Select Discography

This is a list of compact disc recordings available in the United Kingdom in 2014 of many of the symphonies discussed in the book. One recording per symphony (there may be others) is listed in chronological order of composition.

Spohr, Louis

Symphonies Nos 1 and 2 Orchestra della Svizzera Italiana/Shelley   CDA 67616
Symphonies Nos 3 and 6 Orchestra della Svizzera Italiana/Shelley   CDA 67788
Symphonies Nos 4 and 5 Orchestra della Svizzera Italiana/Shelley   CDA 67622
Symphonies Nos 7 and 9 Orchestra della Svizzera Italiana/Shelley   CDA 67939
Symphonies Nos 8 and 10 Orchestra della Svizzera Italiana/Shelley   CDA 67802

Kalliwoda, Johann

Symphonies Nos 2 and 4 Die Kölner Akademie/Willens   cpo 777469
Symphony No. 3 Hamburger Symphoniker/Moesus   MDG 329 1387–2
Symphonies Nos 5 and 7 Das neue Orchester/Spering   cpo 777139
Symphonies Nos 5 and 6 Hofkapelle Stuttgart/Bernius   Orfeo 677061

Burgmüller, Norbert

Symphonies Nos 1 and 2 Hofkapelle Stuttgart/Bernius   Carus 83226

Lachner, Franz

Symphony No. 1 Singapore Symphony Orchestra/Choo Hoey
   Marco Polo 8.220360
Symphony No. 5 Slovak State Philharmonic Orchestra/Robinson
   Marco Polo 8.223502
Symphony No. 8 Slovak State Philharmonic Orchestra/Robinson
   Marco Polo 8.223594

Verhulst, Johannes

Symphony in E Hague Residente Orchestra/Bamert　　　　Chandos 10179

Gade, Niels

Symphony No. 1 Stockholm Sinfonietta/Järvi　　　　BIS 339

Schnyder von Wartensee, Franz Xaver

Symphony No. 3 Württembergische Philharmonie Reutlingen/Fifield
　　　　　　　　　　　　　　　　　　　　　　　Sterling CDS-1073–2

Franck, Eduard

Symphony in A Saarbrücken Radio Symphony Orchestra/Frank　　Audite 20.025
Symphony in B♭ Saarbrücken Radio Symphony Orchestra/Frank　　Audite 20.034

Reinecke, Carl

Symphony No. 1 Berner Symphonie-Orchester/Moesus　　　cpo 777 105–2

Abert, Johann Joseph

Symphony (*Columbus*) Op. 31　　　　Bayer Records BR 100 160 CD

Bargiel, Woldemar

Symphony in C Siberian Symphony Orchestra/Vasilyev　　　TOCC 0277

Volkmann, Robert

Symphony No. 1 Nordwestdeutsche Philharmonie/Albert　　　cpo 999151

Raff, Joachim

Symphonies Nos 1–11 Bamberger Symphoniker/Stadlmair   Tudor 1600

Bruch, Max

Symphonies Nos 1 and 2 Kölner Philharmoniker/Conlon   EMI 7243 5 55046 2 3

Dietrich, Albert

Symphony in D minor Oldenburgisches Staatsorchester/Rumpf   cpo 777 314–2

Draeseke, Felix

Symphony No. 1 Wuppertal Symphony Orchestra/Hanson   MDG 335 0929–2
Symphony No. 2 Radio-Philharmonie Hannover/Weigle   cpo 999719

Gernsheim, Friedrich

Symphony No. 1 Staatsphilharmonie Rheinland-Pfalz/Köhler   ANO 636350

Goetz, Hermann

Symphony No. 2 North German Radio Symphony Orchestra/Albert   cpo 999939

Index

Aachen 44, 48, 110, 127, 174, 184, 219, 261
Abert, Johann Joseph 130, 186–8, 191
    Symphony No. 4 *Columbus* 187
Abraham, Gerald 131
Adam, Adolphe 14
Adelaide, Queen 136
Albert, Prince 136
Altenburg 95, 152
Alvensleben, Gerhard von 106
Ambros, Wilhelm 203
Amsterdam 96
Ansbach 106
Arndt, Ernst Moritz 203
Ashton, Algernon 71
Auber, Daniel 14, 86
    La Muette de Portici 14
    Overture: *Fra Diavolo* 86
Augsburg 66, 106

Bach, Johann Sebastian 5, 7, 13–16, 131, 134, 136, 144, 145, 197, 213, 217, 232
    Concerto for three pianos 126
    St Matthew Passion 13, 169
Bache, Constance 142–3
Bache, Francis Edward 142–3
Bache, Walter 142–3
Baden-Baden 109
Bagge, Selmar 77, 175, 176, 180, 199
Balakirev, Mily 185
    Symphony No. 1 185
Banister, Henry 139–41
Bargheer, Carl 269, 278
Bargiel, Woldemar 130, 169, 186, 188, 191, 218, 233, 253, 267, 279
    Symphony in C 188–9
Barmen (Wuppertal) 179
Barnett, Clara Kathinka 143
Barnett, Domenico Dragonetti 143

Barnett, John Francis 143–4
    The Ancient Mariner 143
Barnett, Rosamunde Liszt 143
Barth, Richard 269
Basel 166, 261
Bayreuth, 252
Becker, Albert 203
    Symphony in G minor 203
Becker, Carl Ferdinand 136
Beethoven, Ludwig van 1–12, 14–19, 25, 27, 33, 34, 36, 39, 47, 50, 52, 53, 55, 56, 61, 71, 72, 75, 77–9, 81, 84, 87, 90–93, 96, 100–103, 107, 109–14, 117, 127, 131, 132, 141, 143, 145, 149, 151, 159, 167, 178, 180, 181, 187–9, 196, 199–201, 203, 209, 210, 217, 218, 224, 225, 231, 232, 237, 238, 250, 251, 253, 256, 267, 277–9, 281, 284
    Choral fantasy 100
    Fidelio 111
    Overture: *Coriolan* 4, 230
    Overture: *Egmont* 188
    Overture: *Leonore* No. 3 66
    Overtures 45, 113
    Piano concerto No. 4 61, 154, 167
    Piano sonata Op. 27 *Moonlight* 140
    Piano sonata Op. 13 *Pathétique* 79
    Piano sonata Op. 53 *Waldstein* 176
    Piano sonata Op. 111 170
    String quartet Op. 127 69
    String quartet Op. 131 140
    Symphony No. 1 8, 25, 113
    Symphony No. 2 128, 189, 280
    Symphony No. 3 *Eroica* 8, 18, 96, 117, 128, 214, 243, 254
    Symphony No. 4 128
    Symphony No. 5 8, 34, 51, 69, 99, 117, 128

Symphony No. 6 *Pastoral* 8, 12, 13, 18, 40, 42, 43, 45, 84, 86, 90, 111, 128, 174, 234
Symphony No. 7 18, 47–9, 51, 91, 111, 128, 213
Symphony No. 8 15, 25, 51, 95, 128, 186
Symphony No. 9 1–4, 8, 12, 18, 19, 31, 35, 45, 49, 60, 65, 69, 71, 81, 83, 110, 113, 117, 119, 128, 134, 139, 153, 192, 197, 206, 213, 239, 270, 277, 280, 281, 284
Violin concerto 25
Violin sonata Op. 47 *Kreutzer* 79
Bellini, Vincenzo 7, 108
    Scene and aria from *Il Pirata* 88
Berger, Francesco 142
Beringer, Oscar 145
Berlin 25, 66, 67, 70, 79, 82, 86, 92, 99, 103, 108, 111–15, 126, 127, 133, 136, 140, 142, 147, 148, 150, 160, 165, 166, 169, 186, 187, 214, 217, 233, 237, 238, 268, 269
    Berlin Arts (Music) Academy 188, 233
    Berlin Philharmonic Orchestra 133, 147
Berlioz, Hector 13, 83, 86, 99–101, 108, 111, 122, 134, 142, 151–3, 173, 199, 203, 206, 225
    Damnation de Faust 111
    Lélio 111
    Queen Mab Scherzo 214
    Roméo et Juliette 100, 111
    Symphonie fantastique 10, 13, 65, 99, 134, 153, 206, 208, 214
    Te Deum 251
Bern 118
Bernsdorf, Eduard 229
Birmingham 127, 142, 143, 145
Bischoff, Ludwig 9
Bizet, Georges 111, 168
    Symphony in C 168
Bloch, Ernest 139
    Symphony in C♯ minor 139
Blümner, Heinrich 133, 134
Bobéth, Marek 266
Bonn 233, 252

Borodin, Alexander 185, 198, 211
    Symphony No. 1 185
    Symphony No. 2 192, 193, 211
Bournemouth 266
Brahms, Johannes 2, 5, 15, 25, 48, 49, 54, 56, 62, 76, 82, 91, 92, 104, 107, 110, 127, 130, 151–3, 158, 163, 165, 167, 168, 188, 192, 193, 198, 200, 202, 203, 205, 209, 210, 217–19, 225, 227–9, 230–33, 235, 236, 249, 251–4, 256, 258, 264, 267, 270, 277–81, 284
    German Requiem 168, 193, 219, 224, 228, 252, 254, 270, 280
    Hungarian dances 109
    Liebeslieder Walzer 197
    Piano concerto No. 1 167, 168, 185, 193, 254, 258, 279, 280
    Rhapsody for piano Op. 119 274, 276
    Scherzo for piano in E♭ minor Op. 4 152
    Serenade No. 1 185, 193, 252, 254, 280
    Serenade No. 2 168, 252, 254, 270, 280
    Sextet 252
    Sonata for piano No. 1 in C Op. 1 167
    Sonata for piano No. 3 in F minor Op. 5 167
    Sonata for two pianos 168, 279
    Symphony No. 1 3, 48, 130, 185, 200, 231, 232, 234, 243, 256, 258, 261, 277–81, 283, 284
    Symphony No. 2 11, 48, 185
    Symphony No. 3 195, 196
    Symphony No. 4 198
    Tragic Overture 217
    Triumphlied 203, 270
    Violin concerto 258
    Violin sonata (Scherzo) F-A-E 233
Brandenburg, Ferdinand 106
    The Nightmare of Three Islands 106
Braunschweig (Brunswick) 94, 99, 115
Breitkopf and Härtel 12, 19, 71, 83, 179, 221, 279
Bremen 90, 91, 179, 190, 228, 229
Brendel, Franz 152, 169, 170, 237–9
Breslau 25, 66, 79, 93, 160, 184
Breunung, Ferdinand 130, 184, 261, 262
    Symphony in E♭ 261, 262

Brion, Marcel 2
Bronsart, Hans von 152, 168
Brown, Clive 11, 13–16
Bruch, Max 20, 56, 61, 88, 104, 130, 149, 153, 174, 180, 185, 190, 195, 218–33, 235, 240, 250, 252, 253, 259, 269, 279–81
   Das Lied vom deutschen Kaiser 203
   Die Loreley 219, 222, 233
   Frithjof 219
   Intermezzo 220–23
   Odysseus 221
   Scottish Fantasy 224–6
   String octet 219
   String quintet in A minor 219
   String quintet in E♭ 219
   Symphonies (1852, 1853, 1861) 218
   Symphony No. 1 212, 219–31, 235, 240, 250, 254, 258
   Symphony No. 2 231, 232, 240, 254, 256
   Symphony No. 3 221
   Violin concerto No. 1 in G minor 219, 220, 222, 231, 254, 256
   Violin concerto No. 2 in D minor 231
Bruckner, Anton 34, 56, 127, 152, 163, 193, 218, 220, 238, 240, 249, 250, 270, 273
   Symphony No. 3 270, 271, 274
   Symphony No. 4 193, 195
   Symphony No. 7 240
   Symphony No. 8 250
Brussels 110, 159, 165
   Brussels Conservatoire 131
Budapest 192
Bull, Ole 131, 146
Bülow, Hans von 15, 16, 56, 147, 168–70, 191, 215–17, 232, 237, 243
Bünau-Grabau, Henriette 136
Burgmüller, Friedrich 43, 44
Burgmüller, Johann 43
Burgmüller, Norbert 21, 43–56, 60, 77–9, 100, 128, 130, 151, 262, 279
   Piano concerto 44
   Symphony No. 1 44–9, 56
   Symphony No. 2 48–56, 58, 60, 188, 213, 243

Busoni, Ferruccio 36
Buths, Julius 252

Cambridge 138
Chemnitz 184
Cherubini, Luigi 7, 108, 114
Chopin, Frédéric 10, 117, 151, 152, 160, 173
Chorley, Henry 15
Chrysander, Friedrich 3, 9, 229
Coburg 238
Cologne 43, 111, 133, 149, 150, 160, 162, 175, 178–80, 188, 217, 218, 227, 229, 230, 253, 280
   Concert Association 174
   Conservatoire 112, 174, 252
Copenhagen 100, 101, 179
Cornelius, Peter 237
   Der Barbier von Bagdad 237
Cowen, Frederic 145, 146, 148, 266
   Symphony No. 1 185
Cranz, August 229
Crefeld 229
Crotch, William 132
Czerny, Carl 11, 92, 143
   Symphony No. 5 87

Dahlhaus, Carl 1, 11, 82, 164
Damrosch, Leopold 184
Dannreuther, Eduard 149
Danzig 88
David, Félicien 110, 111, 115
   Ode-symphonique *Le Desért* 110, 111
David, Ferdinand 88, 100, 126–9, 131, 136, 137, 143, 148, 149, 152, 165, 166, 171, 231
   Concertino for trombone 88
Davies, Peter Maxwell 284
Dehn, Siegfried 11
Delibes, Léo 111
Delius, Frederick 149
Dessau 88
Dessoff, Otto 137, 169
Dietrich, Albert 130, 165, 185, 190, 230, 231, 233–7, 251, 253, 259, 267, 274, 279–81
   Symphony (1854) 233

Symphony in D minor 233–7, 274
Violin sonata (first movement) F-A-E 233
Dobrzyński, Ignaz 65, 66, 78, 128
Doles, Johann Friedrich 134
Donaueschingen 16, 17, 29, 32, 33, 41, 82
Donizetti, Gaetano 7, 108
Dörffel, Alfred 25, 39, 41, 66, 88, 95, 101, 106, 127–9, 131, 134, 141, 164, 170, 171, 179, 233
Dorn, Heinrich 111, 112, 174
  Symphony in C 112
Dortmund 269
Draeseke, Felix 169, 218, 237–50, 279
  Christus-Mysterium 238
  Germania 238
  Jugendsinfonie 238–40
  König Sigurd 237
  Symphony No. 1 239–45
  Symphony No. 2 239, 243–50
  Symphony No. 3 (*Symphonia tragica*) 238–40, 249, 250
  Symphony No. 4 (*Symphonia comica*) 249
Dresden 56, 67, 68, 82, 89, 99, 114, 115, 126, 127, 131, 133, 137, 147, 150, 152, 166, 169, 171, 172, 174, 179, 217, 229, 243
  Conservatoire 238
Dreyschock, Alexander 137, 148, 168
Drobisch, Karl 106, 107, 128
  Symphony in G minor 106, 107
Dürr, Albrecht 19, 24
Dürrner, Johann 106
Düsseldorf 43–5, 48, 53–6, 126, 127, 152, 169, 174, 175, 252
Dvořák, Antonín 11, 18, 87, 185, 249
  Cello concerto 254

Edinburgh 106
Eggert, Joachim 33
Einstein, Alfred 153
Eisenstadt 82
Eitner, Robert 187
Elgar, Edward 149, 208, 252
  Dream of Gerontius 252
  Enigma Variations ('Dorabella') 212
  In the South 206

Erkel, Ferenc 90, 192
Erfurt 91
Esterháza 82
Eulenberg Editions 192
Eybler, Joseph 60

Falke, Matthias 199
Falkenstein, Johann Paul von 133, 136
Ferdinand I, Emperor of Austria 68
Fesca, Alexander 94
  Symphony No. 1 94
Fétis, François-Joseph 44, 110, 132, 135, 159
Feuchte, Andreas 160
Feuchte, Paul 160
Fibich, Zdenko 145
Fink, Gottfried Wilhelm 4, 8, 9, 11, 29, 66, 68–70
Finscher, Ludwig 35, 36, 42
Franck, Albert 160
Franck, César 204
Franck, Eduard 160–64, 197, 274
  Symphony in A 160–62, 182, 274
  Symphony in B♭ 160, 162–4
Franck, Hermann 160
Frank, Ernst 262, 263
Frankfurt 7, 66, 68, 83, 86, 111, 127, 165, 213, 215, 216, 218
  Hoch Conservatoire 202, 217
  Theatre and Museum Concerts 110, 118, 159, 160
Franz, Robert 233
Frederick Augustus II of Saxony, King 169
Fritsch, Ernst Wilhelm 192
Fuchs, Robert 264
  Symphony No. 2 264

Gade, Niels 86, 92, 100–106, 113, 123, 126–31, 136, 140, 160, 165, 166, 168–70, 175, 180, 229, 233, 259, 279
  Overture: *Efterklange af Ossian* 101
  Overture: *Im Hochland* 113
  Symphony No. 1 100–106, 123
  Symphony No. 3 102, 168
  Symphony No. 4 102, 168
  Symphony No. 7 185
Gährich, Wenzel 66, 78

Gänsbacher, Johann 60
Gathy, August 11, 25
Gehring, Franz 202
Geibel, Emanuel 175
Geneva 118, 243
Gernsheim, Friedrich 130, 174, 230, 251–6, 258, 259, 267, 269, 277, 279, 281
  Salve regina 230
  Symphony No. 1 253–60
Glass, Philip 284
Gluck, Christoph Willibald 7, 56, 131, 229
Godfrey, Dan 266
Goethe, Johann Wolfgang von 54, 60, 126, 160, 165, 251
Goetz, Hermann 130, 261–7, 277
  Der Widerspänstigen Zähmung 262
  Symphony No. 1 in E minor 261
  Symphony No. 2 in F 261–7
Goetz, Laura 266
Goldmark, Carl 218, 250, 264
  Rustic Wedding Symphony 264
Goltermann, Georg 130, 165
Gotha 25
Göttingen 268, 269, 280
Gounod, Charles 27, 168, 252, 262
Gouvy, Henriette 252
Gouvy, Louis Théodore 129, 130, 165
Grieg, Edvard 145–7, 185
Grimm, Julius Otto 130, 253, 267–81
  Suite for strings in canon form 267
  Symphony in D minor 267–82
Grotjahn, Rebecca 8, 169, 174, 175, 184
Grove, George 266
Grove's Dictionary of Music and Musicians 9, 43, 128, 214
Grund, Friedrich 66
Guhr, Karl 110, 118
Gyrowetz, Adalbert 60

Habeneck, François-Antoine 251
Hallé, Charles 160
Halle 25
Hamburg 56, 66, 70, 88, 92, 103, 216, 229, 270
Handel, George Frideric 7, 14, 15, 131, 145, 270
Hanover 84, 168, 279

Hanslick, Eduard 7, 152, 217
Härtel, Raymond 71
Haslinger, Tobias 65, 66, 71, 72
Hauff, Christian 251
Hauptmann, Moritz 43, 55, 92, 129, 134, 136, 141–4, 148, 149, 171
Haydn, Josef 7, 8, 10, 14, 15, 26, 27, 33, 47, 56, 57, 70, 78, 79, 81, 83, 90–92, 96, 103, 113, 114, 118, 122, 127, 128, 131, 145, 149, 160, 188, 201, 251
  Symphony No. 7 *Le Midi* 33
  Symphony No. 44 *Trauer* 95
  Symphony No. 45 *Farewell* 33
  Symphony No. 94 *Surprise* 104
  Symphony No. 104 *London* 280
Heap, Charles Swinnerton 145
Heckenast, Gustav 192
Hegar, Friedrich 262
Heine, Heinrich 160
Heller, Stephen 160, 233
Helsted, Eduard 78, 129
Henschel, Georg 202, 270
Hepokoski, James 77
Hermann, Friedrich 128, 130, 165, 167
  Symphony No. 1 167
Herrmann, Gottfried 92–4
  Phantasiestück for piano and orchestra 92
  Symphony in C minor *Pathétique* 92, 93
  Violin concerto 92
Herzogenberg, Heinrich von 218
Hesse, Adolf 66, 79, 93, 128, 129, 140
  Symphony No. 5 79, 93
  Symphony No. 6 93, 94
Hetsch, Ludwig 78, 128, 138
Hiller, Ferdinand 99, 114, 126, 127, 129, 130, 136, 138, 149, 150, 152, 162, 165, 168, 170, 173–8, 184, 188, 203, 217, 218, 228, 230, 231, 243, 252, 253, 279
  Symphony in E minor *Es muss doch Frühling werden* 175–8
  Symphony *Im Freien* 174
Hiller, Johann Adam 126, 134
Hofmann, Heinrich 218
Hoffmann, E.T.A. 4, 9, 11, 55

Holl, Karl 251, 254, 258
Hölty, Ludwig 107
Holmes, Edward 132, 133, 148
Hueffer, Francis 126
Humperdinck, Engelbert 252
 'Humperdinck' rhythm 35
Hundt, Aline 8

Ingemann, Bernhard Severin 104

Jadassohn, Salomon 130, 148, 149
Jahn, Wilhelm 213
Janáček, Leoš 149
Jena 25, 91
Joachim, Amalie 270
Joachim, Joseph 127, 147, 150, 152, 153,
 217, 218, 228, 231, 233, 269, 270,
 279, 280

Kalliwoda, Johann 5, 7, 16–43, 45, 47
 Symphony No. 1 16, 19, 20, 22–5, 28,
  29, 37, 42, 43, 45, 48, 78, 79, 86–8,
  91, 92, 123, 128, 151, 228, 279
 Symphony No. 2 19, 25–9
 Symphony No. 3 25, 29–33, 43
 Symphony No. 4 33, 34, 39, 53
 Symphony No. 5 19, 34–6, 42, 43, 106
 Symphony No. 6 37, 39–41, 43, 155
 Symphony No. 7 37–9, 43, 106
Kalliwoda, Wilhelm 30
Karl-Egon II, Prince 29
Karlsruhe 18, 30, 66, 68, 91, 219, 229, 253,
 261
Kassel 14–16, 43, 44, 67, 68, 83, 94, 103,
 111, 112, 150
Kiel, Friedrich 148
Kirchner, Theodor 218, 233, 267
Kistler, Cyrill 218
Kistner, Carl Friedrich 52, 54, 102, 262
Kittl, Johann Friedrich 83–8, 91, 128, 138,
 140, 153, 187, 234, 279
 Symphony No. 1 83
 Symphony No. 2 *Jagd* 83–7, 91, 162
 Symphony No. 3 83
 Symphony No. 4 86
Kleist, Heinrich von 238
Klengel, Moritz 136
Klingemann, Karl 134

Klitzsch, Emil 151
Klopstock, Friedrich Gottlieb 126
Koblenz 82, 88
Königsberg 25, 66
Königslow, Otto von 88
Königswinter, Wolfgang Müller von 44
Kozebue, August von 238
 Die Unglücklichen 238
Krause, Emil 160
Krebs, Karl August 92
Kretschmar, Hermann 5, 10, 17, 18, 24,
 25, 27, 32, 35, 37, 56, 65, 77, 78,
 88, 158, 192, 196, 197, 225, 226,
 229, 278
Kreutzer, Conradin 60
Krueck, Alan 1, 238–40, 243, 249, 250
Kufferath, Ferdinand 130, 165, 170
Küster, Konrad 1, 42, 66

Lachner, Franz 5, 6, 21, 41, 51, 56–79, 81,
 82, 86–8, 91, 92, 98–100, 123, 128,
 130, 138, 151, 153–9, 165, 168,
 209, 211, 218, 228, 259, 279, 281
 Ball Suite Op. 170 158
 Suite No. 1 Op. 113 158
 Suite No. 7 Op. 190 76, 77
 Symphony No. 1 57–9, 68, 71, 99, 128,
  155, 224
 Symphony No. 2 57, 95
 Symphony No. 3 59, 99, 113
 Symphony No. 4 57, 59, 60
 Symphony No. 5 53, 56, 60–72, 75,
  128, 154, 155, 203, 206
 Symphony No. 6 6, 60, 72–5, 77, 129,
  158
 Symphony No. 7 6, 57, 76, 158, 211
 Symphony No. 8 6, 60, 65, 76, 153–8,
  161, 211
Lachner, Ignaz 56
Lachner, Theodor 56
Lachner, Vincenz 56, 57, 68, 159, 203, 206
Lampert, Ernst 238
Lausanne 243
Leichtling, Avrohom 214
Leipzig 7, 11–14, 16–18, 20, 25, 29, 32,
 33, 36, 39, 41, 42, 45, 55, 56, 65,
 66, 68, 70, 71, 75, 77, 78, 82–4,
 86–8, 92–6, 99–103, 106, 107, 109,

111, 113, 114, 117, 125–31, 133–8, 140–53, 164–71, 173, 174, 178–80, 185, 186, 188, 191, 199, 213, 216, 217, 229–31, 233, 237–9, 251, 253, 261, 262, 267–9, 274, 279
  Conservatoire 83, 88, 131, 133–8, 141, 143–50, 152, 166, 169–71, 174, 237, 251, 267, 269
  Euterpe Concerts 96, 106, 141, 274
  Gewandhaus 11, 13, 18, 32, 36, 41, 42, 56, 88, 100, 106, 109, 113, 115, 117, 126, 128, 129, 133, 135, 138, 140, 143, 144, 146–9, 152, 164–71, 173, 174, 179, 237, 253, 261, 262, 268
  Gewandhaus Orchestra 95, 126, 127, 134, 149, 167, 169
  Historical Concerts 14
  Morning Conversation Concerts 131, 169
  Opera 146, 150, 169–71
  Thomaskirche 88, 126, 129, 133, 134, 136, 148
  University 126, 133, 135, 146
Leonhard, Julius Emil 115, 116, 129
  Symphony No. 1 115, 116
Lessels, Richard 125
Lessing, Gotthold Ephraim 126
Leuchtmann, Horst 214
Levi, Benedikt 170
Levi, Hermann 137, 169, 170, 219, 229, 231, 252, 253
  Symphony in three movements 170
Leyden 137
Lindblad, Adolf Fredrik 128, 131
Lindpaintner, Peter 42, 68, 138
Liszt, Franz 3, 10, 61, 81, 82, 86, 90, 110, 117, 131, 142, 143, 147, 149–52, 158, 164, 166–70, 173–5, 185, 191, 192, 202, 204, 217, 237, 238, 249, 252, 281
  Ce qu'on entend sur la montagne 158
  Les Préludes 90, 158, 169, 170
  Mazeppa 158, 170
  Orpheus 158
  Piano concerto No. 1 170, 174
  Piano concerto No. 2 170

  Piano sonata in B minor 152
  Prometheus 158
  Tasso 158
Litolff, Henri 115
  Concerto-symphonique No. 2 115
  Concerto-symphonique No. 4 115
London 11, 48, 115, 134, 136, 145, 221, 266
  Crystal Palace 144, 266
  Philharmonic Society 15, 19, 71, 129, 141, 142, 174, 266
  Royal Academy of Music 131, 132, 135, 137–9, 143, 147, 149
  St James's Hall 144
Lortzing, Albert 208
Löwenberg 184
Lübeck 91, 92, 229
Lucerne 237
Ludwig II of Bavaria, King 56
Ludwig, Franz 269, 274
Lührss, Carl 78, 89, 90, 129, 165, 170
  Symphony in E♭ 89, 90
Lumbye, Hans Christian 113

Macfarren, George 138–41
  Overture: *Chevy Chase* 140, 141
  Symphony No. 7 139–41
Magdeburg 25
Mahler, Gustav 34, 56, 127, 139, 150, 223, 240, 243, 244, 264
  Symphony No. 1 223, 243
  Symphony No. 5 in C♯ minor 139
Mainz 174, 274
Maitland, John Fuller 188, 189, 218
Mangold, C.F. 233
Mannheim 18, 25, 57, 60, 66–8, 88, 219, 229, 233, 252, 262, 263
  Mannheim rocket 31
Manns, August 144, 266
Markull, Friedrich Wilhelm 78, 88, 89, 129
  Symphony in D 88, 89
  Symphony in C minor 88
Marschner, Heinrich 7, 84, 89, 208
Marx, Adolf Bernhard 11
Marxsen, Eduard 79, 92
  Beethovens Schatten 92
  Symphony No. 5 92

Mason, Lowell 135, 136, 167
Mason, William 141
Matthäi, Heinrich 126, 134
Maurer, Ludwig Wilhelm 128
Mayer, Emilie 8
Méhul, Etienne 78, 131
Meiningen 82
Meissen 191
Mellon, Alfred 144
Mendel, Hermann 42
Mendelssohn, Felix 2, 4–7, 10–17, 20, 21,
    33, 36, 41, 42, 44, 45, 65, 66, 71,
    72, 75, 77–9, 81, 83, 86, 87, 89, 90,
    92, 96, 99–102, 104, 106, 107–9,
    111, 114, 116, 117, 122, 123,
    126–31, 133–45, 147–53, 155, 160,
    164–7, 169–75, 177, 180, 189, 191,
    202, 205, 217–20, 229, 235, 250,
    251, 259, 262, 267, 270, 279, 281
  Elijah 45
  Die erste Walpurgisnacht 89, 100
  Funeral march 44
  Overture: *Calm sea and prosperous voyage* 127
  Overture: *Fair Melusine* 92
  Overture: *Fingal's cave* 95, 103, 127
  Overture: *Midsummer Night's Dream* 30, 103, 127, 144, 214
  Symphony No. 1 127
  Symphony No. 2 *Lobgesang* 1, 81, 100, 106, 110, 165
  Symphony No. 3 *Scottish* 2, 6, 41, 81, 103, 106, 113, 117, 127, 128, 165, 187, 226
  Symphony No. 4 *Italian* 2, 6, 19, 36, 87, 104, 117, 129, 165, 240
  Symphony No. 5 *Reformation* 13, 130
  Violin concerto 81, 116, 220
Messer, Franz Josef 118
Meyerbeer, Giacomo 108, 262
  Dinorah 262
Möhring, Ferdinand 78, 128
Molique, Bernhard 78, 128, 138
Moscow 192, 217
Moscheles, Ignaz 127–9, 137, 141, 143, 144, 148, 149, 237

Möser, Karl 113
Mozart, Wolfgang Amadeus 7, 8, 11, 14,
    15, 17, 20, 47, 56, 70, 78, 79, 81,
    83, 86, 90, 91, 96, 103, 113–15,
    117, 127, 131, 141, 145, 149, 167,
    178, 188, 189, 201, 251, 262, 267
  Cosi fan tutte 22, 23
  Don Giovanni 13, 96, 193
  Overture: *Die Zauberflöte* 27
  Requiem 7
  Symphony No. 36 *Linz* 11
  Symphony No. 38 *Prague* 14, 128
  Symphony No. 39 14, 27, 28, 128
  Symphony No. 40 22, 24, 31, 128
  Symphony No. 41 10, 28, 63, 128, 133, 188
Müller, Christian Gottlieb 91, 95, 128, 138, 167
  Symphony No. 3 128
  Symphony No. 4 95, 128
Müller, Friedrich 94, 107, 128
  Symphony No. 1 94
  Symphony No. 2 107, 108
Müller, Karl 213
Munich 18, 25, 56, 57, 59, 66–8, 70, 72,
    76, 82, 86, 98, 115, 155, 158, 221,
    222, 253, 254, 256
  Lenten Concerts 98, 99
Münster 253, 267–70, 280
Münster am Stein 280

Naumann, Emil 130, 131, 233
Nesselrode-Ehreshoven, Count Franz von 43
Neumann, William 38, 43, 86, 88
Nicodé, Jean Louis 218
Nicolai, W. Frederic 137
Niederrheinisches Musikfest (Lower Rhenish Music Festival) 127, 128, 174, 175, 252
Nietzsche, Friedrich 126
Nikisch, Artur 36, 150, 166, 238, 243
Norman, Ludwig 233
Novello, Vincent 16
Nowakowski, Josef 79

Oldenburg 91, 95, 165, 229, 230, 233, 235, 236, 253
Onslow, Georges 78, 128, 131
Otto, Julius 68

Paganini, Niccolò 10
Palestrina, Giovanni Pierluigi da 5
Pape, Ludwig 78, 91, 128, 129, 140
    Militärsinfonie 91, 92
Paris 44, 48, 99, 108, 109, 111, 114, 115, 125, 159, 160, 165, 174, 251, 252
    Conservatoire 72, 131
Parker, James Cutler Dean 135
Parry, Charles Hubert Hastings 9, 149, 201
Pärt, Arvo 284
Pasdeloup, Jules 159
Pederson, Sanna 5
Penderecki, Krzysztof 284
Pesth 191, 192
Pfeiffer, Carl 13
Pfitzner, Hans 36
Pieper, Antje 166, 167
Pitt, Percy 149
Pixis, Johann Peter 89
Plaidy, Louis 136, 143, 148
Pleyel, Ignaz 229
Pohl, Richard 109, 110, 152
Pohlenz, August 126, 128, 148
Potsdam 79
Pott, August 95, 130, 165
Potter, Cipriani 132, 139
Prague 17, 19, 25, 66, 83, 86, 108, 188, 217
    Conservatoire 68, 83, 86, 131, 132, 148
Prechtler, Johann Otto 238
    Er sucht seine Braut 238
Preising, August 269
Preyer, Gottfried 5, 6, 54, 66, 75, 91
Prokofiev, Sergei
    Symphony No. 7 in C♯ minor 139
Prout, Ebenezer 200, 201

Queisser, Karl Traugott 95, 148

Radecke, Robert 267
Raff, Doris 214
Raff, Helene 214
Raff, Joseph Joachim 5, 130, 148, 152, 168, 185, 187, 190, 200–206, 208, 209, 211, 213–18, 222, 224, 228, 232, 233, 237, 250, 259, 263, 268, 279, 281
    Deutschlands Auferstehung 203
    Suite No. 1 202
    Symphony (1854) 168, 169, 202, 203, 233
    Symphony No. 1 *An das Vaterland* 159, 200, 202–9, 217
    Symphony No. 2 202, 209–11, 213, 216
    Symphony No. 3 *Im Walde* 214, 216, 263
    Symphony No. 4 202, 209, 211–14, 216, 224
    Symphony No. 5 *Lenore* 214, 216
    Symphony No. 6 209, 214–16, 232, 263
    Symphony No. 7 216
    Symphony No. 10 211, 232
Rakemann, Louis 126
Randhartinger, Benedict 66
Reichardt, Gustav 203, 206, 209
Reinecke, Carl 39, 41, 42, 127, 130, 143, 145, 147–9, 166, 168, 178–80, 184, 197, 199, 202, 203, 217, 218, 231, 259, 261–3, 268, 279
    Overture: *Dame Kobold* 179
    Overture: *Hamlet* 179
    Piano quintet 179
    Symphony in A minor 179
    Symphony No. 1 179–84, 200
    Symphony No. 2 *Haakon Jarl* 180
Reinthaler, Carl 186, 189–91, 200, 279
    Symphony in D 189–92
Reissiger, Karl 5, 6, 42, 66, 68, 78, 91, 128, 138
Rellstab, Heinrich 9
Rellstab, Johann 9
Rheinberger, Josef 130, 218, 225
    Symphony (*Wallensteins Lager*) 225
Richter, Ernst Friedrich 137, 141, 144, 148
Richter, Hans 243
Riehl, Wilhelm 106, 107
Riem, Wilhelm Friedrich 90, 91
Ries, Ferdinand 78, 91

Ries, Hubert 92
Rietz, Eduard 169
Rietz, Julius 39, 41, 48, 86, 106, 126–30, 137, 143, 144, 147, 149, 152, 164, 166, 168–72, 174, 178, 179, 184, 217, 237, 243, 251, 259, 279
   Concert overture in A 171, 179
   Der Korsar 169
   Symphony No. 3 168, 171–3
Rimsky-Korsakov, Nikolai 185
Ritter, August Gottfried 91, 92
   Symphony in C minor 91, 92
Rochlitz, Johann Friedrich 9, 11–14
Roeder, Erich 238
Roland, Sophia 43, 44
Rome 99, 125, 160
Rosa, Carl 143
Rosenhain, Jakob (Jacques) 78, 109, 110, 129, 138, 139, 159, 160
   Symphony No. 1 109
   Symphony No. 2 110
   Symphony No. 3 *Frühlingsklänge* 109, 159, 160
Rossini, Gioachino 7, 20, 26, 34, 39, 67, 108, 122, 252, 268
Rostock 56
Rotterdam 96, 188, 252
Rubinstein, Anton 130, 131, 252
   Ocean Symphony 165, 168, 169, 185
Rudolstadt 94, 107, 108
Rudorff, Ernst 147

Saarbrücken 252
Sahr, Heinrich von 137, 279
Saint-Saëns, Camille 111, 168, 252
Schäffer, Julius 233
Scherchen, Hermann 118
Schicht, Johann Gottfried 126, 134
Schiller, Friedrich 261–3
Schindler, Anton 159
Schleinitz, Conrad 148
Schlesinger, Adolf 115
Schmitt, Aloys 83, 92
Schneider, Friedrich 7, 78, 88, 91, 128, 138
   Symphony in A 88
   Symphony in F minor 88
Schneider, Theodor 184

Schnyder von Wartensee, Franz Xaver 33, 68, 100, 118, 122, 123, 215, 232
   Symphony No. 2 *Erinnerung an Haydn* 118
   Symphony No. 3 33, 118–23, 213, 215, 232
   Toy Symphony 118
Schott, Franz 84, 159, 174
Schubert, Ferdinand 1, 50
Schubert, Franz 1, 12, 20, 25, 27, 30, 36, 50, 51, 54, 56–8, 62, 63, 75, 77, 78, 81, 83, 92, 102, 107, 109, 113, 153, 180, 187, 189, 220, 244, 251, 253, 256, 262, 267, 270, 274, 279, 280
   Overture: *Fierrabras* 71
   Erlkönig (D.328) 79
   Sehnsucht (*Trauerwalzer* D.365/2) 69
   String quintet 39, 57, 58, 155
   Symphony No. 4 20
   Symphony No. 5 25
   Symphony No. 8 45, 51, 130
   Symphony No. 9 1, 2, 5, 7, 12, 19, 21, 45, 50, 51, 54, 57, 65, 70, 71, 76, 78, 81, 87, 91, 114, 127–9, 187, 226, 243, 251
Schuch, Ernst von 238, 243
Schulz, Johann Philipp Christian 126, 148
Schumann, Clara (née Wieck) 48, 71, 89, 100, 126, 127, 131, 147, 152, 153, 167, 174, 188, 218, 219, 228, 233, 270, 279, 280
Schumann, Robert 1, 2, 5–7, 9, 10, 12–14, 19–21, 24, 25, 29, 32, 35, 36, 41–3, 48, 49, 51–4, 56, 60, 68–71, 75–7, 79, 81, 84, 86, 90–92, 96, 104, 107, 108, 113, 117, 122, 123, 131, 136, 145, 146, 149–53, 155, 158, 160, 165, 167, 169, 170, 174, 175, 179, 180, 188, 189, 191, 195, 199, 203, 217, 218, 221, 229, 232–5, 237, 238, 250, 251, 264, 267, 278–81
   Jugendsinfonie 81
   Mass in C minor 48
   Overture: *Hermann und Dorothea* 170
   Overture, Scherzo and Finale 230
   Piano concerto 161, 162, 274
   Piano trio No. 3 153
   Prayer from *Genoveva* 170

Symphony No. 1 41, 84, 87, 91, 128, 153
Symphony No. 2 53, 84, 87, 117, 118, 129, 153, 155, 239, 240, 274
Symphony No. 3 36, 104, 129, 130, 153, 184, 197, 198, 220, 232, 278
Symphony No. 4 24, 33, 36, 48, 87, 130, 153, 166, 180, 188, 195, 196
Violin sonata (*Romanze* and Finale) F-A-E 233
Schütz, Heinrich 5
Sechter, Simon 56–8, 158
Seifriz, Max 184
Seyfried, Ignaz von 60, 65
Shaw, George Bernard 201, 266, 267
Simpson, Adrienne 166
Sitt, Hans 149
Smart, George 144
Smetana, Bedřich 104
  Ma Vlast: *Vltava* 104
Smyth, Dame Ethel 149
Solberg, Pauline 145
Sommer, Hans 218
Sondershausen 82, 219–22, 225, 226, 231, 253, 269
Spindler, Fritz 129, 166
Spohr, Louis 7, 11–17, 21, 42, 43, 45, 47, 53, 68, 77–9, 81, 83, 87, 92, 111, 117, 118, 123, 145, 149–51, 153, 168, 173, 219, 253, 279
  Faust 268
  Symphony No. 1 11, 14, 16
  Symphony No. 2 11
  Symphony No. 3 12, 42, 45, 128
  Symphony No. 4 12, 13, 42, 91, 106, 128
  Symphony No. 5 14, 15, 95, 108, 129
  Symphony No. 6 14
  Symphony No. 7 15
  Symphony No. 8 15, 33, 165
  Symphony No. 9 16, 165
  Symphony No. 10 16
  Violin concerto in E 88
St Petersburg 267
Stade, Friedrich 91
Stanford, Charles Villiers 138, 147, 148
Steinbeck, Wolfram 57, 77, 158

Sterndale Bennett, William 132, 137, 142, 147, 170
  Overture: *The Naiads* 88
  Symphony No. 8 185
Stimpson, James 142
Stockhausen, Julius 147, 270
Strauss (family) 56
Strauss, Joseph 65, 66, 68, 78, 128, 138
Strauss, Richard 36, 175, 218, 238, 243, 249
  Alpine Symphony 206
  Aus Italien 206
  Don Juan 238, 243
Strauss-Neméth, Laszló 20, 29, 37, 42, 43
Strunz, Karl 18, 19, 32, 34, 36
Stuttgart 25, 29, 68, 134, 166, 187, 243
Sullivan, Arthur 16, 143–5, 266
  Incidental music to *The Tempest* 144
  Overture: *In memoriam* 144
  Symphony in E *Irish* 144, 145, 185
Svendsen, Johan 130, 131, 145–7, 149, 185
  String octet 147
  String quintet 147
  Symphony No. 1 147
Swanwick, Anna 60

Täglichsbeck, Thomas 78, 128
Taubert, Wilhelm 86, 111–14, 129, 130, 160, 165, 214
  Symphony No. 1 112, 113
Taylor, Franklin 143
Tchaikovsky, Pyotr 15, 18, 185, 210, 211, 232, 249
  The Nutcracker (*Trepak*) 214
  Symphony No. 4 198
  Symphony No. 5 211, 232
  Symphony No. 6 *Pathétique* 13, 192
  Violin concerto 3
Telemann, Georg Philipp 7
Temperley, Nicholas 138
Todd, R. Larry 24, 128, 131
Tovey, Donald Francis 187, 197
Twain, Mark 125

Ulrich, Hugo 130, 166
Umlauff, Michael 60

Veit, Wenzel Heinrich 130, 166
Verhulst, Johannes 92, 95, 96, 98, 123, 274, 279
    Symphony in E minor 95–8, 274
Victoria, Queen 136
Vienna 1, 7, 12, 14, 50, 51, 54, 56, 57, 60, 65–8, 70, 71, 75, 125, 127, 128, 132, 152, 175, 191, 203, 225
    Vienna Conservatoire 131
Vierling, Georg 130, 186, 187, 191
    Symphony in C 186
Vieuxtemps, Henri (*Adagio* and *Rondo* for violin) 170
Vogler, Abt 78, 79, 131
Volkmann, Robert 5, 41, 130, 158, 180, 185, 191–200, 203, 235, 268, 279, 281
    Overture: *Richard III* 192
    Serenade for strings 192
    Symphony No. 1 180, 192–200, 211, 222, 234, 270
    Symphony No. 2 192, 199, 200

Wagner, Cosima 10
Wagner, Richard 1, 3, 10, 16, 56, 81–3, 86, 98, 126–8, 131, 149, 150, 152, 160, 164, 166, 175, 177, 180, 185, 186, 192, 200, 202, 203, 217, 221, 222, 237, 238, 252, 262, 267, 281
    Das Rheingold 185, 221, 222
    Der fliegende Holländer (duet) 170
    Die Meistersinger 3, 56, 185, 221
    Die Walküre 196
    Der Ring des Nibelungen 238
    Kaisermarsch 203
    Lohengrin 164, 251
    Rienzi 221
    Tannhäuser 164, 170, 240, 251
    Tristan und Isolde 185, 218, 219, 237, 250
Walter, August 129, 166
Watts, William 71
Weber, Carl Maria von 5, 7, 17, 18, 39, 46, 47, 79, 83, 102, 114, 131, 149, 166, 172, 205, 208, 262, 267
    Der Freischütz 31
    Euryanthe 56, 67, 88
    Overture: *Jubel* 5
    Symphony No. 1 17, 18, 39
    Symphony No. 2 17, 18, 39
Weber, Dionys 68, 83, 86
Weber, William 7
Weigl, Joseph 60
Weimar 82, 99, 110, 126, 147, 150–52, 169, 175, 202, 206, 217, 237, 238
Weingartner, Felix 81
Weinlich, Theodor 148
Wenzel, Ernst Friedrich 136, 146
White, Maude Valerie 149
Wichmann, Hermann 111, 112
    Symphony No. 1 111
    Symphony No. 2 112
Wieck, Maria 89
Wiesbaden 169, 202, 213
William IV, King 136
Wilsing, C.F. 233
Wolf, Hugo 56
Wüerst, Richard 130, 166
Wüllner, Franz 238, 252
    Two Lieder for female chorus 230

Zürich 261, 262